PROHIBITION ENFORCEMENT

ABOUT THE AUTHOR

Martin Alan Greenberg is a professor of criminal justice at Ulster County Community College in Stone Ridge, New York. He has worked as a probation officer, senior court officer, campus security officer, and volunteer police officer. During the 1970s, Professor Greenberg was an auxiliary police deputy inspector with the New York City Police Department. He earned degrees from the Graduate School and University Center of the City University of New York, John Jay College of Criminal Justice, New York Law School, and Queens College. He holds the Certified Protection Professional credential from the American Society for Industrial Security and serves as a security officer educator in the State of New York. Professor Greenberg is also the author of the book: *Auxiliary Police: The Citizen's Approach to Public Safety.*

PROHIBITION ENFORCEMENT
Charting A New Mission

By

MARTIN ALAN GREENBERG

Ulster County Community College
Stone Ridge, New York

Charles C Thomas
PUBLISHER • LTD.
SPRINGFIELD • ILLINOIS • U.S.A.

Published and Distributed Throughout the World by

CHARLES C THOMAS • PUBLISHER, LTD.

2600 South First Street
Springfield, Illinois 62704

© *1999 by* CHARLES C THOMAS • PUBLISHER, LTD.

ISBN 0-398-06997-2 (cloth)
ISBN 0-398-06998-0 (paper)

Library of Congress Catalog Card Number: 99-35710

With THOMAS BOOKS *careful attention is given to all details of manufacturing
and design. It is the Publisher's desire to present books that are satisfactory as to their
physical qualities and artistic possibilities and appropriate for their particular use.*
THOMAS BOOKS *will be true to those laws of quality that assure a good name
and good will.*

Printed in the United States of America
TH-R-3

Library of Congress Cataloging-in-Publication Data

Greenberg, Martin Alan
   Prohibition enforcement : charting a new mission / by Martin
Alan Greenberg
      p.   cm.
   Includes bibliographical references (p.   ) and index.
   ISBN 0-398-06997-2 (cloth). -- ISBN 0-398-06998-0 (paper)
   1. Narcotics, Control of--United States--History. 2. Drug abuse-
-United States--Prevention--History. 3. Prohibition--United States-
-History. 4. Temperance--United States--History. I. Title.
HV5825.G6963   1999
363.4'1'0973--dc21   99-35710
                                                                CIP

IN MEMORY OF

Gerald R. Neuhoff
(Jay)

FOREWORD

Although parts of Martin Greenberg's study involves events which happened more than a century ago, America's leaders and citizens are still challenged by the inherent difficulties regarding prohibition laws and their enforcement. The concerned officials are now different as are the people they serve, but some key issues remain the same. For example, in the 1920s, there were many illicit stills and distilleries; today, there are many clandestine drug labs producing methamphetamine and crack cocaine. On the other hand, while in the 1920s there was widespread disrespect for the liquor law, today there is widespread support for law enforcement and concern regarding the dangers related to the abuse of controlled substances.

However, the search for solutions remains controversial. For example, in the early part of 1999, New York City became the first city in the nation to seize the cars of motorists arrested for drunk driving. The new policy caused civil libertarians to attack the initiative as overly excessive. Under the New York City seizure program, it is possible for motorists who have been acquitted of drunk driving in criminal court to still lose their cars in civil court. This may occur because such civil proceedings have a standard of proof involving only a preponderance of the evidence. In contrast, the criminal courts require proof beyond a reasonable doubt (Williams, 1999).

Meanwhile, Deputy U.S. Attorney General Eric Holder has cautioned that the number of young men in their late teens and early 20s, the most crime-prone years, will grow by 15 percent over the next 15 years. Furthermore, although the nation has experienced a sharp decrease in violent crime in recent years, there has been an increase in drug trafficking in rural America (Hughes, 1999).

Professor Greenberg contends that if public officials can successfully harness the existing public support for law enforcement, a breakthrough will be achieved in the field of drug enforcement. In order to demonstrate his purpose, he presents an overview of the history of the use and control of alcoholic beverages and other drugs as well as related aspects of the criminal justice system. In particular, the author considers the problems encountered by enforcement officials, the actions taken by local police and federal officials, and the resulting consequences for both bystanders and offenders.

The work concludes with a wide range of tasks for citizens to undertake who are concerned about the drug problem. A new occupational title for some of the nation's police is proposed: the Drug Control Police Specialist. The latter position is recommended in order to replace the current informal, often happenstance, and primarily reactive response of the nation's police with respect to intoxicated and addicted persons.

The primary role of drug control police specialists would be to seek out drug addicts in the community and refer them to the most appropriate treatment agencies and facilities. They would also serve as consultants to a wide variety of institutions seeking to participate in drug abuse prevention efforts. In carrying out their responsibilities, these specialists would be expected to work in a systematic, proactive and creative manner. They would also have the assistance of carefully screened and trained citizen police volunteers who would work under their supervision and direction.

Professor Greenberg's book provides a timely and thought-provoking analysis of prohibition enforcement issues. It comes at a time when one of New York's most prominent officials, Chief Judge Judith Kaye, has come out and said what many politicians apparently think but are afraid to say, namely, that the state's 1973 Rockefeller drug laws need to be eased. She advocates that trial court judges be given more discretion in sentencing, including diversion of appropriate defendants to drug treatment. Governor George Pataki is giving careful consideration to the plan proposed by Kaye. Similar attention should also be given to the novel recommendations made in this book.

J. Richard Bockelmann, Sheriff
Ulster County, New York

PREFACE

The present book is about the drama of everyday life and the exercise of governmental power for the regulation of everyday conduct. It illustrates our nation's incessant struggle to maintain civil order without diminishing civil liberties. Today, this issue is especially relevant as American society tries to cope with: school and family violence; media presentations of violence; the growth of the Internet; and the ravages of substance abuse.

The problem of substance abuse and control is given more attention in order to narrow the scope of this book. It is the only social problem among the foregoing that has actually been the subject of a specific Constitutional amendment (the Eighteenth). A direct consequence of America's experience with the enforcement of the 18th Amendment has been a long line of highly significant cases regarding constitutional principles involving searches and seizures. In addition, school and family violence usually involve mental health and substance abuse matters.

The adoption of a Constitutional Amendment is a rare, historical event. In its 212-year history, the Constitution has been amended only 27 times. The first ten amendments are the Bill of Rights; they were adopted in 1791. The prohibition amendment (Eighteenth Amendment) and its repeal represent two out of the seventeen amendments passed since the Bill of Rights. The amendment was aimed at eliminating the saloon and the consumption of liquor. The prohibition amendment is especially significant since it is the only amendment which has ever been repealed.

The topic of substance abuse and control is presented by considering: the events leading to national prohibition in 1920; the enforcement of prohibition; and the more recent issues and trends regarding overall drug enforcement. A final section of the book describes several ideas concerning a new mission and role for modern prohibition enforcement agents.

MARTIN ALAN GREENBERG

ACKNOWLEDGMENTS

No book is ever complete nor is any list of an author's acknowledgments. For the twin gifts of love and time, my heartfelt gratitude to my wife Ellen Wertlieb. For the gifts of joy and hope, my thanks to my son Eddy. For invaluable editorial assistance, my everlasting appreciation to my special colleague, Joan Neuhoff.

Inspiration for the preparation of this book is due to the opportunity I had during the Spring of 1998 to attend the doctoral level Seminar on Criminal Justice History offered by Professor Eli Faber at John Jay College of Criminal Justice.

Finally, special thanks to Sheriff J. Richard Bockelmann for contributing the book's foreword and to all the men and women who have been assigned the difficult tasks involving prohibition enforcement. Of course, all of the ideas expressed in this book are solely the author's responsibility.

CONTENTS

PROHIBITION ENFORCEMENT

INTRODUCTION

"Hauling dope, it has no race, it has no religion. Age doesn't matter. I've locked up a grandmother and her grandkids for hauling marijuana."[1]

DEAN WILDAUER, TROOPER, INDIANA STATE POLICE

Joseph McNamara, the former police chief of San Jose, California, stated in March of 1997, that anyone "who looks objectively at America's drug war will see that it is racist, violent, corrupt and unsuccessful" (McNamara, 1997, p. 538). Dwight Heath, professor of anthropology at Brown University, believes that many of the ills associated with the nation's drug problem "derive more from the prohibition policies that are in effect than from the use of drugs" (Heath, 1992, p. 285). On the other hand, Lee P. Brown, the mayor of Houston, who has held such positions as police chief in Houston, police commissioner of New York City, and director of the White House Office of National Drug Control Policy (ONDCP), indicates that contrary to popular belief "we have had some significant success in reducing the rate of casual drug use" (Brown, 1995, p. 628). The current director of the ONDCP is Barry McCaffrey, a retired U.S. Army four-star general. He is more optimistic than Brown and about a light-year away from McNamara's perspective. During his confirmation hearing before the Senate Judiciary Committee, he remarked: "our current national drug policy is basically sound and features many successful programs" (McCaffrey, 1996, p. 325).

Generally, it appeared that the mood of the country on the eve of the new millennium was that in order to make progress against drug abuse, the nation should not give up hope and that all Americans needed to share in the responsibility to address this problem. A major purpose of this book is to provide appropriate background materials for everyone to have at least a summary knowledge about the enforcement aspects of the drug problem. Each of us has a positive role to play, whether we be government officials, students, law enforcement officers, factory workers, teachers, coaches, religious leaders, sales agents, family members, health care providers, retired persons, entertainers or journalists. Although this book deals mostly about the adoption and enforcement of laws that restrict the distribution and production of various types of drugs (especially, alcohol, opiates and marijuana), it is also about how ordinary people have become or may become involved in various solutions.

Since prehistoric times mankind has used opium. It was one of the first drugs to be discovered (Booth, 1996). It is naturally derived from the ripe seedpod of the opium poppy (*papaver somniferum*). Both the leaves and seeds of the poppy plant are edible. The term "opium" is from the Greek word opion, meaning the juice of the poppy. Throughout the ages, it has been used medically as a pain reliever. Chinese immigrants operated commercial "opium dens" during the latter part of the nineteenth and early part of the twentieth centuries (Abadinsky, 1997). Two opium derivatives, morphine and heroin, were in common use by the latter half of the nineteenth century. They were distributed by drug and grocery stores and by mail order without the need of a prescription (McWilliams, 1990, p. 29).

Marijuana and hashish are derived from the hemp plant, scientifically referred to as *cannabis sativa L.* This plant grows wild in many tropical and temperate regions of the world, but it has also been cultivated for at least 5,000 years. Plant products include rope and paint (Abadinsky, 1997). "When the dried leaves of the marijuana plant are smoked like tobacco, perceptual changes occur that vary widely according to the strength of the substance, the person smoking the marijuana, and the environmental conditions" (Abadinsky, 1997, p. 51). By the year 500 A.D. marijuana was being used throughout most of Europe (Ferguson, 1975, p. 78). Marijuana was cultivated and used in colonial America. In 1765, it may even have been grown on George Washington's Mount Vernon plantation (McWilliams, 1990, p. 29).

Alcohol is a colorless flammable liquid. A chemist would refer to it as ethanol. Combining sugar, water, yeast, and heat produces the most basic forms of alcoholic beverages. Yeast consists of the collective cells of certain tiny fungi. Yeast is the key ingredient, since it is necessary for the beginning of fermentation (Garner, 1979, pp. 5-6). "Fermentation is the chemical interaction by which the yeast acts upon other substances present to produce ethyl alcohol, a waste product given off by the living yeast organisms. It is given off as a natural life process whenever those organisms are 'fed' sugar" (Garner, 1979, p. 6). For example, beer is produced when grain is first treated with malt. The malt changes the starches in the grain to sugar. The yeast then acts on the newly produced sugar (the fermentation process). After fermentation, the fluid is separated, carbonated, and pasteurized. At earlier phases of the beer manufacturing process, filtering occurs as well as the addition of selected varieties of plants known as hops for flavoring. The final product usually contains not more than 4 percent alcohol. Generally, in order to produce alcoholic beverages with a content of more than 15 percent alcohol, a process known as distillation is used. Distilled spirits include rum, brandy and whiskey (Garner, 1979, pp. 6-8).

In 1998, archaeologists in Spain's northeast Catalonia region scraped the residue from the bottom of a 3,000-year-old broken red clay jar. From this residue, professors at the University of Barcelona with the help of a nearby beer plant were able to recreate a fresh amount of Europe's oldest known beer ("Researchers in Spain Serve Bronze Age Beer," *The Daily Gazette,* November 28, 1998, p. D1). The practice of drinking the alcoholic beverage known as wine is referred to in several passages of the Bible including Genesis IX: 21 and Genesis XIX: 32-36.

During the Prohibition period (1920-1933), the most common ingredient in bootlegged liquor was industrial alcohol. Industrial strength alcohol was supposed to be used for producing such products as paint, cosmetics and ink, but it ultimately accounted for half the booze drunk in the 1920s. According to Gray (1998), to give it the taste and color of scotch, caramel, prune juice, and creosote were added (p. 19).

In the history of drug abuse and control, several legal developments stand out. The ancient common law, upon which much of American law is based, divided criminal conduct into two categories: *mala in se* (wrong in themselves) crimes and *mala prohibita* (bad because it is forbidden) crimes. A *mala in se* crime involved conduct that was patently wrong (e.g., murder or rape), while a *mala prohibita* crime would not usually be considered wrong absent a specific statute declaring it to be so (e.g., traffic regulations, illegal gambling,) (Wrobleski & Hess, 1997, p. 231). In other words, if there were nearly universal agreement about the harmfulness of the conduct it was considered a *mala in se* type of crime, otherwise it was a *mala prohibita* offense. Under early English common law, public intoxication was not, in itself, a crime. Drunkenness was tolerated unless it resulted in some form of breach of the peace or disorderly conduct. In England, mere intoxication in public was first made a criminal offense in 1606 (4 James I, c. 5). Similar laws were enforced in colonial times and well after the achievement of American independence.

In America, several major legal events associated with drugs took place during the first half of the twentieth century prior to the advent of World War II. *The Food and Drug Act of 1906* declared it unlawful to manufacture any article of food or drug that is adulterated or misbranded and to sell that article in interstate commerce. In 1914, the *Harrison Narcotic Act* gave the federal government the power to regulate the sale of cocaine and other narcotics. The primary ingredient in many of the "patent medicines" of the nineteenth century was cocaine. In 1908, a government report listed over forty brands of soft drinks that contained cocaine (Abadinsky, 1997). On January 20, 1920, the Eighteenth Amendment to the Constitution banning the sale, manufacture and transportation of alcohol became effective.

The implementation of the Eighteenth Amendment was made possible through the passage of the *National Prohibition Enforcement Act* (also known as the *Volstead Act*) in 1919. It defined as intoxicating liquor any beverage containing more than half of 1 percent of alcohol and placed the administration of the law under the Bureau of Internal Revenue, and its commissioner.

The actual enforcement of national prohibition was placed in the hands of 48 separate state prohibition directors and their subordinates (reduced to 24 in 1925 as a result of reorganization). In 1920, a Prohibition Unit was organized in the Bureau of Internal Revenue. In November of 1921, a supplementary act (the *Willis-Campbell Act*) limited the use of liquor by medical prescription and extended prohibition to the Hawaiian and Virgin Islands. In 1927, a separate Bureau of Prohibition was created within the Treasury Department and the former Prohibition Unit was dissolved. The new Bureau was charged with the enforcement of all laws prohibiting or authorizing the manufacture, sale, and use of intoxicating liquors and narcotic drugs.

In 1928, Congress authorized the advance of money to narcotics agents to purchase drugs in order to obtain evidence of sale. Prior to this congressional action, an agent was required to make purchases with his own funds and only afterwards seek reimbursement from the Treasury Department. In the same year, Supreme Court Justice William Brandeis wrote his famous dissent in the case of *Olmstead v. U.S.* (277 U.S. 438), in which he stated: "In a government of law, the existence of the government will be imperiled if it fails to observe the law. If the Government becomes a lawbreaker, it breeds contempt for law; it invites every man to become a law unto himself; it invites anarchy." Federal prohibition agents had conducted wiretaps in the *Olmstead* case in spite of the fact that a state law existed prohibiting them. In 1929, the *Jones Act* increased the penalties for violation of the *Volstead Act*. Throughout the prohibition period, the prevention of smuggling was the primary work of the Bureau of Customs and the Coast Guard. In 1937, the *Marijuana Tax Act* was adopted. It placed a prohibitive tax on cannabis ($100 an ounce). By 1938, the Food and Drug Administration had been given expanded powers which included approving of all new drugs.

America's "drug war" has primarily focused upon opium-based substances since 1914 when the *Harrison Act* was adopted. For more than 50 years, this federal statute was the main basis of narcotics regulation in the U.S. as interpreted by the Supreme Court. The laws and various amendments related to the *Harrison Act* were consolidated in the *Comprehensive Drug Abuse Prevention and Control Act of 1970*. This legislation reflected a fundamental change in interpretation of the commerce clause of the Constitution, "thus eliminating the need to portray a police function as a revenue measure" (BJS, 1992, p. 77). In June 1986, a well-known professional basketball player, Len Bias, died from an overdose of crack cocaine. Shortly thereafter, several tough federal drug laws were adopted, including the *Anti-Drug Abuse Act of 1986* which established severe penalties for most participants in drug trafficking (Champion & Rush, 1997, p. 279).

In 1983, Dominican gangs in New York popularized crack cocaine. It consisted of a recipe consisting of: two parts cocaine hydrochloride, mixed with two parts of "comback," and one part of baking soda. Add water and bring to a boil. After cooling, break into little pieces. "Comeback" is the chemical filler that adds weight and bulk to the final product so that it can be cheaply sold. Baking soda serves the same purpose. The original "comeback" was a chemical similar to the prescription anesthetic lidocaine. The term "crack" is derived from the crackling sound that the drug makes when smoked (Benjamin & Miller, 1991, pp. 90-91). Inciardi (1990) has noted that

> In actuality, crack is *not* smoked. "Smoking" implies combustion, burning, and the inhalation of smoke. Tobacco is smoked. Marijuana is smoked. Crack, on the other hand, is actually inhaled. The small pebbles or rocks, which have a relatively low melting point, are placed in a special glass pipe and heated. Rather than burning, crack vaporizes, and the fumes are inhaled. (Inciardi, 1990, p. 25)

In 1983, the Dominican dealers were able to produce 2,000 "hits" of crack from just two ounces of cocaine powder, plus two ounces of comeback and one ounce of baking soda. In that year, an ounce of cocaine sold for about $2,000. Each hit sold for between $5 and $10. In this way, cocaine the drug of choice for the more affluent became available in diluted form to the masses (Benjamin & Miller, 1991, pp. 90-91).

According to Skolnick (1992), an important question that must be considered before any drug control policy is developed or evaluated "is whether the sale or use of drugs is more comparable to illegal betting (use) and bookmaking (sale) or to armed robbery and homicide?" (p. 135). Skolnick (1992) indicates that America's current drug strategy appears to be based on the view that not only the sale, but also the use of illegal drugs is *mala in se*, rather than *mala prohibitum* (p. 135). In accordance with such a viewpoint, the main thrust of America's drug control strategy has focused on expanding the role of law enforcement and increasing penalties. In the words of the noted historian Lawrence M. Friedman, since the passage of the *Marijuana Tax Act of 1937*, "the federal government, and most state governments have never looked back, never wavered, always stuck like glue to a single policy of prohibition, prohibition, and more prohibition: interdiction at the source, the arrest of users and pushers, draconian punishments, and, on the official level, no understanding, no mercy, no letup in the war" (Friedman, 1993, p. 356).

There is nearly universal agreement that alcohol abuse is a more serious problem than marijuana, opium and various other types of narcotics combined. Nevertheless, the Eighteenth Amendment was repealed in 1933 while the penalties involving these other drugs have been periodically increased. Although alcoholic beverages are no longer prohibited, they are heavily regulated and sales are restricted to those above a certain age. The taxes paid for the right to manufacture and distribute alcoholic and tobacco products are important sources of federal and local revenue. In fact, from 1883 to 1914 the enforcement activities of the Bureau of Internal Revenue were mainly confined to the collection of liquor and tobacco taxes (Schmeckebier, 1929, p. 2). However, alcohol remains a contributing factor in nearly half the total number of murders, suicides, and accidents occurring yearly in the United States. Today, alcohol is considered to be the direct cause of 80,000 to 100,000 deaths annually, and alcohol-related auto accidents are the leading cause of teenage deaths (Abadinsky, 1997, p. 10).

By the late 1970s, marijuana had become the largest cash crop in California, Hawaii and Oregon (Falco, 1992, p. 3). In recent years, marijuana has become recognized as an effective treatment of severe muscle spasm, glaucoma, and the severe nausea which accompanies chemotherapy (Lewis, 1992). By 1998, several states including California, Washington, Oregon, Nevada and Arizona had enacted laws permitting marijuana use under a doctor's recommendation (Greimel, 1998). In order to identify patients who are entitled to use marijuana and thereby protect them from arrest, states have established state registries and/or issued identification cards. District of Columbia Police Chief Charles H. Ramsey, president of the Major City Chiefs Association, criticized these measures by calling them a "major step backward in the fight against crime in our nation's cities" (Queary, 1998, p. A8).[2]

This book emphasizes the social, legal and political aspects of prohibition enforcement in the twenties and many other aspects of criminal justice history in order to place the modern-day prohibition of controlled substances into an appropriate historical context. The book tries to reconcile a variety of opposing views about substance abuse and control in the hope that a more effective solution to the problem can be found. Alternatives to the current criminal-police-military approach are developed after the origins of prohibition laws and their enforcement are traced. In seeking this goal, several well-known historical works are relied upon. However, a variety of lesser known materials are also drawn upon, such as a forgotten court transcript involving an actual trial of the period and its associated events. The transcript concerns a case involving gross police misconduct and it is presented in order to include precise details about the onset of the prohibition period.

The selected case minutes includes the testimony of the defendant, a New York City police detective. In many ways, an analysis of the trial and career of New York City Detective Sergeant Charles Tighe can help to illustrate the delicate balance between individual freedom and social order. When he was 32 years-old, his name became synonymous for all that was wrong with police work. The account of Tighe's activities and subsequent trials can help to focus attention on Prohibition's impact on the quality of life of average people. More precisely, the court and newspaper reports indicate what some city residents were experiencing in their lives on a hot summer afternoon on Thursday, July 28, 1921. Their accounts of that day provide eyewitness testimony about the events of that time, place and era. The incident received considerable press notoriety and several of the gaps in the official court record are filled-in by press reports.

Tighe had two separate trials on assault charges. The first case was a misdemeanor assault on a seven-year-old girl. It was held before a three-judge panel in the Court of Special Sessions. The other case consisted of a full jury trial involving a felonious assault charge based on the complaint of Emma Lennon. The numerous press accounts as well as the actual surviving transcript of his second trial provide useful insights about various aspects of: police professionalism; gender and class distinctions; early types of undercover police work; the saloon business after the adoption of national prohibition; state and local politics; protective services for children; the reserve platoon system; occupations after World War I; individual and societal responses to deviancy; trial defense strategies; bookmakers; newspaper reporting (especially, regarding issues involving mental health and police corruption); the handling of civilian complaints charging police abuse; as well as the consequences of national and local efforts to enforce various types of prohibition.

Although the present book does not analyze every one of the foregoing issues, it does highlight many of them through three separate parts. Part 1 is a presentation of the historical background regarding national prohibition and includes chapters dealing with: the nature of the drug enforcement problem (Chapter 1); criminal justice in colonial times (Chapter 2); early temperance efforts (Chapter 3); the wide range of progressive criminal justice reforms at the beginning of the twentieth century (Chapter 4); and the nature of saloon life prior to the 1920s (Chapter 5). Part 2 contains two chapters describing the Tighe case (Chapters 5 & 6). Chapter 7 deals with an analysis of the Tighe case as well as the *Olmstead* case, one of the earliest cases to reach the U.S. Supreme Court regarding the issue of electronic surveillance. The remaining two chapters in Part 2 provide an overview of the enforcement of prohibition (Chapter 9) and Chapter 10 covers the unprecedented battle against "rum row" waged by the Coast Guard. Post-World War II developments are addressed in Part 3. Chapter 11 discusses the escalation of the drug war. Chapter 12 considers current trends in drug enforcement. Chapter 13 discusses the issues traditionally debated regarding victimless crimes. Chapter 14 (the final chapter) relates the concept of community policing to a variety of recommendations regarding a citizen's role in drug enforcement and presents five specific recommendations for reducing the drug problem. The final chapter concludes with a section about the need for a new mission regarding prohibition enforcement and provides details about how that mission should be focused. In particular, it takes note of the current lack of any societal agent who is charged with the proactive task of discovering drug abusers and then helping them to find appropriate treatment.

In general, this book emphasizes the activities of early vice control advocates, political leaders, and police reformers. They have exercised a great amount of influence upon the social and legal institutions of America. At no other time in American history was the drive to rid urban centers of vice more intense, than in the period between the 1890s and the end of the First World War. The activists of the period (known collectively as "the progressives") consistently associated the occurrence of social problems with moral concerns. In addition, they were motivated by popular literature and field studies conducted by social scientists. For example, the popular book by Lincoln Steffens', *The Shame of the Cities*, published in 1904, called attention to the links between organized gambling, prostitution, and political corruption. In an effort to reduce the exploitation of women factory workers, Louis D. Brandeis argued before the Supreme Court of the United States in 1908 that having to spend long hours at work undermined the moral fiber of women and drove them to "alcoholic stimulants and other excesses" (Boyer, 1978, pp. 196-97). Moreover, the *Pure Food Act of 1906* was adopted largely because of the publication of the novel *The Jungle* by Upton Sinclair. In his book, Sinclair graphically described how food companies marketed tainted meats and other products.

The following themes and topics are developed throughout the book: the roots of America's criminal justice system; portraits of the figures associated with the nation's long obsession with chemical use and dependency; governmental and political misinformation campaigns; and the enforcement mechanisms that have been developed to contend with drug use, especially during the Prohibition era. The work is mindful of the old adage of George Santayana: "Those who cannot remember the past are condemned to repeat it."

The prohibition era took place throughout the twenties and into the early thirties. This span of time is given special emphasis since the events that occurred, while well chronicled, have been largely erased from the public's collective consciousness due to the passage of time. Nevertheless, that era can be used to provide object lessons for today. Moreover, the prohibition era never really ended, but has continued to manifest itself by virtue of the enforcement effort aimed at various other types of drugs.

It was once believed that the smuggling operations that took place during prohibition were of such great magnitude that they would never be repeated. However, the development of America's criminal justice agencies for the last quarter of the twentieth century has been primarily guided by anti-drug policies. The current proliferation and use of personal firearms by lower level drug dealers has vastly increased the stakes for all Americans. Moreover, it appears unlikely that these trends will change after the year 2000 unless public awareness creates a demand for new strategies.

This book also attempts to bring together the disparate threads of American culture that have shaped the criminal justice system. Special attention is given to the particular style of law enforcement that was common to the prohibition period. The story that is revealed is filled with the zeal of reformers and the down-to-earth struggles of average people to live with the consequences of that enthusiasm. The relevance of the saloon to the people and business interests of that era are also presented for a better understanding of those times. All governments possess an awesome power for dealing with social problems. An essential objective of this work is to unravel the nature and sources of this power and to assess its limitations.

It is appropriate that as we enter the next millennium and reign-in the close of the twentieth century, that we revisit the issue of prohibition and its enforcement. We can see how interpretations of those events played out and learn new insights about our collective prospects and ultimate destiny. There is much at stake; for on the one hand, is the civil liberties perspective that calls attention to how our government has tried to control what we seek to ingest into our own bodies, while on the other hand is the knowledge that a high percentage of domestic violence, child abuse and other crimes and social problems are associated with alcohol and other types of drug abuse. Chapter 1 further addresses the current issues involving substance abuse and control.

ENDNOTES

1. Huppke, Rex W. (1999, January 17). Drug Smuggling on Interstates a Challenge for Cops, *Sunday Times Union*, p. F1.
2. For a more detailed history of the evolution of drug abuse in the United States, see James A. Inciardi, *The War on Drugs: Heroin, Cocaine, Crime, and Public Policy* (Palo Alto, CA: Mayfield, 1986). Opium, peyote, cocaine, and heroin are also discussed in historical context by David Musto in *The American Disease: Origins of Narcotic Control*, rev. ed. (New York: Oxford University Press, 1989). Coca and cocaine are given special attention in Lester Grinspoon and James Bakalar, *Cocaine: A Drug and Its Evolution*, rev. ed. (New York, Basic Books, 1985). For an important critique of the war on drugs, see Arnold Trebach and Kevin Zeese, *Prohibition and the Conscience of Nations* (Washington, D.C.: Drug Policy Foundation, 1990).

Part 1

HISTORICAL BACKGROUND

Chapter 1

ENFORCEMENT PROBLEMS

"A crisis in drug use is plaguing our youth and our
Nation. More than half our high school seniors report
having used illicit drugs, and young people are using
mood altering substances at increasingly younger
ages."[1]

SHAY BILCHIK, ADMINISTRATOR
OFFICE OF JUVENILE JUSTICE AND
DELINQUENCY PREVENTION (1998)

This chapter concerns various trends and estimates of the extent of substance abuse and related enforcement issues (e.g., national prohibition,
zero tolerance, and sentencing). However, before providing relevant information about these topics three specific terms (i.e., prohibition, demand
reduction, and supply reduction) need to be defined since they constantly
arise when policies and strategies involving the drug problem are encountered.

Prohibition is the policy that bans the distribution, possession, and use of
specified substances made illegal by legislative or administrative order.
Prohibition violators are subject to criminal penalties. Prohibition differs
from "regulation," in that regulations do not ban the possession of specified
substances, but rather place controls (e.g., various restrictions) on their use
and distribution. Both demand reduction and supply reduction are types of
strategies for enforcing prohibition. Demand reduction strategies seek to
decrease the use of drugs by changing the behavior of current or potential
users. Demand reduction strategies include drug abuse treatment, education,
and social services. Supply reduction involves taking official actions to curtail drug use; for example, by apprehending, convicting, and punishing drug
offenders as well as by seizing and destroying illicit drugs. Although thought
of as having primarily supply reduction goals, the use of criminal sanctions
also have demand reduction effects by discouraging drug use (Bureau of
Justice Statistics, hereinafter referred to as "BJS," 1992, pp. 74-75).

Trends and Estimates of Drug Use

Thirty years after the repeal of the Eighteenth Amendment, America was still struggling with the problem of excessive drinking of alcoholic beverages. The issue has both formal (arrest) and informal (nonarrest) aspects. Formally, in 1964 the FBI reported 1,458,821 arrests for public drunkenness by 3,977 agencies covering a population of 132,439,000. This figure accounted for over 31 percent of the total number of arrests for all offenses. The addition of alcohol-related offenses (driving while intoxicated), disorderly conduct, and vagrancy) to this percentage, raises the arrest figure in 1964 to nearly half of all reported arrests (FBI, 1965). However, the police also use a variety of informal means to contend with this problem; for example, warning and escorting the inebriated home, or by arranging for a cab or relative to perform the same function. Thus, the true extent of police involvement with inebriates may be unknown.

The identification of the magnitude of drunkenness is further complicated by the trend to refer nondisorderly inebriates to civil detoxification and mental health centers. These centers are common divisions of most community hospitals and county public health systems. Their patients include persons who abuse a wide array of drugs and other dangerous substances. A large percentage of substance abusers arrive at these and other treatment centers on a voluntary basis. However, as Abadinsky (1997) has pointed out "reducing the consumption of drugs by increasing law enforcement and large-scale treatment programs does not solve such significant sociological problems as lack of educational and employment opportunity and residential instability" (p. 357).

As the twentieth century concluded, newspaper headlines reflected both a national concern for drug prohibition as well as its consequences. A sampling of these headlines included:

1. "Role Models? NBA Players' Drug Use Must End"
2. "Elite Mexican Drug Officers Said to Be Tied to Traffickers"
3. "Woman Learns Costly Lesson When She Drives Home Drunk"
4. "Enforcing Marijuana Laws a Waste of Precious Resources"
5. "Limits on Cash Transactions Cuts Drug-Money Laundering"
6. "No Death Sentence for Drunken Driver in Student Killings"
7. "Drug Trade Feeds on Payoffs at Mexico Line"
8. "Marijuana Measures Aim at Compassion of Voters"
9. "Penn State Students Riot as Bars Close"
10. "President Targets Drug Users: War Requires Diverse Strategy, Report States"[2]

While these were frequent and common headlines, when the Associated Press released the results of its poll of 299 American newspaper editors and broadcast executives at the end of 1998, they had only one story related to drugs in their top ten list. In tenth position was the report that the tobacco companies had agreed to the largest settlement in American history. The tobacco industry agreed to pay to 46 states the sum of $206 billion in order to reimburse them for health care related to smoking. They also agreed to eliminate several forms of advertising. However, the same poll collected through a public ballot posted on the AP's Web site and at the Newseum in Arlington, Virginia, a museum about newsgathering, indicated that this story failed to make the general public's top ten choices (Levinson, 1998).

The National Household Survey on Drug Abuse (NHSDA) is the only survey that regularly produces estimates of drug use among members of the civilian, noninstitutionalized population age 12 and older in the United States. The survey is conducted through personal interviews with a large national probability sample and is considered to be an effective way to estimate drug use in virtually the entire population of the United States. The presentation of highlights from one of its more recent surveys appears to be an appropriate way to begin to consider the topic of prohibition enforcement.

The 1994 NHSDA survey disclosed that about 65 million (31%) of the 209 million persons represented by the survey reported marijuana use in their lifetimes. Almost 22 million (10%) of the 209 million persons represented by the 1994 survey reported cocaine use in their lifetime. An estimated 18 million persons (8.7%) reported ever using inhalants or hallucinogens (e.g., LSD). Tables 1.1 and 1.2 present a more detailed analysis of the use of hallucinogens and inhalants by type and age group. About 4 million persons (1.9% of the surveyed population) reported crack use in their lifetime. Less than 1 percent reported heroin use in their lifetime. However, in 1994, alcohol was the most commonly used drug in the United States. Approximately 176 million (84%) reported alcohol use in their lifetime, 140 million persons (67%) reported use in the past year, and approximately 113 million persons (54%) reported current use (in the previous month). Table 1.3 presents a more detailed age analysis for alcohol use. The data in Table 1.3 is useful for assessing the percentage of underage (illegal) drinking (Substance Abuse and Mental Health Services Administration, 1996).

In 1995, the United States recorded its highest drug arrest total; an estimated 1.5 million people were arrested for either the sale and/or manufacture or possession of illegal narcotics. Arrests for possession constituted three out of every four drug arrests in 1995. The following drug categories were included in this estimate: opium or cocaine and their derivatives (morphine, heroin, codeine); marijuana; synthetic narcotics (Demerol®, methadone); and dangerous nonnarcotic drugs (barbiturates, Benzedrine®). A governmental analysis of national drug arrest trends by drug type was

Table 1.1
PERCENTAGE REPORTING HALLUCINOGEN USE IN THEIR LIFETIME, BY
HALLUCINOGEN TYPE AND AGE GROUP: 1994

| HALLUCINOGEN | AGE GROUP (YEARS) | | | | TOTAL |
	12-17	18-25	26-34	35	
Any Hallucinogen	**4.0**	**14.5**	**15.5**	**6.2**	**8.7**
LSD	3.4	11.1	12.3	5.2	7.0
Peyote	0.3	1.4	2.0	1.8	1.6
Mescaline	0.4	1.9	3.9	3.2	2.8
Psilocybin	1.1	7.2	8.8	2.9	4.3
PCP	1.0	2.5	5.4	2.5	2.8
Ecstasy	0.8	3.1	2.4	0.7	1.3

NOTE: Due to improved survey procedures, these estimates are not comparable to previous
year estimates and should not be used for trends with pre-1994 data.
LSD=lysergic acid diethylamide
PCP=phencyclidine ("Angel Dust")
Source: Office of Applied Studies, SAMHSA, National Household Survey on Drug Abuse,
1994-B.

Table 1.2
PERCENTAGE REPORTING INHALANT USE IN THEIR LIFETIME, BY
INHALANT TYPE AND AGE GROUP: 1994

| INHALANT TYPE | AGE GROUP (YEARS) | | | | TOTAL |
	12-17	18-25	26-34	35+	
Any Inhalant	**7.0**	**10.0**	**11.1**	**3.1**	**5.8**
Gasoline	2.8	2.0	1.3	0.5	**1.1**
Lighter gases	1.1	0.7	0.1	0.1	**0.3**
Spray paints	1.3	0.6	0.5	0.2	**0.4**
Aerosol sprays	1.4	1.0	0.7	0.2	**0.5**
Glue	2.9	1.5	1.4	0.5	**1.0**
Laquer thinners	1.5	1.0	0.5	0.1	**0.5**
Amyl nitrite	0.9	3.0	6.6	1.8	**2.7**
Ether	0.3	0.3	0.3	0.1	**0.2**
Nitrous oxide	1.5	5.0	4.9	1.0	**2.3**
Correction fluids	1.6	1.3	0.8	0.2	**0.6**

NOTE: Due to improved survey procedures, these estimates are not comparable to previous
year estimates and should not be used for trends with pre-1994 data.
Source: Office of Applied Studies, SAMHSA, National Household Survey on Drug Abuse,
1994-B.

made for 1980-1995. The analysis indicated that marijuana arrests dominated the first part of the 1980s, but toward the end of that decade, these arrests were outpaced by heroin and cocaine arrests. However, in the 1990s the pendulum was swinging the other way as the number of marijuana arrests began to increase (FBI, 1996, p. 280).

In 1990, during the height of President George Bush's campaign for a drug-free America, Robert Stone warned that governmental policy with respect to drug abuse appeared to be based on the premise "that if we can't get our people to stop taking drugs, we'll put them all in jail" (Stone, 1990, p. 69). In many respects, the harsh Rockefeller drug laws of the early 1970s were based precisely on this point of view.

Indeed, by January 1998, the National Center on Addiction and Substance Abuse (CASA) at Columbia University issued a major report that found that

Table 1.3

PERCENTAGE REPORTING ALCOHOL USE IN THEIR LIFETIME, THE PAST YEAR, AND THE PAST MONTH, BY AGE: 1994

AGE GROUP	(Unweighted N)	TIME PERIOD		
		LIFETIME	PAST YEAR	PAST MONTH
TOTAL	**(17,809)**	**84.2**	**66.9**	**53.9**
12-17 Years Old	**(4,698)**	**41.7**	**36.2**	**21.6**
12-13	(1,607)	20.3	16.5	8.9
14-15	(1,611)	42.3	36.5	21.6
16-17	(1,480)	64.7	57.6	35.7
18-25 Years Old	**(3,706)**	**86.3**	**78.5**	**63.1**
18-21	(1,845)	82.5	75.8	58.1
22-25	(1,861)	90.1	81.3	68.1
26-34 Years Old	**(5,223)**	**91.8**	**78.8**	**65.3**
26-29	(2,080)	90.2	78.3	64.9
30-34	(3,143)	92.9	79.1	65.5
35 Years and Older	**(4,182)**	**89.0**	**66.2**	**54.1**
35-39	(1,318)	92.2	78.7	65.0
40-44	(983)	92.2	73.5	60.1
45-49	(860)	92.9	77.1	60.4
50+	(1,021)	85.9	57.1	47.0

NOTE: Due to improved survey procedures, these estimates are not comparable to previous year estimates and should not be used for trends with pre-1994 data.

Source: Office of Applied Studies, SAMHSA, National Household Survey on Drug Abuse, 1994-B.

alcohol and drugs were implicated in the incarceration of four out of five prison and jail inmates. At the time of its publication, the study was believed to have been the largest ever conducted of the connections among drugs, alcohol, and incarceration. In particular, the report found that approximately 80 percent of the 1.7 million federal, state, and local prison and jail inmates had either: violated drug or alcohol laws; were under the influence of drugs or alcohol at the time of their crimes; stole property to buy drugs; had a history of drug and alcohol abuse or addiction; or shared some combination of those characteristics. Of further significance was the fact that alcohol was determined to be more closely linked to violent crime than illegal drugs because of its capacity to alter brain functioning. For violent offenders, the changes in brain function included the lowering of inhibitions and the intensification of aggressiveness. For victims of violence, alcohol use decreased the ability to handle unexpected or threatening situations. The study states that alcohol is: "a bigger culprit in connection with murder, rape, assault, child and spouse abuse than any illegal drug. Alcohol addiction and abuse is public enemy number one with respect to homicide and other violent crime." (CASA, 1998). Yet, alcohol has been legal throughout most of this nation's history, except during the Prohibition Era (1920-1933).

Current Enforcement Problems

As we have already pointed out, supply reduction strategies have a major impact on the criminal justice system. The more drug sweeps that take place using police saturation patrols, the more likely that arrests will be made. In turn, these cases will need to be adjudicated in some manner, so that more judges and other court personnel will be needed. If enforcement efforts are directed at high level drug lords, the burden will even be greater. Such cases are more complicated and they will probably require interagency cooperation. On the other hand, if more demand reduction strategies are utilized, an increased burden will probably be placed upon local treatment programs. If the courts refer more cases for treatment, a community's capacity for providing such care may become overburdened (BJS, 1992, p. 77).

In drug control, many law enforcement agencies may have jurisdiction. In drug cases coordination is a key factor for effectiveness as well as information sharing. Sometimes problems have arisen because different types of police officers possess different kinds of arrest authority. Local police officers are empowered to enforce the laws of their state and locality, while state police enforce state laws but not local ordinances. Significantly, neither may arrest and charge persons with violations of federal law unless they are specifically authorized. Conversely, federal law enforcement officers enforce federal laws and may not enforce state or local laws unless so designated.

Moreover, not all federal agents enforce all federal laws. In addition, but only on a limited basis, the cross-designation of officers and prosecutors between state and federal levels of government and between agencies have begun to be used to broaden jurisdictional authority. For example, Drug Enforcement Administration (DEA), state, and local task forces have been established. In such task forces, the local and state police officers "are designated task force investigators and have the authority to enforce Federal drug laws like DEA agents" (BJS, 1992, p. 142). In this way, it is possible to create a multijurisdictional approach to confront drug traffic that crosses municipal, county, and state boundaries.

More than 200 years ago, the founding fathers' solution to the need to protect America from the activities of smugglers was the establishment of "the Revenue Marine"; subsequently, renamed the "Coast Guard." Although the U.S. Coast Guard is the smallest branch of the armed forces, it is the most active and versatile. Moreover, today it has the most visible role of all the governmental agencies that are engaged in humanitarian missions as well as antidrug smuggling operations. It currently deploys hundreds of cutters, planes and helicopters to intercept and deter the smuggling efforts of the world's well-armed drug cartels (Schreiner, 1990). Subsequent chapters will not only highlight the role of the Coast Guard in the current war on illegal drug trafficking, but also its use during the 1920s when the United States declared war on alcoholic beverages.

Today, the availability of new technologies is dramatically changing traditional enforcement strategies in the battle against narcotics. Some of these innovations involve greater levels of governmental intrusion than others. For example, new infrared technology can now detect the number of people and their locations in buildings and ion scanning equipment can detect cocaine residue on money. Special streamlined courts for handling narcotic cases have also been established and such penalties as fines, community supervision (e.g., probation) and shock imprisonment are being used to discourage further drug use. In addition, the concept of "zero tolerance" has fostered the use of "checkpoints" for the control of drunken drivers, drug users and illegal gun owners. While some of these developments are more intrusive than others, a lot depends upon the discretion, skill and knowledge of the agents of enforcement.

Zero Tolerance

There are currently over one hundred federal laws that permit the forfeiture of property upon conviction of a crime. During the Middle Ages, the penalty of forfeiture of a person's property was required punishment for most serious crimes. Present day forfeiture laws have resulted in the confiscation of valuable homes, yachts and automobiles because occupants or owners may have possessed various quantities of drugs. Permanent loss of such property is based on the principle that these properties may have facilitated the commission of crime or been purchased with criminally obtained funds. The frequent occurrence of property forfeiture is representative of a type of "zero tolerance" enforcement policy that has been authorized by state and federal lawmakers during the last quarter of the twentieth century (Senna & Siegel, 1998, pp. 386-87). Former San Jose, California police chief, Joseph McNamara, has indicated that as of 1997 asset seizures have surpassed the $4 billion mark (McNamara, 1997, p. 538). Zero tolerance policies are based upon the view that illegal drug distributors, buyers, and users should be held fully accountable for their offenses under the law (BJS, 1992, p. 75).

Another related type of "zero tolerance" involves neighborhood sweeps by police for "quality of life" offenses (e.g., loiterers, illegally parked cars, sanitary code violations, etc.). During the last few years of the twentieth century the concept has also been applied with respect to just about any effort by authorities to "get tough" with offenders. Between 1920 and 1933, the people of the United States were subjected to another example of "zero tolerance" enforcement when their individual and collective freedom to visit saloons and other drinking establishments were outlawed. In order to shed light on current drug enforcement strategies, this book highlights various aspects of America's greatest "zero tolerance" measure—national prohibition.

A fundamental issue that has existed throughout American history has been the struggle to maintain a proper balance between effective law enforcement and individual freedom. The United States Constitution, the opinions of the Supreme Court, and other sources of law have consistently focused on the goal of maintaining the maximum degree of individual liberty that is consistent with social order. For these reasons, this book gives special consideration to the adoption and repeal of the Eighteenth Amendment of the U.S. Constitution.

The actual process of working out the best desirable balance between law and liberty has often been difficult. Historically, the branches of government have often been at odds with one another. At various times, segments of the same branch of government have had conflicts about this issue. Moreover, the American people have been just as divided, but no less concerned about personal liberty and preserving order. One of the unique features of the American criminal justice system is that unlike many nations of the world, the United States has never had a national police force. This fact has remained a constant despite America's participation in two world wars, a civil war, several major international conflicts and an infamous "Cold War" that lasted for nearly fifty years during the last half of the twentieth century. Instead of such a national police force there are some 17,000 local, municipal, county, and state law enforcement agencies. They are the most visible aspects of the machinery of justice designed to provide Americans with a system of "ordered liberty."

National Prohibition

During the first 15 years of the twentieth century, a fervor for reform spread across most of urban America. It was known as the progressive movement and its supporters sought to enhance the quality of life of the average worker by dealing with social and economic problems through the use of governmental intervention. Many persons associated with the progressives were convinced that temperance and prohibition made sense, since "in a modern society, liquor both reduced men's efficiency and spawned a multitude of social, political, and economic evils" (Kyvig, 1979, p. 8). The progressive era not only coincided with America's long fixation with intoxicating beverages, but it was a time when the middle and upper classes were interested in preserving their gains. They were concerned about the impact of a flood of new European immigrants, particularly Catholics and Jews. They literally launched a crusade to preserve their primarily Protestant values. They initiated a reform agenda and created numerous organizations to contend with vice and disorder. They lobbied throughout all levels of government for stricter controls regarding drinking, gambling, prostitution, and policing. They sought to suppress the perceived breeding grounds of disorder: the saloons, dance halls, and movie theaters (Fogelson, 1977, p. 41).

A much studied and complex case study involving the concept of "ordered liberty" was the encounter that the American people had with its forces of law enforcement during the Prohibition Era. From January 16, 1920 until December 5, 1933, Americans were forbidden by the Eighteenth Amendment from manufacturing, selling, or transporting any intoxicating liquor. Since no national police force existed or was ever created to contend with the enforcement problems engendered by prohibition, state and local police forces were expected to enforce the applicable laws as part of their routine assignments. Moreover, the most outspoken supporters of prohibition strategically underestimated the policing effort that prohibition enforcement would require. They believed that only a small addition to America's police establishment would be needed and this was accomplished with the establishment of a special Prohibition Unit within the Department of the Treasury (Kyvig, 1979, p. 23).

The advent of prohibition climaxed a hundred-year controversy about the need to forbid the use of liquor within the United States. The years of national prohibition (1920-1933), were some of the most turbulent in American history. Moreover, it is believed by many that the era strengthened the interests of organized crime and an illegal merchandising system that today is responsible for the importation and distribution of many of today's controlled substances, especially, narcotics (Coffey, 1975). Indeed, the techniques of "bootlegging" (i.e., the logistical methods for uniting sellers and purchasers) reached new levels of sophistication during the prohibition era. It also increased the amount of local police corruption and spurred "the creation of a federal law enforcement presence that impacted on a large segment of American society for the first time" (Deakin, 1988, p.110).

In America, during the latter half of the nineteenth century and especially during periods of substantial immigration, the semipublic spaces of saloons, often provided relief for the masses of urban tenement dwellers from their cramped living spaces. Saloonkeepers were happy to supply cheap beer and other alcoholic beverages when there were shortages of clean water and safe milk. Before its disappearance, the saloon served as the principal neighborhood gathering place, information exchange, paycheck casher, employment bureau and political club (Kyvig, 1979, p. 189). On the other hand, social reformers of va ious kinds looked upon the saloon as an unsavory institution that weakened family ties and "that left the breadwinner an inefficient worker, more likely to be unemployed" (Duis, 1983, p. 111).

During prohibition the speakeasy replaced the saloon. However, whereas the saloon was often situated on the corner of a block with a swinging door, the speakeasies were typically located in a basement, a back room, or an upstairs apartment. Speakeasy doors were locked and had a peephole. Oftentimes, the front portion of the establishment had the appearance of a legitimate business (e.g., drugstore, coffeehouse, etc.). In 1929, Police Commissioner Grover Whalen stated that there were 32,000 speakeasies in New York City (Cashman, 1981, p. 43). The operators and owners of these speakeasies were "dependent on corrupt policemen and agents who drank too much of their liquor and extorted too much of their profit" (Cashman, 1981, p. 44).

The experiment of national prohibition in the United States was one of the liveliest issues in American politics throughout the twenties and early thirties. One commentator wrote that the experiment had one hope of success and that hope was in the power of the generally law-abiding to stand by it. However, "as a matter of simple fact, the establishment of national prohibition is being made impossible by the refusal of those classes to recognize and obey the law of the Republic" (Ratcliffe, 1925, p. 721). Several decades after the prohibition movement had ended Hofstadter (1955) reflected that the prohibition experience was one of the leading clues to help explain the end of the progressive era. "For Prohibition, in the twenties, was the skeleton at the feast, a grim reminder of the moral frenzy that so many wished to forget, a ludicrous caricature of the reforming impulse...that it is both possible and desirable to moralize private life through public action" (Hofstadter, 1955, p. 289).

Today, the Office of National Drug Control Policy is the agency within the executive branch of the federal government most responsible for guiding and directing strategies to contend with America's drug problem. At the time of the preparation of this book, its 1998 comprehensive plan to reduce drug use in America was the most current. Its stated goal was to reduce drug use by more than 50 percent over the next ten years. The plan was created with the assistance of law enforcement, policymakers, and other stakeholders. Significantly, it omitted any reference to the lessons learned during the Prohibition Era; neither did it refer to the extraordinary political activities that have led to the passage of more and more stringent federal statutes regarding drugs. For example, the document entirely disregards the period when the U.S. Coast Guard and the U.S. Customs Service "were engaged at times in a shooting war with the rumrunners" (Whitehead, 1963, p. 84). Moreover, the report fails to make any reference to the two main methods individuals and gangs used to illegally transport intoxicating liquors into the United States 80 years ago: transoceanic ship traffic, and transcontinental small boat, plane and automobile traffic. Then and now, smugglers have used every possible conveyance to take their controlled substances to the marketplace.

The prohibition experience is sometimes cited when the legalization (or regulation) of drugs is raised as a method for dealing with our current drug problems. During prohibition, many of the same problems we are now experiencing involving America's "drug culture" were also taking place. These common problems include: easy access to controlled substances; uncertainty about quality of substances available through the black market; smuggling activities including money laundering; indiscriminate violence; rising health costs; loss of tax revenue; corruption; wasteful competition between enforcement agencies; inconsistent governmental control policies; and the growth of criminal organizations. Prohibition enforcement in the 1920s and early 1930s involved the combined efforts of state and national agencies of social control. Similarly, the enforcement of current drug laws has required the intervention of local authorities and many federal branches of government. Strategically, during the Prohibition Era the existence of a concurrent power of state and federal enforcement was cited as one of the major reasons for the demise of national prohibition. Significantly, local enforcement efforts varied widely and the need for a better prepared federal agency of enforcement was recognized too late.

A key aspect of enforcing any law relates not only to the array and quality of the assembled personnel, but the type of procedural law that serves to guide such workers in their quest for justice. Significantly, in the 1920s the majority of the provisions of the Bill of Rights had not yet been extended to the court systems of the states. In particular, the federal exclusionary rule was not yet applicable to states through a Fourteenth Amendment interpretation. Thus, the enforcement of the National Prohibition Law (i.e., the *Volstead Act*) oftentimes involved situations where evidence was obtained by state and local police officers that violated the search and seizure provisions of the Fourth Amendment, but was nevertheless admissible in federal courts. In 1921, in *Burdeau v. McDowell*, 256 U.S. 265, the U.S. Supreme Court stated that the Federal government may not use evidence which the government itself has obtained in violation of Constitutional principles.

> But strange to relate, it may use evidence which anybody else has stolen....Such evidence is perfectly admissible in federal courts, no matter how secured by the state officers who, to the federal courts, are merely like any other private thieves of evidence. Hence it follows that in certain jurisdictions the federal authorities rely almost wholly on state discoverers....In more than one jurisdiction it is the daily practice. (McBain, 1928, pp. 97-98)

McBain (1928) pointed out other strange anomalies in the legal system of the United States that became more prominent because of the efforts to enforce prohibition. In 1927, he attempted to explain some of the legal difficulties associated with national prohibition policy in a series of six lectures delivered at Cornell University and the University of Richmond.

Sentencing Problems

The avoidance of injustice after arrest and conviction is dependent upon the penalties established by legislators and the competencies of court and correctional personnel to carry out legislative mandates. The greatest suffering may occur when lawmakers, law enforcers, judges and penal authorities become overzealous in their pursuit of law enforcement. At the end of 1998, lobbying by various groups and individuals was being sharply directed at New York's Rockefeller era drug laws. Such laws mandate a sentence of 15 years to life for possessing 4 ounces of a controlled substance or selling two ounces. The effort included a series of 60-second radio ads that tell the true stories of people unable to be with their families over the holidays because they are serving lengthy prison sentences for relatively low-level drug offenses under the New York laws. The ads appeared after the state's governor for the first time announced that he would not be granting any clemencies for the remainder of the holiday season. New York's governor, George Pataki, had only granted 13 petitions for clemency since taking office in 1994. Eleven of the 13 had been for persons convicted under the Rockefeller laws. Several of the former state senators who had initially sponsored the laws were now calling for their reform as well as a bipartisan coalition of conservative criminal justice experts, religious leaders, retired judges and minority group advocates (McCaffrey, 1998b).

In New York, executive clemency does not guarantee release from prison but it requires a parole hearing. However, parole board members typically go along with the governor's recommendations. Prisoners are eligible for clemency after they have served half of their minimum sentence. Since 1980, only a total of 108 inmates have been granted clemency in New York State. Of these, 69 were drug offenders sentenced under the Rockefeller laws. At the time of Governor Pataki's refusal to grant clemency to any of the hundreds of prisoners who applied, some commentators speculated that his decision may have been inspired out of political concerns since the Republican governor is known to have higher political aspirations (McCaffrey, 1998a).

The problems associated with the nation's drug control policies also involve the thorny issue of race. In 1996, the federal government reported that one of every three black men aged 20-29 was either in jail, awaiting trial or on probation or parole. Experts in the field of law have pointed to the more lengthy sentences imposed for crack than for possession of other drugs (e.g., powder cocaine) as a partial explanation. In fact, under the current federal law, in order for a powder cocaine offender to get the same sentence as a crack cocaine offender, the former would have to have 100 times more the amount of crack. However, crack is made from powder cocaine. Even though more crack users are white, many more blacks than whites have been arrested for possession of small quantities of crack (Carter, 1996, p. 292). These disparities persist despite the criticism of a federal Sentencing Commission and many federal judges (Jackson, 1997). Furthermore, African-Americans and Latinos compose 94 percent of the drug offenders in New York State prisons, although a majority of people who sell and use drugs in New York are white (Green, 1998).

The foregoing has provided a brief overview of the current problems associated with drug enforcement. It is with this background in mind that we now begin to consider the formal history of drug enforcement.

ENDNOTES

1. Bilchik, Shay. (1998, December). From the Administrator. *Juvenile Justice: Journal of the Office of Juvenile Justice and Delinquency Prevention, 5* (2), 1.
2. The sources of these headlines, listed consecutively as they appeared in this chapter are: (1) *The Sunday Gazette,* October 4, 1998, p. E4 (reprinted from *The Washington Post*); (2) *The New York Times,* September 16, 1998, p. 1; (3) *Daily*

Freeman, September 19, 1998, p. 10; (4) *The Sunday Gazette,* September 20, 1998, p. F3; (5) *The New York Times,* March 11, 1997, p. A1; (6) *The New York Times,* May 7, 1997, p. 1; (7) *The New York Times,* March 24, 1997, p. A1; (8) *The Daily Gazette,* October 23, 1998, p. A8; (9) *The Daily Gazette,* July 13, 1998, p. D8; and (10) *The Sunday Gazette,* July 12, 1998, p. 1.

Chapter 2

CRIMINAL JUSTICE IN COLONIAL AMERICA

"Ministers shall not give themselves to excess in
drinkinge, or riott, or spending their tyme idellye by day
or night."[1]

STATUTE ADOPTED BY THE VIRGINIA
COLONIAL ASSEMBLY (1630)

Throughout American history, liquor reform has been an important
theme. It reached its pinnacle of interest during the progressive era,
especially after 1908, when the political efforts of the Anti-Saloon League
were most intense. But the path that ultimately led to the implementation of
the Eighteenth Amendment in 1920 was probably first traversed by the
Pilgrims of 1620 and their immediate followers from across the Atlantic. In
fact, the Pilgrims aboard the *Mayflower*, regularly consumed beer during their
perilous voyage. It was deemed a safer beverage than the water supply they
had loaded at the start of their journey (Harris, 1994, p. 23). In 1630, the
Arabella, which carried John Winthrop to the Massachusetts colony to serve
as its new governor, "had aboard '42 tuns of beer, 14 tuns of water,' and the
ratio of three drinks of beer to one of water was about average for pioneer
voyagers" (Severn, 1969, p. 14).

In this chapter, the maintenance of the social order in Puritan New
England, Middlesex County in the Massachusetts Bay Colony, colonial
Maryland and New York is examined. These materials can provide a social
and legal context for a better understanding of the temperance movements
of the nineteenth century and the final achievement of national prohibition
within the first quarter of the twentieth century.

Chapin (1983) found that America's earliest systems of criminal justice
established in Virginia, Plymouth, Massachusetts Bay, Maryland, Rhode
Island, Connecticut, and New Haven prior to 1660 were the most efficient
that America has ever had (p. 98). "Courts met regularly, normally every
month, and usually cleared their dockets in each session" (Chapin, 1983, p.
97). Demographic patterns, small populations, and relatively short distances
contributed to their efficiency (Chapin, 1983, p. 97). Moreover, "if the success of a criminal justice system is to be judged by the rate of recidivism, all

of the colonial jurisdictions receive high marks," (Chapin, 1983, p. 142) since the rate of recidivism was minuscule.

Unlike the court system in their native England, the colonists that traveled to the New World shaped a rational system of courts by giving all of their courts a general jurisdiction which combined both actions in law and those in equity. Moreover, in three colonies–Plymouth, Connecticut, and New Haven, virtually all criminal cases were heard "in a single central court" (Chapin, 1983, p. 97). This was a marked improvement upon the English system.

In addition, the colonists brought the office of constable with them. The constables acted "as the line peace officers in every jurisdiction" (Chapin, 1983, p. 96). The New England towns elected these officers of the peace for a one-year term following the English pattern and in Virginia and Maryland the governors appointed them (Chapin, 1983, p. 96). The overall responsibilities of constables were expanded in the New World. Their duties included:

> (1) Apprehending all minor offenders and suspicious persons encountered; (2) the execution of warrants and other orders of the courts; (3) initiating and pursuing the hue and cry; (4) inspecting taverns to see that all patrons were orderly; (5) establishing and supervising the town watch; (6) collecting local taxes; (7) supervising the sealing of weights and measures; (8) maintaining custody of all lost goods; (9) identifying and arresting runaway servants; (10) insuring family cohesion; (11) serving as town coroner; (12) acting as the chief election official; (13) escorting offenders to court and presenting the charges; (14) recommending that certain persons secure a bond (also called a recognizance) for the peace or good behavior; and (15) placing accused or convicted persons in the stocks or jail (Chapin, 1983, pp. 28, 31, 52, 96-97).

It is of interest to note that Rhode Island authorized both its constables and tavern keepers the right under warrant to search homes to ascertain the existence of any quantities of liquor (Cherrington, 1920, pp. 23-24).

"The recognizance system" was an early form of community crime prevention that involved warnings, the posting of bonds for good behavior, and monitoring whether or not persons were meeting the conditions of the bond. The system was effective because communities were small prior to 1660 (Chapin, 1983, p. 28). Today, most of these responsibilities are handled by a variety of specialized regulatory agencies and their agents. The "hue and cry" involved raising one's voice or shouting so that all in hearing distance could aide in the capture of a criminal suspect or contend with some other threat to the community's safety. Male citizens have had this responsibility at least since the time of Alfred the Great (849-899 AD). It is commonly believed that this practice was the origin of the concept of citizen's arrest (Wrobleski & Hess, 1997, p. 6).

The less complex nature of colonial society permitted greater reliance upon the church, the family and the community for the purpose of maintaining social control. In general, primary concern focused on the need to return an offender back to the community as soon as possible. The sentencing of criminals aimed at producing public shame and humiliation for the offender. This proved to be an effective means of preventing future wrongdoing not only for the particular offender, but also for the community at large. Significantly, when most towns had less than a thousand residents, attended the same church and travel was rare, everyone had a good opportunity to know one another and the threat of public embarrassment was a strong deterrent to misconduct. Obviously, the stranger or newcomer could not be as easily subjected to shame and most colonial towns were quite wary of such persons. Special ordinances were adopted to try and cope with strangers who had no visible means of support. The majority of these laws were designed to encourage strangers to return to their place of origin or risk such corporal punishment as whipping.

During the colonial period, there was a good deal of drinking. There was no scientific understanding about the harmfulness or healthfulness of alcoholic beverages. Native American leaders often objected to the sale of alcohol and their appeals continued into the nineteenth century. For example, in 1801, Little Turtle, chief of the Miami Nation, visited President Jefferson for the express purpose of preventing sales of liquor to his people. For the administrators of the white settlements, the most important issue was the use of intoxicants that led to disorder. For the landowners and merchants, there was concern that drink contributed to idleness among servants and apprentices. Churchmen regularly drank and liquor was consumed during many church events. By the early part of the eighteenth century, rum shipped from American ports had begun to be used as a means of obtaining slaves from Africa (Cherrington, 1920, pp. 10-14, 60).

Colonial Massachusetts

In 1633, a citizen of the Massachusetts Bay Colony was required to wear a red "D" around his neck for one year because of his repeated drunkenness. In 1637, it was decreed that in order to discourage drunkenness that no person would be allowed to stay in any inn "longer than necessary occasions, upon payne of 20 shillings for every offense"; and two years later it was forbidden to make toasts wishing good health (Cherrington, 1920, pp. 17-19). In 1645, the law of 1639 relative to drinking toasts was repealed, but a new law providing for fining innkeepers 5 shillings for permitting drunkenness was imposed (Cherrington, 1920, p. 21). In 1670, a law was passed that required selectmen to post drunkards' names in public houses and to prohibit sales to them. In 1751, the selling of liquors to any "Negro, Indian or mulatto slave" was prohibited; however, the law was later repealed (Cherrington, 1920, pp. 27 & 35).

Thompson (1986) studied colonial court records in Middlesex County, in the Massachusetts Bay Colony during the latter half of the seventeenth century. In part, he attributed the effective functioning of the justice system in those days to the inquisitorial role of the examining magistrates. In this process, judges specifically questioned defendants about their actions prior to the actual trial and thereafter pronounced their judgment. Significantly, such examinations "often served as the real trial when the examining magistrate decided in his own mind on the guilt or innocence of the accused" (Thompson, 1986, p. 7). Significantly, the conviction rate not only in Middlesex, but in other surrounding courts was about 90 percent (Thompson, 1986, p. 7). Similarly, before 1660 "in most courts there was a grand or presentment jury whose findings in small offenses amounted to a conviction" (Chapin, 1983, p. 30). Convictions for the crime of fornication frequently met with such punishment as: being whipped, fined, put in the stocks, and/or being forced to marry (Friedman, 1998, p. 187).

Unlike future developments in some major midwestern cities, such as Chicago, the New England colonies developed a special culture concerning the inns and their operations. Inns were essential for the well being of early travelers (and in many respects they still are). They had to make available rooms, food and beverages at anytime during the day or evening, including Sundays. Thus, when other types of establishments for the selling and consumption of alcohol developed, many communities provided an "innkeeper's exception" (Duis, 1983, p. 9). For example, "until the early 1900s the hotels of Boston could sell liquor at any time, when other types of sellers were denied the privilege. Tradition held that customers were legally the friends of the innkeeper, who entertained them in his home, and the imposition of temporal restrictions was an invasion of his privacy" (Duis, 1983, p. 9).

On the other hand, colonial legislators were also mindful that such an "innkeeper's privilege" might be abused. In colonial Massachusetts, as noted above, various statutes were adopted to limit liquor sales (e.g., to children, native Americans, drunkards, etc.). In order to insure that the innkeepers knew who the "drunkards" were, local authorities prepared and circulated a list of persons who could not be sold a drink. This law survived the colonial period and in 1798 a new law was adopted that encouraged leading citizens in the Boston area to regularly visit taverns in order to report any violations. Moreover, between 1637 and 1645 other laws were adopted that required that innkeepers only sell to strangers or nonresidents. This restriction was quickly modified to permit local residents to enter inns, but it still sought to limit public drinking by regulating the amount of time that could be spent at inns. In 1698, a law was adopted that required inns to be erected only at major intersections (Duis, 1983).

Colonial Maryland

As did both Thompson (1986) and Chapin (1983), Semmes (1966) in his study of colonial Maryland also relied heavily on court records. The early settlers of Maryland were encouraged to bring with them servants and it was considered essential for any "gentleman" to have at least one. Servants would help build houses, clear fields, plant and harvest crops, take care of livestock. etc. The services of boatwrights, brickmakers, coopers and other skilled workers were especially needed (Semmes, 1966).

Most of the servants in early Maryland were indentured, although many worked for wages (sometimes in the form of tobacco, clothing, land, etc.). An indenture was a contract between a servant who agreed to work for a master for a number of years, in exchange for food, clothing, shelter and in consideration of the cost of transportation to the colony in the New World. The average period of indenture was five years; however, skilled workers could bargain for smaller periods and other favorable terms (Semmes, 1966).

While many agreements were voluntarily entered into while the parties were still in England, some servants were simply kidnapped, especially younger persons. The practice was known as "spiriting" and was usually conducted by sea captains. (Semmes, 1966, p.84). Since English laws governing the practice of indenture were not formalized until 1682, many servants arrived in the colony without any indenture. Colonial assemblies adopted laws governing the problem beginning in 1654. These laws required younger servants to serve longer periods and local justices of a court determined the age of the new arrival. Masters could earn substantial profits from utilizing the services of even unskilled workers (about 250 pounds sterling for a 5 year period). The work of a servant was hard and long. Indentured servants could be sold or assigned to new masters during the period of the indenture. Typically, masters were obligated at the end of the indenture to provide servants with some goods and even land so those servants could become self-supporting. Under the provisions of a 1654 law, servants no longer received 50 acres of land at the expiration of their indenture because their masters now only received 50 acres of land for having paid "for the transportation of the servant to the colony, whereas formerly a master was entitled to receive 100 acres" (Semmes, 1966, p. 92). There were many successful lawsuits by servants to recover the promised end of period goods (Semmes, 1966, p. 92).

Maidservants who were mistreated by their masters were most likely to be ordered either freed or sold to another master. Masters who brutalized their servants might receive a light fine to be paid with tobacco, but some were required to pay nothing (Semmes, 1966, p. 100). Runaway servants were often recaptured. The "hue and cry" would be raised and masters paid a reward of 200 pounds of tobacco for their capture. This bounty was doubled if a servant was returned who had fled to some other colony. Indians were promised "a matchcoat as a reward" (Semmes, 1966, p. 110). Any person who helped to transport a runaway servant or harbored or in any way protected such a servant "had to pay the servant's master all damages he had sustained by the loss of the servant's services" (Semmes, 1966, p. 112). By 1666, a law was passed that imposed a progressive fine for such activity and there were many cases where colonists were accused of aiding runaway servants (Semmes, 1966).

The penalties that recaptured servants faced included two extra days of service for each day of absence as well as an additional seven years. However, whippings could be substituted for additional service. By 1662, a pass had to be carried by servants who traveled more than ten miles from their masters' house and all colonists were empowered to stop all strangers and inquire about their identity (Semmes, 1966, pp. 116–117).

There was quite a lot of drinking done in early Maryland. At least a couple of men drank themselves to death. The legal penalty for drunkenness was 100 pounds of tobacco. However, if the offender was a servant without means to pay such a fine, he could be set in stocks or bilbos, without food or water for 24 hours. A second offense could bring a whipping or fine of 300 pounds of tobacco. A third offense would lead to a loss of civil rights such as voting and holding office for three years. However, in some cases violators only received a reprimand and a fine for court costs for his first offense. Popular drinks of that era included brandy made of peaches or apples, sack (a strong white wine), punch made of brandy and rum, malt beer, cider, many types of wine, cordials, mumm (a type of strong ale and beer) and metheglin (a mixture of fermented honey and water) (Semmes, 1966, pp. 147–148). Maryland began putting drunkards in the stocks in 1658 (Sann, 1957).

During the seventeenth century, inns or taverns in Maryland were known as ordinaries. They played an important role in the life of the early colonists, affording some respite for weary travelers. The principal means of travel included: boats, horses, or walking. Provincial courts and assemblies often met at such locations. Licenses were needed to operate an ordinary where food, liquor and public lodging were available. Ordinary owners and keepers were required to maintain order and in 1671 laws were passed to regulate the prices of the alcoholic beverages. For example, a third of a gallon of mumm cost one shilling. Fees were also set for a meal (one shilling) and six pence for one night's lodging for a bed (but not in a separate room). Later, bargaining was substituted for the fixed price list for drinks, except for beer. Ordinary keepers bought their beverages from merchants at the best price they could get (Semmes, 1966, pp. 153–54).

Colony officials fined each instance of profanity or swearing with a fine of 10 pounds of tobacco. Repeat offenders "might be punished as the members of any court thought fit" (Semmes, 1966, p. 162). Rigid views were also held and enforced regarding Sabbath observance. Sabbath violators (swearing, drinking or working) could lead to a fine, public repentance and a third time violator might be whipped. Innkeepers who permitted drinking or gaming on the Sabbath could lose their licenses and have to pay a fine of 2,000 pounds of tobacco. A constable of St. Mary's made inspections to see that these regulations were enforced (Semmes, 1966, pp. 163 & 165).

People who denied that Jesus Christ was the Son of God or cursed God or other aspects of the faith could be put to death and have their possessions confiscated. This fate nearly happened to Jacob Lumbrozo, a chirurgean, in 1658. Chirurgery involved purges and bloodletting, the most usual treatment for sick persons in those days. He was saved from possible conviction for blasphemy when the governor of Maryland issued a pardon to all persons who had criminal cases pending or had been convicted (Semmes, 1966, p. 167).

Sorcery was also a capital offense. Rebecca Fowler was the only person to be executed in Maryland for witchcraft, but there were other cases in which this was an issue. Moreover, two women on two separate voyages to Maryland from England were hung as witches. In one of these cases, the great grandfather of George Washington, Colonel John Washington, filed a complaint against the vessel's owner–Edward Prescott. Prescott was acquitted when Colonel Washington did not appear at the trial and Prescott's statements in his own defense went unchallenged (Semmes, 1966, pp. 172–173).

Provincial courts could punish adultery and fornication in any manner they deemed appropriate short of taking of "life or member" (Semmes, 1966, p. 174). Captain Mitchell, a member of the governor's council, was fined 5,000 pounds of tobacco for these crimes as well as causing an abortion. He also had to give a bond for future good conduct. In addition, he was later forced to resign his governmental position and forbidden to hold any office by Lord Baltimore. His servant/companion received 39 lashes and was no longer required to provide service. Other colonists besides those holding office were involved in cases of immorality and in most of these cases, severe punishment was ordered. Women appeared to suffer physical punishment in greater numbers than the men. For example, in some cases of adultery, or of fornication, the man was only fined, while the woman was whipped, especially when the woman had no means to pay a fine or friends to help her pay it (Semmes, 1966, pp. 176-183).

In early Maryland, it was not uncommon for some masters or other persons to have sexual contact with their women servants. If a child was born, the servant's master or mistress could seek compensation from the father for the welfare of the child. On the other hand, a servant woman who could not or would not identify the father could be required to perform additional service for the time she lost in serving her owner by having a child. Thus, she alone had to bear all the punishment. If the father was also an indentured servant, his master might be required to provide a bond to insure that the child would be supported in the event the two servants could not maintain the necessary child care and support. In other situations, suitable arrangements were made for child maintenance (Semmes, 1966, pp. 188-190).

In 1640, persons seeking to marry had to post public documents at least three days prior to the marriage so that anyone who had some reason to object could do so. The words used to perform the marriage ceremony were almost identical to that used in modern times. At first two witnesses were required, later five were necessary. It cost 220 pounds of tobacco or nearly two pound sterling to get married in early Maryland (Semmes, 1966, p. 199). Failure to abide by the stated formalities could result in heavy fines being charged to the marriage official as well as the parties to the marriage. In time, even persons coming from other colonies were also subject to the various licensing requirements. Semmes found only two cases of bigamy in the early records. The harshest prescribed punishment in such cases was death or being burned on the hand (Semmes, 1966, p. 205).

The New England Puritans

However, as in modern times, the role of the colonial courts and other official agencies of the criminal justice system in maintaining order were secondary to the role of the family. Then, as now, family values and mores played a leading role in society's quest for social order. For a time, during colonial times, due to the homogeneity of society, there existed a distinctive set of such family traits and values known as "the puritan ideal."

The puritan ideal was centered on the patriarchal family and other values common to the seventeenth century puritan settlers. In order to accurately discuss the customs of this period, Thompson (1986) studied the testimony of some 500 witnesses in nearly 200 court cases. In such cases can be found a variety of their intimate situations and everyday crises and "the norms, values, aspirations, and inhibitions of ordinary people can be vividly exposed" (Thompson, 1986, p. xvii). The essential features of the patriarchal model in the puritan family required: "the father to become the minister of his dependents, disciplining them, catechizing them, praying with them, reading the Bible to them, generally putting the fear of God into them" (Thompson, 1986, p. xvi).

In the early court records, Thompson (1986) found evidence regarding the prevalence of premarital sexual relationships and bridal pregnancy. Explanations for such behavior might include: the frequent promises made by suitors; the existence of true love; economic and political instability; and role of fathers in censuring courtships. Thompson (1986) always remains cautious about drawing conclusions based on the surviving court records, especially due to the small number of cases in the reports. He cites evidence to indicate that family government (also referred to as patriarchal authority) was most often invoked only after adolescent signs of rebellion (Thompson, 1986, p. 69). He concludes that youthful rebelliousness was just a passing phase and that the "typical youth of the county exercised exemplary self-control" (Thompson, 1986, p. 82). Thus, by the time these young persons reached middle age they became refocused on traditional family values. Nevertheless, after the late 1650s patriarchal powers and related puritan ideals "were in retreat" (Thompson, 1986, p. 96).

Morgan (1966) considered the waywardness of the puritan youth as much more important than a mere "passing phase." He concluded that "The Puritan system failed because the Puritans relied upon their children to provide the church with members....their children were not up to the task....they wrote, they preached, they threatened—but to no avail....in 1721, it was long since clear that grace was not hereditary" (Morgan, p. 185). Thus, according to Morgan (1966) the effects of adolescent culture was not transitory or a mere phase on the road to conversion in middle age as asserted by Thompson (1986, p. 105), but an overriding problem for the puritan patriarchs and at least partly responsible for the ultimate decline of the puritan ideal. Other reasons proposed for this decline are the facts that the puritans had "grown prosperous and comfortable, and prosperity had proved as always an enemy to zeal" (Morgan, 1966, p. 186). Morgan (1966, p. 185) suggests that puritan parents should have looked elsewhere (rather than to their children) to save their church. Perhaps, they should have looked inward and reaffirmed the basic tenets of their church; or maybe, they should have undertaken significant steps to reform its tenets to help insure its survival into the next century.[2]

Despite the fact that Puritanism may have failed because the grown-up children were not becoming converted in sufficient numbers, several aspects of the puritan way of life stand out as illustrations of how the earliest American communities maintained social order. These aspects included: the practice of requiring single persons to find patriarchal families to live with; dispatching selectmen to check to see if families were attending to the edu-

cational needs of their children; and selecting tithingmen to generally oversee the good order of groups of 10 to 12 families (Morgan, 1966, pp. 145-49).
Finally, it should be noted that the puritans in Virginia "outlawed" drunks in
1619, the year before the *Mayflower* voyaged to America. Thus, they gave us
the first liquor law in the New World (Sann, 1957, p. 21).

Colonial New York

Drug trafficking has been implicated in the naming of the most valuable
island in America. In 1609, when Henry Hudson first landed on an island
in New York Bay, he is said to have encountered a small group of native
Americans who were fishing. The surprised Delawares were offered a liquor
beverage by Hudson and his crew. They drank until they could no longer
remain awake.   Thereafter, the Delawares referred to the island as
"Manahachta-nienk" ("the island where we all became intoxicated"). Later,
white settlers transformed the words of the Delaware language into
"Manhattan" (Cherrington, 1920. p. 16).

In 1638, Dutch settlers on Staten Island become the first to distil brandy.
Six years later, the first excise taxes on beer, wine and brandy are imposed.
In 1664, the production and sale of malt liquors in New York was declared
illegal and in 1671 Deputy Governor Loverlace of New York decided to leave
to the discretion of the military officers the selling of liquor to native
Americans. In 1687, rum was officially imported into New York and in 1697,
the frequenting of tippling houses was forbidden on Sundays. In 1712, a fine
of five pounds was authorized for selling liquors without a license. Seven
years later, a law was passed providing a fine of 3 shillings on any
"Christians" who are convicted of drunkenness, cursing or swearing, and a
number of strips at the discretion of the court on "Negroes and Indians"
guilty of the offenses. By 1738, an additional law was adopted restricting tav-
ernkeepers from selling strong liquors to servants or apprentices and from
"giving large credit to others" (Cherrington, 1920, pp. 18-34).

In colonial New York during the eighteenth century, 37 percent of about
5,300 court cases resulted in neither conviction nor acquittal. The court system's inability to carry cases to final judgment had to do with the lack of an
effective criminal justice system in most regions of the colony (Greenberg,
1976, p. 71). For example, there were instances in which appointed constables refused to take their oath of office or to perform their required duties
(Greenberg, 1976, p. 66). However, in Suffolk County, the most homoge-
neous region of the colony, guilty verdicts were more frequently the norm.
The conviction rate throughout New York was only about 50 percent. In
general, the inefficiency of this early system was likely due to the following

factors: rapid demographic and economic growth; more heterogeneous groups; greater political divisiveness; rapid and intense urbanization; and a greater population base spread over a wide area. Moreover, after 1750 New York City experienced a sharp increase in the percentage of cases involving disorderly houses and thefts and the entire colony saw a rise in serious crime (Greenberg, 1976, pp. 215-216). Greenberg (1976) has summarized the status of colonial New York's criminal justice system: "In almost every particular—from the quality of the constabulary to the weakness of the jails, to the ignorance of the judges, to the indifference of juries—New York's judicial system was locked into a cycle of increasingly enfeebled law enforcement (p. 217)."

Civil Rights in Colonial America

On the other hand, during this era there were some positive developments regarding civil rights. Generally, by the mid-eighteenth century, "public officials were surprisingly accessible and responsive to petitioners, often pardoning convicted defendants when the interests of justice seemed to be served" (Greenberg, 1976, p. 216). However, New York's African slaves were treated as a group apart and this caused "a profoundly unsettling influence" (Greenberg, 1976, p. 218). As for women, the phrase "civilly dead" aptly explains their legal status until the early part of the twentieth century. Moreover, women remained largely socially subordinate until the latter half of the twentieth century. In August of 1775, Thomas Paine, editor of *Pennsylvania Magazine*, featured a landmark essay on their underprivileged position. In 1776, his publication of the pamphlet *Common Sense* helped to convert thousands of colonists to the idea of independence.

On April 19, 1775, the battles at Lexington and Concord took place, marking the beginning of America's War for Independence. Less than two months later, George Washington was officially appointed commander-in-chief of the Continental Army. One year later, Richard Henry Lee, chairman of the Virginia delegation to the Second Continental Congress offered the following resolution: "That these United Colonies are and of right ought to be free and independent states," and that a plan of confederation be submitted to the several colonies. On July 2, 1776, Congress adopted Lee's resolution declaring independence. On July 4, 1776, Congress also adopted the draft of the formal Declaration of Independence prepared by a committee chaired by Thomas Jefferson. On October 19, 1781, Cornwallis surrendered at Yorktown and Congress officially proclaimed the end of the war on April 19, 1783, just eight years after the battles of Lexington and Concord.

Although the end of America's colonial experience marked the beginning of a new nation, most colonial criminal justice institutions were continued with one notable exception. In the field of penology, the institution of the prison took the place of America's earlier reliance upon public shame and embarrassment. Such humiliations as whipping, the use of stocks and pillories, branding and the rituals associated with public executions were not necessarily replaced by the prison, but rather moved into a closed setting—inside the prison walls. Moreover, while branding and the wearing of scarlet letters faded away as forms of punishment in the nineteenth and twentieth centuries, many might argue that more insidious criminal sanctions have taken their places. For example, in 1998, the state of Delaware adopted a law requiring that the driver's licenses of convicted sex offenders be issued with the letter "Y" on the reverse side. The law was justified on the grounds that the "Y" designation would alert authorities regarding the status of the offender, especially when such an offender moved to another state and applied for a new driver's license ("The Letter of the Law," 1998, p. 16).

A composite list of procedural rights available at the end of the colonial period included:

1. No search or seizure without warrant.
2. Right to reasonable bail.
3. Confessions out of court invalid.
4. Right to have cause determined with reasonable speed.
5. Grand jury indictments in capital cases.
6. Right to know the charges.
7. Straightforward pleading with double jeopardy barred.
8. Right to challenge jurors.
9. Process to compel witnesses for the defense.
10. Right to confront accusers.
11. Trial by jury.
12. Limitation of punishment (e.g., no forfeiture).
13. No cruel or unusual punishment.
14. Equal protection of the law (e.g., women, children, and servants have access to the courts).
15. Equal execution of the law (e.g., no capricious mitigation or application of penalties).
16. A limited right of appeal. (Bodenhamer, 1992, p. 19)

Although this list of rights appears impressive, Bodenhamer (1992) is careful to point out that they are more representative of a set of attitudes than a reality and that even a brief examination of the colonial criminal justice period should quickly dispel "any notion that the rights of defendants embodied modern definitions in anything other than embryonic form" (p. 20). Significantly, while the language of the enumerated rights resembles criminal procedures common to modern America, their substance was different. Thus, during the colonial period general procedural fairness was important, "but the good order of society took precedence over the liberty of the individual" (Bodenhamer, 1992, p. 28).

Additional materials regarding the nature and origins of America's justice system are discussed in Chapter 4. However, the next chapter interrupts this narrative in order to provide additional background about America's experience with the consumption and control of alcohol and opium.

ENDNOTES

1. Cherrington, Ernest H. *The Evolution of Prohibition in the United States of America.* Montclair, NJ: Patterson Smith, 1920, 1969, p. 17.
2. In studying materials from this period, there is a critical need to distinguish between "the ideal" (found by historians in sermons and conduct books) and "the real" (that can be found carefully described in court dockets and the depositions found in court files). Of course, there are serious difficulties in using court records. A summary of the advantages and disadvantages of the use of court records to discern social history is found on p. 18 of Thompson (1986). Thompson's (1986) discussion of various occurrences of prenuptial fornication and various other sexual activities seem at odds with Morgan's (1966) discussion of the strict rules of the puritan family concerning such issues as sex in marriage, disciplining children, reverence for parents, restrictions on church membership, good habits, and family government. The difference appears to be in the nature of the primary research materials that were used by each author. While Thompson relied heavily on the descriptions found in court records, Morgan placed his emphasis on prescriptive sources such as the sermons, tracts and commentaries by the writers and leaders of the puritan period (e.g., Thomas Cobbett, John Cotton, John Davenport, Thomas Hooker, Cotton Mather, Increase Mather, Samuel Sewall, Benjamin Wadsworth, Samuel Willard, & John Winthrop). The use of such early contemporary sources clearly dominates Morgan's work. The dangers of relying on such evidence is that it is not uncommon for discrepancies to exist between the preachments and the practices of historical figures (see Thompson, p. 14).

Chapter 3

TEMPERANCE MOVEMENTS

"I gave to Miss Willard the ardor of a personal devotion, which drew to itself the religious fervor of that Holy War. Her words were to me, almost as sacred as the spirit of the movement itself."[1]

JUDITH ELLEN FOSTER
CO-FOUNDER, WTCU

The present chapter traces the origin of America's preoccupation with intoxicating beverages and the various public and governmental responses to the use of rum and other intoxicating spirits during America's first century after independence. The unusual personalities and events of the period are described and details are provided about their relative impact on local and national policies. Particular emphasis is given to the role of the temperance organizations that were formed in the nineteenth century.

Rum, its assorted concoctions and cider were the most popular drinks of the early colonists. Whiskey, derived from grain, was first distilled by the farmers in western Pennsylvania for their own use. The commercial production of whiskey started "when the farmers discovered that a horse could carry four bushels of grain to market over the rough trails of the western country, but could carry the whiskey made from twenty-four bushels" (Asbury, 1968, p. 11). At the time of the Revolutionary War, when good rum was unavailable, whiskey was issued as a ration to the troops of the Continental Army (Asbury, 1968).

Rum was commonly used in place of money for wages and other types of commerce. In most of the colonies there was a custom of closing offices and businesses each morning at eleven and at four in the afternoon for the purposes of consuming rum or other types of spirits. Similar communal drinking was practiced at public gatherings, such as barnraisings and hayings, town meetings and even court sessions (Asbury, 1968). It was "almost the universal beverage, especially of the middle classes" (Asbury, 1968, p. 9). The production of rum became an important aspect of the early economies of New England, especially Rhode Island and Massachusetts. In 1807, forty distilleries were in Boston and by 1810 there were over 14,000 distilleries nationwide (Asbury, l968, pp. 7 & 12).

Throughout the eighteenth century most members of the clergy were heavy drinkers, whether they resided in towns and cities or in more rural country villages. Drinking was customary when parishioners and clergy met at homes, ordinations or after funerals and on other occasions (Asbury, 1968).

> In those days the clergyman was a man of great importance in the community; to offer him a drink was to show respect and esteem. If he refused it, he was looked upon as a hypocrite, and the donor felt insulted or at least slighted.... Drinks were served almost continuously during his visit....and if he made twenty calls in one day....It is small wonder that many preachers were continually in a more or less pleasant state of befuddlement. (Asbury, l968, p. 16)

The excessive use of hard liquor concerned the colonists and drunkenness was a considerable problem. Individuals could be fined, whipped, placed in either stocks or pillory or even expelled from a colony for such conduct. From 1735 to 1742, the English Government prohibited the importation of rum and brandies into Georgia. According to Asbury (1968), the consequences were remarkably similar to what happened in the United States during the 1920s in that rumrunners, bootleggers, and speakeasies soon appeared throughout the settlements. The rumrunners came from South Carolina and unloaded their boats along the remote sections of the Georgia coast. From such locations, local bootleggers took possession of the liquor for distribution throughout the colony. This experiment was abandoned when local juries invariably found in favor of anyone accused of violating America's earliest prohibition law and a system of licensing taverns was established in its place (Asbury, 1968, pp. 21-23).

The availability of rum proved to be the undoing of many native Americans and caused some of the worst periods of violence during the colonial period. Pontiac, one of the most notable leaders of the Indians was slain by a member of the Kaskaskia society for a bribe of rum provided by a white trader. In 1639, a group of the Pequod nation under the influence of rum attacked a settlement in the colony of Connecticut. In response, the colonists killed every male and family member of a Pequod village. The village's death toll was estimated to be 600.

The most destructive war took place in the late 1670s. The Wampanoags and the Narragansatts were defeated by the union of Rhode Island, Connecticut, Plymouth and Massachusetts Bay colonists. However, before the bloodbath ended, more than a tenth of the colonists were dead. The war began after the leader of the Wampanoags, Metacomet, whom the English called King Philip, arrived in a white settlement for peace talks. He came seeking an end to the selling of spirits to his people as well as the release of

100 Indian prisoners who had been sentenced by local authorities and were soon to be sent to the West Indies as slaves (Kobler, 1973, p. 39). However, their convict status was at least partly caused by resident slavers who devised a system for capturing new slaves. "They would make them drunk, and when they committed some violence, as they frequently did, the courts would sentence them to servitude in the West Indies. A hundred such offenders were awaiting transportation, and King Philip included their freedom in his terms of peace" (Kobler, 1973, p. 39). The deputy governor of Rhode Island and his council refused to consider Metacomet's requests and war ensued. Metacomet was captured and killed and his wife and two children were sold as slaves. Thereafter, parts of his body were hung from trees and his head was displayed on a pole in Plymouth for nearly twenty-five years (Kobler, 1973, pp. 39-40).

One of the first well-known temperance advocates was the Philadelphia physician, Dr. Benjamin Rush. He was considered a leading patriot of his day and was a signer of the Declaration of Independence. During the Revolution, he was the Surgeon General of the Continental Army. In 1785, he published a forty-page pamphlet, which was reprinted many times. In addition, short excerpts from it were frequently reprinted in newspapers and almanacs. He urged that hard liquor should be used only upon the advice of a doctor since it had many health risks. However, he did not call for total abstinence; rather, he recommended the consumption of beer and light wines as a healthy addition to one's diet (Asbury, 1968, pp. 26-28).

Numerous local temperance societies appeared after the wide dissemination of Dr. Rush's pamphlet. Most of them were organized on the principle of moderation. Beginning in 1826, the published sermons of the Reverend Lyman Beecher, the pastor of the Presbyterian Church at Litchfield, Connecticut and the father of Harriet Beecher Stowe, also contributed to the growth of the early temperance movement.[2] About the same time. a series of thirty-six published sermons by the Reverend Calvin Chapin also proved influential. However, the work of the Reverend Justin Edwards from Boston was even more important since he served as the catalyst for the formation of the American Temperance Society. On behalf of the Society, he toured the Eastern half of the country, reviving old societies and organizing new ones. By 1836, the Society became the American Temperance Union and it now advocated total abstinence. Significantly, any drinking was now perceived as a great sin and the movement took on the appearance of a religious crusade. By that time, there were eight thousand local organizations with about 1.5 million members. Some of these organizations were composed of special populations, such as members of Congress and state legislatures as well as workingmen (Asbury, 1968, pp. 32-37).

The temperance attitudes of the period were also supported by an emerging collection of child-rearing books that were the work of laymen, rather than members of the clergy. These books became popular between the 1830s and 1850s and included such bestsellers as: Lydia Child's *The Mother's Book*, Jacob Abbott's *The Rollo Code of Morals*, and Catherine Beecher's *A Treatise on Domestic Economy for the Young Ladies of the Home*. The child-rearing books focused on the necessity of maintaining family cohesion and discipline. The message of many of these volumes was that youngsters "had to learn obedience within the family or would all too predictably move from the candy store to the tavern and brothel, and then to a prison cell" (Rothman, 1971, p. 220).

Temperance efforts also were given a significant boost by the efforts of a group known as the Washingtonians, headed by John Hawkins. This movement was unlike the Union group lead by Edwards in that they advocated neither a religious or legislative point of view. Rather, their "speakers simply related their experiences with liquor, and when it was judged that the emotions of the audience had been aroused to the proper pitch, all drinking men were urged to come forward and sign the pledge" (Asbury, 1968, p.53). The Washingtonians flourished in the 1840s, but the movement faded since it lacked a national organization and the support of the more established temperance societies of that period (Asbury, 1968, p. 53).[3] When the Washingtonians visited Springfield, Illinois in 1842, they invited Abraham Lincoln, a four-term state legislator, to be their "orator of the day." Lincoln was a teetotaler all his life, but he never endorsed compulsory prohibition. In the year 1855, when he ran unsuccessfully for the U.S. Senate, he was asked where he stood on the issue. Lincoln replied: "I am not a temperance man, but I am temperate to this extent–I don't drink" (Kobler, 1973, p. 63).[4]

Today, probation is the most common type of criminal sanction other than the use of fines. It involves the supervision of an offender within the community by an agent of the court. The concept resembles the common law practice of judicial clemency and stays of execution. Its first well-known use within the criminal justice system in the United States occurred in 1841 when John Augustus, a temperance campaigner from Boston agreed to take charge of a man charged with drunkenness. He subsequently helped nearly 2,000 people to remain law-abiding. In 1878, the first paid probation officer was appointed to the Boston Criminal Court as a direct result of Augustus' pioneering achievements in the field of probation work. According to Senna and Siegel (1998, p. 370), "Augustus had an amazingly high success rate, and few of his charges became involved in crime again."

By the early 1850s, thirteen states and two territories had adopted prohibition. The way was led by Maine in 1851 due to a decade-long effort by Neal Dow, a wealthy businessman. He devised the "one issue" political strategy that involved campaigning only on behalf of legislative candidates who favored the desired result (Asbury, 1968, pp. 57-59). However, in a short span of years after these dramatic results had been achieved, state after state began to repeal their prohibition laws and reinstated licensing systems. Temperance leaders blamed these setbacks on: (1) the hundreds of thousands of immigrants who arrived in America from Germany and other central European countries who brought with them their customary drinking practices; (2) preoccupation by the nation with the Civil War and the abolition movement; (3) a wartime Massachusetts Legislative study indicating that prohibition was an arbitrary infringement of individual rights; and (4) the adoption of the first national revenue law that imposed a tax on the distillers and sellers of liquor and beer. The latter measure was intended as a means to raise funds for the North for the duration of the war and remains to this day one of many "sin taxes." In addition, the beer industry created the first organized opposition to the temperance movement with the establishment of the United States Brewers' Association in 1862. Ironically, since the adoption of this revenue measure, prohibitionists have had to contend with the argument that prohibition would mean a serious loss of revenue for the national government (Asbury, 1968, pp. 60-63).[5]

Temperance Issues in Indian Territory

Throughout the nineteenth century, various Native American populations attempted to limit the use of intoxicating beverages. In the 1820s, the Cherokee Nation tried to curtail the sale of liquor within its territory. In the 1850s, the Chickasaw and Choctaw Nations prohibited liquor within their borders. In 1886, various Native American populations residing in the Indian Territory of the United States, including the Cherokees, Choctaws, Chicakasaws, Creeks, Seminoles, Comanches, and Wichitas agreed to suppress the use of liquor. In 1862, a federal law was passed making it a crime to sell liquor to Native Americans under the supervision of a superintendent or an agent, whether on or off a reservation. By 1895, the sale of liquor was proscribed by the federal government for the entire Indian Territory. A special agreement was entered into in 1898 by the Creek Nation with the Commission to the Five Civilized Tribes concerning restrictions on the sale and use of liquor (Cherrington, 1920).

Beginning about 1820, many Native Americans were forcibly moved from the southeastern region of the United States. They were told that they would be moved to a special Indian Territory in the far west that would become their new homeland and that they would be able to live in this new land undisturbed forever. There was untold suffering and hardship during the move. The majority of the Native Americans on this journey were members of the Cherokee, Chickasaw, Choctaw, Creek, and Seminole Nations. Whites referred to them as the "Five Civilized Tribes" because of their knowledge of the customs of the whites. The word "Oklahoma" is derived from the Choctaw words "okla humma," or "okla homma," meaning "red people." The Oklahoma Territory was organized in 1890 and U.S. citizenship was granted to the members of the "Five Civilized Tribes" in 1901.

Native Americans residing in Indian Territory were especially concerned about whether the new state of Oklahoma would be a dry state in accordance with the many previous agreements regarding the maintenance of prohibition within the Indian Territory. Discussions about this issue took place among the "Five Civilized Tribes" in Eufaula, Oklahoma Territory on November 28, 1902. A similar meeting was held the following year. When the Oklahoma statehood bill passed in 1906, Congress included a provision that prohibition would continue for at least a period of 21 years in the Indian Territory portion of the proposed new state. Moreover, in 1907 the first Constitution for the state of Oklahoma was adopted with a prohibition clause. The success of the antiliquor forces in Oklahoma gave encouragement to similar groups in other parts of United States, especially in the south (Cherrington, 1920, pp. 272-74, 281). In 1911, Congress allotted $80,000 for the suppression of liquor trafficking among Native Americans (Cherrington, 1920, p. 309). Unfortunately, the problem of substance abuse is still a significant issue for some Native Americans. In 1998, the federal government through its Office of Juvenile Justice and Delinquency Prevention provided a $400,000 grant to an Arizona corporation, Indian Rehabilitation, Inc., to develop a model program for reducing drinking by Native American youth.

Temperance and the Civil War

During the Civil War, the survival of the union took precedence over regional temperance efforts. However, the use of liquor by Union forces was a topic of major importance. In 1861, Congress outlawed the selling or giving of alcoholic drinks to soldiers, but liquor was still authorized as a daily ration for dealing with excessive fatigue and exposure. In 1862, General McClellan discontinued the ration and directed that instead hot coffee be served. In addition, the spirit ration for Union Naval personnel was eliminated (Cherrington, 1920, pp. 154-155). Later, when President Abraham Lincoln was informed that General Grant was an alcoholic, it was said that he replied: "I only wish I knew what brand of whiskey he drinks. I'd send a barrel or so to some of my other generals" (Harris, 1994, p. 5). At the end of the Civil War, a celebration was held in the nation's capital and 200,000 Union troops were assembled. All liquor sales were discontinued for the event (Cherrington, 1920, p. 158).

Perhaps, an unexpected outcome of the Civil War was morphine addiction. Since colonial times opium had been used as a therapeutic medicine.

According to historian Martin Booth (1996), opium was widely used during the War of Independence by both American and British forces. When it was short in supply, some doctors, like Dr. Thaddeus Betts, grew their own. An addiction, also known as physical dependence, "is the compulsive taking of drugs which have such a hold over the addict he or she cannot stop using them without suffering severe symptoms and even death" (Booth, 1996, p. 83). During this period opium was commonly used as a treatment for malaria and dysentery by both the Union and Confederate armies (Booth, 1996, p. 73). However, the opium poppy was being cultivated as early as 3400 BC in Mesopotamia. The earliest known find of opium was in Egypt. It came from the Tomb of Cha, about 1500 BC. Most opium is derived from just one of the over 250 species of the poppy flower, *Papaver somniferum* (the sleep inducing poppy) (Booth, 1996, pp. 1 & 15-16). During the Civil War, this type of poppy was especially cultivated in Virginia, Tennessee, South Carolina and Georgia. From opium, morphine was refined for use as a painkiller for the wounded. After the war, thousands of veterans continued to use opium for gastric problems. In addition, the sale of patent medicines greatly increased. Consequently, opiate addiction became common and it soon became known as the "Soldier's Disease" (Booth, 1996, p. 73-74 & 192). "The American soldier was not unique. British troops in the Crimean War injected morphine to escape the terrible conditions in their camps and, in the Franco-Prussian War, both French and Prussian soldiers drowned their sorrows in not only alcohol but also in morphine" (Booth, 1996, p. 74).

From the middle of the 1850s to the early 1870s, the temperance achievements suffered a steady decline. Moreover, the "saloonkeepers ignored the laws; they kept open on Sundays, and sold liquor to whoever wanted it, regardless of age, sex, or condition....the unholy alliance of liquor, politics, and crime was in visible process of formation" (Asbury, 1968, p. 71).

The Women's Crusade Against Liquor

Then along came a new leader in the person of a part-time medical practitioner, Dr. Diocleasian Lewis. By his gifted rhetoric, he inspired the women of the midwest, particularly in Ohio, to take prayerful action against the retailers of liquor, especially the saloonkeepers. He was a prolific author and advocated for the equal rights of women. Groups of women organized in twenty-two states. Upon the recommendation of Dr. Lewis, the women focused their efforts on the smaller towns and villagers of their respective states. As their ranks and demonstrations increased saloons began to close. Sometimes the women suffered insults, physical abuse and some were arrested. However, in many instances "the more they were reviled and abused the louder they sang and prayed" (Asbury, 1968, p. 82). Their leaders included: Eliza J. Thompson, Annie Wittenmeyer, Mrs. E. D. Stewart, and Fran E. Willard. The women's crusade against liquor was reported in the eastern city press as well as in the most popular magazines of the period: *Harper's Weekly* and *Frank Leslie's*. While no precise records of the results of the crusade were ever tabulated, it was estimated that at the height of the crusade as many as thirty thousand saloons were closed. Nevertheless, the whole movement was short-lived and soon "every town which had been involved in the crusade...had as many saloons as before the movement" (Asbury, 1968, p. 85).

However, the crusade did lead to the establishment of the National Women's Christian Temperance Union (WTCU). Under the leadership of Frances E. Willard, the union became the most powerful temperance organization in the world. She began her role in the WTCU in 1874 as its first corresponding secretary and became its president five years later. She held that office until her death in 1898. At that time she was one of the most well-known persons of her day. Willard had resigned her position as Dean of Women at Northwestern University in order to devote the rest of her life to the temperance movement (Asbury, 1968, pp. 86-87).

Under Willard's leadership the WTCU became involved in a series of matters related to the welfare of women. One manifestation of this policy was improving the treatment of female prisoners. In the 1870s, under the leadership of the WTCU, the first significant use of "police matrons" took place. In Portland, Maine, in 1877, the local chapter of the WCTU contributed the full salaries of police matrons. Only over time did the city agree to assume the full cost of such personnel. Largely through the efforts of the WTCU, in the 1880s, police matrons were appointed in various major cities (e.g., Buffalo, Chicago, Philadelphia, Boston, Baltimore, St. Louis and Milwaukee). By the next decade, the use of police matrons became commonplace in most urban areas. Reformers concerns not only for confined female prisoners but for the breeding grounds of delinquency and vice led to the appointment of the first policewomen during the progressive era (Walker, 1977, pp. 85-86).

One of the pioneer policewomen was Alice Stebbins Wells. She was born in Kansas in 1873 and was a graduate of Oberline College. She married and became the mother of two children while working in the Oklahoma Indian Territory as the leader of a small church. In order to achieve her entry into police work, she gathered the support of more than 100 of the leading citizens of Los Angeles. When Wells joined the Los Angeles Police force, it consisted of 350 members. All officers worked every day of the year, except for 15 days of vacation. In 1911, one year after she was appointed a member of the Los Angeles Police Department, the WTCU arranged a speaking tour that took her to 31 different cities within a 30-day period. Wells became the president of the International Association of Policewomen in 1915 (Walker, 1977, pp. 85-86; Schulz, 1995, p. 23 & 29).

Other notable figures also emerged as a result of the temperance experience and the emerging national prohibition movement. In 1899, a local county leader of the WTCU in Kansas, Carry Nation, began her ten-year career as a one-woman crusader with a hatchet. She made news throughout the country each time she used her hatchet to strike a blow against both illegal and legal saloons. Her activities brought comic relief to the movement, but when she was disparaged by the press, her supporters would become more energized in their pursuit of temperance. Her supporters included the WTCU and most of the Protestant clergy (Asbury, 1968, pp. 117-119).

The later stages of the prohibition movement were led not only by the Woman's Christian Temperance Union (WTCU), but by the well-organized activities of the Anti-Saloon League, founded in 1893. In its beginning, the Anti-Saloon League was primarily concerned with the dangers of saloon life; it later became focused on achieving national prohibition. However, the WTCU was also concerned with other dangers besides alcoholic beverages. For example, the WTCU focused attention on the need for improving worker safety in the mining and timber industries, rescuing prostitutes, raising the age of legal consent for sexual conduct, and participating in suffrage campaigns (Blocker Jr., 1989). Moreover, Frances Willard undertook considerable efforts to control prostitution out of fear for the welfare of the family due to the consequences of venereal disease. It was one thing for men to drink up their wages and abuse their wives, but it was even more callous for men to transmit prostitutes' venereal diseases to their wives and children. In one New York study, it was discovered that nearly one-third of the infected women were married and that they had been infected by their husbands (Rosen, 1982, pp. 52-53). A further notable activity by the Temperance Union was having laws passed in every state and territory (except Arizona) requiring temperance teaching in the public schools as well as specialized teacher training for the delivery of temperance instruction (Blocker Jr., 1988, p. 82; Sinclair, 1964, p. 43). The curriculum endorsed by the WTCU consistently referred to alcohol as a poison and by constant repetition of the word "poison" and "by similar exaggerations, the WCTU-approved textbooks seemed calculated to frighten children into total abstinence" (Timberlake, 1963, p. 49).

It might be interesting to speculate about how many members of the WTCU or similar organizations during the late nineteenth century were opium or morphine addicts. According to Booth (1996), "amongst the well-off, morphinism spread with the introduction of the hypodermic syringe, many of the addicts being society ladies" (p. 192) who could afford to see doctors and purchase medicines. Significantly, prior to the 1920s most addicts became addicted through medicinal use. Consequently, such persons were not seen as an evil threat, but rather as persons who had suffered a misfortune not of their own making and they were treated accordingly (Booth, 1996, p. 193). In addition, many women became alcoholic without realizing it because of the consumption of patent medicines. In either case, women typically hid their addictions to avoid any chance of social criticism. Of course, such secrecy diminished any chance for treatment. During this era no public funding was ever approved for the treatment of female alcoholism or opium addiction, although the issue was part of the concerns of the WCTU beginning in 1874 (Harris, 1994, pp. 63-64).

The Anti-Saloon League

Beginning in the 1890s, the main agenda of the Anti-Saloon League "was not to advocate prohibition in the broad sense, but was to rally the divided temperance forces for the more modest task of saloon suppression" (Timberlake, 1963, p. 127). It concentrated its early efforts on the dangers of the saloon rather than the entire liquor traffic. Initially, the Anti-Saloon League sought to achieve prohibition through "local option." This was a method by which separate political entities (e.g., an election district within a city or town, or an entire county) could pass laws to limit the selling of alcohol. The League's field tactics included efforts to educate the public and to discredit the saloon (Cashman, 1981, pp. 246–247).

However, by 1913, the League was specifically advocating on behalf of national prohibition and claimed that it represented the churches and the majority of Americans. It had already successfully navigated the *Webb-Kenyon Act* through Congress as well as the vote that overrode its veto by President Taft. The act outlawed the shipping of liquor into dry states. During the following three years, the League continued to lead the efforts for the adoption of individual state prohibition laws. In order to make as strong a case as possible for their cause, statistics were regularly used. League publications "fairly bristled with charts, tables, and graphs purporting to establish positive or negative correlations between the saloon and death rates, arrest rates, tax rates, divorce rates, wages, insanity, pauperism, bank deposits, industrial efficiency, housing investment, and public-school enrollment" (Boyer, 1978, p. 199).

By 1917, the total number of states that had passed antiliquor laws was twenty-three (Engelmann, 1979, p. 66). Also in 1917, the prohibition movement was aided by the American Medical Association when it voted its own opposition to the use of alcohol (Sinclair, 1964, pp. 49, 61 & 68). In the same year, at the League's annual convention, the Reverend A. C. Baine announced the League's intention to bring about international prohibition (Timberlake, 1963, p. 180-181).

Linking the saloon and the liquor trade with the brothel and venereal disease provided further grounds upon which to argue for the elimination of the saloon. The issue first became apparent as a result of an error in legal draftsmanship. In 1896, a revision in New York State's licensing laws made it possible for saloons to become hotels by adding bedrooms. When such "hotels" spread into upper-class neighborhoods, the protests began (Boyer, 1978, p. 193).[6] Citizen vice commissions in several American cities hired investigators. Although not perhaps intended, their reports shed interesting light on the complexity of urban prostitution in the early part of the twentieth century. Significantly, a careful scrutiny of these reports might have revealed "that organized prostitution might sometimes function as a stabilizing and conservative urban social force" (Boyer, 1978, p. 202). Nevertheless, the central theme of the Anti-Saloon League was "that prohibition would remove at a single stroke most of the political, social, and moral problems associated with the city" (Boyer, 1978, p. 208).

America's entry into World War I greatly accelerated the earlier momentum that was generated on behalf of national prohibition. A period of wartime prohibition was initiated with the passage of the *Lever Food and Fuel Control Act* in August of 1917 and the *War Prohibition Act* in November 1918. The former measure banned the production of distilled spirits for the duration of the war, while the latter outlawed the manufacture and sale of all intoxicating beverages (including wine and beer) of more than 2.75 percent alcohol content until the end of wartime mobilization (Kyvig, 1979, pp. 10-11).

Meanwhile, the Anti-Saloon League successfully lobbied in Congress for a resolution submitting the Eighteenth Amendment to the states. The Senate adopted the resolution on August 1, 1917 and the House approved it on December 18, 1917. Only two states failed to ratify the amendment, Rhode Island and Connecticut (Asbury, 1968, pp. 132-133).

The necessary state ratification of the Eighteenth Amendment took place in 1919 and it went into effect on January 16, 1920. According to Asbury (1968), the rather quick ratification was due to the fact that the Anti-Saloon League had been manipulating "state legislatures for some ten years, and that the drys had brought most of them into the fold before they went after Congress" (Asbury, 1968, p. 131).

When national prohibition's major enforcement statute, the *Volstead Act* (which limited the alcoholic content of beer to 0.5 percent) was passed on October 28, 1919, it provoked a nationwide drinking spree over Christmas and New Years that led to some awful consequences when individuals experimented with homemade recipes. "More than a hundred people in New York drank whiskey distilled from wood alcohol and died" (Cashman, 1981, p. 28).

The threads of this history will be taken up in Part 2 when an overview and assessment of prohibition enforcement is considered. The remaining chapters in Part 1 address the temperance and prohibition movements from the progressive viewpoint. A final chapter considers the cultural significance of the saloon. The progressives supported a wide variety of legislative initiatives that were designed for the improvement of the urban environment. The progressives believed that unfavorable environmental conditions were the leading causes of social disorder and that remedies could be fashioned through the proper blend of governmental and private interventions.

ENDNOTES

1. Kerr, Austin K. *Organized for Prohibition: A History of the Anti-Saloon League.* New Haven, CT: Yale University Press, 1985, p. 47.
2. In 1852, Harriet Beecher Stowe's *Uncle Tom's Cabin* was first published. Litchfield, Connecticut was also the site of the first law school in the country. Founded in 1784, it lasted until 1833 and was quite successful in its day. The full course took little more than a year. There were no entrance exams or final examinations. There was instruction every day (Friedman, 1998, p. 278).
3. On April 5, 1841, on the first anniversary of the founding of the Washingtonians, six thousand persons celebrated in a parade through the main streets of Baltimore. In the parade was a legion of one thousand boys and girls who were members of a juvenile temperance society called the Cold Water Army. The organization was founded in 1836 by the Rev. Thomas P. Hunt who formed units of his "army" when he visited Sunday school classes as a traveling agent for various state societies. They wore bright red and blue uniforms and chanted their official pledge:

> We do not think we'll ever drink,
> Whiskey or gin, brandy or rum,
> Or anything that'll make drunk come
> (Asbury, 1968, p. 51)

With these verses to recite, the Cold Water Army seems like a forerunner of the well-known Drug Abuse Resistance Education (DARE) program which was developed jointly by the Los Angeles Police Department and the Los Angeles Unified School District during the last quarter of the twentieth century. DARE's goals include teaching school age children about the nature of tobacco, alcohol, and drugs; how to resist peer pressure; how to build self-esteem; and how to identify and use constructive alternatives. The program is taught by specially trained police officers and is currently offered to millions of students (Senna & Siegel, 1998, p. 126).
4. In 1833, one year before Lincoln was first elected a state legislator, he was issued a license, authorizing him to sell whiskey, gin and wine in a country store in New Salem, Illinois (Kobler, 1973, p. 63).

5. The United States Brewers' Association was organized in New York on November 12, 1862. A similar organization for the distillers was begun in 1879. They followed the same tactics that were used successfully to establish Maine as the nation's first dry state; namely, they sought to influence and control elections and "from the beginning the brewers displayed an uncanny affinity for politicians, and a remarkable knack of getting things done in the national capital" (Asbury, 1968, pp. 63-64). Apparently, this legacy has continued to this day as it has become the customary practice for companies and interests in pending legislation to make large political contributions. For example, a recent Associated Press report, indicated that members of the alcohol industry were able to eliminate a proposed national standard for drunken driving from a pending highway bill. This success coincided with the following donations: Anheuser-Busch, the makers of Budweiser beer, gave $50,000 to the Democratic Senatorial Campaign Committee; E & J Gallo Winery gave $50,000 to the Democratic Congressional Campaign Committee; and Seagram Co. contributed $1,000 to the National Republican Senatorial Committee (see "Mircrosoft Gives $100K to GOP," *The Daily Gazette*, May 30, 1998, p. C8).

6. The 1896 statute outlawed Sunday liquor sales except when provided with a meal in a hotel. A hotel was defined as having at least ten bedrooms. The same competition among saloonkeepers that led to the need to encourage drinking with a free lunch now led to the addition of the necessary ten bedrooms (typically, tiny and shabby) out of the need to keep open on Sundays. These extra rooms "quickly became the haunts of prostitutes and their customers" (Boyer, 1978, p. 219).

Chapter 4

CRIMINAL JUSTICE AND THE PROGRESSIVES

> "I want to say that the only reason we have a govern-
> ment is to do right and justice. And that's a moral pur-
> pose, and it is in carrying out that purpose that this
> Government will be tested."[1]
>
> JUSTICE FLORENCE E. ALLEN
> SUPREME COURT OF OHIO (1923)

This chapter concerns the reforms regarding criminal justice that took place mainly during the progressive (1900 to 1914) and national Prohibition periods (1920-1933). Included among the many topics addressed are: the development of penal reforms; the advent of probation and parole; the early social service role fulfilled by police; the creation of novel youth educational programs, such as the "Junior Police"; the origins of state police agencies; the introduction and early role of women police; and the nature of the eugenics movement.

In addition, extra attention is given to the development of the Federal Bureau of Investigation (FBI) and the appointment of J. Edgar Hoover to the position of director. The creation of the FBI, known primarily as the Bureau of Investigation until the mid-1930s, was an important milestone for the development of more professional law enforcement standards throughout the nation. Its appearance in 1908, "marked the intervention of the federal government into the law enforcement picture in a manner that was without precedent" (Walker, 1977, p. 77). Historian Richard Hofstadter (1968) has indicated that followers of the progressive movement consisted largely of male college graduates with professional careers, who came from urban and middle-class backgrounds. They were mostly native-born Protestants and held membership in the Masons. Powers (1987) noted that "J. Edgar Hoover's resemblance to Hofstadter's ideal progressive type is uncanny, even to the detail of Masonic membership" (p. 519).

Prior to America's independence, justice was administered by lay judges, soldiers, clergymen, constables, various administrative officers (e.g., gover-nors appointed by the English King) and by legislative assemblies. An important legacy of the colonial period was a system of petty courts manned by laymen (e.g., rural justices of the peace). On a broader scale, the Constitution of the United States, drafted in 1787, sets forth the structure of the legal system of the federal government. Former Chief Justice of the United States, Warren Burger, has declared that the "Constitution has had as great an impact on humanity as the splitting of the atom" (Bowen, 1986, p. x). According to Bowen (1986), Alexander Hamilton was "the most potent single influence toward calling the Convention of '87" (pp. 5-6). During the war he acted as Washington's aide-de-camp; however, James Madison's total commitment to the actual work of the convention has earned him the title of the "Father of the Constitution." The central government established by the Constitution was one of limited powers with most common police powers reserved for the states.

After independence and the adoption of the Constitution, there was an extended period that lasted until 1873 during which state legislatures eliminated the earlier common practices of public whippings and hangings. At the same time, local courts shaped the laws to meet the needs of America's rural settlements and agricultural areas (Pound, 1930). Significantly, the basic and familiar machinery of the current justice system including the courts, substantive and criminal procedural law were introduced during the nineteenth century. It was a time of relatively "simple problems and straightforward tasks to lawmaker, prosecutor, judge, and jurist" (Pound, 1930, p. 141). The majority of the legal profession was trained through the apprentice method of law office practice. It was a system marked by lack of organization, decentralized responsibility, and little cooperation (Pound, 1930, p. 149). It has produced for the practice of criminal law a "type of politician lawyer, of little standing at the bar, or of the lowest stratum of the profession" (Pound, 1930, p. 159). At the beginning of the twentieth century, Pound concluded that much of this system had become a burden for the progressive development of America's urban industrial centers (p. 155).

In the two-decade period just prior to the full-fledged eruption of the work of the progressives, several dramatic and violent events took place as a result of encounters between labor activists and the police. One of these events took place on the evening of May 4, 1886, in Chicago's Haymarket Square, when an unknown person threw a bomb at police. The police had been assigned to break-up the rally and before the night was over five persons were dead and scores wounded. In 1892, violence also erupted when the members of a Pinkerton security force clashed with strikers at Andrew Carnegie's Homestead steel works near Pittsburgh. Moreover, in 1894, an American Railway Union strike in support of striking Pullman railroad car workers led to "violent confrontations in Chicago, Los Angeles, Hammond, Indiana, and other rail centers. In Chicago, where more than 14,000 federal troops, deputies, and police patrolled the troubled areas, at least thirteen persons were killed and substantial amounts of railway property destroyed" (Boyer, 1978, p. 126). Undoubtedly, such significant incidents of labor unrest, Depression era anxieties between 1893-1897, and popular media depictions of degrading conditions among the urban poor, contributed to the uneasiness of the middle and wealthier classes. In turn, these emotions helped to stimulate the progressive impulses of some of the more secure members of American society.

Criminal justice officials become especially motivated to act when public indignation is strong or the public interest is sufficiently aroused. Pound (1930) noted that the influence of public opinion on the formulation of criminal justice policies during the nineteenth century can be discerned through four attitudinal perspectives: the pioneer attitude; the natural rights attitude; the democratic attitude; and the entrepreneur attitude. A similar influence on the criminal justice system can be detected at the start of the twentieth century by examining the progressive movement or attitude.

The pioneer attitude has left a strong stamp on the justice system. It is best characterized by self-reliance, righting wrongs, and a preference for short-cuts. However, an obvious problem arises when efforts are made to transfer such practices to urban areas. Illustrations of this nineteenth century attitude include: a reluctance to convict persons seeking to defend family honor; a preference for letting a neighbor go free; and a distrust of experts (Pound, 1930).

The natural rights attitude is characterized by the belief that there exists rights above and beyond the law which cannot be bargained away. In practice, jurors have been encouraged to return not guilty verdicts in cases where the law violation involved matters concerned with natural rights (Pound, 1930, p. 139). This theory also helps to explain the early disregard for antidueling laws, violations of the *Fugitive Slave Laws*, and the resistance to the *Stamp Act*. A natural rights argument was certainly raised by the wets during Prohibition and eventually led to its repeal. This view is still a critical topic by those who advocate for the liberalization of various controlled substance statutes.

The democratic perspective places emphasis on: rights as contrasted to duties; checks upon government; the existence of law depending upon the consent of the governed; and the supremacy of the legislature. Illustrations of this attitude are reflected in the establishment of an elected judiciary, short terms, recall of judges, and recall of judicial decisions (Pound, 1930).

The entrepreneur attitude is represented by the needs of business interests beginning with the birth of the industrial age. The enterprising spirit is the successor of the earlier pioneer attitude and epitomized by the view that law should not stand in the way of economic progress, especially when the law appears to be outmoded and geared for any earlier age (e.g., an agricultural society) (Pound, 1930).

The progressive movement, according to Hofstadter (1955), lasted from about 1900 to 1914. In several respects the progressive period resembled the democratic and entrepreneurial perspectives discussed by Pound (1930), except that the latter spirit was tempered by the need to insure social justice. Progressive programs were "the invention of benevolent and philanthropic-minded men and women" who came "from the world of the college, the settlement house, and the medical school" (Rothman, 1980, p. 5). The general theme of the progressive movement was the restoration of "a type of economic individualism and political democracy that was widely believed to have existed earlier in America and to...bring back a kind of morality and civic purity that was also believed to have been lost" (Hofstadter, 1955, pp. 5-6). With regard to the advent of national Prohibition, it would be doing an injustice to hold the progressives responsible for Prohibition since "they had been generally antagonistic, or at the very least suspicious, of the prewar drive toward Prohibition" (Hofstadter, 1955, p. 289).

The mission of the settlement house was to gather and analyze the social science data derived from the "natural laboratory" of the slum. Progressives sought to use the case method to study and resolve social problems and they possessed an abiding belief in the benefits of achieving middle-class status. Their key tenets were: the individualization of treatment; trust in the power of the state to do good; and the need for the state (i.e., the public sector) to lead the way in "equalizing opportunity" and acting for the common good (Rothman, 1980).

The progressives were so enthusiastic about their proposals and methods that they never stopped to contemplate that they might be causing more harm than good. They knew that the prisons (the invention of the Jacksonian reformers) had degenerated "into more or less lax, corrupt, and brutal places" (Rothman, 1980, p. 18) where staff survival, rather than inmate treatment was the main concern. They also knew that asylums and prisons had inept board members who consistently deferred to the will of institutional superintendents. Most prisons "sold inmate labor to the highest bidder" (Rothman, 1980, p. 27), so that state legislators and taxpayers had little cause to worry about the costs of incarceration. However, states typically paid the costs for operating insane asylums.

Progressives may have disagreed about the causes of an individual's problem (e.g., environmental, psychological, etc.), but they agreed that treatment had to be based on a case by case analysis. In other words, different persons had to be treated differently. Thus, individualized treatment was a major goal and they decried the uniformity and rigidity of those institutions, which denied such a discretionary response to the needs of the particular clients. However, they falsely believed that institutions (e.g., prisons or mental hospitals) could work closely with community alternatives and that the creation of such alternatives (e.g., probation, outpatient clinics) could eliminate the need for institutionalization in many cases. According to Rothman, the progressives "were convinced that their innovations could satisfy all goals, that the same person and the same institution could at once guard and help, protect and rehabilitate, maintain custody and deliver treatment" (Rothman, 1980, p. 10).

An early forerunner to the new reform movement was the creation and celebration of a different type of penitentiary for first-time felons—the Elmira Reformatory in New York State. Its pioneering features were the use of the indeterminate sentence and an elaborate grading system to help officials from the prison determine release dates (Rothman, 1980, pp. 33-35). Elmira opened in 1876. Zebulon Brockway, a prominent penologist, conceived it. He served as the institution's first superintendent. Elmira was the first prison in the country where the term of imprisonment depended upon the observable progress made by the inmate. All sentences were indefinite with the maximum being the period specified in the Penal Law for the particular crime. The minimum term was set by the Board of Managers based on the inmate's previous criminal record and his conduct, work and school progress while at Elmira. The institution is credited with introducing parole as a regular part of correctional programs in the United States. The program at Elmira was highly publicized and many other states followed New York's lead by establishing similar adult reformatories throughout the 1880s and 1890s.

However, a number of investigations by state legislators and the State Board of Charities indicated a wide disparity between the publicized success and reality at Elmira. For example, it was discovered that officials at the reformatory regularly used brutal punishments and the system involving the indeterminate sentence, parole, and vocational training was carried out in an abusive manner. In particular, investigators discovered widespread violence, drug use, suicide, homosexuality and other patterns of breakdown. While changes at Elmira finally took place by the end of the nineteenth century, the promise of the use of adult reformatories as a means of achieving prisoner rehabilitation was severely set back.

Nevertheless, at the beginning of the twentieth century, the progressives adopted the concept of the indeterminate sentence (marked by the philosophy that the prisoner carries the key to the prison in his own pocket) and advocated for such well-known practices as: probation (with its comprehensive presentence report), parole, juvenile courts, and outpatient clinics for the mentally ill. They also actively lobbied for better housing conditions, organized playgrounds, safer worker places, and improved health policies (Rothman, 1980).

Ironically, the Elmira Reformatory was developed in reaction to the perception that the Jacksonian penal philosophy had failed. The tenets of that older philosophy included such tenets as:

1. the penitentiary can cure the criminal by isolating the prisoner from all contaminating influences (including fellow prisoners);
2. the methods for curing the roots of deviancy rest in creating the ideal prison routine (e.g., rules of silence, the lockstep, long work hours, longer periods of isolation, restrictions on mail, and curtailment of visits);
3. the prison would serve as a model for society; and
4. rehabilitation will arise through the perfection of "bell-ringing punctuality and steady work habits" (Rothman, 1980, p. 118).

On the other hand, the penal philosophy of the progressive movement focused on the following ideals:

1. discretionary justice is in everyone's best interest;
2. criminal justice agencies do not compete with one another;
3. the penitentiary can cure the criminal by respecting individual needs and facilitating an eventual return to society;
4. the penitentiary is to be modeled on normal society as nearly as possible so that rehabilitation can be achieved;
5. inmates are to be treated as individuals and helped to adjust to the democratic quality of community life;
6. the lockstep and the striped uniform should be eliminated;
7. inmate correspondence, visitation and expanded recreational opportunities should be encouraged; and
8. since "it is liberty alone that fits men for liberty" (Rothman, 1980, p. 120), it is appropriate to permit inmate self-government.

Warden Osborne of Sing-Sing briefly tried one illustration of these reform-minded views. He advocated the use of inmate self-government using a Mutual Welfare League approach. This program was based on the premise that the administration of the law inside the prison should approximate the workings of the law in the community. In this way, inmates would be better prepared for reentry into free society (Rothman, 1989, pp. 120-21).

The progressives also developed "the medical model" or psychiatric approach for dealing with various types of deviancy. They believed that deviancy is rooted in psychological factors and must be dealt with through a medical treatment model. The key goal is correct diagnosis and the delivery of appropriate treatment. In this regard, Hofstadter (1955) pointed out that one cannot ignore "the diagnostic significance of prohibitionism" (p. 289). "For Prohibition was a pseudo-reform, a pinched, parochial substitute for reform....It was linked not merely to an aversion to drunkenness and to the evils that accompanied it, but to the immigrant drinking masses, to the pleasures and amenities of city life, and to the well-to-do classes and cultivated men" (Hofstadter, 1955, pp. 289-90).

In the field of penology, the medical model called for the prison to assume the characteristics of a hospital, especially with regard to the diagnostic stage of treatment. Thus, the model led to the creation of diagnostic centers or reception centers for all new inmates. In such new institutions, doctors and social workers would assign inmates to the appropriate setting (Rothman, 1980).

Thus, there needed to be a variety of institutions to serve the special needs of offenders. Five broad categories were created for purpose of the treatment and placement of criminals: those capable of learning a trade; those best suited for agriculture; the insane; the defective; and the psychopathic. Systems of classification and segregation were based on the inmate's capacity for rehabilitation involving minimum, medium, or maximum security custodial settings. The process of inmate classification and segregation appealed to other reformers, including wardens because it eased custodial concerns (Rothman, 1980).

Fundamental to these penal reforms was the belief that it was proper to permanently segregate the "defective" and "psychopathic" criminals from the rest of society so long as they were considered dangerous. The primary programs for rehabilitation included education programs; vocational training programs; and work assignments. Social adjustment would be measured by the progress demonstrated by the inmates in their respective programs. A significant reward would be early release on parole (Rothman, 1980).

The progressive movement experienced mixed success. In the United States, the use of probation became common between 1900 and 1920. The first probation law in New York State was passed in 1901. The law provided for the appointment of probation officers by justices of various courts. In 1907, the New York State Probation Commission was established to supervise the work of all probation officers. In 1901, the "visiting agents" of the New York House of Refuge, a juvenile reformatory, became parole agents. Founded in 1825, the New York House of Refuge was one of the earliest institutions of its kind in the United States.[2] However, it did not appoint its first visiting agent until 1894. These early types of parole agents were needed to replace the indenturing system of discharging inmates. They visited the homes of new inmates and the home and prospective employer of each inmate to be paroled to ensure that an appropriate placement would occur. In addition, they made similar visits while inmates were on parole to check on their progress.

Nationally, by 1923, almost half of all inmates sentenced to state prisons were under an indeterminate sentence, and a little over half of all releases were under parole. However, not all of the progressive's agenda was implemented and those items that were implemented took place on a piecemeal basis.

The outlandish design of prison uniforms (e.g., bold stripes) was changed except in four southern states by the mid-1930s. Inmates were given the "freedom of the yard," but only for brief periods. Prisoners were allowed to hear radio programs, attend weekly movies, engage in letter-writing, and read newspapers; however, the overall atmosphere of the prison community remained abnormal. Oftentimes, visitations took place under frustrating circumstances (Rothman, 1980, p. 131). Inmate self-government was not very successful nor widely used.

Some psychiatrists and other professionals were hired and some diverse types of prisons were initiated (e.g., in New York State, Dannemora for the criminally insane and psychopathic, Napanoch for the defective, etc.). The limited numbers of new professionals did not lead to any real progress in the psychiatric and psychological treatment of criminals. Classification schemes were static and descriptive, not dynamic and analytic. Diagnosis did not lead to prescriptions for treatment. The lack of quality teaching and the limited number of teachers employed in prisons did not foster meaningful educational programs. Vocational training only reached a small number of prisoners and what skills were learned often were not relevant for employment upon release (e.g., the production of automobile license tags). Prisons found it difficult just to keep inmates busy. The convict lease system was abolished. The state-use system for prison-made goods was not profitable due to governmental inefficiency (Rothman, 1980).

The inconsistent goals of maintaining custody and delivering treatment defeated most program reforms, since conflicts were always resolved in favor of security needs. Many of the key staff positions (e.g., wardens, etc.) were filled by persons who possessed only law enforcement backgrounds. Moreover, prison guards were low paid, untrained, undereducated, and overworked. Prison discipline was often cruel and arbitrary. The use of witnesses and the opportunity to cross-examine accusers were not allowed. Guards were forbidden to counsel inmates. The whip was replaced by administrative segregation and solitary confinement (Rothman, 1980, p. 152). If solitary confinement proved insufficient, small cages and the use of restraints were available. Prison practices and prison walls presented an ever-present obstacle to rehabilitation. Appellate court decisions sided with prison officials by adopting a "hands-off" policy with respect to prison conditions and the treatment of inmates.

Wardens especially welcomed the practice of the indeterminate sentence since it gave them significant influence regarding inmate release. It enhanced their discretion. Judges liked the concept of probation because they controlled this sentence and the nature of its conditions. Furthermore, probation and parole gave prosecuting attorneys room to negotiate pleas. On the other hand, police officials were unhappy with probation and parole since these practices appeared to diminish their authority to take offenders off the streets (Rothman, 1980).

Some of the most important reforms achieved by the progressives were in the areas concerning probation and parole. Generally, probation involves release to the community under supervision and the suspension of any applicable jail or prison time by order of the sentencing court. Parole involves early release from prison under supervision based on the decision of parole board members. In addition, each parolee and probationer has to follow a tailor-made list of conditions in order to satisfy a personalized rehabilitation plan. However, while the use of such practices has become nearly universal throughout the nation, the fulfillment of the promises of individualized treatment as contained in the conditions set forth for the probationer and the parolee remain highly problematic.

There was inadequate training for probation, parole officers and parole board members. The qualifications for probation and parole personnel were minimal and their salaries were inadequate. Caseloads were too high and working conditions (e.g., proper office space) were dismal. Presentence reports were poorly prepared. The great majority of revocations of probation and parole were for new offenses and not for violations of conditions. Supervision was little more than a formality.

Probation systems were administered and funded locally so that poorer communities were reluctant to incur its costs unless it was used to reduce the costs of local jails by keeping minor offenders out of them.

Probation persisted because it facilitated the work of prosecuting attorneys, judges, and defense lawyers by relieving an overburdened system through plea-bargaining. However, this linkage was carefully kept private. Attempts by legislators to restrict the grant of probation were undermined by judges and prosecuting attorneys still seeking the convenience of offering this option. All that was required was the reduction of charges.

The advent of probation probably increased the number of persons brought under the control of the criminal justice system. It had an "add-on" quality whereby the scope of state action and surveillance was expanded. Proponents of probation who were aware of its negative aspects continued to support its use out of fear that its abolition might result in "a massive increase in retribution" (Rothman, 1980, p. 114).

Parole has also survived, but it is "undoubtedly the most unpopular of all reform measures" (Rothman, 1980, p. 159). Parole boards spend little time on their cases and decisions were often made in an arbitrary and capricious manner. Parole supervision was lax or nonexistent. The parole system persisted because of the support of prison wardens, since its removal could lead to inmate unrest. In addition, state legislators believed that it served as a safety valve for prison overcrowding. There is evidence to indicate that parole has actually increased the state's period of control by adding to the period of incarceration a further period of supervision. There is also some evidence to indicate that in some jurisdictions parole boards have exacted more time from inmates than have the courts; especially, with respect to the recidivist (Rothman, 1980, p. 196).

Pound (1930) assessed the status of the administration of justice in the early 1920s. He urged the need to make the office of the prosecutor responsible to central authority and removed from politics (Pound, 1930, p. 183). He called for the reform of the petty criminal courts, separating the bench from politics, and improved methods of bench and bar discipline (see pp. 190-196). Pound concluded that the system of probation, despite its insufficient resources was "one of the outstanding good features of our criminal justice" (Pound, 1930, p. 197). However, he cited the following as obstacles for improving conditions within the justice system: false ideas of democracy; behavior of the press; the rural orientation of state legislatures; the lack of central authorities within states for the administration of justice: and the needless regimentation by means of the criminal law (e.g., censorship of public meetings when views in disfavor with police officials were advocated). Finally, Pound called for lawyers and universities to take leading roles in the reshaping of the institutions of social control.

The centerpiece of America's criminal justice system is usually considered to be its trial courts. Some writers have even referred to them as "temples of justice." They certainly represent the intersection where the major parties of the system are likely to encounter one another (e.g., defendant, prosecutor, defense attorney, judge, juror, witness, police officer, and probation officer). In reality, most criminal trials of the nineteenth century were abbreviated affairs. According to Friedman (1998, p. 195), trials of that era "were short, routine, cut-and-dried." Moreover, in 1839, in New York State, one out of four criminal defendants pleaded guilty. In New York City, by the 1920s, such pleas accounted for the dispositions in 88 out of 100 cases (Friedman, 1998, p. 196). Currently, such pleas are the rule rather than the exception and governmental studies indicate that nationally 94 percent of all convictions result from them (Schmalleger, 1997, p. 229). In 1971, the U.S. Supreme Court summarized the reasons for the prevalence of this practice. The court stated: "The disposition of criminal charges by agreement between the prosecutor and the accused, sometimes loosely called 'plea bargaining' is an essential component of the administration of justice. Properly administered, it is to be encouraged. If every criminal charge were subjected to a full-scale trial, the States and the Federal Government would need to multiply by many times the number of judges and court facilities." (*Santobello v. New York*, 404 U.S. 257) In 1973, the National Advisory Commission on Criminal Justice Standards and Goals recommended the elimination of the plea bargaining system of justice. At least since that time, the subject of guilty pleas has been a major controversy. In recent years, criticism has been voiced over the creation of drug courts where cases may be treated in assembly-line fashion. Similar complaints have also been raised regarding the use of grand juries in New York City. In New York, every felony indictment must be approved by a majority of the members of a 23-person grand jury. In 1998, a retired newspaper reporter and former grand juror remarked: "I've often heard the aphorism that a district attorney could indict a ham sandwich. And I think that's probably true" (Rohde, 1998, p. B5). However, these issues did not appear to be items that stood out on the agenda of the progressives in 1900.

The reform impulse that pervaded American life around 1900 did, however, extend to the administration of municipal police services, but only in sporadic developments. Most of these took the form of: new training requirements; achievements related to administrative efficiency; the introduction of some women into the police service; and the adaptation of the lab sciences to the field of policing. However, a more fascinating aspect of police reforms during the progressive era and shortly after had to do with "the idea that police should play a positive role in the general reform of society" (Walker, 1977, p. 79). In many respects, the changes that were taking place in the other major parts of the criminal justice system were being adapted for the police officer, or more accurately the average beat patrolman. Significantly, during the early part of the twentieth century, police in many communities were assigned roles more related to the ideals of rehabilitation and diversion, than of punishment and incarceration. Although this trend was short-lived, these early accomplishments could be summarized as representing a social-work orientation to police work. Several aspects of this work resurfaced under the heading of "community policing" during the last two decades of the twentieth century. The final few chapters in Part 3 consider the revival of this spirit. Moreover, the book's final chapter specifically calls for the creation of a new professional occupation in the field of police work that relates back to the ideals of rehabilitation and diversion.

The foremost advocate of a social service role for the police was August Vollmer. Vollmer began his illustrious career in police service when he was elected the city marshal of Berkeley, California in 1905. However, the year before as a letter carrier he had distinguished himself by leaping aboard a runaway flat-car and breaking it just in time to avoid a crowded passenger train (Carte & Carte, 1975, p. 37). He was the first to seek out college graduates for policing and to facilitate college level instruction for in-service personnel. He shared his views in speeches and publications in order to convince his fellow police chiefs about the merits of his philosophy. Vollmer believed that police should do more than merely identify and arrest criminal suspects, rather they should take an active role in diverting potential law-breakers. He coined the term "predelinquents" to refer to this group and urged that police work closely with schools and other community institutions so that the most appropriate resources would be found to help any wayward youth. Moreover, he proposed that every police officer should take advantage of opportunities to inform the public about the needs of the underclass and urged them to support the creation of any needed services (e.g., youth centers, etc.) (Walker, 1977).

In 1925, Vollmer organized a Crime Prevention Division and recruited Elisabeth Lossing to serve as its supervisor. The division employed social workers that assisted young boys under 12 and women under 21. This was a pioneering achievement that has seldom been duplicated. The division was "the first attempt to bring professional social workers into a police department on a full-time basis" (Carte & Carte, 1975, p. 48).

Unfortunately, while Vollmer was able to introduce many new ideas to the world of police he was unable to see them become widely accepted. According to Walker (1977, p. 82), "Vollmer's passionate belief that each patrolman could become a 'practical criminologist' was advanced with an excess of rhetoric and a shortage of practical suggestions.

Walker (1977) has been able to catalog the following list of innovative and surprising activities that were taking place in 1915:

1. The Los Angeles Police Department set-up an anti-smoking clinic that targeted community members, especially youth.
2. The New York City Police raised money for homeless men and distributed meal tickets to them redeemable at local restaurants.
3. Washington, D.C. had two officers investigating child labor.
4. The Seattle Police had three truant officers and Rochester, New York had six.
5. New York City Police had thirteen boiler inspectors.
6. Council Bluff, Iowa; Cincinnati; and New York City had "Junior" or "Boy Police" programs (Walker, 1977, pp. 83-84).

The New York City Police Department conducted one of the largest youth oriented programs and it was similar to the Boy Scouts of America organization, except that it had a career orientation. It was created through the efforts of a Captain Sweeny and adopted by Commissioner Arthur Woods. Sweeny was concerned about the boys in the various districts of his police precinct. He was aware of the power of peer pressure to shape human character. His goal was to create a club where the boys could channel their energies into something constructive. He met with the youth of his precinct and shared his vision of turning the "gangs" of boys in each of the districts into more structured groups focusing on the field of police work. The idea was accepted and the first group consisted of 21 boys. Sweeny personally appointed five of the boys to serve as leaders and they were given the usual military style ranks (Captain, Lieutenant, & Sergeant). The group was organized from the school that they attended and Sweeny made a point of carefully defining the geographical boundaries of the territory in which they would be able to carry out their activities. The zone extended a few blocks from their school. Several residents donated funds for police style uniforms and the group's activities received other favorable responses. Shortly, inquiries were received from other parts of his precinct and eventually units were organized throughout the city. Each of the units held regular meetings, performed assigned duties, attended drills, participated in games (e.g., dodge ball, etc.), attended first aid training, and received identification cards and shields. The receipt of the police shield was dependent upon a good record of attendance and required a fifteen-cent deposit. Moreover, a formal pledge and motto had to be learned in order to obtain initial membership. In addition, each boy was required to study the twelve duties of the Junior Police force and a system of merit and demerits was used. The duties focused on such health and safety issues as: refraining from smoking, breaking windows, jaywalking as well as keeping sidewalks and fire escapes clear of obstructions (Crump, 1917, pp. 277–84). At its peak, the New York City Junior Police program had enrolled 6,000 boys between the ages of eleven and fifteen (Walker, 1977, p. 84).

Chief Vollmer also organized a junior police program. In 1915, several hundred boys were involved in the program and they, too, participated in military drills and were involved in community projects (Carte & Carte, 1975, p. 34).

In later years, such well-known law enforcement figures as Vollmer, O.W. Wilson, and J. Edgar Hoover expressed greater interest in the crime fighting aspects of police work, so that the social service aspects were lost sight of (Walker, 1977, pp. 79-80). Traces of this crime fighting emphasis can be found in the progressive period. Significantly, such major police agencies as the Federal Bureau of Investigation (FBI) and the New York State Police were being nurtured at this time.

The FBI did not start off bearing its well-recognized name, rather it was simply known as the Bureau of Investigation for nearly three decades. This branch of the U.S. Department of Justice was the idea of President Theodore Roosevelt's attorney general, Charles Bonaparte. Bonaparte was a grand-nephew of Napoleon. Until its creation in 1908, the attorneys in the Justice Department had to rely on the services of the agents in the Secret Service Division of the Treasury Department or hire the temporary services of the Pinkerton Detective Agency. Bonaparte had requested Congress to approve such an investigatory branch in 1907 and 1908. Thus, when he created the Bureau, it was entirely a unilateral effort. Ostensibly, on each occasion his request was denied on the grounds that such an agency would evolve into a type of federal secret police force and in such a capacity could endanger the basic freedoms of the American people. It is critical to note that two members of Congress had recently been indicted for land fraud and that the Secret Service Division had gathered evidence in these cases. Moreover, Congress in various appropriation bills had attached additional legislation expressly stating that Secret Service agents were not to be hired with the appropriated funds. Shortly before Bonaparte left office due to the election of President Taft in 1908, he again addressed members of Congress and this time won a reluctant approval. Bonaparte accomplished this dramatic turnaround by promising that:

> First, particular care would be taken to recruit high-quality professional investigators. Second, the attorney general would personally assume supervisory responsibility over the initiation and operations of investigations. And, third, the newly created investigative division would not investigate political beliefs and affiliations or strictly personal matters; its investigations would be confined to violations of antitrust and interstate commerce laws. (Theoharis & Cox, 1988, p. 43)

Both Attorney General Bonaparte and President Theodore Roosevelt left office in March of 1909. According to the FBI's Office of Public and Congressional Affairs Internet fact pages (June 1998), it was actually Bonaparte's successor, Attorney General George Wickersham, who on March 16, 1909, first officially used the designation "Bureau of Investigation."

The following year Congress passed the *Mann Act* which made it a federal crime to transport any woman across state lines for "immoral purposes." In 1912, Congress outlawed the interstate transportation of prizefight films. In 1919, the *Dyer Act,* made the movement of stolen vehicles across state lines a federal crime. These laws and many more to come added to the responsibilities of the new Bureau of Investigation and created specific mandates for federal investigators. Significantly, the opportunity for any future attorney general to "personally assume supervisory responsibility" over particular cases became more and more remote. J. Edgar Hoover obtained his first job with the Justice Department in 1917 as a clerk and soon was given a promotion to the position of Justice Department attorney because of his wartime expertise in deportation matters. In the coming months, his zeal in enforcing the *Sedition Act of 1918* was to result in massive dragnet raids and the arrest and detention of thousands of suspected alien radicals. Under this law any alien belonging to an organization determined to be anarchistic or revolutionary could be deported at the sole discretion of the Secretary of Labor (Theoharis & Cox, 1988, pp. 46-50).

After a bomb exploded on the front porch of Attorney General A. Mitchell Palmer and at least a dozen more bombs were simultaneously exploded in other parts of the country on June 2, 1919, the new attorney general, appointed Hoover his special assistant for investigating radicals of any kind (Theoharis & Cox, 1988, p. 55). The public's fear generated by these bombings reached even greater proportions when in September of 1920, a bomb exploded in front of J.P. Morgan's Wall Street offices, killing thirty-eight and wounding several hundred persons (Horan, 1967, p. 496). Hoover was empowered to establish his own General Intelligence Division within the Bureau of Investigation and he began his lifelong career of compiling reports on individuals and organizations. He began to target various Communist sympathizers and arrange for their arrest and possible deportation. This period has come to be known by historians as the "Red Scare." Hoover became the assistant director of the Bureau on August 22, 1921 and its acting director in May of 1924 (Theoharis & Cox, 1988).

On December 19, 1924, Attorney General Harlan Fiske Stone, a future chief justice of the United States, appointed Hoover to a permanent position as director. Stone, had been appointed attorney general by President Coolidge as part of Coolidge's effort to distance himself from the scandals of the Harding administration. At the time of his appointment, Stone was the dean of Columbia University's School of Law. Coolidge was Harding's vice president and he became president in August of 1923 after Harding suddenly died in a San Francisco hotel room. Coolidge was later elected President with the backing of Wayne Wheeler, the acknowledged leader of the prohibition movement. Stone was appointed attorney general after Coolidge fired Attorney General Harry Daugherty for his conduct relating to the Teapot Dome affair. In a private meeting Hoover had been able to convince Stone that he played an unwilling role in the past misdeeds of the agency and that he was and would be a loyal subordinate (Powers, 1987; Theoharis & Cox, 1988).

Herbert Hoover, the Secretary of Commerce, originally recommended J. Edgar Hoover to Stone and he was later elected President of the United States. Stone also received a good report about J. Edgar Hoover (who had no kinship to Herbert Hoover) from Mabel Willebrandt, the Justice Department's attorney in charge of prohibition enforcement. Commerce Secretary Hoover learned about the reputation of J. Edgar Hoover from his confidential assistant, Larry Richey, a former member of the Secret Service presidential guard. Willebrandt told Stone that Hoover was "honest and informed and one who operated like an electric wire, with almost trigger response" (Powers, 1987, p. 143).

Hoover's appointment drew little press attention, except in the *Daily Worker*, the chief publication of the Communist Party in the United States. In part, its front-page report on December 22, 1924 stated: "After public excitement over the Teapot Dome graft scandal and the corruption exposed in the department of justice died down, the promises made by the government prior to the election were conveniently forgotten. Now that the excitement is over, we find J. Edgar Hoover slipping his feet in Burns' shoes" (Theoharis & Cox, 1988, p. 100).

William J. Burns had headed the Secret Service Division of the Treasury Department. He resigned in 1909 and established his own private detective agency. He was appointed to head the Bureau just four days prior to Hoover's selection as its assistant director. In the early part of 1924, Attorney General Harry Daugherty ordered Burns to investigate the activities of Senator Wheeler after he had publicly charged that Daugherty was blocking the investigation of the sale of the navy's oil reserves at Teapot Dome, Wyoming. Senator Wheeler had called for Daugherty to resign for failing to investigate the Teapot Dome affair. Later, Burns was forced to resign by Stone as part of the house-cleaning efforts of the new Coolidge administration. His forced resignation came shortly after he admitted before a Senate committee that he had not spoken-up after hearing his former boss, Attorney General Daugherty lie about ordering agents to investigate Montana's U.S. Senator Burton Wheeler. Indeed, Burns had helped to cover-up Daugherty's dishonesty by remaining silent and his subsequent resignation tarnished an otherwise honest and loyal reputation. J. Edgar Hoover was Burns' chief assistant and also well aware of Daugherty's lack of probity. On the other hand, Hoover was able to remain in his position until a heart attack, in his sleep, caused his death on May 2, 1972 (Powers, 1987; Theoharis & Cox, 1988).

According to the June 1998 Internet fact pages posted by the FBI's Office of Public and Congressional Affairs, when Hoover was selected to head the Bureau in May of 1924, the agency had approximately 650 employees, including 441 special agents. At that time, Hoover was 29 years old and an honors graduate of the George Washington University Law School's evening division. He immediately fired those agents he considered unqualified and proceeded to professionalize the organization. For example, regular inspections of field offices were held and the seniority rule of promotion was eliminated and replaced by a uniform system of evaluation. Subsequently, all new agents had to be between the ages of 25 and 35, attend a formal academy training program, and a preference for persons who had law or accounting education was given. Moreover, by 1926 law enforcement agencies throughout the nation began contributing their fingerprint cards to the Bureau's Identification Division (Office of Public and Congressional Affairs, June 1998).[3] He also introduced a strict code of personal behavior for special agents, which included a strict ban on the use of liquor during the prohibition era, whether off or on duty (Powers, 1987, p. 152).

Of course, throughout the prohibition period, profits from organized bootlegging did much to raise a criminal underworld. During the 1930s, Hoover was able to capitalize on the public's fear of gangsters, crime and general disorder. The result was expanded duties for the FBI. In fact, according to the FBI's Office of Public and Congressional Affairs (June 1998), public confusion between the Bureau of Investigation Special Agents and Prohibition Agents led to a new name for the former group. In 1935, the Bureau of Investigation became the Federal Bureau of Investigation.

In 1917, Pennsylvania had the most recognizable state police department because of the nature of its' organization and extensive authority. In every sense, it resembled a military force, complete with various troops housed in barracks throughout the state. Its role in policing labor strikes associated with the coal industry and other disputes involving the average working man made it very unpopular. While most scholars acknowledge these facts, they also cover their words by making reference to the Texas Rangers that have a history traceable to the year 1835. (Walker, 1977, p. 75). The New York State Police followed the lead of Pennsylvania, but for reasons quite different than an immediate concern for the need to suppress the activities of striking workers.

A crime in 1913 and the response by two women were directly responsible for the establishment of the New York State Police. The crime took place in Westchester County, New York, near the site of a home under construction for M. Moyca Newell in Bedford Hills. Four men attempted to rob Sam Howell, the foreman of the home construction project. Although he was shot several times, he managed to deliver the payroll he was carrying to the carpenters at the site. He died three days later, but he was able to identify two of his assailants as men he had hired. The suspects remained close to the scene of the crime when local police arrived. Even though the general location of the prime suspects was known, they were not pursued and none were ever arrested ("The New York State Police," 1967).

Newell was with her friend Katherine Mayo, a writer, when they witnessed the ineptitude of the local police officials at the scene of the crime. Justly outraged, the two women initiated an effort to create a state police force that would bring adequate police response to the state's rural areas. Through their direct efforts, a lobbying committee was established. Mayo also authored a book about the purposes of state police which included research about the Pennsylvania State Police. Although organized labor, Democrats, and some upstate Republicans were opposed to it, a bill for the establishment of the New York State Police was drafted. The bill gave nearly unlimited power to the head of the proposed organization with respect to the selection of personnel. This caused some critics to take the position that the bill was not in keeping with civil service reforms and was merely designed to benefit existing interests. At the time, New York's Governor Charles Whitman strongly favored the bill and a new clause was inserted, stating that the use of state police shall be prohibited "within the limits of any city to suppress rioting and disorder except by the direction of the Governor or upon the request of the Mayor of the city with the approval of the Governor." In addition, Governor Whitman urged that the shortage of National Guard recruits could be alleviated by the adoption of this act, since members of the Guard would no longer be required to perform domestic police duties. In the past, these duties had taken guardsmen away from their families and regular employment, resulting in substantial inconvenience and personal financial loss. The state legislature approved the bill by a small majority. It became a law on April 11, 1917, just five days after Congress had declared war on Germany ("The New York State Police," 1967).

A surgeon from Kingston, New York, as well as a Major in the Army, George F. Chandler became the first superintendent of the New York State Police. Besides writing their first orders, he recruited the first troopers, personally conducted all the physical examinations, oversaw their training, and arranged for their barracks and equipment. Near the end of 1923, when the time came to return to his Kingston medical practice, he even selected his successor with the blessings of Governor Smith. Perhaps, his most important contribution at that time to the emergence of police professionalism was successfully convincing New York State's new governor, Alfred E. Smith, of the value of the new force. In 1919, Smith had recommended that the newly created state police should be abolished ("The New York State Police," 1967).

Certainly, one of the most important aspects of the progressive era and the development of the criminal justice system was the introduction of some women into the police service. Although women had been serving as police matrons (involving the supervision of female prisoners) for nearly two decades prior to 1900, their attainment of full police powers took time. The hiring of policewomen, as had been the case with the appointment of the first police matrons, required the lobbying efforts of organized women. For example, "even in reform minded Cleveland...the struggle for policewomen took eight years" (Walker, 1977, p. 88). From 1916 to 1923, the Women's Protective Association actively campaigned for policewomen and even hired their own "special investigator" to counsel and assist young women. The organization of this private association was initiated after a teenage girl was murdered by an employee of a local men's club (Walker, 1977, pp. 87-88).

Throughout most of the first three-quarters of the twentieth century, the duties of women police officers have been limited. Typically, those duties have involved: cases involving juveniles; missing persons; consumer frauds; vice enforcement; and, of course, searching and guarding female prisoners. The interrogation of female suspects and crime victims have also become essential aspects of their role. In general, the educational requirements for policewomen tended to be much higher, especially in the first decades of the twentieth century. Moreover, they had to serve in separate units. The early women pioneers in this field were not issued regular police uniforms. According to Walker (1977, p. 89), two major reasons for this policy included: (1) reducing the criticism that they were taking on a traditional male occupation; and (2) for the practical advantage it might provide for the performance of detective work. By the 1930s, members of the women's bureau of the New York City Police routinely patrolled in uniform at large public events. However, by mid-century only a minority of jurisdictions permitted women to be promoted. In a survey conducted in 1946, it was found that only 21 cities with a population of over 25,000 permitted women to be promoted (Schulz, 1995, pp. 108-109).

The role of women in policing did not change dramatically until two Indianapolis policewomen, Betty Blankenship and Elizabeth Coffal were assigned to engage in routine marked patrol car duty. This event took place in September of 1968. The greatest impetus to the hiring of women police throughout the nation occurred as a result of the passage of *Title VII of the 1964 Civil Rights Act* in 1972; the 1973 amendments to the *Omnibus Crime Control and Safe Streets Act of 1968*; and the *1973 Revenue Sharing Act*. The provisions of these federal laws meant that local jurisdictions that discriminated against women could be denied substantial federal aid. The FBI did not hire its first female special agents until after Hoover's death. In July 1972, two women began FBI special agent training (Schulz, 1995, pp. 131-34). At that time, the FBI had only 70 blacks and 69 Hispanics out of a total of 8,659 agents. However, it was not until William Webster became FBI Director in 1978, that the FBI began to actively recruit women and minority group agents. During Webster's nearly ten years of service as director, the number of minority agents doubled; and the number of women agents increased five-fold, from 147 to 787 (Kessler, 1993, pp. 398-400).

Throughout most of the twentieth century, environmental factors have been consistently cited as contributing to the roots of criminality. The progressives made great strides in the field of preventive medicine in order to reduce such conditions. For example, they helped to establish city and state diagnostic laboratories for the identification of infectious diseases and commenced public education regarding the bacteriological origins of many diseases as well as the basics of modern hygiene in order to prevent disease transmission. As part of the lattermost effort, nurses, medical inspectors and physicians visited schools, tenements and other places of public accommodation in order to reach the most at-risk children and their parents. By 1915, the infant death rate in New York City dropped from 273 per thousand live births in 1885 to 94. The work of local and state departments of health in the dissemination of educational services has continued since that era (Lubove, 1962, pp. 84-88).

Prior to and at the same time that the progressives were instituting a variety of criminal justice and public health reforms that were to shape the institutions of social order for the remainder of the twentieth century, a British "scientific" development was attracting attention known as the "eugenics movement." In the United States, eugenics played a part in shaping policies and campaigns involving peace, immigration, prohibition, and birth control.

The eugenics movement exerted a major influence upon educated Americans during the first three decades of the twentieth century. The movement had its formal beginnings in England. Sir Francis Galton (1822-1911) is considered the founder of the movement and the person who gave eugenics its name. His first studies utilized the backgrounds of famous men to show that mental abilities were inherited. Galton favored a program to raise the inherent abilities of mankind through the replacement of inferior races by the superior (Haller, 1963, p. 11). However, he underestimated the environmental influences involved in the development of individual personality and of cultural differences among races (Haller, 1963, p. 12).

The major developments in the eugenics movement took place in the United States. Many leading professionals in the fields of crime, insanity, mental retardation (called "feeblemindedness" in the first half of the twentieth century), and poverty embraced the ideas of the movement and incorporated them into the progressives agenda. In addition, particular leaders in the field of eugenics such as Charles Davenport, Alexander Graham Bell, Henry H. Goddard spearheaded the movement. They believed that many of the nation's social problems could be alleviated by preventing the unfit from breeding more of their kind, and that either long-term custodial care or sterilization could serve such a purpose. The enactment of laws restricting marriage among the "feebleminded," whites and blacks, and insane were precursors for more drastic measures. In 1931, 27 states had laws permitting the sterilization of persons deemed unfit due to hereditary conditions (Haller, 1963, p. 137). By the end of 1931, over 12,000 sterilizations had taken place in the United States and by 1958 the number exceeded 60,000. A third of all sterilization occurred in the state of California. A major boost for the advocates of sterilization took place in 1927 when Justice Oliver Wendell Holmes declared on behalf of the U.S. Supreme Court (*Buck v. Bell*) that "Three generations of imbeciles are enough" (Haller, 1963, p. 139). The case, with only one dissent, gave approval for the Virginia sterilization law.

Eugenics also played a part in shaping policies and campaigns involving peace, prohibition, and birth control. For example, Margaret Sanger (who coined the term "birth control") fought an uphill battle against the laws that classified information on contraception with those involving obscenity. Her efforts were supported by many of the respected and scientific eugenicists of the day since birth control could limit the breeding of the unfit. Peace advocates argued that "war did not mean victory of some vague entity called nation or race; it meant the slaughter of individual combatants, often the choicest stock from both sides" (Haller, 1963, p. 88). Thus, most American eugenicists, as well as many in England, believed that prevention of war was a eugenic good (Haller, 1963, pp. 88-92).

In the United States, three different groups contributed to the major eugenics activities of the first 30 years of the 20th century. The first group included psychiatrists, psychologists, and social reformers interested mainly in the prevention of crime, mental illness, and disease. A second group consisted of "mostly old stock Americans, proud of their heritage and heredity" (Haller, 1963, p. 93) and alarmed by the new waves of immigrants at the beginning of the 20th century. The third group was the researchers from the universities.

The eugenics movement also attracted a fair share of racists and immigration restrictionists who praised the merits of the Anglo-Saxon and warned that America faced contamination from lower classes and from "inferior" races. The most significant development in eugenics after 1930 was its rapid decline in popularity and prestige (Haller, 1963, p. 179). The Nazis showed graphically what use could be made of an emphasis upon biological theories of heredity. They espoused a creed of Aryan purity and superiority. In 1935 alone, they sanctioned 72,000 sterilizations and in the fall of 1939 about 50,000 insane, "feebleminded," and deformed were put to death in gas chambers (Haller, 1963, p. 180). A similar approach was decreed for millions of Jews and other minority group members beginning in 1941.

During the 1930s and through World War II, knowledge concerning the complexity of human heredity and revulsion against the atrocities of the era brought disrepute to the eugenics movement. Today, the promise of DNA research has spurred great interest in the potential of curing diseases through genetic engineering. However, the old word "eugenics" is seldom used.

Thus, the concept of species manipulation was inherent in the eugenics movement. A somewhat less controversial subject that was also developed at the time of the progressive era was the concern for both individual and governmental "efficiency." In order to achieve, economic and governmental forms of efficiency, social reformers hoped "within the existing urban framework to redistribute at least in part some of the amenities of middle-class life to the masses" (Holli, 1974, p. 141). They sought to accomplish these goals through the provision of less expensive public utilities, the reorganization of municipal government, and eliminating corruption. The eventual creation of the strong city-manager form of government was an illustration of this type of reform effort (Holli, 1974, p. 142). In pursuit of such efficiency goals, many progressive advocates were inclined to attack corrupt political parties in their home quarters. In the urban environments of the times, the purchase of a few drinks often bought political support. However, the ingestion of alcohol was also known to reduce worker efficiency and lead to unsafe work habits. In the opinion of many progressives, new studies regarding the effect of alcohol upon the organs of the body added to the existing needs for liquor control.

Concern for the efficiency of workers in the emerging auto industry caused some employers to undertake extreme measures to maintain the sobriety of their workforce. For example, the "REO Motor Car Company hired private detectives not only to report workers who drank but also those who smoked and voted against prohibition" (Engelmann, 1979, p. 14).

The following chapter primarily addresses the nature of saloon life in the years prior to the adoption of national prohibition. "In the five or six decades before 1920, the saloon was an almost ubiquitous structure on the American landscape" (Engelmann, 1979, p. 3). The urban saloon typically served as the storefront offices of local politicians and as "election-day recruitment centers where drinks bought votes" (Kyvig, 1979, p. 9). In most cities, the saloon provided a variety of social services, which were of strategic value for members of the working class and recent immigrants. On the other hand, the urban saloon also became a primary target of the progressives who associated it with the brothel and other aspects of moral decay (Boyer, 1978).

ENDNOTES

1. Allen, Florence E. The Courts and Law Enforcement in Fred B. Smith, ed. *Law vs. Lawlessness: Addresses Delivered at the Citizenship Conference, Washington, D.C. October 13, 14, 15, 1923.* New York: Fleming H. Revell Co., 1924, p. 60.
2. Such major eastern cities as New York, Boston and Philadelphia established the trend for the creation of the earliest juvenile reformatories, known as houses of refuge. They took in "several types of minors–the juvenile offender, convicted by a court for a petty crime, the wandering street arab, picked up by a town constable, and the willfully disobedient child, turned over by distraught parents. Its administrators were disinclined to bring the protections of due process to these minors (Rothman, 1971, pp. 207 & 209). An interesting experiment for homeless boys in Boston and New York City was begun in the late 1860s. School ships were used to train neglected boys for careers as seamen. The program was designed, in part, to offer an alternative to the houses of refuge and as a way of preventing escapes from the houses of refuge. For the youth of New York City, a packet style vessel was used named the "Mercury." It could accommodate 300 boys. A sketch of the schoolroom that existed between decks appears as Illustration 4.1 as it appeared in the article "The School-Ship *Mercury*," in *Harper's Weekly*, November 27, 1869, at page 756.

Illustration 4-1. School between decks of the school-ship "*Mercury.*"

3. The U.S. Department of Justice created its first Bureau of Criminal Identification in 1905 in order to provide a centralized reference collection of fingerprint cards. In 1907, the collection was moved, as a money-saving measure, to Leavenworth Federal Penitentiary, where prisoners staffed it. Understandably suspicious of this arrangement, police departments formed their own centralized identification bureau maintained by the International Association of Chiefs of Police. Until 1924, it refused to share its collection of records with the Bureau of Investigation until Congress intervened and both the federal government's collection of fingerprints and that of the police chief's association were eventually merged. (See "A Short History of the Federal Bureau of Investigation," Internet Fact Pages, FBI Office of Public and Congressional Affairs, June 1998.)

Chapter 5

THE CULTURE OF THE SALOON

"A man who is sober can do more work than a man who is drunk; a man who puts his money in a savings bank does better than the one who spends it on intoxicating liquor."[1]

WILLIAM JENNINGS BRYAN
SECRETARY OF STATE (1923)

In *The Jungle,* novelist Upton Sinclair, observed that during the period of America's industrial era, when employees were particularly hard pressed and their livelihoods depended on the benevolence of their employers, there was one deliverance, they could drink. The business of the saloon was to assist men in this endeavor. According to Duis (1983), in the five decades prior to 1920, the saloon touched almost every aspect of city life. For example, their presence near schools might give rise to public outrage about rising rates of delinquency or their location near certain housing tracts might lower home values. Moreover, saloons were connected with governmental corruption, the assimilation of immigrants, and as a necessary source for the collection of lucrative business taxes.

This chapter explores the development of the saloon, including both its manifest and latent functions in American society. A concluding section summarizes various aspects of the Harlem Renaissance that coincided with the northern migration of blacks during the prohibition period.

In colonial seventeenth century America, alcoholic beverages were primarily sold to the middle and lower classes at taverns and tippling houses. However, the early licensing of such establishments also gave rise to the first speakeasies. In the eighteenth century, came the wide availability of rum. Its sale was highly profitable and the character of drinking establishments plummeted when a new lower class of men took up the retail trade. Moreover, with a few exceptions, the quality of taverns also declined. According to Asbury (1968) "a new type of resort began to appear—the dramshop and the gin mill, housed in rude shacks and attracting thieves, ruffians, loafers, and other ornaments of a developing world" (p. 8).

However, the taverns served as important locations for political discussions and many important events involving the early history of the United

States took place in them. It is said that even George Washington grew some rye at Mount Vernon and produced whiskey from this crop (Harris, 1994, p. 35).

A further change in the style of drinking establishments took place in the middle of the nineteenth century when the production and sale of beer greatly increased. The impetus for this growth was the new immigrants who tended to settle together in the cities. They brought with them their old world establishments, such as the beer garden. Typically, such places "were large, fairly elaborate, provided music and sometimes entertainment, and catered to family parties. Smaller places, of varying degrees of depravity, were known as saloons. The term 'saloon' caught the popular fancy, and was soon applied to every resort where liquor was sold, both malt and distilled" (Asbury, 1968, p. 62).

One of the most notorious types of saloon was known as the "concert saloon." With some exceptions (e.g., in Massachusetts), they were quite popular by the 1860s in most East Coast cities. The multistory concert saloon offered a "mixture of musical showmanship, liquor and sex" (Duis, 1983, p. 237) with different forms of entertainment on each floor. In 1882, a survey was conducted for a twenty square block area in Chicago. The results indicated a total of over 1,000 "concert halls," 500 saloons, and 500 brothels. This area known as the Levee, became a target of reformers for a long time, but it was not until 1912 that the infamous red light district (i.e., an area set aside for vice) was ended (Duis, 1983, pp. 237-238; 269-273).

Vice was also associated with saloons in other parts of the nation. It has been estimated that in 1876 nearly half of the 8,000 saloons in Philadelphia were involved with prostitution (Harris, 1994, p. 75). Moreover, in addition to Chicago's Levee, most major cities had red light districts. From today's point of view, the most nostalgic included: "Gayosa Street in Memphis; San Francisco's Barbary Coast; New Orleans' Storyville (named after the alderman who drafted the statute establishing its boundaries); 'Hooker's Division' in Washington, an appellation immortalizing the Civil War General who had confined prostitutes to that section" (Boyer, 1978, p. 192).

When the first internal revenue law was passed in 1862, more speakeasies were created in order to circumvent federal and/or local taxes. Significantly, in 1890, when a saloon license in Pennsylvania cost an annual fee of $500, the city of Pittsburgh had 92 legal retailers and 700 speakeasies. Since federal licenses were often less expensive than state licenses, many establishments held only the federal license. Without both licenses, many saloons could only be classified as speakeasies (i.e., illegal saloons), because they were operating illegally under state laws (Asbury, 1968, p. 113).

Saloonkeeping offered employment opportunities to many immigrants, especially during the great waves of European immigration during the closing years of the nineteenth century. It was a common practice for shop-keepers to open a business on a lower level of a building and to live above it. Thus, many saloons were located at street level, while the proprietor's family lived a floor or two above. George Herman (Babe) Ruth, Jr. was born in 1895 in Baltimore, Maryland. His parents owned a saloon in the city's waterfront district and they lived above it. On many occasions he drank the last drops of alcoholic beverages from the glasses left behind by the bar-room's patrons (Macht, 1991, pp. 13-14). Today, in the far centerfield of Yankee Stadium a monument stands that bears a bronze relief of Babe Ruth and the following inscription:

> "GREATEST DRAWING CARD IN HISTORY
> OF BASEBALL. HOLDER OF MANY HOME
> RUN AND OTHER BATTING RECORDS.
> GATHERED 714 HOME RUNS IN ADDITION
> TO FIFTEEN IN WORLD SERIES."

In 1909, there was one saloon for every three hundred persons in the cities and at the beginning of national prohibition there were 177,790 legal saloons in the United States (Sinclair, 1964, pp. 76 & 79). Moreover, there were over 1,200 breweries and over 500 distilleries (Harris, 1994, p. 86). In 1910, there were 10,775 saloons in New York City. By 1916, after an assortment of legislation was passed to control liquor sales, the number had declined to 9,667. In 1915, there were approximately 23,000 licensed saloons in the entire State of New York. Nationally, during 1917, various new restrictions went into effect, chiefly due to American entrance into the First World War when it became necessary to conserve food items and transportation. From 1917 to 1918, the number of saloons throughout New York State decreased from 20,000 to 15,000 largely due to local option measures. By 1918, New York City had just over 2,000 saloons and by 1919, the whole state had decreased to about 11,000 (Corradini, 1925, pp. 3-11). These figures do not include any illegal enterprises that may have been in operation during this period.

The saloon has been described as "the church of the poor" (Sinclair, 1964, p. 73). According to Sinclair (1964, p. 73): "Both took money and dispensed comfort. Both provided an escape from the world. While the minister advised and aided his flock, the bartender performed the same service for his regular patrons."

However, the saloon also had features that surpassed those of the average church. For example, saloons provided free lunches (although often dry and salty) with the purchase of a five-cent glass of beer and were easy to enter (no doorstep, swinging doors, long business hours). They also provided: "newspapers, billiards, card tables, bowling alleys, toilets, and washing facilities. And above all, the saloon provided information and company" (Sinclair, 1964, p. 74).

In 1907, a moderate depression throughout the nation and the presence of numerous railway connections, brought an estimated 75,000 drifters to the Chicago area. They sought out every available inexpensive or free sleeping space and overburdened local charities. Homeless persons during the early history of America, particularly during the age of the saloon and the prohibition era, were known as hobos, tramps, bums, panhandlers or drifters. City parks and "hobo jungles" along transportation routes were the outdoor residences of many of these people during the warmer seasons of the year, whereas the often unsanitary conditions of flophouses served as their winter quarters. For most of the members of this special population, drinking alcoholic beverages "provided an escape from misery, while at the same time being a central reason for the downfall of those who were formerly respectable" (Duis, 1983, p. 88). These homeless Americans drank wine because it was inexpensive and whiskey because it was easily stored and consumed. In the districts of the cities where such transients congregated, competition among saloonkeepers for any business was usually intense. Although mission meals were often available, transients preferred to go hungry or seek out a saloon, since there was no requirement to participate in church services (Duis, 1983, pp. 87-89).

There exists a scholarly debate about just how generous or friendly saloons were, especially, with regard to an obviously poor customer. Some were clearly more hospitable than others and some less so. No doubt a lot had to do with the demeanor of patrons as well as the attitude of bartenders. Duiz (1983) concluded that "whether a saint or scoundrel, the saloonkeeper hosted a mixed army of transients...young boys and old men, criminals and noncriminals, professional hobos and heads of families who were temporarily dislocated" (p. 91).

Most saloon customers were not professional hobos since they had regular or permanent shelter. Members of the poorer classes lived in tenements and tried to get by as best as possible. Junkmen and pushcart peddlers were common occupations. Young mothers often substituted beer for milk and water to give to their children because of fear of unsafe supplies. Beer could be "consumed at room temperature; unlike milk, it would not spoil" (Duis, 1983, p. 96). In those days, women and children used a tin pail referred to as a "growler" to receive and store about a half-gallon of beer that was purchased from a saloon in almost all immigrant neighborhoods (Duis, 1983, p. 102). There was a large "growler" or "can trade" in those days. The tin pail also had other uses, particularly when it was lined with tar. When men went off to work at local factories or other jobs, a lined pail "could protect a lunch from the jostling bumps of a streetcar crowds or from the weather. It carried coffee and a small bottle of whiskey for consumption during the working hours of the morning" (Duis, 1983, p. 102).

A lined pail also produced fewer suds and more beer because of reduced friction. In order to save extra effort at lunchtime, the workers would pay a penny to local youths to have their pails filled with beer and returned to them at the gates of their places of employment. Beginning in the 1880s, saloons charged between five and ten cents to fill one pail with beer and that price remained constant until the start of prohibition. This common practice was known as "rushing the can" and some boys could carry several pails at once by carefully placing them along a pole. In Chicago, various initiatives and alliances between liquor interests and progressive leaders were aimed at ending the practice of having children carrying and purchasing pails of beer. None of these efforts proved satisfactory, even though a local city ordinance was passed that outlawed the practice (Duis, 1083, pp. 102-103).

Boston had strict statutes for the licensing of saloons. One requirement was that they be located in more commercial sections of the city and this along with a heavy demand by drinkers created a cottage industry—the kitchen barroom. In order to avoid detection and arrest by honest police officers, it was important to maintain the secrecy of their locations while at the same time struggling to maintain a worthwhile group of customers. Occasionally, when concerned police decided to make an arrest, they temporarily switched to different precincts in an effort to avoid any additional embarrassment (Duis, 1983, p. 106).

Oftentimes, barkeepers had access to useful information and could help secure work for those in need of employment. Perhaps, no other institution in American life was as friendly to the new immigrant as the saloon, since jobs and help could be obtained by the contacts made there. "The ward heelers and barkeepers were the first welfare workers of the slums. The saloons were the first labor exchanges and union halls" (Sinclair, 1964, p. 75).

The immigrant minorities in the cities were mostly Catholics and Jews and there was little support for the "dry" cause among these minorities (Coffey, 1975, pp. 10-11, 176). In 1926, one member of the New York City clergy remarked: "It was the saloon that the working men in those days held their christening parties, their weddings, their dances, and all other social functions" (Sinclair, 1964, p. 75).

In many towns and cities, saloons served as a respite from the chaos of everyday events. In large cities, saloons and city streets were the only havens away from the overcrowded tenement rooms. Companionship and friendly listeners could be found in saloons. Discontents could be aired and tensions released (Engelmann, 1979, p. 7).

However, to many persons the typical preprohibition saloon was an offensive setting and "respectable women would go blocks out of their way to avoid passing such a place" (Asbury, 1968. p. 112). Studies in Wisconsin and Chicago found a close connection between prostitution and saloon life.

Significantly, the back rooms of saloons were described as those areas in which customers would be most likely solicited. It was not uncommon for bartenders to pretend to serve good brands of liquor by refilling premium labeled bottles with inferior quality beverages (Asbury, 1968, pp. 114-15). Moreover, saloonkeepers could make their best profits "from the drinks bought by customers who accompanied prostitutes to the rear booths or upstairs rooms used for sexual activities" (Rosen, 1982, p. 77). "In addition to the booths and upstairs rooms, saloons frequently provided 'vaudeville' shows in the rear rooms....Half-naked, stripping dancers encouraged male customers, already plied with drink from waitresses, to accept prostitutes' offers" (Rosen, 1982, p. 84).

Since the latter part of the nineteenth century, many states have adopted laws that specifically make the sellers of liquor to underage drinkers or inebriates, subject to civil lawsuit for endangering the health of minors and/or the occurrence of any other resulting damage or harm. Collectively, these laws are known as the "dramshop laws or acts." Their effectiveness depends on the ability and willingness of persons who have been injured to undertake the necessary legal proceedings. Beginning in 1877, after a series of strikes caused deaths in several major cities, civic organizations were formed to gather evidence against violators of the dramshop laws and to encourage interested parties to pursue their rights under such laws. The pioneer group in this regard was known as the Citizens' League of Chicago for the Suppression of the Sale of Liquor to Minors and Drunkards. In 1878, for a limited time, the Chicago organization was granted authority to make arrests. Such groups recruited volunteers and paid agents to work as investigators and court watchers for the express purpose of visiting saloons and courtrooms watching for cases that might lead to dramshop suits. Some of these citizen investigators were beaten for their efforts. For a time, these groups did succeed in substantially raising the number of dramshop act lawsuits. The Boston Citizens' Law and Order League disbanded in 1901. Most of the groups were either absorbed by other groups, such as the Anti-Saloon League, or folded because of a loss of public support (Duis, 1983, pp. 97-99). According to Duis (1983):

> It became nearly impossible to find men willing to risk life and limb as an agent. The leagues also gradually lost their uniqueness, in part because other temperance groups imitated their use of the dramshop law and also because the leagues themselves widened their activities to include lobbying for other antisaloon legislation . . . and most important, the press and the judges tired of the growing excesses of the leagues. (Duis, 1983, p. 99.)

Depending on their location, ownership, customer support, and other critical factors, saloons could operate quite differently from one another. In New York City, just prior to the advent of prohibition, the Harlem branch of the Women's Christian Temperance Union was very pleased when black saloonkeepers began offering nonalcoholic beverages, such as tea and cocoa, in order to attract new customers. Moreover, special rooms were set aside for groups to listen to music, especially ragtime. This innovation became known as "afternoon tea" and was so successful that other saloons began presenting them. Some saloons added the opportunity for dancing and "tango teas" became popular (Anderson, 1982, p. 71). Later, in the years after the establishment of national prohibition, Harlem was a center of entertainment and its finer late-night speakeasies became a magnet for thousands of white visitors (Anderson, 1982, pp. 139–140). Moreover, liquor was not only available in many Harlem saloons, but along Lenox Avenue, liquor could be obtained in the most unlikely places—delicatessens, shoe shops, newsstands, stationery stores, soda fountains, cigar stores, and drugstores. "They were really cheap speakeasies, stocking large amounts of moonshine behind a thin camouflage of legitimate merchandise.... It was estimated that the number of Harlem drugstores more than doubled during the first three years of Prohibition" (Anderson, 1982, pp. 146–147).

In New York City, beginning around the middle period of prohibition, the black cultural movement known as the Harlem Renaissance, took place. It was a time when many famous black artists, entertainers, writers, and scientists began to achieve fame for their notable contributions to American society. This movement has grown throughout the twentieth century and has spread to all parts of the nation as blacks have been able to experience racial equality in America.

It was hardly likely that the Harlem Renaissance could have begun in any southern city. By the 1890s, most southern communities had disenfranchised and segregated their black populations. This took place through the phenomenon of "Jim Crow" laws. Even in the District of Columbia, the capital of the United States, Jim Crow took hold. Blacks were banned or discouraged from participating in civic groups, such as the Women's Christian Temperance Union. By the end of World War I, "the only public accommodations that were not segregated were the trolleys and buses, the public libraries, and the grandstands at Griffith Stadium" (Powers, 1987, p. 10). Furthermore, conditions were worse in other communities throughout the south and varied in northern areas. In Boston, by 1914 there were no independent black saloonkeepers because the city's licensing authorities simply refused to grant liquor licenses to blacks. On the other hand, in Chicago, black saloonkeepers were an essential aspect of the local business scene (Duis, 1983, p. 159).

During the progressive era, several of the oldest and best-known black civil rights organizations were established by coalitions of black and white leaders. For example, in 1909, the National Association for the

Advancement of Colored People (NAACP) was founded; and in 1910, the National Urban League was formed. On behalf of the legal rights of blacks, the NAACP brought lawsuits and lobbied Congress and other branches of government; while the League, sought to improve living conditions and employment opportunities. However, progress was agonizingly slow. In the years between 1914 and 1920, the black populations of such cities as Philadelphia, New York, Pittsburgh, Chicago, and Detroit tripled. In 1919, at least 26 race riots occurred. In 1921, the NAACP was able to have an anti-lynching bill introduced in Congress. Southern senators kept the bill from coming to a vote and similar bills were defeated in 1935 and 1940. Housing and better employment opportunities became scarce in the North and racial tensions ran high. Consequently, such alternative groups, as Marcus Garvey's Universal Negro Improvement Association (formed in 1916) became popular. This organization supported a "return to Africa" movement. A similar, but more separatist theme was later echoed by the Nation of Islam, founded in 1930 (Redding, 1979).

Before the adoption of prohibition, Duis (1983) noted that at least four separate approaches were used to control the saloon and its most likely customers. Firstly, temperance organizers tried to educate the masses about alcohol's adverse effects; secondly, civic groups undertook to enforce the dramshop acts themselves; thirdly, zoning regulations were adopted to curtail the spread of saloons in residential areas and their placement near schools; and fourthly, the creation of settlement houses and classes in domestic science for homemakers sought to provide better alternatives for saloon-bound husbands. The saloonkeepers who prospered or at least survived these attacks, were most likely those who were astute enough to appreciate the ethnic differences of their clientele and to cater to them. They also appreciated that the nature of the street life surrounding their places of business oftentimes required additional services (e.g., hours of operation, food, bathrooms, etc.). However, saloonkeepers that adapted to these conditions by supporting gambling and prostitution greatly contributed to the undoing of the entire enterprise. Moreover, these illegal activities also required saloonkeepers to hand out bribes and encouraged unscrupulous officials to engage in shakedowns.

During prohibition the speakeasy replaced the saloon. However, whereas the saloon was often situated on the corner of a block with a swinging door, the speakeasies were typically located in a basement, a back room, or an upstairs apartment. Speakeasy doors were locked and had a peephole. Oftentimes, the front portion of the establishment had the appearance of a legitimate business (e.g., drugstore, coffeehouse, etc.). In 1929, Police Commissioner Grover Whalen stated that there were 32,000 speakeasies in New York City (Cashman, 1981, p. 43). The operators and owners of these speakeasies were "dependent on corrupt policemen and agents who drank too much of their liquor and extorted too much of their profit" (Cashman, 1981, p. 44).

In cities, such as Detroit, the illicit manufacturing and distribution of intoxicating liquor became the city's second largest industry. Retail sale and consumption took place in speakeasies that were known as "blind pigs." This rather derogatory term arose when the more established downtown Detroit liquor dealers felt that their business was being absorbed by amateur dealers who quickly set up operations all over town to take advantage of the new clandestine market for spirits. They were "pigs" for seeking their business and they were "blind" because they had to hide themselves from confrontations with law enforcers and local dry residents. Basements, garages, apartments, attics as well as barber shops and other business sites could be used as blind pigs so long as the owner could provide adequate concealment and possessed "the necessary nerve and money" (Engelmann, 1979, p. 128). "Blind pigs ran into very little trouble if they were adept at distinguishing undercover police officers, WCTU matrons, Anti-Saloon League crusaders, federal prohibition agents, and state troopers from serious boozers. And they were extremely talented in making such distinctions.... In 1925 the police department estimated the number of blind pigs to be at least 15,000" (Engelmann, 1979, p. 126).

The experiment of national prohibition in the United States was the liveliest issue in American politics throughout the twenties and early thirties. One commentator wrote that the experiment had one hope of success and that hope was in the power of the generally law-abiding to stand by it. However, "as a matter of simple fact, the establishment of national prohibition is being made impossible by the refusal of those classes to recognize and obey the law of the Republic" (Ratcliffe, 1925, p. 721). America's great moral crusade withered away because of the difficulty of converting social mores into laws that could be clearly understood and accepted by the masses.

On December 5, 1933, only 288 days after Congress had sent the 21st Amendment to the states, ratification of the repeal of prohibition took place. Repeal made it possible for states to decide how liquor control would take place and "nearly every state moved quickly to establish statewide alcoholic beverage regulations" (Kyvig, 1979, p. 186). Initially, the fear of the return of the saloon prompted most states to either eliminate or severely restrict the on-site sale and consumption of liquor. For example, any on-site sale and consumption also required the business location to sell food. Other common restrictions included: no ownership by brewers or distillers; no Sunday sales; no sales to intoxicated persons or minors; maintaining a certain distance from schools and houses of worship; limits on advertising; no gambling; and no concealment of the interior from the street. Gradually, the use of the name of the saloon faded away and was replaced by the label "bar" or "tavern." By 1941, most liquor was packaged for home consumption and sold in nonreusable containers. Thus, the old "saloon" as the main community gathering spot and political club vanished from the landscape of America (Kyvig, 1979, pp. 188-189).

Part 2 deals with the unusual case of Detective Sergeant Charles Tighe of the New York City Police Department. It is presented to illustrate the impact of prohibition upon the lives of everyday people. The case arose out of the need to enforce yet another form of vice law: the prohibition of public gambling.

ENDNOTES

1. Bryan, William Jennings. The Fruits of Prohibition in Fred B. Smith, ed. *Law vs. Lawlessness: Addresses Delivered at the Citizenship Conference, Washington, D.C. October 13, 14, 15, 1923*. New York: Fleming H. Revell Co., 1924, p. 114. Bryan ran three times for the presidency of the United States as the Democratic Party's candidate and he was defeated each time. Bryan resigned his position in the cabinet of Woodrow Wilson after disagreeing with his prewartime strategies. One of the most famous orators and statesmen of previous decades, he died a few days after serving as the prosecutor in the famous Scopes trial held in Dayton, Tennessee on July 26, 1925. After Scopes was convicted for teaching about the theory of evolution contrary to the laws of the state, many high school textbook publishers removed the topic of evolution from their existing texts. At the trial, Clarence Darrow served as counsel for the defense. The media heavily covered the case. It became the first trial to be covered through the use of radio (Perrett, 1982, p. 200). The most famous moment of the trial came when Darrow called Bryan as an expert witness on the Bible. When Bryan died of a heart attack, millions of his grief-stricken supporters "eulogized him as a true Christian martyr, fallen in defense of the faith" (Parrish, 1992, p. 129). He was buried at Arlington National Cemetery and etched on his tombstone are the words, "He kept the Faith." Scopes received a gift from a local businessman that enabled him to attend the University of Chicago and he later became a well-known geologist. He never returned to Tennessee. The case was never appealed to the federal courts, because the Tennessee Supreme Court reversed Scope's conviction on a minor technicality. Although the court also upheld the legality of the law under which Scopes was convicted, no one was ever prosecuted again for its violation (Perrett, 1982, pp. 201-202).

Part 2

THE ERA OF NATIONAL PROHIBITION
1920-1933

Chapter 6

THE RAID ON COEN'S SALOON

"The saloon has been well-nigh destroyed, and with it
the vast corrupting power of the liquor interests in politics. The practicability of the enforcement of prohibition is being substantially proved."[1]

REV. JOSEPH FORT NEWTON
CHURCH OF THE DIVINE PATERNITY
CITY OF NEW YORK (1923)

The dawn of the 1920s witnessed a shell-shocked world trying to recover
from the wounds of World War I and a desire by Americans to come
"back to normalcy." In 1920, of all the words uttered by Warren G. Harding
during his successful campaign for the presidency of the United States, that
one phrase received the most approval (Sullivan, 1939).

However, the decade was anything but "normal." On August 26, 1920 an
estimated 9.5 million additional women became eligible to vote as a result of
the passage of the Woman's Suffrage Amendment to the Constitution. For
the first time in American history women in every state had the right to vote.
The Prohibition Amendment had already been in effect for over six months
when women's suffrage became a matter of national policy, rather than local
initiative. Urbanization had also taken place since more than half of the population now lived in or near cities. Urban growth was fostered by at least five
causes: (1) the migration from the farm to the city as a result of better farm-
ing techniques; (2) the development of manufacturing centers and other
expansions of industry; (3) improved systems of transportation including rail-
roads and some new highways linking the cities of the nation with rural
areas; (4) the development of elevated and underground urban electric rail-
ways with low fares; (5) and successive waves of immigrants, especially from
eastern and southern Europe and Asia.

The conditions within the cities, as we have seen, gave rise to a new sense
of "social consciousness" when the progressives began to introduce their programs. However, by the 1920s, the tide of progressivism had begun to
recede. President Coolidge, who succeeded Harding, after the latter's

untimely death in August of 1923, is today remembered for having "chloro-formed the remnants of the progressive movement" (Parrish, 1992, p. 52). Coolidge believed that the country had too many laws and that it would be better off if it didn't have any more. He stated: "The greatest duty and opportunity of government is not to embark on any new ventures....It does not at all follow that because abuses exist...it is the concern of the federal gov-ernment to attempt their reform" (Parrish, 1992, p. 52).

The advent of the 1920s also witnessed a rebirth of the Ku Klux Klan after having been dormant for fifty years. Although there was no actual connec-tion with the original Ku Klux Klan of the days of Reconstruction following the Civil War, the new organization adapted its rituals and dress (Slosson, 1958, p. 308). Consequently, the figures of white-robed and masked figures began to assemble in both southern and northern states (Sullivan, 1939). On June 24, 1922, a mass initiation of Klansmen took place on a pasture range near Tulsa, Oklahoma. According to a press report, over one thousand men were inducted into Tulsa Klan No. 2 in a ceremony witnessed by a huge crowd in over ten thousand automobiles. The ceremony took place after dark and lasted for several hours. Two fiery crosses illuminated it. The larg-er cross had a dimension of 70 by 20 feet. One young boy who witnessed the spectacle said: "It was awful solemn and spooky. White figures were every place" (Sullivan, 1939, p. 574). The new Klan viewed Jews, Roman Catholics and recent immigrants with equal hostility. Its feelings about blacks was summarized by Hiram Wesley Evans, a Texas dentist, who became the Klan's new Imperial Wizard in December of 1922: "The Negro is not a menace to Americanism in the sense that the Jew or the Roman Catholic is a menace. He is not actually hostile to it. He is simply racially incapable of understanding, sharing in or contributing to Americanism" (Slosson, 1958, p.309). From October 1920 to October 1921, newspaper reports revealed four killings, one mutilation, one-branding with acid, five kidnappings and forty-three persons driven out of their communities (Slosson, 1958, p. 311). It has been a subject of dispute whether or not all of these and subsequent similar acts of brutality were committed by Klan mem-bers or pretenders. Perhaps, the truth falls somewhere in between. Nevertheless, screening of Klan applicants was minimal and "membership became a convenient refuge for criminals who wanted protection and politi-cians who wanted a ready-made 'machine'" (Slosson, 1958, p. 312).

One of the goals of the *Volstead Act* was the elimination of all saloons and liquor stores. New York City, the biggest city in America, was also one of the least amenable to going dry. Throughout the decade, it received the constant attention of the news media and federal officials. Legally, saloon and liquor storeowners had two choices: either renovate for a replacement business or go out of business. In Manhattan, the heart of New York City, most saloon and liquor stores were on the Avenues. In 1918, the most licensed liquor stores and saloons were located on Third and Eighth Avenues. Third Avenue had 205 saloons and 28 liquor stores while Eighth Avenue had 188 saloons as well as 28 liquor stores. By 1922, most of these businesses had been converted to other types of establishments and 32 locations were now vacant. Typically, the new businesses related to foods, clothing and dry goods. On these two avenues, a total of 74 restaurants, 29 grocery stores, 21 soda fountains, 15 candy shops, and 31 other assorted meat, fish and produce markets took the place of the former saloons and liquor stores. In contrast, the most frequent types of nonfood related stores on these two avenues were: 49 specialty clothing shops (e.g., baby and ladies clothing, etc.); 29 dry goods; 21 men's wear; 11 laundries; and 20 assorted shoe, hat and clothing stores (Corradini, 1925, pp. 8 & 11).

On March 4, 1921, Warren G. Harding and Calvin Coolidge were inaugurated President and Vice-President. On April 25, 1921, Congressman Andrew Volstead, who wrote the prohibition enforcement statute, introduced additional legislation in order to prohibit the sale of beer even though a doctor's prescription had first been obtained. On July 2, 1921, President Harding signed the joint Congressional Resolution declaring peace with Germany and Austria.

On Tuesday, July 27, 1921, the major headlines on the front page of the *New York Times* announced that U.S. Secret Service agents and members of the Italian squad composed of local New York City police detectives had just completed two raids. They arrested six men, three of them printers and seized $2 million dollars worth of counterfeit revenue stamps. The revenue stamps were copies of the federal government stamp that is pasted over the cork of liquor bottles. The six-inch long stamps stated that the contents of the bottle were filled "in bond under the supervision of the Unites States Government, 100 proof and tax paid." In addition, the raid netted several printing presses, thousands of forged labels of well-known brands of liquor, forged liquor withdrawal permits, cuts and dies, and a great quantity of related evidence. Law enforcement authorities stated that the arrests and evidence seizures indicated the great extent to which bootlegging had become a big business and represented a widespread effort to undermine prohibition measures. It was said that the printing operations were being conducted along the lines similar to any traditional business, in that there existed the manufacturer, who sold to the jobber, who in turn sold to the retailer ("$2,000,000 Bogus Rum Stamps Seized in Raids; Six Held," *NYT*, July 27, 1921, pp. 1 & 5).

During the last days of July, the city was in the midst of a heat wave. On July 28, 1921, just a couple of days after the large seizure of counterfeit revenue stamps had taken place, five persons died from the heat and more than a score were prostrated. The heat drove thousands to the beaches and another four persons drowned in nearby waters. All of the shorefront resorts within close proximity to the city reported record-breaking crowds ("Heat Kills Five; Score Overcome; No Relief Today," *NYT*, July 29, 1921, p. 1). New Yorkers didn't need an automobile or trolleys to reach Coney Island. For a nickel, a rider could take the newly completed subway line that extended from the upper Bronx to the Atlantic Ocean (Lyman, 1975, p. 240). Those who could not get away sought relief in the city's indoor swimming pools or hoped to find a breeze out in the city's parks. In the evening, hundreds of persons slept on park benches or on the grass of the parks. They did so with the mayor's blessing. He had declared them to be open due to the hot and stifling weather ("Heat Kills Five; Score Overcome; No Relief Today," *NYT*, July 29, 1921, p. 1).

At the same time, Franklin D. Roosevelt, the future governor of New York State and president of the United States, was summering with his young family in Campobello Island. After several days of sailing, fishing, jogging and swimming, he became the most famous American to ever become a polio victim. Later, Roosevelt's eternal optimism would aid and inspire the American public to overcome two of the greatest calamities in its history: the Great Depression and World War II (Parrish, 1992, pp. 277-278).

In New York City on July 28, 1921, the temperature reached 89 degrees at around three in the afternoon and remained at that level for at least an hour. A few customers were in Coen's restaurant, located at the southeast corner of 43rd Street and Ninth Avenue, taking a break from the heat of the day. The establishment was formerly a licensed saloon, but with the advent of national prohibition the owner had converted it into a lunchroom. Police officers, who made a later search of the premises, indicated that the only drinks sold there were soft drinks and near beer. According to the initial *New York Times* report, there were only four customers inside the business. Three were at the counter, where a chef was serving them. The fourth person, a man believed to be nearly 80 years old, was seated at a side table. Suddenly, three men entered and one of them, later identified as Detective Tighe, announced that they had come to raid the saloon ("Sleuth Runs Wild," *NYT*, July 29, 1921).

Alphonse Delgrosso, the counter man and chef in the lunchroom, said "the moment Tighe entered he swept his club along the counter, breaking every bit of glassware and crockery and knocking most of it to the floor. Then he came behind the bar and started after me." Delgrosso also said that Tighe struck him several times and dragged him to the back room ("Detective Who Blackjacked 40 Reduced to Ranks," *NYT*, July 30, 1921).

Tighe was heard to state "What the hell are you all doing here?" As he said that one of the officers with him advised him to use quieter tactics.

Eventually, after Tighe repeated his question, one of the men at the counter responded that they were waiting for food and to get the baseball results as they came over the telegraph ticker buzzing away in the center of the restaurant. When Tighe shouted for them to get into the back room, each obeyed except for the old man at the table. One of the officers who had entered with Tighe tried to calm him, but Tighe responded "Look out, look out. I'm here to clean the place out." This officer was later identified as Detective Milton Kaufman ("Sleuth Runs Wild," *NYT*, July 29, 1921, p. 1).

After securing the three men in the back room, Tighe turned his attention to the old man at the table. He asked him what he was doing there and the old man said: "I am waiting for some more soup." According to witnesses who later reported their complaints to the desk lieutenant at the West 47th Street Police Station, Tighe then picked up the old man's soup plate and hurled it to the floor. He then drew out his blackjack and struck the man over the head. He then seized him and pushed him into the back room. While all this was happening the other detectives were still trying to calm him. He then seized the glass covering of the baseball ticker and hurled it to the floor and then ran out to the street. Once on the street, Tighe proceeded to use his blackjack on men and women and dragged them into the rear room of the restaurant. In all, the press reported that between 25 and 50 persons, including six women and two children were assaulted and "then made prisoners in a stifling back room for two hours" (*NYT*, July 29, 1921, p. 1).

After several of Tighe's forays onto the streets, a large crowd gathered outside Coen's restaurant. Tighe's actions also attracted the attention of the priests in the rectory of Holy Cross Roman Catholic Church on West 42nd Street, between Eighth and Ninth Avenues. One of them was said to be Father Francis P. Duffy, the chaplain of the famous 69th Regiment. He reported the incident to the police by calling the West 47th Street Station (*NYT*, July 29, 1921, p. 3).

After the reported violence, 27 men who had been in the back room were taken to the Men's Night Court on 57th Street near Third Avenue for the purposes of being charged with disorderly conduct. However, before being taken to the night court, they had been brought in the late afternoon to the West 47th Street Station. The desk lieutenant refused to book any of them (*NYT*, July, 30, 1921). A similar response occurred in Night Court:

> Before the policemen could make a complaint, Magistrate Thomas E. Nolan summarily dismissed the twenty-seven prisoners and indignantly upbraided the arresting officers. "This is an outrage," he declared, "and it must stop or else I shall personally take action. If you detectives bring in any more men on such a flimsy pretext"–the detectives had said they found the prisoners "congregated around a ticker getting baseball results"–"I am going to make a complaint of oppression against you" (NYT, July 29, 1921, p. 1).

On July 29, 1921, a day after the incident, Tighe was suspended from his position by Chief Inspector William J. Lahey and transferred back to the uniformed force and told to report daily to the West 33rd Street Station. Tighe had been assigned to a special squad under the command of Lahey. While Tighe was not at this point arrested for his alleged actions, it was stated in the press report that Police Commissioner Enright had ordered his immediate arrest and that several of the women who had been beaten said they intended to bring assault charges. Although witnesses stated that Tighe had the odor of alcohol on his breath, no action was taken in this regard. No action was taken against Detective Milton Kaufman, also a member of the Chief Inspector's squad, who was with Tighe. Witnesses had said he took no part in the numerous assaults, but that he did little or nothing to prevent them from happening. No further newspaper articles nor any of the trial witnesses referred to the presence of a third detective as had the original press report ("Detective Who Blackjacked 40 Reduced to Ranks," *NYT*, July 30, 1921, p. 1).

Subsequently, at each of Tighe's assault trials, the central facts in dispute were whether he used force in an unjustified manner. If force was used, did he injure anyone and what was the extent of those injuries? Did he use a deadly weapon? In addition, precisely who did he detain in the back room of Coen's former saloon and for what reasons?

Tighe's Previous Disciplinary Record

In an unusual coincidence, three weeks prior to the incident the Chairman of the Joint New York State Legislative Investigating Committee, Senator Schuyler M. Meyer, had received Tighe's disciplinary records through a subpoena. The subpoena had been issued because Tighe was one of several New York City detectives under suspicion for having brutalized prisoners and who seemed to be immune from punishment because of favoritism within the Police Department. The record revealed to the press by Senator Meyer indicated that Tighe had joined the force in 1912 and since then had been charged with seven different duty-related complaints. The following is the full text of Tighe's record as published in the *New York Times* (p. 4) on July 30, 1921:

Dec. 3, 1915–(1) Absent from post, standing at bar in licensed liquor saloon. (2) Failed to obtain permission. (3) Failed to make entry. Reprimand.

June 20, 1916–Struck a prisoner with his fist and baton while conveying him to the station house. Reprimand.

June 20, 1916–Struck a prisoner with his baton while conveying him to the station house. Two days' pay.

March 15, 1917–Improper patrol. Complaint dismissed.

March 18, 1918–(1) Absent from post, lying on platform of subway station. (2) Intoxicated. (3) No permission. (4) No entry. Reprimand.

Aug. 27, 1919–(1) Struck colored man with baton and used improper language to him. (2) False Arrest. One day's pay.

Aug. 27, 1919–(1) Assaulted woman in station house with his night baton. (2) Falsely arrested a woman. Complaint dismissed.

The last two charges according to additional materials in the record grew out of a raid on a craps game in which the black man struck by Tighe was James Harris. The woman who accused him of striking her with his club was Mrs. Dorothy Gibbins of 60 East 134th Street. According to the record revealed by Senator Meyer, Mrs. Gibbons testified that she had entered the station house to make arrangements for the care of a child of one of the persons arrested (*NYT*, July 30, 1921, p. 4).[2]

With respect to the intoxication charge of March 18, 1918, the following report of Police Surgeon Thomas A. McGoldrick was also included in the record and published in its entirety in the *New York Times* (July 30, 1921, p. 4):

To the Police Commissioner: (Through Official Channels) Sir: At 4 A.M., March 18, 1918, I visited the 146th Precinct Stationhouse and examined Patrolman Charles Tighe, Shield 6,237, of that precinct, and found him unfitted for duty by reason of the use of intoxicants. Findings: In deep stupor from which he could be aroused only with difficulty. Breath very foul and alcoholic in odor. Clothes very soiled with dust. Pupils of eyes dilated. Pulse 72, full and regular. Face flushed. When aroused could not stand or walk steadily. Brain action slow. Thoughts disconnected. Recognized the police surgeon and could read time on a watch correctly.

Respectfully,
THOMAS A. McGOLDRICK, Surgeon Twelfth District.

Dr. McGoldrick was born in Brooklyn in 1875 and in 1893 graduated from Manhattan College. Three years later he received his medical degree from the Long Island Hospital College of Medicine. He became an internist and specialized in the treatment of tuberculosis and other lung diseases. He was appointed a police surgeon on January 4, 1907 (NYT, March 10, 1956, p. 17).

Senator Meyer commented that the only punishment Tighe received for his conduct of March 18, 1918 was a reprimand. He said: "That certainly looks as though he were a policeman with a pull" (*NYT*, July 30, 1921, p. 4). He then went on to describe an incident where a sergeant evidently had no "pull." This officer had been assigned to a Liberty Loan parade in 1919 and had been disrespectful to a high-ranking civilian police official, but whose actual duties are not well known by the uniformed force. His punishment was the loss of twenty days' pay. Finally, Senator Meyer concluded that records show there were many other instances of policemen being protected in wrongdoing by inadequate punishment. He stated that this was a cause of low morale within the Police Department and that his committee would attempt to ascertain why the police authorities had been so lenient with Tighe and other policemen and so stern with others (*NYT*, July 30, 1921, p. 4).

Senator Meyer's comments provoked the following response from the New York City's Commissioner of Accounts, David Hirschfield:

> From the records of the Police Department it appears that during the Mitchell Administration, when the Police Department was under Arthur Woods, Tighe was up on charges on four distinct occasions. In each instance the charges were of a character which would, under any efficient police administration, have resulted in his being discharged from the service. The records show, however, that in each instance he got off with a small fine or a few days' suspension. For Senator Meyer's information I would refer him to charges made against Tighe on Dec. 3, 1915; June 20, 1915; another on the same date, and on March 15, 1917. If Tighe had a pull he didn't have it under this administration. (*NYT*, July 31, 1921, p. 18)

In subsequent days and weeks, the rhetoric between representatives of city government and Senator Meyer heated-up. Investigators for Senator Meyer's committee had spent the previous two months gathering evidence about the New York City municipal and borough governmental operations. Public hearings were scheduled to begin August 9th in the City Hall Building. Meyer said that his investigating committee, which had thus far spent half of its $100,000 appropriation, had discovered evidence of graft, extortion and misrule. In addition to his previous comments about the need to eliminate violent policemen with Tighe as his number one exhibit, he now took the opportunity to focus attention on general graft and corruption among members of the New York City Police Force. Hirschfield responded with a call for an immediate showdown with respect to Meyer's allegations ("Graft and Misrule Charged by Meyer," *NYT*, August 2, 1921, p. 15).

> Senator Meyer has got to make good this thieving charge, and do it today, or he is a liar. He has made a general statement here, trying to besmudge the whole department. He has issued an indictment against 10,000 men. If he has got anything, it is his business to come out and prove it. If he hasn't he will be shown as trying to scandalize the Police Department for political purposes. Investigating bodies should be fair. (*NYT*, August 2, 1921, p. 15)

Tighe's Civilian Career

Prior to joining the police force, Tighe, worked for the Devlin Stables in Manhattan and Brooklyn. Edward Devlin, the owner of this business, had employed Tighe as a hearse driver and had discharged him for a reason he said he could no longer remember. He revealed that Tighe visited him on

the same day as the raid on Coen's place, but earlier. He was surprised to
see him. It had been a long time since they had met. According to Devlin,
when Tighe walked into his office at 405 West 42nd Street, he appeared to
be angry about Devlin's appearance as a witness in a previous investigation
of an alleged slush fund involving the Police Endowment Association
("Swann Will Rush Tighe Prosecution," *NYT*, August 2, 1921, p. 28).
Ironically, David Hirschfield headed that investigation!

Devlin reported the conversation that next transpired between Devlin and
Tighe as follows: "'I've a good mind to lock you up.' 'Well, you try it, and
you'll get locked up yourself. 'This piece of tin will take you to the police station.' 'That's for the judge to decide.'" At that point, according to Devlin,
"Tighe placed his hand in his hip pocket and when I saw the motion I knew
he was going to reach for a blackjack or something, so I reached into my safe
and got the jump on him. He and the policeman with him left without
exchanging further words" ("Swann Will Rush Tighe Prosecution," *NYT*,
August 2, 1921, p. 28). When Devlin was asked by a press reporter if he
intended to make a complaint against Tighe regarding this incident, he said:
"I don't suppose I will, because what's the use when there are so many complaints already lodged against Tighe?" (*NYT*, August 2, 1921, p. 28).

Tighe's Arrest

On July 30, 1921, suspended Detective Sergeant Charles F. Tighe was
arrested for assault in the third degree. The charge was based upon his having slapped Mrs. Ella Fitzgerald of 329 West 43rd Street, tearing her dress,
and dragging her to a patrol wagon. The press report pointed out that this
was one of the least of the alleged violent actions that Tighe had engaged in
at the time of his raid on Coen's cafe. Detectives Dennison and Fitzgerald
first went to Tighe's home at 2742 Eighth Avenue and then took him to the
West 47th Street Police Station. At the station, the Precinct's Captain,
Thomas Donahue, formerly arrested him. After turning in his shield and
other equipment, he was released on $500 bail posted by his brother-in-law,
Samuel Dann of 74 West 108th Street. Interestingly, the bail was in the form
of "Liberty bonds" which the precinct Captain accepted in lieu of cash. He
then left for his home with his brother-in-law ("Tighe Arrested in 'Selected'
Case," *NYT*, July 31, 1921, p. 1). According to the press report, Tighe had
not been lodged in a cell and did not appear worried over his predicament.
He refused to talk about the case (*NYT*, July 31, 1921, p. 1).

The police blotter entry at the West 47th Street Police Station showed that
Tighe was arrested and charged by Mrs. Fitzgerald with grabbing her about
the left arm, causing slight contusions, and that she received no medical
attention (*NYT*, July 31, 1921, p. 18).

On the same day of Tighe's arrest, a summons was issued by Magistrate George W. Simpson of the West Side Court returnable on Monday August 1st on a charge that Tighe had assaulted a seven-year-old child, Helen Coen on the day of the initial disturbance. Helen was the daughter of Patrick Coen, the owner of the raided establishment. The summons was issued based upon an investigation conducted by Joseph F. Kenehan, a special officer for the Society for the Prevention of Cruelty to Children. Although Kenehan had specifically requested that a warrant be issued for Tighe's arrest, only a summons was granted. Kenehan testified before Magistrate Simpson along with seven-year-old Helen Coen and her mother. Kenehan told the court that Tighe had picked up the child by her neck and had thrown her across a room in the restaurant. When the child's mother appeared, Tighe dragged both into the rear room of the restaurant. In court, the child exhibited bruises, which she said were caused by Tighe (*NYT*, July 31, 1921, p. 1). However, Kenehan also admitted that Tighe had told young Helen to get out of the room because she was in danger during the raid and that he was informed by the child's mother that Helen was all right and that she had not been struck. Furthermore, he stated that he was unable to find any marks indicating that Helen had been choked (*NYT*, August 1, 1921, p. 1).

After Kenehan had left the courtroom with the summons, Magistrate Simpson told reporters that he refused to issue the warrant because he did not want to humiliate a police officer. He stated: "I have known Tighe for many years and I know that he will respond to the summons just as quickly as he would to a warrant" (*NYT*, July 31, 1921, p. 1).

Tighe's First Court Appearance

On July 31, 1921, Tighe appeared in a courtroom for the first time to face charges arising out of his conduct at the time of his raid of Coen's restaurant. The presiding Magistrate was George W. Simpson. Simpson was born in Baltimore in 1870 and became an attorney in 1892 after graduating from Columbia Law School. He served one term as a state senator before Mayor Hylan appointed him as a temporary magistrate in 1918. He was appointed to a full 10-year term the following year (*NYT*, August 18, 1951, p. 11).

In the West Side Court, Tighe was arraigned on the following charges: simple assault, felonious assault, and attempted felonious assault. The simple assault charge was based on the complaint of Mrs. Ella Fitzgerald, age 53, previously described. Tighe's bail was fixed at $500 for this charge. The second offense, felonious assault, was based on the complaint of Mrs. Emma Lennon, 38, who alleged that Tighe accosted her on the sidewalk in front of Coen's place, dragged her into the place, and thrust her into the back room, where he struck her several times with a blackjack on the arm and on the back. He was held on $1,000 bail for this charge. The third charge, attempt-ed felonious assault, was founded on the allegations of Mrs. Catherine Gaiety, 37, who maintained that Tighe accosted her on the street in front of the raided restaurant and struck at her with a blackjack, but only landed a blow with his fist. On this charge his bail was set at $1,000. Joseph B. Rosenback, an attorney, of 306 West 54th Street, represented Tighe. The total bail in the amount of $2,500 was provided by a surety company ("Comrades Go to Aid Accused Detective," *NYT*, August 1, 1921, p. 1).

According to the press, the suspended detective appeared wearing a neat light gray suit and with the greatest self-possession. Upon his arrival, he was accompanied by at least three fellow detectives who attempted to shield him from the press at points outside and inside the courtroom. Just outside the courtroom, they used their hats to cover the defendant's face when press photographers closed in. One of the men protecting Tighe, threatened to smash a camera held by one of the photographers'. Once inside the court-room, his fellow officers congregated in front of the press table and by stand-ing shoulder to shoulder, they made it difficult for the reporters to hear the arraignment proceedings (*NYT*, August 1, 1921).

For the first time, Tighe revealed his side of the case. When the arraign-ment was over he said to the press:

> There are always two sides to every story. So far the newspapers have failed to publish my side of this matter. I know several newspaper men very well, and I cannot understand the action of the papers. The situation was this: My partner Kaufman and I had received instruction to watch Coen's place, as there had been several complaints made against it, and we had the place under observation about half an hour on Thursday before we entered the saloon and arrested several men whom we had seen violating the law. We placed them under arrest and put them in the back room. I then went to telephone for a patrol wagon, and was compelled to go to Ninth Avenue and Forty-second Street, where was the nearest signal box. When I returned to Coen's place I found that several of our prisoners, who had number about twenty-five in all, had escaped through a side door. I rushed out into the street and started to push back those who, I know had been placed under arrest. Then followed a struggle in which several women friends of the men took part. I suppose they were roughly handled in the excitement, but I was not drunk or crazed with the heat, as the papers have stated. Do I look like an insane man? (*NYT*, August 1, 1921, p. 1)

On the day after Tighe's arraignment, an editorial appeared in the *New York Times* criticizing the leniency that had been shown to Tighe in the past for his misconduct on duty, condemning the fact that he had been promot-ed soon after he had been found drunk and in uniform in 1918, castigating Magistrate Simpson for refusing to "humiliate" a police officer by issuing an arrest warrant, and warning city political leaders that the community would no longer tolerate a return to old and brutal police methods ("Pull in the Police Force," *NYT*, August 1, 1921, p. 10).

Tighe's Second Court Appearance

Tighe's second court appearance was less dramatic then had taken place the previous day and only garnered back page mention in the *New York Times*. He was now being charged with two additional crimes: simple assault and felonious assault. Again, the arraignment proceedings took place in the West Side Magistrate's Court, before Magistrate Simpson. The simple assault case concerned his conduct with respect to Helen Coen. A few days earlier, Tighe had been issued a summons to appear on this matter. Charles Green, who was employed in the restaurant as a bootblack, lodged the more serious charge. Today, the words to refer to Green's occupation would be a "shoeshine stand operator." Before Tighe was arraigned on these additional charges arising out of the incident, Helen, her mother and Mr. Green were called to testify. Green witnessed what had happened to Helen and her mother and he testified that when he asked Tighe if he were drunk. "Tighe answered, 'I'll show you whether I'm drunk or crazy,' and he pushed me, knocking the crutch from under my arm" ("Swann Will Rush Tighe Prosecution," *NYT*, August 2, 1921, p. 28).

Bail on each of the new assault charges was $1,000 and his total bail amount was now $4,500. All of the cases pending against Tighe and any additional ones were assigned to be prosecuted by Assistant District Attorney Frederick J. Sullivan. Sullivan was informed by his supervisor that he should devote his full attention to these cases and give them his highest priority. The announcement of his selection as prosecutor was made by District Attorney for New York County Edward Swann, who had just returned from a vacation, arriving at Grand Central Station (*NYT*, August 2, 1921, p. 28). At that time, Swann was quoted in part as follows:

> If only a fraction of what the newspapers say is true, and I have no doubt it is all true, we will be justified in clearing the tracks and recommending immediate trial. Of course, the judges control the calendar, but I will certify that public interests demand it be tried as soon as possible.... I have instructed Mr. Sullivan to put the case ahead of everything else and give all his time to it. I have instructed him to give it his best attention and to bring it to trial as soon as possible. (*NYT*, August 2, 1921, p. 28)

Tighe's Third and Fourth Court Appearances

On August 3, 1921, Tighe went before Magistrate Simpson for the third time since the incident at Coen's restaurant had occurred. The purpose of this appearance was an opportunity for Tighe to challenge the validity of the charges brought against him. A preliminary hearing regarding the charge by Mrs. Catherine Gaiety was held. However, defense counsel waived similar hearings with respect to the complaints of Green and Lennon. During Mrs. Gaiety's appearance she informed the court, that she smelled the odor of whiskey in her encounter with Tighe. Mrs. Gaiety testified that she and her husband were returning to their home at 345 West 43rd Street after seeing a motion picture. They were standing across the street from the Coen restaurant when Tighe approached them by running across the street. She stated that he grabbed her husband and that she started to follow the two of them with her baby in her arms. Tighe tried to chase her away. After he brought her husband to the back room, he came out and tried to strike her with a blackjack. She dodged the blow, but was dragged with her infant in her arms into the back room. She said she stayed there for an hour, until Tighe told her to "get out." She then followed the patrol wagon to the West 47th Street Station and was arrested again. However, no charge was brought against her and after another hour she was told to go home by a different police officer ("Smelled Whiskey on Tighe's Breath," *NYT*, August 4, 1921, p. 17). At the conclusion of the hearing, Magistrate Simpson upheld the charge filed by Mrs. Gaiety. Simpson indicated: "There was no excuse for the arrest and assault of this complainant. If there is anything that the citizens of New York have a full right to expect it is safety on the streets of New York as well as in their homes, especially from the sworn officers of the peace" (*NYT*, August 4, 1921, p. 17).

Since Tighe waived preliminary examinations involving the other two assault cases arising out of the complaints filed by Mrs. Emma Lennon and Charles Green, the court referred a total of three felony cases to the grand jury. A fourth case concerning the simple assault charge brought by Mrs. Ella Fitzgerald, was referred to the Special Sessions Court. The press accounts consistently noted that Mr. Green was "a crippled Negro bootblack" ("Smelled Whisky on Tighe's Breath," *NYT*, August 4, 1921, p. 17).

On August 22, 1921, suspended Detective Charles Tighe was arraigned on charges of assault in the first and second degree as contained in the grand jury's indictments. Specifically, three indictments were voted on, each containing two counts each for assaults on Mrs. Emma Lennon, Charles Green, and Catherine Gaiety. The arraignment took place at the Court of General Sessions before Judge Nott. Tighe was represented by Samuel Furstenberg and pleaded not guilty to each of the indictments ("Indict Tighe, Fix Bail at $3,000, for Assault," *NYT*, August 23, 1921, p. 6).

Collateral Developments

The chief collateral development in the Tighe case was his police disciplinary trial before First Deputy Police Commissioner John A. Leach. After at least one postponement at the request of Tighe's counsel, the hearing regarding Tighe's misconduct got underway in the latter part of the month of August 1921. The hearing was conducted at police headquarters in the special trial room of the Deputy Commissioner. Tighe's counsel was Samuel Furstenberg ("Tighe's Police Trial Postponed," *NYT*, August 6, 1921, p. 3; "Calls Witness Liar in Blackjack Trial," *NYT*, August 26, 1921, p. 8).

On August 24 and 25, 1921 a number of witnesses were called including Alfonso Delgrosso, the cook at the lunch counter in the former saloon; Charles Green, the bootblack; Michael Durkin, a customer at the counter; Harry Wright, a witness; James Reid, a witness; Hugh Lavery, a local pawnbroker; and Father Terrence F. McNulty (*NYT*, August 26, 1921, p. 8).

On the same day that Tighe's police trial commenced, the giant British-built dirigible R-38, nearing the end of a 35-hour test flight, after which it was to be delivered to the U.S. Navy, burned with a loss of 42 lives including 16 Americans (Sullivan, 1939).

Alfonso Delgrosso, the cook at Coen's former saloon, testified that Tighe had gone behind the counter and struck him on the knees with a blackjack. However, under cross-examination by Furstenberg he said that he paid no attention to the activities taking place a few feet away at the ticker since he was too busy. During his questioning, Furstenberg had pointed out that Delgrosso had previously indicated that he had worked for four months in the counter area, implying that he had more than adequate time to observe events in the former saloon. When Delgrosso stated that he presumed that the men gathered around the ticker were merely reading the news, Commissioner Leach interrupted: 'Do you mean to say that you worked only two feet away from that ticker and did not know what was going on there?' 'No, I did not know what was going on.' 'Get off the stand! You are a liar!' (*NYT*, August 26, 1921, p. 8)

Charles Green, the bootblack, admitted under cross-examination that after Tighe had put him into the back room, he escaped and aided five others in escaping. On the strength of this admission, Furstenberg made a motion to dismiss the proceedings against Tighe, but Commissioner Leach denied the motion (*NYT*, August 26, 1921, p. 8).

Next, Michael Durkin was called as a witness on behalf of Tighe. He said he had been a customer at the counter and had seen money pass between men receiving the results of horse races at the ticker. He said that when Detectives Tighe and Kaufman entered they arrested the men around the ticker and herded the men into the back room. Then, Tighe went to call for a patrol wagon. By this time, Durkin said he was on the street and observed Green lead several persons outside through a door from the back room. He said Tighe also saw the escape and he went through the crowd arresting men he recognized as having been in the back room. He observed that several women interfered with Tighe's efforts and called him vile names while trying to take his prisoners away from him. Furthermore, Durkin said he didn't see a blackjack in Tighe's hand. Similar testimony in support of Tighe was provided by Harry Wright and James Reid (*NYT*, August 26, 1921, p. 8).

Hugh Lavery, a pawnbroker, testified that he had talked with Tighe shortly before the raid and had not smelled any liquor on Tighe's breath or noticed any other sign of drinking. Finally, Father Terrence McNulty, a priest from the Church of the Resurrection, 151st Street and Eight Avenue, was called by the defense. Father McNulty testified that on the evening of July 28, after the raid, he went to Tighe's home, which is in his parish, to meet another priest. At that time, he observed no signs of intoxication. The police trial was then adjourned until September 14, 1921 (*NYT*, August 26, 1921, p. 8). No decision in this matter was announced by Deputy Commissioner Leach until after Tighe's criminal trial involving his alleged assault on Mrs. Lennon.

At about the same time as Tighe's disciplinary hearing, rumors had been heard that mysterious ships had been sighted off the coast of New Jersey. Less than a week after Tighe's police trial, the U.S. Coast Guard announced that it had seized the schooner *Marshall* and several other vessels, which were found to be carrying liquor intended to be smuggled into the United States. This was one of the earliest examples of liquor-smuggling vessels hanging off the Atlantic coast. In due course, a strip some twenty or more miles distance from this coastline would come to be known as "Rum Row" (Sullivan, 1939).

There were other hearings being held during this same time period involving New York City police affairs. Most of these matters were reported on in the press. Potential jurors in the Tighe case might have been aware of them and they shed additional light on Tighe's activities. New York State Senator Meyer and New York City Commissioner David Hirshfield conducted these hearings. On August 3, 1921, testimony before the Joint Legislative Investigating Committee, chaired by Senator Meyer, was given by John William Black, the assistant general purchasing agent for the Aniline and Chemical Company. In February 1919, he was standing on the Century Roof, which sits above the famous Coconut Grove nightclub. Black and his friend, Captain Sheldon Wittlesly of Opelika, Alabama had just left the Coconut Grove. Wittlesly was in his army uniform since he had just returned from overseas service. They saw a man slapping a young woman and when they successfully intervened, they were interrupted by a man later identified as Detective Sergeant Charles Tighe. Whereupon, with Tighe speaking first, the following remarks were exchanged: 'Who the hell are you!' 'I might ask who you are.' 'I'll show you who I am.' At that point, Tighe called him "a foul name" and John Black hit him. Tighe then struck Black with his blackjack and Black continued fighting believing Tighe was a robber who was holding up the place. After more blows from the blackjack, Black was stunned and went down. Tighe kept up the attack. Captain Wittlesly then came to his friend's defense and received blows on his arm. After that, Tighe let Black get up and placed him under arrest, revealing for the first time that he was a police officer. Black was taken downstairs from the Century Roof and handcuffed between Tighe and another police officer. He was dragged from their present location on 62nd Street to the 68th Street Police Station. Along the way Black received a constant barrage of punches and strikes with two blackjacks. Wittlesly had followed his friend down the steps and protested the action of the officers. He was also arrested and later turned over to military authorities ("Meyer Told of Old Beating by Tighe," *NYT*, August 4, 1921, p. 17).

John Black had more to say. His initial testimony was only the beginning of his tale of mistreatment. Once he was delivered to the station house he was taken into a dark room. Unknown police officers were present, some wearing uniforms. They threw him to the floor and one of them kicked him in the face and broke his nose. While he was being escorted to be booked before the precinct desk lieutenant, he was told to say that he fell down the stairs or if he didn't do as he was told "we will crucify you" (*NYT*, August 4, 1921, p. 17).

Black went along with his captives, but when his bail was put at $500 he had to spend the night in the precinct's cell. He had asked to make phone calls, but he was told it was too late. Black didn't sleep, but just sat on the cell's bench for the remainder of the night. In the morning, he was first taken to the precinct's basement and told by the escorting officer to keep quiet and again threatened with reprisals if he failed to do so. The same officer took him to the West Side Magistrate's Court. However, before he was taken inside the courtroom, he encountered Tighe and was told to say nothing and he would only have to pay a fine of five or ten dollars. He said nothing and was fined five dollars. Tighe met Black outside the courthouse and offered to buy him a drink, Black refused. Instead, he immediately went to the Knickerbocker Hotel where Wittlesly was staying to call his wife; while there he was seen by the hotel doctor. The doctor told him that it was remarkable that his skull had not been broken. His head was swollen and his eyes were black and blue. He needed stitches to close-up his head wounds. When Senator Meyer asked Black why he hadn't made a complaint at the Police Department, Black responded: "Not after going through a thing like that, where they had you absolutely in their power. They would not let me telephone for outside assistance. They would not let me get in touch with a lawyer. I suggested two or three people who might come down to help me, but they would not let me telephone" (NYT, August 4, 1921, p. 17).

After Black had completed his testimony, Senator Meyer made the following comments:

> One of the most amazing stories of police brutality which has been brought to the notice of this committee is that of the experience of Mr. Black with Clubber Tighe, the policeman whose record has been placed before the public, thanks to the committee's efforts. Mr. Black appeared voluntarily as a citizen because he was persuaded for the first time that an agency was at hand to protect him from the vengeance which Tighe's associates promised him if he made any attempt to secure redress. It is a shocking indication of the collapse of police morale and discipline that an incident such as befell Mr. Black could go uninvestigated.... Mr. Black's story seems to reveal the tactics of a police mafia. (*NYT*, August 4, 1921, p. 17)

The other parallel event at the time of the Tighe scandal and the hearings being conducted by Senator Meyer's committee, was the hearing conducted by Commissioner of Accounts Hirshfield. He was looking into charges of undue influence regarding the passage of a state law increasing the salaries of various municipal employees including police detectives and making all of their positions permanent. Senator Clayton R. Lusk had sponsored this legislation. During the hearing, Hirshfield called such witnesses as Detective Sergeant Edward M. Burns, President of the New York City Detective Endowment Association; and Miss Louise Hart, assistant professor in the Classics Department at Hunter College.

Specifically, Hirshfield's inquiry focused on whether presents had been made by city employees in an effort to influence the law that had not only increased detective salaries but also that of teachers at Hunter College. Hirshfield concluded that there were enough discrepancies and contradictions in the testimony taken to warrant bringing the matter before a grand jury (*NYT*, August 4, 1921, p. 17).

Tighe's First Trial

On September 12, 1921, Tighe was tried before a three-judge panel in the Court of Special Sessions. The court consisted of Justices Murphy, Healy and Moss. The seven-year-old daughter of the owner of Coen's Restaurant was the principal witness called by the prosecution. Helen Coen said she was on her way to her home over the restaurant, and had started to enter it from the rear side door, when Tighe appeared. He squeezed her neck with his hands and pushed her into the street. Under cross-examination, she admitted her parents had told her what to say on the witness stand, and that she was not prevented from breathing when her neck was squeezed. Her mother testified that she heard her child's cries and ran down to the street. She found red finger marks on her daughter's neck. Mr. Green also testified for the prosecution and said that he saw Tighe grab the child by the neck ("Tighe is Acquitted of Child's Charge," *NYT*, September 13, 1921, p. 7).

Tighe testified that when he first entered the restaurant he found thirty-five men standing close to the ticker. He said he and Detective Kaufman arrested twenty-four of these men for disorderly conduct. He left the prisoners in charge of Detective Kaufman and when he returned from his call for a patrol wagon, he discovered that some men had escaped. While searching for these persons, he saw Helen run into the rear room and he put her outside. He further testified that he did not squeeze her neck and that he placed her out of the back room because "it was no place for her" (*NYT*, September 13, 1921, p. 7). At the conclusion of the trial, the court found that the evidence did not support the complaint. Thus, Tighe was acquitted of the misdemeanor assault charge (*NYT*, September 13, 1921, p. 7).

ENDNOTES

1. Newton, Joseph Fort. The Message of the Citizenship Conference to the American People in Fred B. Smith, ed. *Law vs. Lawlessness: Addresses Delivered at the Citizenship Conference, Washington, D.C. October 13, 14, 15, 1923*. New York: Fleming H. Revell Co., 1924, p. 181.
2. Today, second thoughts by all parties involved would occur before releasing such detailed information about an officer who had a pending case. In a matter involving police in the City of Schenectady, New York, local officials even refused to divulge the names of officers involved in misconduct. On June 4, 1998, the Appellate Division of the New York State court system ordered that the city of Schenectady had to reveal the names of 18 police officers involved in an off-duty egg-throwing fracas in the previous year, thereby reversing a lower court ruling that had supported the confidentiality of the information. However, on April 6, 1999 in a unanimous 15-page decision, the Court of Appeals, New York's highest court, reinstated the lower court's ruling (Laura Suchowolec, "Court Backs Schenectady," *Daily Gazette*, April 7, 1999, p.1). The lawsuit was initiated by the *Times Union* of Albany and Schenectady's *Daily Gazette*. The incident took place after-midnight in May 1997 and involved a rolling bachelor party in a rented school bus. The off-duty officers were accused of throwing eggs and beer cans at a car and its driver. In exchange for the police officers admissions, Schenectady's police chief had promised to keep their identities a secret (Morgan Lyle, "Egg Throwers May Be Named," *Daily Gazette*, June 5, 1998, p. B1).

Chapter 7

TIGHE'S SECOND TRIAL

At the time of Detective Sergeant Tighe's second trial, at least three other cases were pending against him. These consisted of two untried indictments involving assaults on Mrs. Gaiety and Mr. Green and a misdemeanor assault case where Mrs. Ella Fitzgerald was the alleged victim.

As previously stated, the incident arose on the afternoon of July 28, 1921 (a Thursday) during a gambling raid at Coen's Restaurant, a former saloon on the corner of Ninth Avenue and 43rd Street in the "Hell's Kitchen" area of New York City. The press reports of that era inconsistently referred to Coen's establishment as a lunchroom, cafe, former saloon, and a hotel. Mrs. Lennon, the victim in the present case, resided at Eleventh Avenue and 50th Street. In addition, as previously indicated, the police had received other complaints of assault with a blackjack and about other types of misconduct concerning Detective Tighe on that day and earlier in his career. Tighe and fellow officer Milton Kaufman claimed that they had been observing the former saloon for several months based on information that the establishment was permitting gambling on horses and that known bookmakers were on the premises. On the afternoon of July 28, 1921, they arrested about two dozen persons at the saloon's location for disorderly conduct. All the cases were dismissed before the end of the day.

The following sections present a summary of the testimony of the witnesses called by the prosecutor (Mr. Frederick Sullivan) and the defense attorney (Mr. Samuel Furstenberg) during a two-day trial that began on October 6, 1921. At the start of the trial, the prosecuting attorney asked that the first-degree assault charge in the grand jury indictment against the defendant be dropped, leaving only one count of second-degree assault. The motion was granted by Justice Thomas C. T. Crain, the presiding judge of the Court of General Sessions of the Peace, County of New York, Part VI.

Judge Crain was born on E. 14th Street just a short distance from the original Tammany Hall on May 25, 1860. He was the son of Dunham Jones Crain, a former Democratic Assemblyman and United States Consul in Milan, Italy. His mother, Hannah Ann Crain, came from an old New York family, which had traceable roots to a *Mayflower* family. His grandfather, Col. William Crain, fought in the American Revolution. Young Thomas Crain traveled with his father to his diplomatic post in Europe and became adept in three foreign languages. He studied law in Europe and on his return to New York City, he studied law with the firm of Platt & Bowers, a famous old law office. Within two years he was admitted to the practice of law in New York State. His first significant political position was as the private secretary to the Mayor. He held this position for two years and in 1890, he became the City Chamberlain. From 1894 to 1905, he served as Tenement House Commissioner. He resigned this post when he became at odds with Mayor McCllellan over enforcement of the tenement house laws in connection with the burning of a tenement in which 18 lives were lost. He obtained his position as General Court Sessions judge in 1906 and was reelected in 1920. He became a State Supreme Court Justice in 1924 and was elected District Attorney of New York County in 1929 at the age of 69 ("Thomas C.T. Crain, Ex-Justice, Dies, 82," *NYT*, May 30, 1942).

In May, 1930, five months after taking office as District Attorney, his office investigated the murder of Arnold Rothstein. Rothstein was one of the most celebrated crime figures of his day. He was killed in a New York hotel and Rothstein was behind the most famous sports scandal in American history. (In recent years, his participation in fixing the outcome of the 1919 Baseball World Series has been well chronicled by the mass media.) A grand jury was impaneled, but was discharged with the statement that it was unable to solve the slaying. In another case, where job buying was alleged involving a former Magistrate named George F. Ewald, Governor Franklin D. Roosevelt superseded Crain's office, by appointing a special assistant attorney general to take over the case. While indictments were returned, several trials ended in jury disagreement. In early March 1931, the City Club accused Crain of general negligence in the conduct of his office and urged his dismissal (*NYT*, May 30, 1942).

Samuel Seabury was appointed by Governor Roosevelt to head a commission to investigate 27 different allegations. After an extended hearing, at which Crain and others from his staff testified, the Seabury Commission recommended that 24 of the 29 charges be dismissed. On leaving his post as DA, he was appointed a Supreme Court referee. He held this post until his death in May of 1942 at the age of 82 (*NYT*, May 30, 1942).

The People's Main Presentation of the Case [1]

Mrs. Emma Lennon testified that on the afternoon of July 28, l921 she was suddenly grabbed from the rear and pushed into a nearby saloon. It was only by chance that she happened to be passing by on her way to do an errand in the neighborhood. Inside the saloon she was struck "twice right across the back" and as she screamed a man (later identified as Tighe's partner Officer Kaufman) rushed from "out of the rear of the saloon and he threw himself" between Mrs. Lennon and Officer Tighe and said "For God's sake, Charlie, don't strike that woman" (p. 6). Kaufman was struck by the third blow that had been intended for Mrs. Lennon. Lennon stated that Officer Tighe grabbed her again and threw her into a rear room. At the same time, he called her a "whore, cunt and cock sucker" and she said she was struck again "right across the arm three of four times" (p. 8). She was made to stand with men who had also been taken to this part of the saloon. Mrs. Lennon also stated that Tighe said he "would tell the judge that I was in the room soliciting all the men for a dollar a piece" (p. 8). She was later allowed to leave by Tighe and she went to the 47th Street police station to file a complaint. On cross-examination, Mrs. Lennon revealed she had a brother-in-law who was a former police officer and therefore knew that she had been struck with a blackjack. Overall, she was consistent in her direct testimony during cross-examination.

Other witnesses called by the prosecutor included: Joseph Smith, a driver for a beef packer and slaughterhouse and Police Officer Joseph Gaynor, of the 26th Precinct.

Smith testified on direct that he witnessed Mrs. Lennon being struck in the rear room with a small object covered in leather and that he heard a woman scream just prior to seeing Mrs. Lennon "getting shoved into the back room" (p. 21). On cross-examination, Smith indicated that he had never been to the saloon before Officer Tighe (pp. 26-27) shoved him inside. He stated that he "was shoved into the raid" (p. 30).

On direct examination Officer Gaynor testified that he saw Officer Tighe grab Mrs. Lennon and take her into the saloon. On cross-examination he was asked if the reserves were called out and if he knew that the Precinct Captain had arrived. The questions were objected to by the defense. The objection was sustained and no answers were given to them. He indicated that he couldn't say whether Officer Tighe had a blackjack because he didn't look (p. 36). On redirect he was read back a portion of his grand jury testimony in which he stated that when he went into the saloon he saw a blackjack in Tighe's right hand. Although pressed hard by the prosecutor, he could only now indicate that Tighe had something in his hand, but he couldn't tell what it was (p. 38).

The People rested at that point and the defendant's counsel moved to dismiss on the ground's that "the People have failed to make out a case of assault in the second degree" (p. 39). The motion was denied and the defense counsel asked that the jury be instructed that the court's decision should not in any way be "construed as an expression" of the judge's opinion. This seemed to be a very prejudicial event. Today, such motions are rarely made in front of a jury. The court's response was "I do tell them that" (p. 39).

The Main Case of the Defense

The defense called the following witnesses: Burt Lenn, a resident of West New York, New Jersey, who operated cafeterias for an automobile concern known as the Willis Corporation; Harry Wright of Elmont, Long Island, a florist during the season and a chauffeur out of the season; James Reid, Newark, New Jersey, the head of the Mail Order Department at Arnold Constable; Michael Durcan, a local resident and former railroad worker who has been unemployed for the past 12 months; Police Officer Milton Kaufman with only about one year of service on the force; and Police Officer Charles F. Tighe with nine years of New York City police service.[2]

Lenn said he was attracted by a crowd of about 300 to 400 people at the scene of the "performance" (p. 40) while he was on his way to visit his butcher. On direct examination he also testified that he saw Officer Tighe go into the crowd to retake some men who had escaped through a side exit. He said he did see Officer Tighe grab a woman by the shoulder and "tore her waist" (p. 42). He indicated that the woman was part of the crowd who resisted being pushed back into the crowd. The same crowd that the witness was a part of. He said he didn't see Mrs. Lennon. On cross-examination he was questioned about how he came to be subpoenaed. He said someone in the crowd must have given his name. He indicated that when Officer Tighe came after the men on the street that had escaped through a side door, the crowd was between 1,200 and 1,500 people (p. 46).

The second defense witness was Harry G. Wright, who had only recently moved to Elmont. At the time of Tighe's various trials he was living in Corona, Queens. He was on his way to visit his mother in Yonkers when his trip was interrupted by the events on Ninth Avenue and Coen's saloon. He stated he took subway trains from Corona and a cross-town shuttle to reach the area of Coen's saloon and he went inside primarily to use the bathroom. He was having a soda at the bar when police officers (Tighe and Kaufman) came in and announced to the crowd inside that they were under arrest (p. 48). Under redirect he clarified that only the persons around the ticker were placed under arrest (p.59). Wright said at that point he "stepped out to the corner" (p. 48) and when he walked out he did so with others at the bar and didn't leave the area until the last patrol wagon was filled with those arrested. He indicated that Mrs. Lennon interfered with Tighe's duties by coming up from behind the officer and grabbing both his arms as he was about to arrest a man outside the saloon. He said he heard Mrs. Lennon say "You haven't got anything on this man, I have lots of weight here in this neighborhood and I can have you broke" (pp. 49-50). Wright only saw Tighe push Mrs. Lennon away and did not see her taken or pushed into the bar. He never got to visit his mother on that day (p. 57).

Wright was also asked about how he had come to be a witness in this case and indicated that he had volunteered his name after reading in the newspaper that Tighe had been described as an officer who had on this occasion gone mad. He testified that he was in his "hack" (cab) parked in front of the Vanderbilt mansion on Park Avenue and 34th Street when he gave his name to a nearby police officer. The officer responded "Well, this Tighe is a pretty good friend of mine and I will be able to let you know in about an hour or two" (p. 52).

The third defense witness was James Reid. He saw the crowd by the saloon when he left his employment for lunch and joined it as a bystander. He testified that he didn't see Tighe attack anyone. He wrote a letter to Tighe to inform him of his availability as a witness.

The fourth witness for the defense was Michael Durcan, an unemployed railroad worker. He said he was at the saloon's bar with a friend and was not arrested. He frequently visits the saloon and knows the owner well since he lives just three blocks away. He said he saw men gambling by the ticker and he witnessed how Tighe put about 30 men into the back room. He never saw Mrs. Lennon, but he did see persons interfering with Officer Tighe's efforts to arrest people. He said he went to Officer Tighe's house to volunteer to be a witness after he saw the newspaper report of the incident. He indicated he got Tighe's address from a newspaper article.

The fifth witness to be called by the defense was Officer Kaufman. At the time of the incident, he was a plainclothes member of the Chief Inspector's Squad. He denied seeing Mrs. Lennon struck at any time. He said he had been Tighe's partner for six months at the time of the incident and that they were friends. Although some men escaped from the back room which he was guarding, he said he never pulled out his service weapon since there was "no necessity" (p. 98). He said that although he visited the saloon to observe conditions on at least 10 to 15 previous occasions he never checked the back room and hence was unaware that a back or side door existed. He stated that all the persons were arrested for disorderly conduct and that Magistrate Nolan dismissed all the cases. Kaufman was the last witness to be called on October 6, 1921 and the trial resumed the next day with the testimony of Officer Tighe.

Testimony of Officer Charles F. Tighe, The Defendant

The sixth witness for the defense was called on the morning of October 7, 1921. Tighe had been a member of the New York City Police Department for nine and one-half years, was married and had one child. He said he had been observing Coen's saloon for two months and on the day of the incident he and his partner, Officer Kaufman arrested about 35 men who were around the horseracing ticker. The saloon was under suspicion for being "a race horse pool room." The persons arrested were taken to the saloon's back room and Officer Kaufman guarded them while Tighe went outside to call for patrol wagons (p. 92). While he was doing this, some men got out through a rear door. Their escape was assisted by "a colored man now known as Green," who held the door open for them (p. 93).

In the process of looking for the escaped men, Tighe stated that he was interfered with by three different women including Mrs. Lennon, the complaining victim/witness in this case. He claimed that Mrs. Lennon came from behind and took hold of first his right arm and then both of his arms. This occurred while he was trying to bring back to the saloon one of the escaped men. Mrs. Lennon was protesting that Tighe had the wrong man and Tighe said in the courtroom that he did "the best I could to push her off, to push her away" (p. 94). Tighe testified that he warned her at least twice that she should not interfere with his arrest and that she stated to the man being arrested: "If I were you I wouldn't go with the cock sucker" (p. 95).

After Officer Tighe succeeded in bringing this man back to the saloon, he came out again and by this time additional police had arrived and a crowd estimated to be between 1,200 and 1,500 persons had gathered (p. 95). He then saw Mrs. Lennon and remarked to a police officer at the scene that he was going to arrest her. Tighe testified: "I took hold of her" (p. 96) and we entered the bar together. Tighe said he released her when she said she would make no further trouble if allowed to go home. He denied at anytime striking her with a blackjack, calling her any vile names, or punching her. He admitted to having such a weapon in his pocket, but denied striking anyone with it (p. 96).

The total number of persons actually arrested for disorderly conduct was 24 out of the original 35. Oddly, Tighe said he did not accompany the prisoners to the Magistrate's Court because he said: (1) he had a previous appointment with two clergymen at his home that evening; (2) that the case was "very light"; and (3) that he was only the "assisting officer," not the arresting officer (p. 98).

During cross-examination by Mr. Sullivan, Tighe stated that he never arrested anyone at the saloon for gambling, just the 24 for disorderly conduct. He admitted to seeing one of the arrested men, a known bookmaker, tear up a betting slip, but didn't believe that his testimony would be needed at the Magistrate's Court (p. 101). He justified the disorderly conduct charges on the grounds that "we hand nothing on any one particular individual. We arrested them in general for disorderly conduct" (p. 103). Such a crowd "necessarily creates quite a noise and nuisance, so to say, to the community in that particular vicinity" (p. 103). After being pressed on the point, Tighe admitted that he only had "information, not complaints" (p. 103) about noise from the saloon! At a later point during his examination by the prosecutor, Tighe was again asked about why he didn't appear in court for the trial of the men he assisted in arresting. This time he gave a more elaborate legal explanation:

> where we cannot prove that a man took at least three slips, the Magistrate will not hold a defendant in case of that kind, and we are so used to having defendants discharged on a charge of violation of 986 of the Penal Law, which is bookmaking, that unless we get evidence of conversation with at least three men, and taking three slips, we don't need any corroboration in Special Sessions or in the Magistrate's Court. (p. 116)

Upon further questioning by the prosecuting attorney, Tighe stated that he believed he saw Mrs. Lennon on a couple of previous occasions in the back room of the saloon, but he cannot say so with any degree of certainty. He insisted that he never arrested Mrs. Lennon, but that he let her go just after they got inside the bar area and she said to him: "Officer, please don't humiliate me by putting me back there with those men. I promise you there will be no further interference from me" (p. 109). Officer Tighe admitted to arresting a Mrs. Gaiety, but that he never took her into the saloon (p. 110). Tighe's counsel objected to any questions regarding Mrs. Gaiety on the grounds that she was a complaining witness against him in another case for which the grand jury had also indicted him. The court concurred, but all of the statements were made in open court before the jury (p. 110).

Tighe was also questioned about why he didn't arrest the person who held the door open for prisoners to escape. He said it was a misunderstanding on the part of Officer Kaufman. Officer Kaufman thought that Mr. Green was just an innocent porter who worked at the saloon. Green used crutches and had only one leg. Tighe couldn't remember how he came to know Harry Wright, a defense witness. He couldn't remember if he met him a couple days after the incident at his home or if he had only received a letter from him (p. 114).

At a point when it seemed the cross-examination had ended, Tighe suddenly interjected that "Had I struck anyone, I dare say it would not have been women, but I would have struck somebody that deserved it" (pp. 114-115). It provided another opportunity for the prosecutor to ask several key probing questions concerning why Mrs. Lennon testified in the manner she did. The only explanation that Tighe could offer for Mrs. Lennon to have made her complaint was that she "Knew the man I was locking up" and "had a motive through friendship to get him away from me" (p. 115).

The People's Rebuttal

Mr. Furstenberg objected when several rebuttal witnesses were called to testify. He objected on the grounds that they were called unfairly. In each case, his objection was overruled. The following five persons were called by the People in rebuttal of the defense's evidence: Elias M. Meltzer, 365 West 43rd Street, a recently retired newspaper retailer; John Kraemer, 448 West 43rd Street, a waiter at Coen's saloon; Frank Surdi, Cliffside, New Jersey, a barber who worked next door to the saloon; Alfonso del Grosso, 153 E. 113th Street, the saloon's cook; and Catherine Gaiety, 345 West 43rd Street, a married woman with three children. A sixth witness, the doctor who treated Mrs. Lennon two days after the incident would have been called to testify, but the defense and prosecutor agreed to a stipulation concerning his testimony.

Mr. Meltzer had been selling newspapers from a stand just in front of the saloon for eighteen months. On the day of the incident he saw Officer Tighe carrying a "little club." He pays no rent for the stand, but keeps the area in front of the saloon swept during all seasons. He is well-acquainted with the saloon owner's family. He sells the *Morning Telegraph,* a newspaper devoted to horse racing. He denied selling tips on the races called " Early Birds" and "Lucky Bill's Winners." Meltzer also denied selling newspapers inside the saloon, but indicated he was aware of the ticker.

The second rebuttal witness was John Kraemer. He was inside the saloon, but not working at the time of the incident. He said he ordered a glass of beer and when he encountered Officer Tighe, Tighe said to him "Come out of here, you don't want no beer" (p. 123). Upon objection by the defense, the court struck this testimony out. He stated that he was shoved to the back room and said he saw Tighe with a blackjack and that he saw him hit several men. He indicated that one man was 65 years old (p. 123). Kraemer said that he was the only person at the bar at the time and that no one was around the ticker.

The third rebuttal witness for the prosecution was Frank Surdi. He said he was in the barber shop next door to the saloon when Officer Tighe arrested him and brought him to the back room of the saloon. He claimed that Tighe had a blackjack in his hand at the time of his arrest. The saloon's owner had been his customer on several occasions prior to the incident. Surdi said he volunteered to be a witness and admitted that he would spend a thousand dollars to get even with Tighe (p. 131). However, this admission followed a series of questions that seemed to be designed to provoke the witnesses' anger during cross-examination by Mr. Furstenberg. His initial statement was not precisely to that effect. In response to a question from the court about who asked him to come to testify, Surdi stated: "I want to get a chance at that fellow because he took me in the barber shop for no reason, and suppose I got a thousand dollars I want to charge against him because he had no right to take me from the barber shop without reason" (p. 130). Also, during the course of his direct testimony the witness seemed to be having difficulty understanding questions, he stated: "If you want me to answer you good, you take an interpreter" (p. 128).

The fourth rebuttal witness was Alfonso del Grosso, the former saloon's cook. (The spelling of his name is as it appeared in the transcript. It was spelled "Delgrosso" in the press reports of the incident.) He had been working at the saloon for seven months at the time of the incident. He was also arrested and placed in the back room. He stated that Tighe had a blackjack in his hand. He recognized the weapon because he had worked as a watchman for a trucking company for four years and saw detectives carrying them. At the time of the incident he was in charge of the saloon, but he denies any knowledge of what the men standing around the ticker were doing. Mr. del Grosso emphasized that his job was to serve people lunch, usually stew or corned beef and a soft drink from 9 AM to 9 PM (p. 135-136). On many occasions he brought such meals including "a glass of beer or cup of coffee" (p. 136) into the back room. Although he sees the owner of the saloon every day, he indicated he only spoke to him three times about the case. The cook further stated that he only came to court because the owner told him to come, but not what to say (p. 137).

The fifth rebuttal witness was Mrs. Gaiety who indicated that she had three "living children" and has been married for 15 years. The Gaiety family has lived directly across from the saloon for two years, but according to Mrs. Gaiety she has never been in the saloon nor had her husband. She said she came to the vicinity of the saloon after seeing the "moving pictures" with her husband. At the time of the incident, she had her baby with her. She testified that she saw Officer Tighe with a blackjack in his hand and said that she was taken to the back room where she found her husband, several men, and Mrs. Lennon.

The prosecutor next asked the court to consider a postponement of the case till the afternoon so that a Dr. Louis Staack who treated Mrs. Lennon could be called. Instead of the postponement and at the suggestion of the court, the parties agreed that a letter from the doctor be read to the jury. Dr. Staack treated Mrs. Lennon two days after the incident. The contents included (p. 142):

> This is to certify that Mrs. Lennon is suffering from contusions of the right arm and back.
> Respectfully,
> L. J. Staack, M. D.

The prosecutor rested after the letter was read to the jury. Whereupon, the defense recalled Police Officer Tighe to testify. For the first time in the case,

he now stated that he did have in his hand an object. He said he was holding a "memorandum book" which had been discarded by one of the men
who had been arrested (p. 143). Assistant DA Sullivan asked the very last
question of the trial. After eliciting the response from Tighe that he had once
placed John William Black under arrest, Sullivan asked: "Where did you lock
him up?" Defense attorney Furstenberg objected to the question and Judge
Crain sustained the objection (p. 144). This was the only occasion when
Black's name was brought up at the trial.

Furstenberg again moved to dismiss the case and his motion was denied.
Summations then followed. First by the defense and then by the prosecutor.
The court reporter did not record these summations.

The Court's Charge

Prior to the jury's deliberation in this case, Judge Thomas C. T. Crain
delivered his charge to the jury, which was transcribed. Judge Crain
explained that the jury only had to decide if Officer Tighe had committed
assault in the second degree. Some parts of the definition he gave have not
survived the microfilming process (see p. 146), but he did state that "A person, who under circumstances not amounting to the crime of assault in the
first degree and more particularly in that connection where there is an
absence of an intent to kill, willfully and wrongfully wounds or inflicts grievous bodily harm upon another either with or without a weapon, or who willfully and wrongfully assaults another by the use of a weapon or other instrument or thing likely to produce grievous bodily harm is guilty of the crime
of assault in the second degree" (p. 145). Judge Crain also defined reasonable doubt as "a doubt that is founded in and sustained by reason. It is not
a whim; it is not a caprice; it is not the action of unreasonable sympathy; it
is not a mere subterfuge to which resort can be had in order to avoid doing
a disagreeable duty. It is a doubt back of which there is a because so that a
juror says he doubts the guilt of the defendant for such and such a reason"
(p. 146). In a final section of the charge he called upon the jury to try to
answer some of the important factual questions that arose due to conflicting
testimonies. In particular, he recited the stipulation of Dr. Staack and asked
the jury to consider the following questions:

> Was the complaining witness injured by this defendant? If so, under what cir-
> cumstances did she receive those injuries? Was it while the defendant was
> doing what he had a right to do or when the defendant was doing that which
> he had no right to do? If she received those injuries when the defendant was
> doing that which he had no right to do how extensive were those injuries? Do
> they answer the description of wounds, do they answer the description of griev-
> ous bodily harm? If they do not were they inflicted by the use of a weapon

likely to produce grievous bodily harm when the defendant had no right to use upon the person of the complaining witness such an instrument? These, in brief, are matters for your consideration." (pp. 148-149)

The jury then retired to consider the verdict. It was 12:53 PM. They returned on the same afternoon at 2:27 with a verdict of guilty of assault in the second degree. The case was adjourned one week for sentencing and Tighe was continued on bail, which was described in court as "considerable" (p. 150). The defense indicated that it expected to call character witnesses at the time of sentencing. Tighe's next appearance was a week later on October 14, 1921. Only the first two pages of the transcript have survived. From these we find that there were apparently three persons who testified: Thomas Early, Hugh J. Lavery, and Mrs. Emma Lennon. Both sides sought to have the sentencing postponed for a week, but their motions were denied.

The nature of Tighe's sentence and other relevant facts can be learned from press reports of that period. They will be considered below. However, the section that immediately follows samples the types of information that were contained in newspaper reports at the time of Tighe's jury trial and prior to the jury's deliberation. They contain details about the Tighe case that could have been very prejudicial to the accused.

Pretrial and Preverdict Publicity

On September 29, 1921, the *Times* reported that Tighe's motion to the Court of Special Sessions for an immediate trial on the indictments charging him with both first and second degree assault was denied. Counsel for the defense told the court that suspension from duty made it necessary for Tighe to report daily to a station house without pay until the case was decided. Tighe's attorney argued that in the meantime, his client was unable to obtain other employment for the support of his family. "The court said that the hardship on Tighe was not so severe as that affecting many prisoners held in the Tombs without bail until tried" (See "Tighe Trial in November," *New York Times*, September 29, 1921, p. 9).

A brief story on October 7, 1921 begins with the words "Patrolman Charles Tighe." Thus, a careful reader of previous accounts of the incident could have surmised that along with his suspension he was reduced in rank. This article very briefly refers to Mrs. Lennon's testimony on the first day of Tighe's trial as well as to the testimony of Albert (Burt) Lenn who was the first witness called by the defense ("Tighe Faces Court Trial," *New York Times*, October 7, 1921, p. 6.) However, the subtitle of the article is most damaging: "Witnesses Uphold Woman's Testimony as to Clubbing." Moreover, there is no indication in the trial transcript that the jury was admonished not to read the newspapers concerning this case. The jury rendered a guilty verdict in just one hour the day after this article was published.

The Sentencing

The day after sentencing was imposed, October 15, 1921, the *Times* reported that Detective Sergeant Charles Tighe, age 32, was sentenced to not less
than two years and not more than four years at hard labor in State Prison for
abusing and beating Mrs. Emma Lennon on July 28, 1921. The report stated that Judge Crain used the phrase "ran amuck" to describe how Tighe beat
a number of men, women and children at Coen's saloon. Tighe had been
free on bail of $2,000 at the time of sentencing. The following remarks of
Judge Crain appeared in quotation marks in this report (a copy of all of Judge
Crain's comments as well as a copy of this article is presented in *Appendix A*;
they can help to fill-in part of the missing pages from the trial transcript of
this case contained in the New York State and John Jay College Libraries collections):

> Your record in the police force is a bad one, and it is rather surprising to me
> that you have remained on the force.... You were mentally unbalanced from
> drink, and, to use a colloquial expression, "ran amuck".... Your punishment is
> in part a warning to members of the Police Department that if they overstep
> the law and act brutally toward citizens they will be punished.... ("Two to Four
> Years for Tighe, Clubber," *New York Times*, October 15, 1921, p. 3)

On October 17, 1921, an editorial in the *Times* remarked that "Tighe
thought that he could continue forever to do anything suggested by depraved
fancy. He...has found himself mistaken....The conviction of Tighe...is a conviction of the Police Department.... Whoever protected or tolerated this man
shared his guilt, and, if full justice could be done, would share his punishment" ("Topics of the Times: Justice Slow but Sure," *New York Times*, October
17, 1921, p. 14).

Post-Conviction Legal Actions

On November 2, 1921, the *Times* reported that Tighe's lawyer was seeking
his release from the Tombs pending an appeal of his conviction on the
grounds that "the newspaper references to Tighe's activities created an
atmosphere unfavorable to him, and that General Sessions Judge Crain did
not give him a fair trail" ("Tighe Plea for Freedom on Bail," *New York Times*,
November 2, 1921, p. 9).

Tighe's involvement with the mental health system began when he was
suddenly removed from the Tombs late in the afternoon on November 4,
1921 and taken to Bellevue Hospital for observation upon the recommendation of Dr. Perry Lichtenstein, the prison physician, and a court order signed
by Judge John F. McIntyre. The court order had been obtained by Tighe's
counsel, Emil Fuchs. He was not placed in the psychopathic ward, but rather

in the regular prison ward. Dr. Lichtenstein was quoted as follows: "Tighe has been acting very strangely for the last few days and he displayed certain well-defined symptoms of insanity. There was the possibility that he might at any time become violent....It is not incurable, however, and I think that it ought to clear up in a few days" ("Tighe, Police Clubber Under Sentence, Transferred to Bellevue for Observation," *New York Times,* November 5, 1921, p. 1).

When Dr. Lichtenstein was informed that the keepers at the Tombs (today, known by their title as correction officers) had failed to observe anything wrong with the former policeman's health, he laughed and replied "that it would not have been apparent to the lay eye" (*NYT,* November 5, 1921, p. 1).

Was Tighe's lawyer simply trying to stall his client's transfer to Sing Sing Prison by these legal maneuvers or were they based on genuine issues of fact? By virtue of the court order, the execution of Tighe's sentence was stayed pending the outcome of a mental health examination. However, a two-sentence report in the next day's issue of the *Times* appeared quite ominous: "Former city Detective Charles F. Tighe was visited yesterday by his wife and five-year-old daughter in the prison ward of Bellevue, where he is confined. It was said that Tighe seemed disinterested and gave little sign of recognition ("Tighe in Bellevue Prison Ward," *New York Times,* November 6, 1921, p. 8).

It is unlikely that Tighe's family members could have exaggerated these dire comments. Certainly, Tighe could simply have been depressed when his family visited him, anyone in these circumstances would have been. On the other hand, Tighe could have been faking his symptoms in order to obtain his family's sympathy. Given all we know about Tighe's "pull" in the system, the statements of the Tombs' keepers, the initiation of legal steps to gain his release pending the hearing of an appeal, the rather cavalier remarks of Dr. Lichtenstein and his prediction of a quick recovery from mental illness, and the fact that the doctor remained in public service throughout his career adds some fuel to the speculation that a ploy was used to delay his transfer to Sing Sing in order to allow additional time for further legal maneuvering.

Dr. Perry Lichtenstein, was the Tombs psychiatrist for more than eighteen years. While he was employed at the Tombs, he was able to complete a law degree from Fordham University's School of Law in 1920. This was rather remarkable, because he later commented that the Tombs averaged more than 25,000 annual admissions during his career. In his next appointment, in 1931, he served as the "medical assistant" to the New York County District Attorney for nearly a quarter of a century. When his appointment to the DA's staff was announced, he remarked that in his new post he would be able to continue his studies in criminology. He was a graduate of the Cornell Medical College (1910), spent two years as an intern at St. Mark's Hospital, and was appointed a physician at the Tombs in 1913. Before his death in June of 1954, he wrote more than 300 articles on criminal psychology and two books entitled: *A Doctor Studies Crime* (1934) and *A Handbook of Psychiatry* (1943), the latter in collaboration with Dr. Saul Mouchly Small. After his sudden death in a corridor of the Queens General Court House, Manhattan District Attorney Frank S. Hogan, who had been associated with Dr. Lichtenstein for sixteen years, said that his death was "a deep personal loss to me, to this office and to the people of this city, whom he served so faithfully for so many years" ("P.M. Lichtenstein, Psychiatrist, Dies," *NYT,* June 15, 1954).

The first indication that Tighe would soon be returning to the Tombs and that his sentence would be carried out was on November 11, 1921 (Armistice Day), when the *Times* reported that Tighe had been found to be in fairly good health, mentally and physically. The report also indicated that his final transfer to Sing Sing would depend upon the outcome of an appeal to the State Supreme Court for a certificate of reasonable doubt and a request for a new trial ("Tighe is Found Sane by Bellevue Staff," *New York Times,* November 11, 1921, p. 9).

Also, on Armistice Day November 11, 1921, the people of the nation were enthralled by a demonstration of the new invention called "radio." The voice of President Harding was heard over loudspeakers by a gathering of thousands of people at Arlington National Cemetery. It was also transmitted to New York and San Francisco. Editorial comment about the event included the remark "Will wonders never cease!" (Sullivan, 1939).

Three days later, Tighe was returned to the Tombs. Excerpts of a report prepared by a Dr. Gregory of Bellevue Hospital regarding his condition appeared in the *Times:*

> After careful examination and observation of this man we find that he is neither insane nor a mental defective. On his admission to this hospital he was somewhat nervous, fearful, suspicious and seemed to suffer from hallucinations of sight and hearing, fancying that he was seeing imaginary pictures and figures and hearing imaginary voices. Physically he exhibited evidences of toxemia....The symptoms...are characteristic of a case of toxic delirium, which may be caused by infection, various auto-intoxication and frequently by alcoholic excesses, and occasionally by excessive smoking. Tighe admits to smoking cigarettes to excess, but absolutely denies the use of alcoholic beverages during the past three years. ("Tighe Back in the Tombs," *New York Times,* November 15, 1921, p. 21)

On December 1, 1921, former Detective Sergeant Tighe who had been assigned to the staff of the Chief Police Inspector at time of his raid on Coen's saloon, was received at Sing Sing Prison. However, even this event was not without controversy. The *Times* reported that information had reached prison officials that two or three inmates had planned revenge against Tighe since he had brutalized them when he placed them under arrest. Could this also have been a ploy to further delay the carrying out of Tighe's sentence? When Warden Lewis E. Lawes of Sing Sing was asked about any precautionary measures for Tighe's protection, he indicated that it may be necessary to transfer Tighe to another prison for his own safety. In the meantime, special guards were assigned to protect him from any possible attack by his fellow prisoners. His first meal consisted of stewed prunes, bread and tea. Then he was assigned to a cell. The special press report continued that "although Tighe showed that he had still the fear and shame he felt when imprisoned in the Tombs he had apparently steeled his nerves for the final ordeal here. He appeared glad when it was over and the cell door closed, leaving him as just 'one of the crowd' within the prison walls" ("Guard Tighe in Fear of Convicts' Attack," *New York Times*, December 2, 1921, p. 18).

Tighe, the police officer who "ran amuck," who had imprisoned more than two dozen men and women in the steaming rear room of a former saloon, was now beginning his own imprisonment under the watchful eyes of the warden of Sing Sing prison, Lewis E. Lawes. Lawes said of himself that he believed in neither coddling nor brutality. His philosophy was in accord with the humanitarian spirit of the progressive era, but he knew when and how to be strict. In 1947, he died at the age of 63. Tighe's fate remains a mystery.[3] Lawes was one of the nation's leading authorities on penology. An editorial in the *New York Times* (April 24, 1947, p. 24) stated that "more than any other man who served the state he brought its prisons out of medieval darkness into institutions that give erring men a chance to redeem themselves....Practical penologist and real reformer, Lewis Lawes left a healing touch on one of the sorest spots of our society." Lawes was Sing Sing's warden for 21 years. He retired as warden in 1941, but from 1943 to 1945 he became chief consultant for the prison industries section of the federal government's War Production Board. Through hard work and basic common sense, he rose from the rank of prison guard to the post of warden of one of America's most difficult prisons. His remarkable career is worthy of additional comment.

Lawes was born on September 13, 1883 in Elmira, New York. His father, was an employee at the Elmira State Reformatory. When Lawes was 17, he ran away from home and joined the Army. After three years of military service he became a prison guard at Clinton Prison in Dannemora, New York. His career in corrections took him briefly to Auburn and then to his hometown of Elmira. At Elmira, he became the chief record clerk and gained recognition for his capabilities. After eight years at Elmira, he obtained his first real opportunity to put his penological ideas into actual practice. He was selected by New York City officials to superintend its reformatory located on Hart's Island. He was able to relocate it to larger facilities in New Hampton, located in Orange County, New York. The youthful inmates under his supervision built their own prison! Needless to say, this accomplishment drew widespread attention and late in 1919 he was appointed warden of Sing Sing ("Ex-Warden Lawes of Sing Sing Dies, April 24, 1947, p. 25).

When New York's Governor Alfred E. Smith appointed Lawes to head the administration of Sing Sing prison, the institution was known as the "The Wardens' Graveyard." Within the previous decade Sing Sing had no less than 13 different wardens and a popular joke of that period was that the quickest way to get out of Sing Sing was to become its warden. The first thing he did was to abolish all privileged inmate classes. He replaced the previous policy of permitting inmates to wear fancy silk shirts and neckties with a requirement that all inmates were to wear a prison-made uniform. In addition, prisoners were graded according to their behavior and newly arrived inmates were assigned to hard labor for ten days before receiving a different job. In order to raise funds for prison needs, he permitted inmate theatrical performances open to the public. He also encouraged the establishment of recreational teams and games with outside groups. New safety devices were installed in prison shops and inmates were granted escorted leaves to attend funerals and to visit seriously ill relatives. Although he was vigorously opposed to capital punishment, he was required to supervise 302 executions. He considered the penalty a futile gesture given the large number of people who are murdered each year and the very small percentage that are actually ever executed for such crimes. In the early 1920s, he was the president of the Wardens Association of America and the American Prison Association. Lawes wrote numerous articles and books about penal reform. He also attended several international conferences held in England, Prague and Berlin. His books included: *Life and Death in Sing Sing* (1928); *Man's Judgment of Death* (1926); *Twenty Thousand Years in Sing Sing* (1932); *Cell 202, Sing Sing* (1935); *Invisible Stripes* (1938); and *Meet the Murderer!* (1940). His last major undertaking was a survey of the Massachusetts State Prison in 1946 (*NYT*, April 24, 1947, pp. 24-25).

In the summer of 1924, the New York State Commissioner of Prisons, Leon C. Weinstock, indicated that Sing Sing had 1,400 inmates, the greatest number that had ever been housed there. He attributed the high inmate population to an increasing crime rate associated with prohibition enforcement efforts. In particular, Commissioner Weinstock noted that "the prisons are now filled with more offenders whose crimes can be directly traced to narcotics than ever before" and that prohibition had "driven people seeking stimulant to various drugs and narcotics" ("Prohibition and Crime," *NYT*, July 9, 1924, p. 17).

The following chapter reviews the events of Tighe's trial and the era in which they took place. Gender and class issues are discussed as well as issues regarding journalism, the careers of the prominent professional men concerned with the Tighe case, and the circumstances of cases involving overzealous prohibition enforcement. The facts regarding the Tighe case reveal intriguing details about the maintenance of social equilibrium during the early 1920s. Furthermore, an analysis of the incident at Coen's former saloon can provide insights about the nature of individual and societal responses to deviancy during that era.

ENDNOTES

1. All of the page reference numbers in this section indicate where the summarized or quoted testimony appeared in the original trial transcript. The transcript is located on microfilm roll number 366 for the Court of Special Sessions, New York City, housed in the collections of the John Jay College Library and the New York State Library in Albany, New York. Unfortunately, the transcript did not contain any information regarding the selection and composition of the jury. Nearly all of the witnesses called at the trial consistently referred to Coen's establishment as "the saloon." Of course, all saloons were outlawed with the passage of the *Volstead Act.*

2. Tighe is referred to as a "Detective Sergeant" and Kaufman is referred to as an "Acting Detective Sergeant" in most of the newspaper reports of the period. Yet, in the only available trial transcription that was extensively used for this study, neither police officer was identified as being of any rank other than "Patrolman" assigned to plainclothes duty. Thus, while at one point Tighe was questioned about his rank at the trial, he probably did not discuss his past rank because it would have been prejudicial for the jury to hear about such internal disciplinary proceedings. Of course, any juror who had read the newspapers would have been fully acquainted with these matters. The trial transcription omits what is considered off-the-record discussions between the attorneys and the court. It is more than likely that an agreement was reached at one of these "side bar" conferences to simply refer to the defendant and his partner, as patrolmen performing in plainclothes.

   In addition, the owner of the saloon, Patrick Coen, has his last name spelled as "COHEN" throughout most of the transcript. However, all of the newspaper reports indicated that his name was Coen. I have used the "Coen" spelling since that appears to be correct.

3. On June 16, 1998, the author initiated a request to access whatever records the New York City Police Department had with respect to Charles Tighe and Milton Kaufman under the New York State Freedom of Information Law (FOIL). In a letter dated July 15, 1998 from Lt. Glen Suarez, the author learned that this request was assigned to Paralegal Charles Ellis. A second letter was received

dated August 25, 1998 from Sgt. Richard Evangelista, Record Access Officer. This letter indicated that no personnel records were located for Charles Tighe or Milton Kaufman. However, a redacted photocopy of Milton Kaufman's NYPD Pension Card was enclosed. According to this document, Officer Kaufman was born in 1893 and was appointed to the force on July 7, 1920. His wife's name was Adele and he had one child. He retired in 1946 at the age of 53 after a little over 26 years of service and received an annual pension of $1,875. He died on February 7, 1966. Thus far, the author's efforts to find information about Tighe's post-conviction history have been unsuccessful. No records regarding Tighe at Sing Sing are available according to three public information sources: "Personal Communication," with Bill Evans, NY State Archives, May 27, 1998; "Personal Communication," with Warren Ernest, Clerk, Information Office, Department of Correctional Services, May 28, 1998) and a letter from Mark E. Shepard, Division of Support Operations, Department of Correctional Services, Albany, NY, October 22, 1998 received in response to a FOIL inquiry.

Chapter 8

FRAGILE LIBERTIES

"Agents, at times, get into the force who ought not to be
there, but I give you my word of honor as an official, as
soon as evidence is forthcoming that they are not what
they should be, proper measures are taken to put them
off the force."[1]

ROY A. HAYNES
FEDERAL PROHIBITION COMMISSIONER (1923)

What objective did Detective Sergeant Tighe hope to accomplish by
suddenly announcing a "gambling raid" at Coen's lunchroom on July
28, 1921? Was Tighe's special squad participating in an overall strategy that
combined local and national law enforcement personnel for prohibition's
enforcement? It hardly seems likely. A review of relevant research in the
field of the history of policing and police professionalism can provide useful
insights regarding these questions.

According to Walker (1977) and Nelli (1976), the problem of enforcing prohibition fell largely on federal officials. In New York City, the police rarely
conducted raids on their own initiative. When raids were conducted it was
common practice to turn over any seized liquor to federal agents. Moreover,
the raided establishments typically reopened for business as soon as the
police left (Walker, 1933, pp. 74 & 165). "For the municipal police, national
prohibition represented a strong continuity with earlier traditions of nonen-
forcement and corruption....Prohibition came and went leaving little effect
on the urban police" (Walker, 1977, p. 109).

Fogelson (1977) noted that the police of that era lacked strict discipline,
strong leadership, and quality personnel. He further elaborated that "most
officers followed the paths of least resistance laid out by ward bosses and
precinct captains. Now and then, when pressure from reformers built up,
they raided a joint or arrested a crook; but most of the time they kept out of
sight and away from trouble" (Fogelson,1977, p. 51).

The police were also preoccupied with performing many other tasks that
they had been assigned. Such duties included: supervising elections, cen-
soring movies, operating lodging homes and emergency ambulances. They

also inspected boilers, tenements, markets and factories (Fogelson, 1977, p. 52). Of course, they now had the extra task of disposing of any confiscated liquor and its public destruction often brought out the crowds. On at least one occasion in January 1923, in Plattsburgh (a city near the Canadian border in upstate New York), police had to be especially vigilant to prevent bystanders from grabbing broken bottles before all the contents had drained out. Sometimes various quantities of seized liquor were diverted before reaching the town dump (Everest, 1978, p. 131).

During the Prohibition era, two of the leading authorities on policing were Raymond Fosdick and August Vollmer. They were of the opinion that most new police officers were unqualified for their positions and that the officers remained so throughout their careers. They pointed out that most hadn't finished high school, scored below average on intelligence tests, received little or no training, and earned inadequate salaries. Their views received considerable support during the 1920s (Fogelson, 1977, p. 51). In addition, many police applicants could even slip through the minimum standards established by civil service commissions. "Under pressure from the ward leaders the civil service commissioners sometimes gave out advance copies of the tests and the precinct captains often ran cursory character checks. The civil service commissioners overlooked serious transgressions if they meant disqualifying a candidate with strong endorsements from influential politicians" (Walker, 1977, p. 103).

The evidence in Tighe's record and the testimony of witnesses indicated that he was a rather ordinary type of police officer with a serious drinking problem who had special connections. His drinking got him into difficulty at various points within his career, probably even before he became a policeman. His connections got him out of trouble on nearly every occasion. It appears doubtful that much planning went into his raid on Coen's establishment. There was specific testimony that both he and his partner, Detective Kaufman were not even aware that the former saloon's back room had a nonsecure door. There was also an indication that Coen's lunchroom had a telephone located within its front room that could have been used to call for extra assistance. There were also reports about how Tighe had gone to visit Edward Devlin, his former employer earlier in the day. Devlin had been questioned about a police association slush fund by investigators for the Meyer Committee. At that time, Tighe had sought to threaten or possibly even assault him, but his old boss was able to get his weapon out first! Tighe must have been very angry about having gotten bested again by his former boss.

Tighe's partner on this day and in recent months was a rookie, named Milton Kaufman. Apparently, he was selected to be Tighe's partner on one of the special squads of Chief Inspector Lahey because of departmental policy, which favored the use of new officers for such work. Later, other public officials would call this administrative policy into question. Thus, his pairing with Tighe was probably just an initial random event. On the other hand, could someone have thought that Kaufman (assuming he obtained his position in a meritorious manner) might serve as a good influence on Tighe? This idea seems unlikely since it would be assuming that some essential planning had taken place and many of the events of this period appear to demonstrate that planning was an unusual occurrence. On the other hand, it seems plausible to assume that a rookie was probably assigned to Tighe so that he could learn from him! Kaufman testified that he was Tighe's "friend." There is some indication from the press reports that newer officers were used on these special squads.

Therefore, it could be argued that Tighe's squad was only at Coen's lunchroom to make some arrests to show some activity for their salary. The qualities of those arrests were not as important as the fact that they needed to be made. Moreover, based upon Tighe's mood, his inclination was to get the work over with as quickly as possible and that if he encountered any sign of resistance, he was prepared to use physical means to accomplish his purpose. The same tactics were apparently used on many previous occasions. The heat and his own drinking added extra fuel to his already inflamed state of mind. Moreover, he apparently met with resistance, almost at every turn, even from his partner. Such factors clearly put him way over the edge of reason. Only Officer Traver, who came with the precinct's reserves, along with other officers, was finally able to subdue him.

Yet, even in the aftermath of all that had transpired on Ninth Avenue and inside Coen's restaurant, higher police and possibly local political leaders sought to protect Tighe. Certainly, the rank and file police members and Tighe's fellow squad members were reluctant to testify against him. A desk lieutenant permitted a cash alternative when setting bail and a local court issued a summons, rather than an arrest warrant. His fellow officers used their bodies to shield him from members of the press. Apparently, in order to delay the carrying out of his sentence, political influence even penetrated the walls of the city's prison, the Tombs.

It is now well understood that the police of this period, along with ward leaders and other politicians wielded significant influence. Even reform minded police chiefs and commissioners were often powerless to change the system and their careers were terminated after short periods of service. Especially, in New York City, the police were able to exert significant influence through their many rank and file organizations (e.g., benevolent associations for captains, squad commanders, and patrolmen). Such groups often lobbied against proposals to enhance central authority. When their interests combined with those of the local politicians who dominated city hall, the city council, police boards, local courts and other local agencies, the united groups were capable of forming a solid wall to resist the efforts of reform minded police officials. When Arthur Woods, a reform minded police commissioner in New York City, formed an internal affairs unit to assist in weeding out police corruption, the new Tammany Mayor, John F. Hylan had it abolished and discharged Woods in 1917 (Fogelson, 1977, pp. 76, 100-101). In his place he appointed Lt. Richard E. Enright who had become known as an antagonist to Woods. Woods tried to limit strong-arm measures and the widespread illegal practice of making arrests on only suspicion evidence. Enright possessed his own power base as head of the Police Lieutenants' Benevolent Association and through this post he also influenced power over the larger Patrolmen's Benevolent Association (PBA). Enright was a leader of the rank and file police who opposed such reforms. When Enright qualified for promotion to Captain by becoming first on the civil service list, Woods refused to appoint him (Richardson, 1974, p. 76).

Commissioner Enright demonstrated little sympathy for reform measures. He was police commissioner in New York City from 1918 to 1926 (Fogelson, 1977, p. 101). According to Walker (1933, p. 154), Enright was "a garrulous and extremely ambitious police lieutenant" at the time of his appointment to the post of police commissioner and because of hair color and other characteristics "some people called him Silver Dick."

Class and Gender Issues

The testimony during the second trial of Detective Tighe and contemporary reports about the entire incident revealed a variety of information about the class structure of the period and the roles individuals associated with those classes performed. The men who testified were all from the working classes with mainly "blue collar" occupations. There were possibly a couple of exceptions, but they managed "blue collar" workers. One witness, Burt Lenn managed cafeterias and another witness was the mail order manager for the Manhattan branch of Arnold Constable. None of the working class witnesses seemed to be college educated. In fact, it is doubtful that many of them were even high school graduates. Employment for those men who sought it appeared to be plentiful. There was no indication that these men had seen service in the war that had just ended. Perhaps, they had exemptions due to their ages and marital status. At least one witness, a barber, appeared to be a recent immigrant who had limited English speaking abilities. The business employees appeared to be as loyal to their bosses as much as the wives were to their husbands.

All the women who testified were married and most had children. None had regular employment. They appeared to be loyal housewives when confronted with hardship. The women stayed by their men, whether they were being arrested and dragged off to the back room at the time of the raid at Coen's lunchroom, or being taken away by the patrol wagon.

The customary practice for families to live above their husband's shops during these years was well illustrated by this case. The hazards this might entail for younger members of the family were also plainly revealed. In Tighe's first trial, he was accused of choking Helen Coen, the seven-year-old daughter of the saloon's owner. She testified that while she was on her way to her home over the restaurant, that Tighe squeezed her neck with his hands and pushed her into the street. Her testimony was supported by her mother who said she ran down into the street when she heard her daughter's cries and found red marks on Helen's neck. Charles Green also testified that he saw the detective grab the child by the neck. On the other hand, Tighe explained that while he was searching for the men who had escaped from the back room, the child ran into the room and he put her out, "as it was no place for her." He denied he squeezed her neck. Although, the case was dismissed because the child, under cross-examination, admitted her parents had told her what to say on the witness stand and that she was not prevented from breathing when she was squeezed by the neck, Patrick Coen's daughter clearly experienced some form of trauma as a result of her contact with Tighe. ("Tighe is Acquitted of Child's Charge, *New York Times*, September 13, 1921, p. 7).

Coen's employees appeared to be extremely loyal to their employer. Coen's counterman was literally thrown off one witness stand because of such loyalty. Green, "the bootblack," demonstrated his loyalty not only through his favorable testimony, but tried to help customers escape. He was consistently referred to as the "crippled Negro bootblack" and he was the only black person who was called as a witness. These facts suggest the fact that blacks held positions at a very low end of the employment scale and that persons with disabilities were not well regarded.

The press of that era appeared to have a free hand to publish just about anything except "filthy language." Such words were omitted from the otherwise graphic and dramatic reporting of the period through the use of dashes, although on some occasions the first letter of a word would appear.On the other hand, the courtroom testimony contained the raw language of the streets. Governmental officials seemed much more willing to release personal and sensitive information about individuals than in today's world. Today, oftentimes a lawsuit has to be commenced to release just the names of persons who have been accused of misconduct. It was startling to read descriptions about Tighe's mental health coming from institutional psychiatrists and to see his complete internal disciplinary records displayed in the *New York Times*. Moreover, the freely given comments of the "keepers" at the

Tombs stood out as something that would cause a correctional officer to be harshly disciplined for in today's world.

Two of the most highly educated individuals who participated in this case were Judge Crain and Dr. Lichtenstein. Their backgrounds enabled them to play important judgmental roles regarding Tighe's fate. Crain was a product of the Tammany system. His reputation was tarnished only after he became the District Attorney for New York County. This occurred when his office was investigated by the Seabury Commission appointed by Governor Franklin Roosevelt at the tail end of the prohibition era. The Seabury investigation was an extraordinary event of that day, but the practice of appointing various types of crime commissions has become more commonplace over the intervening years. Perhaps, this is even more so due to the media consciousness of today's elected officials. Walker (1933) compared Judge Crain to the other New York County prosecutors of his era, such as William Travers Jerome and Charles S. Whitman, and noted that Crain was "the gentle, septuagenarian Sachem of Tammany Hall—a poodle set to bring down hyenas" (p. 175).

Dr. Lichtenstein seemed to have obtained his first employment on the merits of his credentials. He came to the Tombs straight out of medical school and after the successful completion of his local medical internship. He stayed within the system becoming a key aid to future Manhattan DA's such as Frank S. Hogan. On the inside cover page of his book on psychiatry, published in 1943, his occupation is listed as "In charge of Psychiatry and Legal Medicine for the District Attorney, County of New York." However, it appears that he was able to move up to that office through an initial appointment made by Judge Crain. This took place soon after Crain's election to the DA's position. Further research may reveal closer links between these two men. Of additional note is that both of these men became authors. In 1940, the Scribner Press published Crain's small book simply entitled *Survey*. In it, he urged the need for a spiritual reawakening in the home and in the church. Crain also advocated for a constitutional amendment providing one six-year presidential term of office. Dr. Lichtenstein's two books are entitled: *A Doctor Studies Crime* and *A Handbook of Psychiatry*. These were published, respectively, in 1934 and 1943 (*NYT*, May 30, 1942; *NYT*, June 15, 1954).

Dr. Lichtenstein's second book summarized the differences between normal and abnormal states of mental health and he took note of the importance of cultural differences. For example, he wrote "the manner in which an individual conducts himself with regard to the accepted moral code and cultural pattern of his community is the index of his normalcy" (Lichtenstein & Small, 1943, p. 9). His comments included:

There is no definite demarcation between normality and abnormality... What is considered normal in one country may be thought peculiar in another. Two Frenchmen kissing each other at a railroad station in Paris would attract little attention, but this would be thought most unusual in our country....in general one adheres to the old saying "In Rome do as the Romans do" to be accepted as a well-balanced personality. (Lichtenstein & Small, 1943, p. 9)

Unfortunately, whatever notes Dr. Lichtenstein may have kept about the Tighe case have never been made public. However, given the importance that he attached to cultural patterns of behavior and his other published comments, it might be possible to speculate that he would agree with the view that the manner in which individuals conduct themselves with regard to the accepted moral code and cultural pattern of the community not only provides an index of their normalcy, but that such behavior is especially vivid during encounters with deviancy.

Significantly, the incident at Coen's former saloon can provide insights about the nature of the normal behavior of the times since it can be contrasted to an abnormal event. For example, many of the witnesses in the case were first drawn to the vicinity of Coen's saloon by the sudden appearance of a crowd. The crowd grew in size with each of Tighe's strikes with his blackjack as well as with the eventual appearance of police reinforcements. Moreover, when press reports about the incident were published, several bystanders became further involved by volunteering to testify.

At times, it even seemed that for the people in and around Coen's saloon on July 28, 1921, that the unfolding events were a form of theater in the streets and that they were the audience. The whole atmosphere took on the air of a kind of spectator sport. One witness at Tighe's second trial, Burt Lenn, the cafeteria manager, even referred to the entire scene as "a performance" (NYC Court of General Sessions, Tighe Trial Transcript, October 8, 1921, p. 40).

Not only does an examination of the events at Coen's former saloon afford a view of routine or commonplace behaviors in the early 1920s, but these and other cultural characteristics may help to explain the maintenance of order and control in those days. According to Cashman (1981), there are various devices for maintaining equilibrium between the conflicting interests of disparate people (e.g., the deviant and observer; the wets and the drys; the working middle class and the working poor; the civil servant and those engaged in free enterprise; the employed and unemployed; whites and blacks; men and women, etc.).

For example, Cashman (1981) points out that team sports were "most important as devices to maintain social equilibrium" (p. 181). In 1920, Babe Ruth became a Yankee and in the season of 1921 Ruth hit 59 home runs. Millions followed his baseball and personal activities. Many people bet on the outcome of the games. Clearly, "the ticker" was another means by which people were able to preoccupy themselves as spectators and vicarious participants through the bets they wagered. Moreover, in the present case we have seen how the occasional disaster or spectacle in the street could bring people running and mesh them into a common "spectator" whole.

Of course, social equilibrium was also maintained through other channels aside from professional sports in the twenties. The advent of paid holidays, radios, motion pictures, and automobiles helped not only to spread social equilibrium, but also "provided new outlets for the libidos of deprived drinkers" (Sinclair, 1964, p. 27).

Furthermore, "Freud saw that the moderate use of liquor was necessary for driven men, who could not find other interests or gratifications against the miseries of the world" (Sinclair, 1964, p. 27). Thus, some persons may have been in the area or on their way there seeking an illegal glass of liquor or seeking other illegal outlets for the release of tensions (e.g. gambling, prostitutes, etc.). Moreover, when the fancier speakeasies of that era became "night clubs," an entire new diversion for recreation was established.

Thus, the various events on that hot summer July afternoon (e.g., Tighe's behavior at the time of the raid, possible illegal activities in a former saloon, etc.), created a chain of mixed reactions. There were bystanders who hung around for the show or "performance." Some of them volunteered to give their accounts on behalf of the defense or prosecution. Some victims of police brutality had to decide whether they would report their abuse. No doubt, a few joined in the general mayhem by trying to either resist or help others at the scene. While others, because of their own embarrassment or fear of the consequences about revealing their presence inside or even near a former saloon, chose to remain silent and slip quietly away.

The police themselves were an interesting group of participants and spectators. They needed to choose a side or remain neutral. Although it was never brought out in the testimony of the second trial, some responding officers actually did take overt action to stop Tighe's rampage. Moreover, when the immediate incident had run its course, these officers had to decide how they were going to testify if called.

According to one account by a newspaper reporter, Tighe's activities were brought to an end in the following manner:

> Under Captain Thomas Donohue, commanding the precinct, the reserves... and the patrol wagon arrived in front of Coen's restaurant. The reserves, led by Captain Donohue, dashed into the eating place. At the curb at the wheel of the patrol wagon was Policeman Frank Traver of the Charles Street Station. The appearance of Traver and the patrol came just as Tighe was engaged in pulling another woman victim down the street toward his place of imprisonment. Traver jumped from the automobile and hurried over to Tighe and his

prisoner. Traver remonstrated with Tighe and was struck over the head with the blackjack. Then Traver, although dazed by the blow, aided by other policemen, took Tighe in charge. (*NYT*, July 21, 1921, p. 3)

The reserve platoon system required police officers to spend additional hours at station houses in order to be available for any emergency (Fogelson, 1977, p. 96).

Generally, the various judges, higher ranking police as well as defense, prosecutorial and correctional officials had to decide how they were going to respond to the case if and when interviewed by members of the press. Certainly, the key legal practitioners in the case–the defense lawyer and assistant district attorney, had to consider various strategies and possible scenarios for the purposes of preparation for trial. Moreover, in the background of the case was an unseen set of performers–friends and family members of witnesses giving advice, court staff and possibly local political leaders advising the judges prior to and during each of Tighe's court appearances, as well as a variety of confidential aides to the higher ranking members of the Police Department. Due to their own unique roles, each of these participants had the opportunity because of the events in the Tighe case to either reinforce their understanding of normal behavior and thus promote social cohesiveness or act, perhaps, in some less stable manner.

The facts of the Tighe case also reveals information about social disorder and upheaval (i.e., social disequilibrium). The Tighe case as well as the countless other trials and conflicts of the Prohibition era offer opportunities to study the forces of social disorder as well as order. All such human interactions involve persons who commit specific actions and those who respond to them. In the Tighe case, a city's working class appeared to be unprepared and largely unwilling participants from the very start of Prohibition. Prohibition meant new pressures for the general working classes (e.g., former saloonkeepers, police, etc.) in urban America. The constellation of events surrounding the Tighe case symbolized the types of instability that can arise when a social movement is out of touch with a given segment of the population.

Thus, the Tighe incident affected many persons living in the neighborhood of Coen's saloon. Some of these persons included: workers in the saloon and neighborhood; those socializing in the saloon; those just passing through the area; a reserve platoon in the police station; those reading about it in the newspapers; those who would be hired as legal representatives; private and institutional doctors who would examine the participants; a caseworker who would examine a young victim; keepers at the Tombs; priests at the nearby rectory; public officials and their associates; and the family members and friends of all.

The Prohibition Mind

Life would be a lot easier if what we deemed to be unpleasant or odious would just disappear. It's a view supported by the old witticism: "out of sight, out of mind." In many ways, it was just such a mindset that contributed to the belief by a large segment of the American population that by simply prohibiting the sale, manufacture and transportation of alcoholic beverages, that alcohol use and abuse would end. We now know the naivete of this belief. However, in the first quarter of the twentieth century, it appeared that prohibition, namely, the forbidding by law of particular actions, seemed to know no bounds.

It was during this period that Americans also: greatly restricted immigration; discouraged international organizations; banned the teaching of evolution in some states; limited the possibility of procreation of insane, retarded, and epileptic citizens in many states by authorizing the practice of sterilization; and in Oregon, briefly banned the attendance of elementary age school children at nonpublic schools. The Oregon law had been adopted through a ballot initiative at the general election held in 1922. In 1925, the United State Supreme Court held the law to be unconstitutional (Sullivan, 1935, p. 613).

In the halls of Congress, the filibuster, whereby Senators can talk indefinitely on any topic was used repeatedly by southern Senators for the purposes of blocking a vote on a federal antilynching statute. Presidential administrations from 1920s to the period of World War II requested and supported such a law, but even the efforts of presidents could not change the tactics used by a few southern senators (Murray, 1969, p. 402).

With respect to the *Volstead Act,* several exceptions existed. For example, in 1923, the United States Supreme Court upheld the policy of allowing American ships to carry and sell intoxicating liquors outside of the three-mile limit; and a United States District Court in New York held that under the prohibition law prescriptions of whiskey by physicians may not be limited. Moreover, a unanimous decision by the Supreme Court upheld the *Willis-Campbell Act* which had been adopted in November of 1921. The law provided that not beer but "only spirituous and vinous liquors may be prescribed for medicinal purposes" (Sullivan, 1939, p. 616).

At the start of the prohibition era, Congress explicitly adopted medicinal exceptions. In recent years, ballot initiatives to permit the use of marijuana for therapeutic purposes have been successful. For example, such an initiative was passed in Oregon in 1998. One seriously ill woman indicated that the use of marijuana reduced her pain in half and eliminated the spasmodic nightmares triggered by her years in Vietnam as a Red Cross volunteer. She said that as a result of the passage of the new law that she didn't "expect to have any problems with the local police, but I don't know about the feds" (Greimel, 1998, p. A6).

Tighe's conduct and that of many of his fellow officers may have been, in some small way, a part of the mindset of his generation. It was a type of mindset that is seen when children are confronted by many family injunctions. They may not always respond as desired. The 1920s turned out to be one of the most lawless in American history. It now appears that at least part of it was generated by the overzealous actions of police in their efforts to enforce prohibition or in other instances, to either ignore it or to personally gain from it. These events are well illustrated by the brief law enforcement career of a Marine Corps general who was dispatched by the federal government to deal with prohibition enforcement in Philadelphia toward the end of 1923.

The Capped Crusader

In October 1923, Pennsylvania's Governor, Gifford Pinchot personally discovered that saloons were operating in clear defiance of the law. His criticisms of the situation coincided with the election of a new mayor in Philadelphia. Mayor Kendrick appealed to the President for assistance. In order to contend with prohibition enforcement in Philadelphia, Brigadier General Smedley D. Butler, was given a leave from the Marine Corps of which he was the head to serve as the city's new director of public safety (Merz, 1931). He had won two Medals of Honor (Perrett, 1982, p. 172). He believed that any law could be enforced "if the men responsible want it done" (Merz, 1931, p. 141). Butler was very serious about getting the job done when he addressed the city's police force in the following manner: "We don't want any help from reformers...men, let's do the damned thing ourselves! Hell! We don't want any pussyfooting squads around. Put on your uniforms and go after 'em" (Sullivan, 1939, p. 610).

Within the first couple of weeks of his appointment, approximately 1,000 saloons were closed and two thousand arrests were made. He suspended eight police lieutenants for failing to rid their districts of saloons on forty-eight hours' notice and he enlisted the services of the city's 1,600 firemen to help enforce the law by searching for illegal liquor. He also put on notice the wealthier classes when he warned them against serving liquor at their society banquets and other gatherings (Merze, 1931, p. 142). On one occasion, armed with a service revolver, he arrested seven suspects. He frequently appeared in full uniform and attached to it a blue cape lined with red silk. In this dress he would go out on patrol riding "in an enormous Packard limousine, its siren blazing, and accompanied by his wife" (Perrett, 1982, p. 142).

At first, the public vigorously supported Butler, but in a short time, his tactics and successes had aroused opposition from many quarters. Butler complained that law enforcement in the city had been effectively "blocked by powerful influences, by legal machinery that should have been an aid, and by the invocation of technicalities" (Merze, 1931, p. 144). In particular, he was distressed that only 212 of the more than 6,000 people arrested during his second year in office had been convicted. By December 1924, President Coolidge revoked his leave from the Marines and he left Philadelphia. According to Perrett (1982), Butler was really ousted from the city because he not only went after members of the lower classes who were involved in bootlegging, but he also began to go after the rich and powerful. Significantly, machine politics found it difficult to function with a General Butler around. Indeed, the people most responsible for governing the city (e.g., the mayor and other elected officials) never really wanted full enforcement, but just enough to fend off their most vocal critics. Overzealous enforcement was dangerous. During the previous year, United States Senator Frank L. Greene of Vermont was seriously wounded on one of the downtown streets of Washington, D.C. when shots were fired by prohibition agents and bootleggers (Sullivan, 1939, pp. 610-611). Additional types of police responses to the demands made by Prohibition are considered below and in Chapters 9 and 10.

Ordered Liberty in a Changing World

However, given enough time, some things do change. Today, our fast paced world and the almost anonymous existence of many city dwellers, mean that an incident similar to the Tighe case is unlikely to be repeated. It is highly unlikely that in today's urban world of constant siren blasting by emergency vehicles, incessant ringing of auto theft alarms, honking of taxis, and the intermittent sound of personal communication devices (e.g., beepers, cellular phones, etc.), that many persons would pay much attention to the presence of police responding to a corner bar in Manhattan. They would not come running and therefore would not be at risk of being assaulted by a police officer. Of course, police brutality is still a fact of life, but today most people have through experience learned "to mind their own business." Moreover, if such an incident should occur on a public street at 3 PM in any large American city, there exists the possibility that it would be videotaped and be seen by millions of viewers within a few hours. This knowledge not only acts as a deterrent to police misconduct, but reassures the public that justice will eventually be done. Thus, although it has taken 80 years, the Tighe case can illustrate that police misconduct and society's response to it can change over time. Furthermore, certain laws may also be changed due to advances in the artifacts of a culture.

By the end of the twenties, Sinclair (1964) concluded that national prohibition was doomed due to such new technology as the automobile, talking movies, as well as radio. Such new instruments brought the city to the country and helped to erode the strength of the drys that was based in small towns. "For better or for worse, the American films of the twenties had spread everywhere the desire to imitate the life of the rich.... And the life of the rich included liquor, its use and abuse.... Moreover, the political use of the radio by Franklin D. Roosevelt gave a great popular support to the economic methods which he advocated, such as repeal" (Sinclair, 1964, p. 324).

In 1921, there were 9 million autos in the United States; by 1929 there were more than 23 million. Cars gave the working man the means to go where liquor was sold and to bring it back to the home. They were also used to take liquor to prospective buyers. "Criminals penetrated the trucking companies and the Teamsters' Union, in order to acquire control of fleets of trucks to transport their supplies of bootleg from still to sale" (Sinclair, 1964, p. 318).

Moreover, the "metamorphosis of the American press itself did not help the dry cause" (Sinclair, 1964, p. 312). Between 1925 and 1930, rural subscriptions to city newspaper doubled and "the city press grew wetter and wetter" (Sinclair, 1964, p. 312). These events both led and reflected the change of the American people in their attitude toward Prohibition. During the 1920s, the press meticulously covered police activities. However, since the printed word requires the services of a reporter, there is an intermediary who must always come between the event and the members of the reading public. On the other hand, while film and television may be edited, these methods of communication are more direct and their impact has been more widely felt.

Ordered Liberty in the Twenties

New York City's Police Commissioner Enright was particularly sensitive to the affects of adverse publicity and on at least one occasion he took the opportunity to warn the superior officers of the department about "leaks" to the press. On November 17, 1924, he mustered nearly 700 of these officers at police headquarters. The men were divided into two groups. The first consisted of 16 inspectors, 100 captains and 150 lieutenants and the second was composed of an audience of 400 sergeants. He met separately with each group. Although Enright delivered a lecture that began with information about preventing crime during the period preceding the Christmas holidays, it also featured advice regarding Rule 142 of the department's regulations. He stated that the rule only authorized commanding officers of precincts, squads and divisions to give information to the press. He asserted that there had been too many "leaks" of information and that this had brought about an interference with the work of the department. He pointed out that revealing information (which he referred to as "inside stuff") can defeat the ends of justice. He especially urged that police detectives should not pose for photographers since such pictures would allow criminals to become familiar with their appearance ("Enright Lectures Police," *NYT*, November 18, 1924, p. 2).

In some cases, the prohibition of liquor gave rise to additional new vices (e.g., gambling) as saloonkeepers sought to maintain their livelihoods. Women often accompanied men to the speakeasies of America and became more liberated as a consequence. Moreover, the era of prohibition institutionalized corruption in American political life which was on a scale previously unseen (Coffey, 1975). The liquor business operated notoriously "and with a knowing wink in the most smug communities, as well as in the more free and easy cities of the eastern seaboard. No person...believes that these organizations...could continue to do business year in and year out without active cooperation of duly constituted police authority" (Driscoll, 1925, p. 170).

Frustration with the way Police Commissioner Enright was dealing with vice and the enforcement of the *Volstead Act* in New York City had reached a boiling point when several Democratic (Tammany) aldermen offered resolutions to reprimand Enright and to abolish his Special Service Squad. The squad was established as the lead division within the department for the suppression of vice and consisted of 500 to 600 men. However, it was Enright's policy or perhaps Mayor Hylan's, that the squad be composed primarily of new members of the department. According to former policeman and Tammany Alderman Edward J. Sullivan, the morale of the department was the lowest in its history. He stated:

> These young men in this squad are open to the contamination of graft. We cannot fool ourselves. We know they are taking money and ruining their careers, and they are also casting a stigma on the honest, two-fisted cops of the department who are out pounding their beats, ready to lay down their lives for you and for me.... It is not fair...to turn...the newly created policemen over to the dirtiest work imaginable. ("Aldermen Charge Police with Graft," *NYT*, November 19, 1924, p. 1)

At the same meeting, Democratic Alderman James F. Kiernan of Coney Island, presented a resolution calling for the reprimanding of Commissioner Enright for specifically having offered a three day's vacation and official commendation to members of the force as an inducement for obtaining the prosecution and conviction of any person attempting to bribe a police officer. Alderman Kiernan declared that such a policy amounted to nothing better than "bribing policemen to do their duty in resisting a bribe" (*NYT*, November 19, 1924, p. 1).

Occasionally, even Republican aldermen joined in the revolt of renegade Democratic members. For example, Republican Alderman William F. Quinn, presented a resolution seeking a full investigation of the charges made and said that the fact that the charges emanated from Democratic aldermen removed the issue of politics from the matter. Nevertheless, as each resolution was presented, the Democratic majority tabled the motions fearful that to do otherwise could prove detrimental to the success of their future political ambitions and the reelection of Mayor Hylan. Shortly after the session, Mayor Hylan sent a letter of thanks to the most vocal opponent of the revolt–William T. Collins. Collins had at first presided at the meeting in the absence of the Aldermanic President (*NYT,* November 19, 1924, p. 1).

Indeed, police practices reached a distinct low point during the prohibition period because of widespread disrespect for the law. With hindsight, it is now believed that the findings of the National Commission on Law Observance and Enforcement (commonly known as the Wickersham Commission) provided strong backing for the forces seeking repeal when it concluded in 1931 that the laws relating to prohibition were basically unenforceable (Bopp & Schultz, 1972, p. 107). However, at the time of its publication, the report was perceived differently because of the inconsistencies in the statements by the various authors of the study.

Ironically, many of the civil liberties problems associated with prohibition enforcement could have been avoided if the leading practitioners of criminal justice had paid greater attention to an earlier report. Significantly, at the very beginning of this era there were distinct problems associated with law enforcement. Segments of the country were actually made aware of the health of federal law enforcement as early as 1920. In that year, a private committee composed of six prominent attorneys including Roscoe Pound and Felix Frankfurter was formed to study the U.S. Department of Justice. They found that Justice Department agents consistently: made searches and arrests without warrants; physically abused prisoners; planted secret agents within radical political organizations who often helped to instigate wrongful conduct; obtained cooperation from suspects through the use of terror tactics; and orchestrated a variety of self-serving propaganda campaigns (Bopp & Schultz, 1972, pp. 100).

In the 1920s, overzealousness by key prohibition agents in the state of Washington set the stage for a landmark Supreme Court decision that significantly curtailed the right to privacy with respect to personal communications for the next four decades.

The Olmstead Case

One of the earliest Supreme Court decisions in the field of electronic surveillance arose during the prohibition era. The legal doctrine that emerged, known as the *Olmstead doctrine*, prevailed as the law of the land until 1967. In that year, the Supreme Court decided the case of *Katz v. United States.* In *Katz*, the Court held that individuals have an expectation of privacy when communicating with another person, whether that communication takes place in a private or public space. The Court stated that the Fourth Amendment protects people, not places. It held that in order for government agents to intercept telephone conversations or to conduct other kinds of electronic eavesdropping, at least two requirements had to be established: (1) that a statute exists for the type of eavesdropping desired; and (2) that government agents obtain a search warrant prior to eavesdropping. In 1968, Congress passed a statute to satisfy the *Katz* requirements known as *Title III of the Omnibus Crime Control and Safe Streets Act.* This new *Act* went further than *Katz* in that it also provided that in certain limited emergency situations electronic surveillance could be conducted so long as government agents sought the appropriate search warrant within 48 hours. In addition, if the nation's national security was threatened, the President was entitled to exercise inherent Constitutional powers to protect the nation (Hickey, 1998, pp. 233-237).

In the *Katz* case, FBI agents acting without a warrant attached a listening and recording device to the outside of a telephone booth used by Katz. They only acted after they believed that Katz was involved in the illegal transmission of interstate wagering information. The electronic eavesdropping evidence was admitted at his trial and he was convicted for violating federal gambling laws. The Supreme Court reversed the conviction and in so doing reversed the legal doctrine expressed in the earlier *Olmstead* case. In *Olmstead*, the Supreme Court had upheld a warrantless wiretap on the grounds that the federal agents had not committed a trespass into any constitutionally protected area in order to install the listening and recording device. Therefore, no violation of the defendant's Fourth Amendment rights had taken place. Unfortunately, the *Katz* decision came too late to save Roy Olmstead from imprisonment.

Similar to the personal histories of most people growing up in Seattle and the world, in his youth, Roy Olmstead had not planned to become a criminal and to go to jail. However, in 1920, at the age of 34, when he was married with two daughters and serving as the youngest lieutenant in the Seattle Police Department, Omlstead had become a part-time rumrunner. After his first arrest and dismissal from the force, he entered into this occupation on a full-time basis. He had always been an ambitious person and he used his administrative talents to become in the language of the newsmen of his day: "the booze baron" (Clark, 1965, pp. 161-163).

By the time Olmstead was finally sent to prison, he had been grossing two hundred thousand dollars a month and delivering daily 200 cases of liquor.

He was careful to sell only the best Canadian liquor and began to entertain in a royal manner. He divorced his first wife, remarried, and purchased Seattle's first radio station. Olmstead was aware of the fact that his phones were being wiretapped, but he continued to use them, believing that the use of any such evidence would be illegal. On January 19, 1925, he was indicted along with ninety other defendants for conspiracy to violate the *National Prohibition Act* since June of 1923. Brazenly, even after being arrested and having had boxes of records seized from his home and that of his attorney, who was also indicted, Olmstead continued to engage in his bootlegging enterprise. On Thanksgiving morning in 1925, he was surrounded and caught unloading a boat and again arrested. At his trial, for his January arrest, the prosecutor remarked to the jury that Olmstead was the unofficial police chief of the Seattle police force. During the course of the trial, Prohibition agents took the witness stand and testified to what they heard over Olmstead's tapped telephones. The defense frequently pointed out that the wiretapping in the case violated a Washington law adopted in 1909 that made it a crime to intercept messages over any telegraph or telephone line (Clark, 1965, pp. 164-173).

Of those indicted who did not initially flee to Canada when out on bail, twenty-three were convicted and sentenced. On March 9, 1926, Roy Olmstead was sentenced to serve four years at hard labor in a federal penitentiary and to pay an $8,000 fine. Defendants who had cooperated with the government's attorneys received one-year sentences. Mrs. Willebrandt, the assistant attorney general in charge of prohibition enforcement, had serious reservations about the legality and morality of wiretapping, but she noted the importance of the outcome of this case with respect to overall prohibition enforcement efforts (Clark, 1965, p. 174).

Out on bail, Olmstead sold his possessions, home and radio station while he awaited the outcome of an appeal to the Federal Circuit Court of Appeals in San Francisco. The conviction was upheld, but a dissenting opinion by Judge Frank H. Rudkin encouraged Olmstead's attorneys to appeal to the Supreme Court. Judge Rudkin wrote:

> Must the millions of people who use the telephone lines every day for lawful purposes have their messages...intercepted? Must their personal, private, and confidential communications to family, friends and business associates pass through any such scrutiny on the part of agents....If such ills as these must be borne, our forefathers signally failed in their desire to ordain and establish a government to secure the blessing of liberty to themselves and their posterity. (Clark, 1965, p. 175)

At first, the Supreme Court rejected Olmstead's petition, but agreed to hear the case upon further review after the filing of a new petition. At this point Mrs. Willebrandt declined to have anything further to do with representing the government's side in the *Olmstead* case. She didn't approve nor agree with the manner in which the wiretaps had been obtained and used, but she did not say so at that time (Clark, 1965, p. 176). The Court was sharply divided. By one vote, a majority of the court upheld Olmstead's conviction. The four dissenters included Justices Louis Brandeis, Oliver Wendell Holmes, Pierce Butler, and Harlan Stone. The dissent prepared by Justice Brandeis took special note of the violation by federal prohibition agents of the anti-wiretapping statute in the state of Washington. It has become a classic statement about the obligations of the government with respect to the people it serves. Justice Brandeis stated: "In a government of laws, existence of government will be imperiled if it fails to observe the laws scrupulously....If the government becomes a lawbreaker, it breeds contempt for the law...it invites anarchy.... Against that pernicious doctrine this court should resolutely set its face" (Clark, 1965, p. 177).

In May of 1931, Roy Olmstead was released from the McNeil Island Federal Penitentiary. In prison, he studied religion and emerged a changed man believing that liquor was sinful. Rumrunning was still a profitable occupation for many in Seattle, but he refused the opportunities offered to participate; instead, he took a job in a credit bureau and became a law-abiding citizen. He also became a Christian Science missionary among the prisoners he left behind at McNeil Island (Clark, 1965, pp. 218; 251-252).

Throughout the remainder of the century, giant strides were made in the field of police professionalization. However, the actual achievement of such an ideal has remained elusive. Events such as the pattern of police corruption uncovered by the Knapp Commission investigation in the early 1970s as well as abuses by the FBI under Hoover during America's civil rights movement were obvious setbacks. Today, the fragile liberties of American citizens are still at the mercy of law enforcers who may be overzealous, misguided, inept or otherwise unprepared for their responsibilities.

No one is immune from the zeal of enforcement agents. In 1998, Kenneth Starr, the independent counsel, who had been initially appointed four years earlier to investigate President Clinton's Whitewater land dealings in Arkansas, successfully used the revelations of Monica Lewinsky because they had been secretly recorded by her friend Linda Tripp. The availability of the recordings served to corroborate Tripp's information and eventually led to President Clinton's impeachment by the House of Representatives and trial in the Senate. At the time of the recordings, the majority of states did not prohibit the taping of a conversation by one of the participants to it. In addition, there was no violation of the federal law regarding eavesdropping (*Title III*), because "by virtue of revealing the information to another, the communicator has lost his or her justifiable expectation of privacy in the information" (Hickey, 1998, p. 238). However, Tripp was a resident of Columbia,

Maryland. As this book was going to press, Tripp was being investigated by a Maryland grand jury for taping her phone conversations with Lewinsky. Maryland law forbids taping another person without their knowledge and consent ("Tripp Seeks Donations," 1999, p. D14).

The following two chapters deal with additional details about the difficult position that both local and federal social control agents were facing in their efforts to enforce prohibition.

ENDNOTE

1. Haynes, Roy A. The Facts of Prohibition Enforcement in Fred B. Smith, ed. *Law vs. Lawlessness: Addresses Delivered at the Citizenship Conference, Washington, D.C. October 13, 14, 15, 1923.* New York: Fleming H. Revell Co., 1924, p. 28.

Chapter 9

THE ENFORCEMENT OF PROHIBITION

"The greatest progress ever made in such a movement
since the world began, has been made in this great work
of prohibition law enforcement."[1]

ROY A. HAYNES
FEDERAL PROHIBITION COMMISSIONER (1923)

Prior to the adoption of national prohibition, various states and their sub-
divisions had adopted prohibition measures. The most organized effort
to establish and enforce these laws was made by the Anti-Saloon League. In
1908, the League was operating in 43 states and territories as well as in the
District of Columbia. Volunteer League attorneys worked in each state.
Their functions included: preparing annotated lists of state liquor laws; drafting laws; assisting local prosecutors by helping to present cases; and public
speaking and fundraising (Timberlake, 1963, pp. 132 & 144).

In some states, the League maintained its own armed detective units in
order to obtain evidence against local violators of temperance legislation.
However, these units were abolished after several episodes involving violence. In 1910, such a unit operating in Newark, Ohio raided a number of
Newark locations and at one location encountered a hostile crowd. In the
course of the struggle, a League Detective, Carl Etherington, aged 17, while
acting in self-defense shot and killed one of his assailants. Although he was
placed in the local jail, he was seized by a mob and lynched in the public
square (Timberlake, 1963, pp. 144 & 218).

After the ratification of the Eighteenth Amendment, the League took on
the task of preparing an appropriate set of guidelines for enforcing it. This
initiative was called the *National Prohibition Act* or more commonly, the
Volstead Act, named for its introducer, Congressman Andrew J. Volstead. It
was approved by Congress in October 1919 and took effect on January 16,
1920. Although President Wilson initially vetoed the legislation, Congress
easily produced the necessary votes for override (Perrett, 1982, p. 169).

Perrett (1982) indicates that Volstead was "hardly the fanatic that the
statute named after him implies" (p. 169). Through the seniority system,
Volstead had obtained the position of chair of the House Judiciary

Committee. In that capacity, he had the obligation to both report out of committee the Eighteenth Amendment as well as its supplemental enforcement statute. In 1922, he lost his seat in Congress to an opponent who had accused him of being an atheist and he was nearly defeated in 1916 when he was challenged by a member of the Prohibition Party (Perrett, 1982, p. 169).

The *Volstead Act* prohibited all drinks with an alcoholic content of 0.5 percent or more. Thus, many common brands of beer and wine were outlawed. The law did permit home brews of cider and fruit juices so long as they were nonintoxicating and liquor that had been stored in homes prior to July 1, 1919. The latter date was when the last special wartime prohibition law had come into effect (Timberlake, 1963, pp. 181-183). Liquor could be used as a prescribed medication and for religious purposes. Denatured industrial quality alcohol was also permitted. "The .5 percent provision—advocated by the Anti-Saloon League and other militant drys—surprised considerable numbers of persons who assumed that, as had been the case with many state laws, only distilled spirits would be banned" (Kyvig, 1979, p. 13).

For the first year of prohibition (1920), Congress voted an appropriation of 2 million dollars for enforcement and for the second year the total allocated was 6 1/2 million dollars. The apparatus of enforcement centered upon the creation of a new federal agency called the Prohibition Bureau. Under the *Volstead Act*, its agents were initially exempted from civil service selection criteria (Sinclair, 1964, pp. 273-274).

The highest authority for the purposes of enforcement of the provisions of the *Volstead Act* was the Commissioner of Internal Revenue who reported to the Secretary of the Department of the Treasury. Thus, the new Prohibition Bureau was located in the Treasury Department as a branch of the Internal Revenue Service. At that time, the Commissioner declared that it was: "the right of the Government officers charged with the enforcement of this law to expect the assistance and moral support of every citizen, in upholding the law, regardless of personal conviction" (Sinclair, 1964, p. 183).

Initially, for administrative purposes the United States was divided into ten departments. An assistant commissioner headed each department. In addition, each state had a federal prohibition director with an assistant and a legal advisor. At the broadest and lowest end of the authority structure for prohibition enforcement were "1,500 recently invested, gun toting revenue agents" (Kobler, 1973, p. 13).

Shortly after the adoption of the *Volstead Act*, Senator Frank Willis of Ohio and Congressman Robert Campbell successfully introduced a new federal law that set limits on the amount of liquor that could be prescribed by physicians. The law was adopted during the summer of 1921 and it limited prescriptions to one pint of liquor per patient during any ten-day period. In *Lambert v. Yellowley*, 272 U.S. 581 (1926), the U.S. Supreme Court by a slim one vote majority endorsed the provisions of the law. It held that the statute was not arbitrary and that the right to practice medicine was subject to governmental authority. However, like the *Volstead Act,* the *Willis-Campbell Act* did not diminish the consumption of alcoholic beverages by those determined to drink and to ignore any law that was in opposition to such a purpose (Kyvig, 1979, pp. 31 & 34).

It is important to indicate that while a tremendous amount of the government's and public's attention was absorbed by national prohibition, another kind of national prohibition had taken place in 1914 and by the 1920s had led to the criminalization of a quarter of a million narcotics addicts.

In 1920, the Treasury Department was responsible for enforcing the *Harrison Act* and it established a Narcotics Division within the Prohibition Unit. There were 175 agents in this division in 1920 and an average of 270 by the 1930s. Although various segments of the health profession were in disagreement, between 1919 and 1921, an effort was launched to treat addicts through medical clinics in many of the nation's largest cities. Most of these efforts involved ambulatory treatment and self-medication. The New York City clinic was established on Worth Street in lower Manhattan, not far from City Hall. It was initially established as a temporary walk-in facility with the goal of establishing inpatient services as soon as such specialized treatment centers could be established and patients referred to them. Such temporary clinics were thought to be better than no treatment at all. However, by the spring of 1921 the experiment was generally over. Many addicts seemed more interested in obtaining their medical supplies than in any long-term cures. Furthermore, as doctors witnessed their patients attitudes, they lost faith in this type of supervised self-dosing program (Morgan, 1981, pp. 111-116).

Moreover, the narcotics agents of the Treasury Department were committed in their efforts to see these clinics closed. It has been estimated that over 50,000 individuals between 1914 to 1922, including many physicians and others who were required to register under the *Act*, were charged with violating it. However, about seventy-five percent of the cases were dropped (President's Commission on Organized Crime, 1986, p. 202). The *Harrison Act of 1914* contained the sentence that a physician could prescribe narcotics "in the course of his professional practice only." The exact meaning of this phrase was interpreted by the agents of the Treasury Department to mean that maintaining addicts with narcotics was not a part of a doctor's legitimate "professional practice" (Gray, 1998, p. 51). When a Pittsburgh doctor challenged this interpretation, the U.S. Supreme Court dismissed the charges against him in a case decided in 1916. Nevertheless, the Treasury Department continued to bring similar charges without pressing for trials, thereby intimidating thousands of doctors and their patients. In 1919, the

Supreme Court reversed its earlier decision, when it found a Dr. Webb indiscriminately selling narcotic prescriptions to anyone who paid him fifty cents (Gray, 1998, p. 60). After this case and a few others, most of the nation's medical profession acquiesced in the prohibition approach engaged in by the government. One of the last doctors to take a stand against this policy was Willis Butler of Shreveport, Louisiana. Under significant federal pressure, he reluctantly agreed to close his clinic in 1923, even though he had the support of the leading members of law enforcement in his local community. Six months later, the press reported that heroin and morphine were being sold on the streets of Shreveport in unprecedented amounts (Gray, 1998, p. 63). Moreover, even though the 1925 Supreme Court decision in *Lindner v. U.S.* appeared to reinstate the view that a doctor could appropriately prescribe narcotics for relief of conditions incident to addiction, the opinion was simply ignored by the Narcotics Division (Gray, 1998, p. 88).

Colonel Levi G. Nutt

Enforcement of the *Harrison Act* was initially assigned to the Bureau of Internal Revenue in the Department of the Treasury. When the *Harrison Act* was initially adopted, $150,000 was allocated for its enforcement. Eighty years later that amount was being spent every three minutes (Gray, 1998, p. 55). After the adoption of the *Volstead Act*, a special Narcotics Division was created within the Prohibition Unit in order to separate narcotics and liquor enforcement work. The division had 170 agents and it was headed by a former pharmacist, Levi G. Nutt, throughout most of the prohibition era.

Colonel Nutt began work at the Internal Revenue Service in 1901. He was transferred to the first narcotics unit of the Department of Treasury when it was first authorized by law in 1915. In 1917, he was appointed chief agent of the Internal Revenue Service. He became head of the Narcotics Enforcement Division in 1920 and served in that capacity for ten years (*NYT*, April 17, 1938, sec. 2, p. 6).

The agents of the Narcotics Division were dispatched to 13 different field offices. Narcotics agents were hired under civil service rules and their reputations for honesty exceeded the public's attitude with respect to prohibition agents. In 1930, when the Federal Bureau of Narcotics (FBN) was created, Levi Nutt was the likely candidate to become its first commissioner. However, rumors began to circulate that agents had falsified their arrest records. Moreover, it was even suggested that Nutt's son, Rolland was working for the notorious gangster Arnold Rothstein (McWilliams, 1990, pp. 32 & 34). At that time, Colonel Nutt was abruptly transferred from his position as deputy prohibition commissioner in charge of narcotics to the position of that of a field supervisor in the Prohibition Bureau and he moved to

Syracuse, New York. Thus, Nutt's service ended in the narcotics unit and his assistant, Harry J. Anslinger was appointed to the newly created position of FBN chief (McWilliams, 1990, pp. 32 & 34).

Nutt retired from government service in 1935. He died at the age of 72, three years later. He was married for 50 years and had five children. When he was transferred from his leadership position in 1930, Assistant Secretary of the Treasury Seymour Lowman said Colonel Nutt "has been an active and zealous officer and the duties he is to assume March 1 are of great importance, and it is felt that because of his wide experience he will render great service to law enforcement in his new position" (*NYT,* April 17, 1938, sec. 2, p. 6). His obituary in the *New York Times* did not mention any of the old rumors.

The history of the enforcement of the *Harrison Act* during the fifteen years following its enactment illustrates the operation of a principle that has been validated repeatedly since that time: drug demand will result in the creation of supply channels to satisfy demand. An effective drug abuse policy requires a systematic and long-term demand reduction component. In fact, not until the mid-1960s was there any concerted effort to formulate demand-reduction strategies. In 1919, a bill "to provide aid from the United States for the several states in prevention and control of drug addiction and the care and treatment of addicts" was introduced, but the bill was not passed (President's Commission on Organized Crime, 1986, p. 204).

A New Structure

It was not until 1927, that federal prohibition agents were placed within the civil service system. In the same year, the office of Commissioner of Prohibition was created by an act of Congress and 27 different administrative districts were created. Each district had a chief administrator who acted largely on self-initiative with only general instructions on matters of policy from the Commissioner. An assistant administrator within each district was in charge of enforcement work for the suppression and control of all illegal traffic in liquor and alcohol. This enforcement office was further divided into three sections: General Enforcement; Major Investigations; and Case Reports (Schmeckebier, 1929, pp. 154-162).

The General Enforcement Section did the police work in connection with ordinary raids and seizures. Its work was generally confined to cases where an overt act was apparent to the agent. The Major Investigations Section dealt with more serious cases that took place within the administrative district's borders, such as conspiracies involving wholesale amounts of liquor with broad distribution networks. If the case had wider ramifications in that it extended outside of district lines, it was generally handled by the Special

Investigation Division, which operated under the direct supervision of the Commissioner of Prohibition. Finally, the function of the Case Reports Section was to review the reports submitted by agents and investigators (Schmeckebier, 1929, p. 162).

Enforcement Operations in New York City

In New York, the first person to be given a jail sentence for violating the *Volstead Act* was the co-owner of the Greenwich Village Inn, Barney Gallant. Gallant was born in Riga, Latvia in 1884. He was of Jewish descent. His great grandfather had founded a large brewery in Riga and Barney had the benefit of home tutors until he arrived in the United States in 1903. He lived with a wealthy uncle in St. Louis and was able to learn English in three months. Prior to coming to New York City in 1910, he worked as a newspaper reporter. In New York, his writing ability led to a position with the Mexican government. Along with several partners, he purchased the Village Inn in 1919. He and six of his waiters were arrested for selling liquor and he offered to plead guilty if the charges against the waiters were dismissed (Walker, 1933, pp. 283-284 & 292-294). Federal District Court Judge Learned Hand agreed to this arrangement and he was sentenced to thirty days. Gallant received a ten day stay of his sentence after serving just four days when the Assistant U.S. Attorney, Joseph Mulqueen appeared before Judge Hand and stated: "May it please the Court, since this man was convicted I have not had a moment's peace or pleasure. I have been besieged with pleas to let this man go. Even a police captain and a priest have come to me. But I am unalterably opposed to leniency in this case" (Walker, 1933, p. 285). His friends had collected more than 20,000 signatures on a petition seeking his release. Perhaps, because of his fame as a result of this case, Barney was able to open his own nightclub after his release and it became one of the most popular and exclusive resorts in the city. He remained in the night club business throughout the twenties (Walker, 1933, pp. 285-287).

About a year after former Det. Sgt. Tighe was sent off to Sing Sing, New York City police officers and federal prohibition agents were busy seizing liquor and arresting sellers. One typical operation took place not far from Coen's former saloon, at the famous Dinty Moore's restaurant, located on 46th Street near Broadway. However, unlike the Tighe case, the detectives in this raid had first obtained a search warrant. The warrant identified the entire five-story building that included the restaurant. On the evening of November 28, 1922, five detectives made a complete search of the premises beginning with the first and second floors that were filled with diners. The sudden appearance of the police caused many diners to get rid of their liquid refreshments as quickly as possible. On the third floor of the building, the restaurant's owner, James Moore lived. On the fourth floor, the police located and seized eighteen cases of whiskey, 200 bottles of wine and another 200 bottles of champagne. It took four trips to the local police station to remove the liquor, with an estimated value of ten thousand dollars. Moore and one of his waiter's, Charles Cusacke, were arrested and charged with violating the *Mullan-Gage Act*.[2] The warrant was based upon the testimony that Det. Thomas Sheehan had previously purchased a pint of "Canadian ale" from Cusacke. At the time of the raid, the news that police were in the process of raiding the popular theatrical district establishment caused a large crowd to assemble. As had occurred in the Tighe case, the appearance of the crowd outside the restaurant made it necessary to call upon the reserve platoon. Moore claimed that the seized liquor had been purchased prior to the effective date of the *Volstead Act*. Local magistrates were required to process prohibition cases such as this one and they carefully scrutinized each case. For example, if the beer seized by the police did not contain more than the legal one-half of one percent, cases had to be dismissed ("'Dinty' Moore Raid Crowds Broadway," *NYT*, November 29, 1922, p. 7).

On December 15, 1922, Magistrate Joseph E. Corrigan was presiding in his Yorkville, Manhattan courtroom when a waiter at a local restaurant was brought in by Patrolman Madden of the Chief Inspector's staff. The waiter was charged with illegal possession of liquor based on a warrant sworn to by Police Officer John J. Casey. Casey had sworn in his application for the warrant that he had found a quart of whiskey in a rear room of the restaurant. When Officer Casey didn't appear in court, Magistrate Corrigan stated to Patrolman Madden: "Bring Casey into court. He is the one who is responsible for the issuance of the warrant. How do I know the facts presented are true. How do I know that the defendant served Casey with liquor. I refuse to tolerate the evidence that is presented. Nine-tenths of these liquor cases are tainted with graft" ("Orders All to Jail in Volstead Cases," *NYT*, December 16, 1922, p. 25).

Cases brought to the federal courts were also carefully reviewed. For example, federal officials had seized the British schooner *Marion Mosher*, on July 27, 1922. It was found to contain over 1,200 cases of whiskey and 20 barrels of other kinds of liquor. The contents of the vessel had to be reloaded when it was determined that the ship's seizure had taken place outside the three-mile limit ("Order All to Jail in Volstead Cases," *NYT*, December 16, 1922, p. 25).

On the same day as the raid on Dinty Moore's restaurant, federal prohibition agents were dropping into former saloons throughout the city. In Manhattan, they seized two cases of whiskey, several cases of beer, ten barrels and ten gallons of assorted wines. In Brooklyn, agents made a dozen arrests involving owners, waiters and bartenders serving alcoholic drinks. At one location on Myrtle Avenue, Frank Honigman, the saloon's owner and his bartender were arrested. The agents recalled that Honigman the previous December had sent an invitation to Ralph Day, then enforcement director, inviting him to attend a New Year's eve party which was to be celebrated in "a fitting manner." Day didn't attend the function, but did send his agents to the party. They arrested Honigman and he was fined fifty dollars and sentenced to one day in jail. On the same day, federal agents and at least one prosecutor were also busy enforcing the prohibition law in New Jersey. Jacob Fiedler, an East Orange pharmacist, was under investigation for filling nearly 700 bogus prescriptions for liquor. Fiedler told authorities that he was unaware that the signatures of the local doctors had been forged ("'Dinty' Moore Raid Crowds Broadway," *NYT*, November 29, 1922, p. 7). This was not an uncommon occurrence. Two years earlier, during the first six months of prohibition, Captain Hubert Howard, Federal Prohibition Administrator for Illinois, estimated that 300,000 spurious prescriptions had been issued by Chicago physicians (Mowry, 1963, p. 92). Meanwhile, in front of the Union County Court House in Elizabeth, New Jersey, a crowd watched the local prosecutor, Walter Hetfield, pour almost 800 quarts of whiskey and gin as well as 28 barrels of beer into a sewer. The liquor had been seized in raids during the last four months and chemical analysis indicated that it was impure and a health hazard. On the other hand, an additional 300 gallons of liquor had tested pure and was being distributed among seven area hospitals ("'Dinty' Moore Raid Crowds Broadway," *NYT*, November 29, 1922, p. 7).

About two years later special city police units and federal agents were still at work trying to enforce the prohibition law. Illustratively, on the morning of September 22, 1924 a large crowd gathered near the intersection of Houston and Sheriff streets to watch police dump into the sewers a very large quantity of bottled home brew valued at more than $30,000. The crowd included young children from the neighborhood who attended Public School 22. At first hammers and axes were used to smash the bottles, but there were so many large explosions and pieces of flying glass that superior officers at the scene required that each bottle be uncorked. On the same day, William P. Finley, "a shell-shocked veteran" of World War I pleaded guilty to selling liquor in Brooklyn Federal Court. The judge ordered that he be returned to his Veterans' Hospital, located in the Bronx. Furthermore, the city of Kingston, New York, located 90 miles north of New York City and directly up the Hudson River, was declared the "wettest spot" in New York State. Ironically, the city was also the hometown of the state's current prohibition director Palmer Canfield. The conclusion was made in a report filed by three federal prohibition agents after conducting a series of raids in upstate New York. On their raiding tour, they arrested 21 men, 15 of whom were arrested in Kingston ("Pour Liquor Into Sewer," *NYT*, September 23, 1924, p. 8).

Padlocks

A unique feature of prohibition enforcement involved the availability of a legal procedure for locking-up any room, house, or building where intoxicating liquor was sold, stored or produced. The procedure involved obtaining a court order known as an "injunction." This could be done for a period of one year once a federal court judge had declared the suspected premises to be a "common nuisance" under the applicable sections of the *National Prohibition Act*. The method was used extensively in Omaha, Detroit, Chicago, and New York City. During a thirteen-month period, one federal attorney was able to have padlocks placed on 500 speakeasies in New York City. In the five-year period from 1921 through 1925, over 11,000 padlock injunctions were issued nationwide (Merz, 1931, pp. 148-150).

In theory, the padlock procedure seemed to be a more effective method of enforcing prohibition than conducting weekly raids on the same establishments since injunctions forced the premises to close for a year. However, in practice, it encountered various difficulties. Civil libertarians voiced frequent objection on the grounds that the padlock procedure was conducted without the benefit of a jury trial and that it penalized innocent landlords who were unaware of a particular tenant's wrongdoing. The padlock procedure also had several inherent faults. Padlocking one warehouse where liquor was sold, stored, or produced, did not prevent the owners of such a facility from investing in the opening of a different warehouse for the same purposes. Frequently, there was difficulty in finding the correct property owner for the necessary service of court papers. Finally, there was a lack of human resources to insure that padlocked premises remained closed (Merz, 1931, pp. 151–152).

The padlock enforcement concept was resurrected in the late 1980s when the city of Fort Lauderdale created a code enforcement team. The team consisted of representatives from police, fire, building, and zone departments who from 1987 to 1991, tore down 124 crack houses, boarded up 587 crack houses, and reduced overall drug activity by 57 percent. Since that time, many other cities including Albuquerque, New Mexico have developed similar approaches. Landlords of buildings occupied by drug dealers and other undesirable tenants are given notice that various hazardous conditions must be removed and repaired or risk facing heavy fines and condemnation proceedings. In most urban areas, this approach can be implemented without the need for new legislation, just stricter and more thorough enforcement of existing housing, construction, electrical, health, and plumbing codes

(Oliver, 1998, pp. 66-67; 97). Nevertheless, many of the same problems that confronted the use of padlock injunctions in the 1920s are still applicable today.

The Canadian Connection

There was a considerable amount of smuggling taking place over land routes between Canada and New York State during the twenties. Bootleggers discovered that it was not only profitable to transport whiskey, beer and wine into the United States from Canada, but also profitable to move raw alcohol into Canada. Canadian distillers were willing to pay $85 for five-gallon tins that originally cost smugglers between $20 to $35. The distillers used industrial alcohol and alcohol made from corn to create inexpensive liquor that was then smuggled back into the United States. According to one state police official, one-half of the automobiles seized in the summer of 1925 contained alcohol destined for Canada. In addition, silks and cigarettes also found profitable markets once inside of Canada (Everest, 1978, pp. 14 & 41-42). These events were possible because during the 1920s Canada did not ban the manufacture and export of liquor, although some provinces did prohibit its sale, consumption and transportation. The fact that liquor exports were forbidden to countries maintaining national prohibition, such as the United States, made bootlegging all the more profitable (Gervais, 1980, pp. 11-12).

After the repeal of the *Mullan-Gage Act*, the primary agents for enforcing prohibition and other smuggling activities at the border were the members of the Customs Patrol and the Immigration Border Patrol. Between Clinton County, New York and the province of Quebec, they received some assistance from Troop B of the New York State Police which was headquartered in Malone. Their task was to stem the flow of liquor over main roads, back roads, and over the railroad. In the passenger cars of trains, individual travelers could conceal liquor, but the bulk of the smuggled liquor was simply loaded onto freight cars. Some freight cars had false ends making detection more difficult. Moreover, until Coast Guard forces could be strengthened customs and immigration officers also had to police such water routes as Lake Champlain, the Great Lakes and the St. Lawrence River. However, all of these units were greatly understaffed given the task presented (Everest, 1978, pp. 61-65).

Concealment aboard the Pullman cars (Pullman was the nineteenth century inventor of railway passenger cars), took place in light fixtures, inside seats, sleeping car mattresses as well as behind the wall panels in staterooms and washrooms. Some passengers tied bottles to strings and hung them out car windows while customs inspectors searched luggage carried on board, while others hid their liquor in special trunks that were made with false sides and bottoms. More serious bootleggers arranged to have "access to empty freight cars in Canada and constructed false ends three feet deep that created space for almost 200 cases of beer at each end" (Everest, 1978, p. 33). Most of the cases involving the seizure of liquor on freight trains never involved any arrests nor the imposition of any penalties since the shipments were made without the presence of the shipper and intended receiver (Everest, 1978, p. 142). However, the same situation did not hold when train passengers could be identified as the owners of smuggled liquor.

During the prohibition era, many persons were found with concealed liquor as they crossed America's northern border from Canada by automobile or train. Prior to the *Jones Act*, minor violators of the law typically settled their cases by paying small fines directly to customs officers under a "civil settlement" policy. For example, the fine for possession of two bottles of beer would be $4, for five bottles of liquor $25. Of course, the outlawed substances were also confiscated. This process actually involved a simple type of judicial procedure whereby the border agents acted as judges, since the federal officers had the power to decide the amount of the fine (Everest, 1978, pp. 61 & 142). According to Everest (1978): "Noncommercial smugglers of a few bottles for personal use, if detected, signed an 'offer of civil settlement' and paid a fine, but they were not arrested. Otherwise the courts would have been swamped with petty cases. Border officers had to decide when the contraband was sufficient in quantity to constitute commercial smuggling" (p. 142).

Occasionally, officials would encounter celebrities in their own private railroad cars. On one occasion, forty bottles of quality liquor were discovered in the car of Geraldine Farrar, a famous singer. The bottles were concealed in a piano, the maid's room, and the ventilators. On another occasion, the private car of the producer of the famous Ziegfeld Follies, Flo Ziegfeld, was searched. It contained 106 bottles of liquor and 42 quarts of Canadian ale. Ziegfeld and his two traveling companions paid a total fine of $614. Ms. Farrar was not fined (Everest, 1978, p. 93).

In the rural border communities of upstate New York, law enforcement officials used a variety of techniques to stop bootleggers. High-speed pursuits were common. Members of the Border Patrol, Customs Patrol and New York State Police were armed. Sometimes they tried to shoot at the tires or gas tanks of fleeing vehicles. Officers also fired warning shots and shouted "halt" when bootleggers abandoned their cars and fled into nearby woods. Six-foot spiked sheets made of iron, heavy chains and car barricades were also used to stop fleeing vehicles. Such tactics, especially when they resulted in the serious injury or death of suspects were condemned by the press (Everest, pp. 78, 81, & 101).

Earl Warren

During the prohibition era, Earl Warren, a young assistant deputy district attorney from Alameda County, California was assigned to work in Berkeley, California. The city had earned an enviable reputation as a "clean town." Residents of Berkeley had to visit Oakland or other cities in order to obtain whiskey. At that time, Warren met August Vollmer and they worked closely together on a number of projects. When Warren was elected county district attorney, he specifically selected Vollmer's department to participate in bootlegging, prostitution, and gambling raids conducted in neighboring jurisdictions. Warren also depended on Vollmer's force for the collection of photographic evidence and other technical assistance. Later, they worked together to set up education programs and to develop state law enforcement agencies (Carte & Carte, 1975, pp. 48-49). After service as attorney general and governor of California, Earl Warren became chief justice of the United States beginning in 1954. His leadership of the Supreme Court continued for the next fifteen years.

During Warren's tenure as chief justice, the decisions of the Supreme Court were notable for their tendency toward judicial activism and they "carried weighty social and political significance" (Blum, 1991, p. 190). For example, in *Brown v. Board of Education* (1954) a unanimous Supreme Court declared that separate schools for black children were inherently unequal and therefore violated the equal protection clause of the Fourteenth Amendment. Moreover, between 1961 and 1969 the Warren Court accomplished what previous courts had resisted. Through the use of the doctrine of selective incorporation, the Court applied nearly all of the procedural safeguards in the Bill of Rights to the states' administration of criminal justice. Moreover, in the landmark decision of *Mapp v. Ohio* (1961) the Court finally agreed that the federal exclusionary rule of evidence regarding unlawful searches and seizures should also apply to the conduct of local police so that such evidentiary seizures could be barred from both state and federal criminal trials. In so doing, the Court did away with the practice known as the "silver platter" exception to the exclusionary rule. By this practice, illegally seized evidence was still admissible in federal prosecutions, if it had been seized by state or local police and then turned over to federal authorities (Bodenhamer, 1992).

Enforcement and Internal Problems

In the first eleven years of the Prohibition Bureau, there were nearly 18,000 agents appointed. Almost 12,000 agents voluntarily resigned and about 1,600 were dismissed for cause. During any one year, the total number of agents assigned to enforcement in the field consisted of between 1,500 and 2,300 men. For the first eight years of the Bureau's existence agent appointments were made without regard for civil service rules and regular agent training did not commence until 1927. When the entire service was finally required to take a civil service examination, only two-fifths were able to pass after two attempts. When the long awaited findings of the Wickersham Commission became available in 1930, the Bureau was transferred to the Department of Justice. However, for most of its life the Prohibition Bureau lacked continuity of service, adequate salaries for its personnel and both public and federal cooperation. Moreover, Congress never adequately funded the Bureau even though there was a dry majority in Congress. Sinclair (1964) commented that an obvious reason for their failure to provide such funds was "fear that large-scale enforcement would change their growing unpopularity into public disgust" (p. 357). Seymour Lowman, who became the enforcement leader of the national prohibition effort in 1927, declared that "enforcement in New York alone would need 30,000 agents instead of the existing 300, and a score of new federal courts" (Everest, 1978, p. 163).

Throughout most of the history of the Bureau, the agency lacked cooperation from the Coast Guard, the Border Patrol of the Bureau of Immigration, and the Customs Service (Sinclair, 1964, pp. 183-86). In 1933, one New York City newspaper editor considered the Bureau's agents "offensive beyond words, and their multifarious doings made them the pariahs of New York" (Sinclair, 1964, p. 184). In a popular pamphlet of that era, the Association Against the Prohibition Amendment claimed that within a period of ten years of the Bureau's existence, more than 1,000 people had been killed as a result of efforts to enforce the *Volstead Act* (Sinclair, 1964, p. 188).

The most sustained opposition to prohibition came from members of the Democratic Party in New York State. In 1920, the New York State Assembly voted to investigate the activities of the Anti-Saloon League and a law was passed authorizing the sale of a 2.75 percent beer. In 1921, as a result of a shift in political power, Republican legislators rescinded the beer measure and instituted a state prohibition enforcement law known as the *Mullan-Gage Act*. However, on June 1, 1923, after considerable political maneuvering and debate, the state's only prohibition law was repealed. New York State Governor Al Smith demonstrated political courage in withstanding the pressures of the prohibitionists who had urged him to veto the repeal measure (Kyvig, 1979, pp. 56-57).

In the first 18 months of prohibition, New York City employed "no fewer than four administrators... each with different systems of organization" (Cashman, 1981, pp. 51-52) for the enforcement of prohibition laws. Moreover, while the national average of fines for violation of the *Volstead Act* was $130 and the average prison sentence was 140 days, the federal court in New York City typically imposed fines of between $5 and $10. When the *Jones Act* of 1929 became law, the fines for violations increased (Cashman, 1981, p. 52).

Early reports about the effectiveness of the 18th Amendment and its supporting laws and law enforcers were indecisive. For example, several mayors and local sheriffs in communities outside of New York City noted that there had been a decline in their local jail populations in 1920. They believed that this had more to do with better employment opportunities than increased respect for the law, since they noted similar declines in applications for charity. In New York City, Mayor Hylan reported that "the number of admissions to the alcoholic ward of Kings County Hospital were more than double during the year 1920 than for the same period prior to prohibition" (Editorial, "Effects of Prohibition," *NYT*, August 16, 1921, p. 14). This statistic might be perceived as a sign that more people were becoming motivated to seek help for their drinking problems. However, the city's Commissioner of Public Welfare indicated that whereas in the past there had been many "beer drunks," the patients received under prohibition were victims of hard liquor of inferior quality that resulted in more serious illness and an increase in deaths. One police chief from a city near the Pennsylvania border was convinced that there were "more places where liquor is sold, and more consumed, than before the Eighteenth Amendment became effective" (*NYT*, August 16, 1921, p. 14). Finally, it was also pointed out by one warden that the state prison population was increasing and that "a great number of the new men are drug addicts" (*NYT*, August 16, 1921, p. 14).

Support from High Places

A series of decisions by the U.S. Supreme Court during the prohibition period favored law enforcement efforts. In *U.S. v. Lanza*, 260 U.S. 377 (1922), the Court unanimously ruled that an individual could be prosecuted and sentenced under both state and federal prohibition laws. The Court held that the Fifth Amendment protection against double jeopardy only barred successive prosecutions by the federal government. In 1923, the repeal of the *Mulligan-Gage Act* had eliminated the double jeopardy issue for New Yorkers. In *Caroll v. U.S.*, 267 U.S. 132 (1925), the Court ruled that federal prohibition agents could search a motor vehicle on a public highway without obtaining a search warrant as specified in the Fourth Amendment. The Court held that officers possessing reasonable cause could conduct a motor vehicle search without first obtaining a warrant since to do so was impracticable as the vehicle could depart long before a warrant was secured.

Furthermore, as indicated in Chapter 8, *Olmstead v. U.S.*, 277 U.S. 438 (1928), involved a five to four decision wherein the Court decided that wiretaps on telephones did not violate, respectively, the provisions of the Fourth and Fifth Amendments regarding reasonable search and seizure and the protection against self-incrimination. The majority members of the Court held that the provisions of the Fourth Amendment were not violated because no trespass had been committed and that nothing tangible had been searched or seized and that there was no violation of the Fifth Amendment since the defendants had voluntarily spoken over the telephone.

The Portia of Prohibition

The federal official responsible for guiding most of these and similar cases successfully through the U.S. Supreme Court was Mable Walker Willebrandt. During the prohibition era, Willebrandt was the country's best-known woman lawyer. Her legal career began in 1910 when she and her husband settled in California, where she worked her way through law school as a teacher. She was appointed to the post of Assistant Attorney General on September 27, 1921 and her varied duties included enforcement of the 18th Amendment (*NYT*, April 9, 1963, p. 31).

In October 1923, she delivered an address before a large audience in the nation's capital regarding progress in enforcement of the Eighteenth Amendment. In her address she carefully outlined the role of the various United States Attorneys and the U.S. Department of Justice with respect to using the federal income tax code to investigate and prosecute known bootleggers. She pointed out that the use of the tax law provisions enabled her staff to seek much higher penalties than would be available under existing prohibition laws. An excerpt of her remarks follows: "Until reverence for our laws, for laws particularly that are embodied in the moral sense of a great nation, are put in the hearts of the people of every locality, law will not be satisfactorily enforced; but in the meantime it will be enforced to the very limit of the ability of the Department of Justice of the United States" (Willebrandt, 1924, p. 93). In 1924, she said: "America's greatest sin today is good-humored indifference to existing conditions. We cannot lay the whole burden of law enforcement at the door of Uncle Sam. On the contrary, it is the duty of every individual, community and state to assist in making successful those policies adopted by the people of the nation" (Mable Walker Willebrandt Dies," *New York Times*, April, 9, 1963, p. 31).

Willebrandt was the highest-ranking Department of Justice official below the Attorney General, charged with overseeing prohibition enforcement. She devised several new methods for conducting prohibition raids, including having women accompany agents during their undercover investigations. It was estimated that under Willebrandt, agents spent $75,000 purchasing liquor just in New York City's night clubs. Despite incessant raiding by her agents, only an insignificant number of convictions were obtained and the speakeasy business continued to flourish (Walker, 1933, pp. 65-68). However, she was instrumental in bringing into the prohibition effort the U.S. Coast Guard. In October 1923, she stated: "They are a courageous lot of men, who, if ordered into the frey, would make the liquor pirates tremble" (Willebrandt, 1924, p. 89).

Within the first six months of his presidency, Herbert Hoover accomplished several notable objectives. For example, he held the first White House Conference on Children; he selected a dedicated conservationist to head the Department of Interior; he increased funding for the Bureau of Indian Affairs; and he obtained the resignation of Mrs. Willebrandt. She stayed on in the District of Columbia as the counsel and chief lobbyist for a California grape growers' association known as Fruit Industries. Willebrandt earned a substantial salary and was instrumental in securing a $20 million dollar loan to the association. Ironically, the grape growers business included the packaging of grape concentrates, the main ingredient used in home winemaking during the prohibition era (Perrett, 1982, p. 318)!

The Masked T-Men: Moe and Izzy

Although Sinclair (1964) noted the low salaries of Prohibition Bureau agents, according to Coffey (1975) a salary of $40 per week was sufficient to attract the interest of Izzy Einstein, a Manhattan postal clerk. When he applied for the post, he was living on the Lower East Side with his wife and four children. Izzy was 40 years old, five feet tall and weighed over 200 pounds. At first, his interviewer didn't think Izzy fit the image of a federal law enforcement officer. But as the interview progressed, he was able to convince the new chief agent for the Southern New York Division of the Federal Prohibition Bureau that he would be a capable investigator. Izzy was also able to convince his old friend Moe Smith to join him on the force. "Moe ran a cigar store on the Lower East side and also managed a small boxing club, having himself fought professionally in his youth. A taciturn, introverted man, he was the perfect foil for the ebullient Izzy" (Kobler, 1973, p. 295). Moe was a little taller than Izzy and about fifty pounds heavier. Their unusual appearances and their ability to use a variety of ruses and disguises helped them to become the most successful agents that the Bureau recruited. Moreover, they appeared satisfied with their forty dollars per week salaries, while other agents decided "to augment their government salaries with regular stipends from the very people they were supposed to arrest" (Coffey, 1975, p. 43). All prohibition agents received small salaries when compared to the money bootleggers were making. The only real law enforcement folk heroes of the prohibition era were dismissed in November, 1925. According to Sinclair (1964, p. 314): "Izzy Einstein and Moe Smith, who made over four thousand arrests and confiscated more than fifteen million dollars' worth of liquor in their brief careers, probably made the front pages more often than any other personages of their time except for the President and the Prince of Wales."

It has been argued that their extraordinary enforcement efforts upstaged the leaders of the Bureau and led to their dismissal after just five years of service (Sinclair, 1964; Kobler, 1973). More likely, they had offended the city's power structure through their aggressive investigatory tactics. For example, Coffey (1975) pointed out that on two occasions in 1925 Izzy had offended many New Yorkers by seizing several thousand dollars worth of sacramental wine from a shop in Brooklyn and "by getting himself elected to a private club for actors on Forty-eighth Street, then using his membership to raid the place" (p. 176). The wine in question was destined for the religious observances of Jews. Additionally, the Catholic Church had already taken a stand on this issue since the use of fermented wine is an essential aspect in the celebration of Mass (Timberlake, 1963). Therefore, one could speculate that the combined interests of both Catholics and Jews prevailed to strip Izzy and Moe of their credentials since "prohibition was no more popular with Jews than it was with Catholics" (Coffey, 1975, p. 176). In addition to thousands of arrests made by Izzy and Moe, it was estimated that they had seized 5 million bottles of bootleg liquor and beer (Sann, 1957, p. 119).

In 1932, Izzy Einstein with the aid of two of his sons published his memoirs in a book entitled *Prohibition Agent No. 1*. Since their sudden termination, he and Moe had worked as insurance salesmen. When a reporter asked Izzy if he believed in the moral principle of prohibition, he appeared bewildered by the question, and responded: "I don't get you." None of the reporters pursued the matter, because it was apparent to all that such a question was entirely irrelevant for Izzy (Coffey, 1975, p. 307). Izzy died in 1938 of an infection following the amputation of his right leg. Moe survived him by twenty-two years, dying in 1960 at the age of 72 (Kobler, 1973, p. 298). Izzy's book only sold 575 copies (Sann, 1957, p. 119).

"Put Your Hands on the Table"

In 1928, the head of the Prohibition Bureau's New York office, Captain Daniel Chapin, called a meeting at which he directed his agents to place both hands on the table. He then stated that "every one of you sons of bitches with a diamond ring is fired." About half of the group had been wearing such a ring (Perrett, 1982, p. 170; Sann, 1957, p. 203).

Cashman (1981) studied the corruption of police and other local officials engendered by prohibition and concluded that the real tragedy was that more than half a million people were convicted of violations of liquor control laws and related crimes and that thousands died in gangland warfare and from poisonous liquor. It is also ironic that the three groups who had been most active in opposing the use of liquor, were in fact the only three groups allowed by law to make, prescribe, or sell it after the adoption of the *Volstead Act*: "the ministers, the farmers, and the doctors and druggists" (Sinclair, 1964, p. 73).

The revitalized Association Against the Prohibition Amendment (AAPA) launched a major media blitz in the late 1920s. This organization issued a series of pamphlets that were widely circulated throughout the United States. They bore such titles as: "Scandals of Prohibition Enforcement," "Cost of Prohibition and Your Income Tax," and "Reforming America with a Shotgun: A Study of Prohibition Killings." Generally, the pamphlets were carefully prepared and except for their titles contained only a relatively small amount of editorial or rhetorical comment. They were cited by newspaper wire services as regular news items and thus served as an effective tool for the antiprohibitionists. In March 1929, the pamphlet, "Scandals of Prohibition Enforcement," was published. It summarized official reports from five major cities involving gross instances of police corruption. The cities included Philadelphia, Chicago, Pittsburgh, Detroit and Buffalo. Another pamphlet, "Prohibition Enforcement: Its Effect on Courts and Prisons," summarized the research conducted by the U.S. Department of Justice. The materials were organized to demonstrate the increased burden that prohibition had placed on federal courts and prisons. The report inferred that key elements of the nation's system of criminal justice were being prevented from dealing with other forms of crime (Kyvig, 1979, pp. 106–108).

Wickersham Commission

In May 1929, President Herbert Hoover appointed an eleven-member commission to study and report on the status of America's criminal justice system. He had promised during his campaign to appoint a commission for the purpose of reviewing the Eighteenth Amendment, but had now broadened its mandate. This change of policy by President Hoover directly caused the disaffection of at least one major Republican supporter—Pauline Sabin. She was a member of the Republic National Committee and the wife of Charles Sabin, the treasurer of the Association Against The Prohibition Amendment (AAPA). Pauline Sabin founded the Women's Organization for National Prohibition Reform. In time, her organization's membership greatly exceeded that of the AAPA. By 1932, its membership had surpassed one million and had added a half a million more supporters by December of 1933 (three times the size of the AAPA) (Kyvig, 1979, pp. 120–23).

The official title of Hoover's study commission was the National Commission on Law Observance and Enforcement, but it came to be known by the name of its chairman, George Wickersham. In 1913, Wickersham was serving as the U.S. Attorney General when the first major legislation supporting national prohibition, the *Webb-Kenyon Act*, was adopted. The statute expressly prohibited the shipment of liquor into states where its sale was against the law. Wickersham counseled President Taft that the statute was a violation of the "commerce clause" of the Constitution and Taft vetoed it. However, the strength of the dry forces was such that Congress overrode the President's veto (Engelmann, 1979, p. 66). In private sessions, the Wickersham Commission heard testimony from both dry and wet advocates and retained leading criminologists for the purposes of gathering information. While these closed sessions were being held, the House Judiciary Committee held public hearings about prohibition enforcement. AAPA's research director, John Gebhart, provided an effective presentation and concluded that the major consequences of the Eighteenth Amendment were increased liquor consumption and the fact that excessive liquor profits were being channeled to criminal groups. In mid-January 1931, President Hoover disclosed the findings of the Wickersham Commission. He asserted that the Commission did not favor the repeal of the Eighteenth Amendment. However, a careful scrutiny of the actual prepared statements of each of the eleven commission members appeared to undermine that assertion. Significantly, two members of the Commission had indicated that they favored repeal of the Eighteenth Amendment and most of the members indicated that they believed that the current system was either unwise or unenforceable. The contradictory statements made by President Hoover and the individual commissioners gave rise to numerous newspaper editorials and other commentary. While nothing had been resolved, the combined findings of the House Judiciary Committee and the Wickerham Commission had highlighted the nation's growing concern about the effectiveness of the Eighteenth Amendment (Kyvig, 1979, pp. 111-114). The Wickersham Commission indicated that 144 civilians and 60 prohibition agents had died as a direct result of enforcement efforts (Engelmann, 1979, p. 98).

Nearing the End

The convention planks of the Republican and Democratic Parties differed on the issue of prohibition in 1932. The Republican plank seemed as confusing as had been the Wickersham Commission's varied pronouncements.

The Republican delegates recommended that an alternative amendment to the Eighteenth should be submitted to popularly elected state conventions. The proposed new amendment was designed to permit states to decide whether or not to ban liquor sales while at the same time guaranteeing that the federal government would serve to safeguard the choices that were made and so long as the return of the saloon and its abuses were prevented (Kyvig, 1979, pp. 154-155). On the other hand, the delegates to the Democratic convention declared that Congress should "immediately pass a repeal amendment to be submitted to the state conventions, that in the event of repeal the federal government help protect states against liquor imports in violation of their laws, and that pending repeal, Congress modify the Volstead Act to legalize and tax the manufacture and sale of beer" (Kyving, 1979, pp. 157-158).

Just prior to the presidential election of 1932, the AAPA published a forty-page pamphlet listing over thirty reasons for repealing the Eighteenth Amendment; for example, widespread crime and corruption; very large enforcement costs; and the loss of one billion dollars in annual taxes. The landslide election of Franklin Roosevelt and other Democratic Party candidates to national office was widely interpreted as a voter referendum for repeal. Four years earlier, Herbert Hoover had received 58.2 percent of the vote, but in this election it was reduced to only 39.6 percent. President-elect Roosevelt had given a major address on the repeal issue to a huge crowd in Sea Girt, New Jersey on August 28, 1932. He had used the opportunity to condemn prohibition on mainly economic grounds, an astute statement of policy during the nation's worst economic depression. Roosevelt also pointed out that the Republican's prohibition plank was ambiguous in that it tried to please both sides of the issue, while he was solidly behind the repeal position of the Democratic platform (Kyvig, 1979, pp. 166-168). On the other hand, Hoover's rhetoric while consistent with his party's plank was perceived as "fence straddling." During the 1932 presidential campaign, Hoover had sought to attract repeal supporters by recommending that each state be allowed to decide for itself whether to allow liquor sales and he attempted to appeal to prohibition advocates by asserting that federal laws should be retained to "protect dry states and prohibit saloons. He succeeded in pleasing no one. The president failed to convince wets that his position was attractive as his opponent's, and he angered many drys" (Kyvig, 1979, p. 165).

By the summer of 1933, the number of prohibition agents in New York City had been cutback to sixty-three and "virtually all of them were known by sight to hundreds of bootleggers, night club owners, waiters, bellboys, bartenders and doormen" (Walker, 1933, p. 72). Earlier, the federal government had terminated funding for wiretapping, the use of informers and other agent expenses (e.g., the money to purchase drinks). The next to the last chief of the Prohibition Bureau in New York was Major Maurice E. Campbell, a former newspaper reporter and press agent. When he left office in the summer of 1930, he stated that he was for repeal of the Eighteenth Amendment and actually began publishing a magazine called *Repeal*. However, "while he had the job he used all the tricks in the book to enforce prohibition" (Walker, 1933, p. 63). He was succeeded by Major Andrew McCampbell, who remained in office until prohibition's last summer in the year 1933 (Walker, 1933, p. 73).

In New York City, during the era of prohibition neither the beat patrolman nor his superiors appeared to favor prohibition. According to Walker (1933), "the police raided usually only on specific complaints from persons who had been robbed or otherwise mistreated, or from neighbors who objected to noise and other forms of annoyance" (p. 74). Several seasoned speakeasy proprietors and other persons interested in the events of that day were of the opinion that if the police really wanted to eliminate the speakeasy, they could have done so in about a week! (Walker, 1933, pp. 160-161).

According to Kyvig (1979), by 1930 illegal stills within the United States were providing the main supply for American liquor consumption. However, the choicest types of liquor were being "smuggled in from Canada and from ships anchored on 'Rum Row' in the Atlantic beyond the twelve-mile limit of United States jurisdiction" (Kyvig, 1979, p. 21). The following chapter describes prohibition enforcement against the rumrunners (referring both to those persons and gangs who smuggled and the ships they used) as waged by the U.S. Coast Guard.

ENDNOTES

1. Haynes, Roy A. The Facts of Prohibition Enforcement in Fred B. Smith, ed. *Law vs. Lawlessness: Addresses Delivered at the Citizenship Conference*, Washington, D.C. October 13, 14, 15, 1923. New York: Fleming H. Revell Co., 1924, p. 23.
2. The *Mullan-Gage Act* was actually a series of bills sponsored by New York's Republican Governor Nathan L. Miller. The statute wrote the provisions of the *Volstead Act* into state law and gave broad authority for state and local law enforcement officers to search and seize liquor. Moreover, under one of its provisions individuals could sue for damages if injured as a result of the actions of any intoxicated person. Miller served as governor from 1921-1922. The law had a two-year life and was repealed in 1923 after the reelection of Alfred E. Smith. Smith, a Democrat, was governor in 1919-20 and again from 1923-28. Thereafter, in New York, enforcement activities were primarily in the hands of federal officers (Everest, 1978, pp. 9-10).

Chapter 10

U.S. COAST GUARD v. THE SMUGGLERS

"In this juncture we look with confidence to the
President of the United States. We ask him to place
every available craft and every available agency which
may lawfully be used for the purpose, to police our
shores."[1]

REV. JOSEPH FORT NEWTON
CHURCH OF THE DIVINE PATERNITY
CITY OF NEW YORK (1923)

Today and throughout most of its history, the U. S. Coast Guard has been
considered to be a primarily humanitarian service because of its core
responsibilities: conducting rescues at sea and other related maritime safety
assignments. For example, one of the most well-known functions of the
Coast Guard is its participation in the International Ice Patrol, established in
1914. The Ice Patrol was made possible by the financial contributions of the
various nations whose vessels sail the North Atlantic. The original impetus
for this effort was the loss of the luxury liner, *Titanic*, in 1912. It struck an
iceberg on its maiden voyage to the United States and due to an insufficient
number of lifeboats, 1,517 people drowned. Today, the Coast Guard is heavily involved in the efforts to curtail trafficking in drugs and to guard against
water pollution from oil spills and other hazardous substances.

The Coast Guard also engages in such diverse activities as: search and rescue; aids to navigation; military readiness; port security; boating safety;
maintaining ocean patrol stations for gathering meteorological and oceano-
graphic information; icebreaking; and oil pollution control (Gurney, 1973, p.
9). In addition to its mainly humanitarian services, the Coast Guard is a
branch of the armed forces of the United States and its organization, administration and methods of operation conform to that status. Not all of these
responsibilities were present from its inception; rather since its origin in 1790,
the Coast Guard has constantly evolved and its tasks have kept pace with
changing times.

The Coast Guard was inaugurated with the commissioning of ten-armed
revenue cutters on August 4, 1790. In that year, the United States was only

a fledgling nation and had incurred a debt of eighty million dollars as a result of its successful war of independence. The cutters were needed to insure that merchant vessels arriving from Europe passed through customs so that new tariffs could be collected based on their cargoes. During the Revolutionary War, the habit of smuggling cargo onto shore was encouraged as a necessary part of the war effort. In fact, John Hancock, one of the leading figures in the founding of the United States and a signer of the Declaration of Independence, was a notorious smuggler in his day. However, it was now necessary to abandon such practices for the sake of the financial security of the new nation. Alexander Hamilton, the nation's first Secretary of the Treasury, carefully selected the first group of captains for the new service. These men had exhibited special heroism and seamanship during the Revolutionary War. Hamilton carefully molded the Coast Guard, then known as the "Revenue-Marine," so that its operations would be the least objectionable to Congress and the citizens of the United States (Bloomfield, 1966, pp. 3-8). For example, he directed the following order to the new officers of the service: "always keep in mind that their countrymen are freemen, and as such are impatient of everything that bears the least mark of a domineering spirit.... refrain with the utmost circumspection from haughtiness, rudeness and insult and overcome difficulties by a cool and temperate perseverance rather than by vehemence or violence" (Bloomfield, 1966, p. 9).

Soon most of the nation's income was obtained through the custom's offices at the nation's seaports and the war debt was discharged. By 1796, the Revenue-Marine was given the expanded authority to defend the United States against any intruders. Eight years after the establishment of the Coast Guard, the U. S. Navy was created. In 1799, Congress gave the President the discretion of placing the Coast Guard under the supervision of the Secretary of the Navy in times of national emergency (Bloomfield, 1966, pp. 11-14). The members of the service performed gallantly during the War of 1812, in the Mexican War, in the Seminole War, in the Civil War and in the War with Spain. In 1837, the duties of the Coast Guard were officially extended to missions involving scientific research and search and rescue operations under severe weather conditions (Bloomfield, 1966, pp. 38 & 107).

It was not until after 1915 that the U.S. Coast Guard was officially given its name. It was known as either the Revenue-Marine Service or Bureau until 1885. From 1885 to 1915, it was referred to as the Revenue-Cutter Service. By an act of Congress, Coast Guard officers only obtained equal rank, pay and retirement benefits with Army and Navy officers in 1902. Enlisted personnel had to wait until 1915 to receive retirement benefits and until 1920 to obtain a pay scale comparable to their counterparts in the Navy. Prior to these changes, Coast Guard personnel had only been able to receive a pension if wounded and disabled while serving as part of the Navy in wartime

(Bloomfield, 1966, pp. 66 & 107). Nearly, 9000 men served in the Coast Guard during World War I. The service had the highest fatality rate of the all the branches of the armed services (Bloomfield, 1966, p. 138).

With the passage of the Eighteenth Amendment, America became a magnet for persons wanting to make it rich by illegally importing intoxicating beverages. The nation was especially besieged by "rumrunners" on its eastern seaboard and northern borders because of their proximity to vessels arriving from Europe. By 1922, the island of Nassau, in the Bahama Islands had become a major staging area for smuggling liquor through the eastern shores of the United States. Imports to that tiny island from Europe were estimated to have increased from 50,000 quarts to ten million quarts (Bloomfield, 1966, p. 146). One of the best known rumrunners of this era was Bill McCoy. He was a speedboat builder and avid sailor. He made his home base in the Bahamas and added to his income by taking whiskey to Martha's Vineyard and other northern beach communities. The expression "the real McCoy" stems from the high quality of his liquor (Behr, 1996, p. 136). He was raised in upstate New York and moved to Florida with his brother in 1898. He was eventually arrested and sentenced for his smuggling activities to nine months in the federal prison at Atlanta (Asbury, 1968, pp. 248-250).

However, nearly two-thirds of the liquor was coming in via water routes from Canada (Bloomfield, 1966, p. 146). In 1928, the Canadians were operating at least 83 breweries and 23 distilleries (Asbury, 1969, p. 260). America's northern border with Canada was particularly difficult to protect from smuggling due to the extensive length of the land boundary (over a thousand miles) as well as the length and narrowness of the water-boundary. The combined water and land border extended for a length of three thousand miles. While the water boundary was patrolled by the Coast Guard and a Customs Marine Patrol, the land boundary was patrolled by Customs border guards, various state police agencies, and the U.S. Immigration Border Patrol. The Immigration Border Patrol was not established until the mid-1920s (Schmeckebier, 1929, p. 16; Everest, 1978, p. 7).

President Harding appointed Roy A. Haynes to be the first Prohibition Commissioner. Haynes pointed out that one of the difficulties in interdicting liquor supplies from Canada was due to the fact that Canadian brewers used "spy ships" to alert rumrunners to the presence of any Coast Guard or Prohibition Bureau cutters (Behr, 1996, p. 151). Typically, the smugglers would enter into the United States by way of the Great Lakes, the Detroit and St. Lawrence Rivers, and Lake Champlain. The St. Lawrence River shares a long border with the many small villages of the uppermost part of New York State. Liquor arriving over the Great Lakes could reach such commercial centers as Duluth, Toledo, Cleveland, Sandusky, Erie and Buffalo.

Canadian brand liquors could also be brought to Plattsburgh, New York and Burlington, Vermont by traveling down Lake Champlain (Asbury, 1969, p. 260).

The lack of roads along the long Mexican border as well as diminished supplies of the most desirable brands of liquor, decreased smuggling along the southern boundary of the United States (Schmeckebier, 1929, p. 16). Nevertheless, because of the advent of prohibition there was a large demand at the United States border for mescal and tequila. Some of this demand was satisfied by Mexican smugglers who either rafted or waded through the shallow waters of the Rio Grande with barrels containing bottles of liquor. Sometimes dogs were used to bring over a rope to a patiently waiting conspirator on the American side. Additional supplies were simply carried over the bridge separating the cities of Juarez and El Paso. Such smuggling was readily accomplished by women "wearing voluminous skirts and bulging ...because of the goat bladders and stomachs filled with mescal and tequila tied about their waists" (Asbury, 1969, p. 260).

In the northeast, there existed a significant problem just outside of the harbor of New York City. According to Bloomfield (1966): "A 'Rum Row' of schooners and steamers, like a floating city, built up in plain sight off Sandy Hook near the entrance to the New York Harbor...There were even a few convictions within the Coast Guard itself of warrant officers and enlisted men who took bribes to look the other way" (p. 146).

During the twenties, it was common to see all types of vessels loaded with liquor from Canada, the West Indies, and Europe stationed along the coasts of New Jersey, Long Island and Massachusetts waiting to unload their cargoes onto smaller boats. The various clusters of ships came to be known as "rum rows." The smaller and faster boats used for off-loading the liquor were termed "rumrunners" by the press (Steffoff, 1989, pp. 49-50). The smaller boats favorite destinations on the East Coast included: New Bedford, the Hamptons, Nantucket, and Martha's Vineyard (Behr, 1996, p. 135). Another rum row operated in the Gulf of Mexico. Such gulf ports as Tampa, Mobile, New Orleans and Galveston were used by the rumrunners (Asbury, 1969, p. 241). Their cargoes could be taken ashore by landing at any of the nearby secluded beaches and inlets. The Bahama Islands and Cuba supplied most of the illegal liquor that reached the Gulf Coast (Gurney, 1973, p. 90). On the West Coast, rumrunners particularly favored Puget Sound since it was a convenient destination for the delivery of illicit liquor originating from either Mexico or other Pacific regions (Behr, 1996, p. 135). However, the western rum fleet "was never as large or as important as the one on the Atlantic coast; it was too far from the main sources of supply and the big eastern markets" (Asbury, 1969, p. 241).

The Coast Guard service estimated that it was intercepting only about five percent of the liquor being off-loaded by merchant vessels onto specially built speedboats for the three-mile dash to shore. In 1923, the situation was becoming so critical that prohibition advocates advanced the suggestion that the U.S. Navy should be directed to join in antismuggling efforts. However, Curtis Wilber, the Secretary of the Navy, insisted the enterprise of prohibition enforcement was a domestic policing responsibility and not the Navy's (Bloomfield, 1966, p. 146).

Finally, Congress acted by authorizing a major expansion of the Coast Guard in 1924. In 1923, Mrs. Willebrandt had pointed out that there was no legal reason to prevent the Coast Guard "from being charged with the duty of policing coastal waters for smugglers" and she declared that they "would make the liquor pirates tremble" (Willebrandt, 1924, p. 89). Within fourteen months, a special fleet of about 200 seventy-five-foot patrol boats were built and put into service. In addition, 103 thirty-six-foot speedboats were constructed for pursuits close to the shores. In subsequent years, even more specially built craft were added as well as hundreds of seaworthy vessels captured from the smugglers. These vessels and many more including twenty-five old destroyers were urgently needed to combat the smuggling of liquor along America's extensive double coastlines with its many different harbors, inlets, coves, bays, rocky islands and gulfs. In the north, special attention would have to be given to the Great Lakes and the St. Lawrence River boundaries and in the south the Rio Grande (Bloomfield, 1966, pp. 147-48).

In order to obtain the necessary crews for all of these new and old ships, the Coast Guard was authorized to enlist 4,500 additional personnel, utilize one-year enlistments, to shorten the length of the Coast Guard Academy curriculum for new officers to less than the required three-year period. As a result of this build-up of ships and personnel during the Prohibition Era, the U.S. Coast Guard tripled its size by the time of World War II (Bloomfield, 1966, pp. 147 & 153).

The Coast Guard Academy's curriculum was expanded to four years in 1931 and it is the only military service academy that does not consider political and geographical factors for admission, but rather relies only on competitive test results. In 1939, the U.S. Coast Guard Auxiliary was formed. Then and now it is composed of thousands of unpaid volunteers. In 1942, a Women's Reserve was created and shortly thereafter, women reserve officer candidates were enrolled at the Coast Guard Academy in New London, Connecticut (Bloomfield, 1966, pp. 266-67; 211-213). Women have only been on regular active duty since 1973 and the Academy only admitted its first female career officer candidates in June 1976. However, the Coast Guard Academy was the first of the military academies to admit women (Nadine & Blue, 1993, p. 41).

Only in 1926 was the Coast Guard sufficiently funded so that two air bases at Gloucester and Cape May, New Jersey and five planes were added to the amount of resources available to this branch of the federal forces engaged in the enforcement of prohibition (Bloomfield, 1966, p. 141). In 1919, Coast Guard Lt. Elmer F. Stone was a copilot on the NC-4 Curtiss-built biplane (also referred to as a "flying boat,"), that made the first successful flight across the Atlantic. Between 1927 and 1930, the Coast Guard air fleet consisting of about six planes flew more than 200,000 miles (Gurney, 1973, p. 97).

Aerial rum-running was not a major tactic used by bootleggers during the prohibition period, but airplanes were used as early as 1920 to ferry liquor from Ontario, Canada to various locations in Michigan. Moreover, at one point during the twenties, the Chicago crime syndicate headed by Ralph Capone had a fleet of 20 airplanes to aid in its bootlegging enterprises. There were a variety of disadvantages in using airplanes during that period for smuggling purposes; for example: flights needed to be made in the day-time, since nighttime flying was considered too dangerous; oftentimes peo-ple would report seeing airplanes land because of their novelty; landing areas had to be frequently changed to avoid attracting police attention; and the early types of aircraft had limited cargo space (Engelmann, 1979, pp. 84-85).

Consequently, most rum-running involved the use of speedboats to tra-verse the waterways between Canada and the United States and between mother ships hovering outside U.S. territorial waters and America's shores. The rumrunners employed a variety of tactics to deliver their precious car-goes. In general, two methods were used to unload cargoes of liquor:

> Under one, arrangements for sale and transportation were made in advance, and the liquor was landed at various points on the coast, loaded on trucks, and carried to the consuming centers. Another method was to hover outside the three-mile limit, and make sales to purchasers who came from the shore in their own boats. Under this system grew the notorious "rum row" of the harbor of New York. (Schmeckebier, 1929, pp. 13-14)

In order to facilitate these methods of distribution and to avoid detection, the rumrunners: deployed decoy boats; made use of smoke screens; encod-ed messages; used high speed watercraft with twin airplane engines; would cut across shallow waters; used armor plating on their pilot houses; estab-lished secret radio stations; stacked fish and ice over liquor cases of liquor bottles; attached cargoes to submerged buoys; created false bottoms on their boats; bribed workers operating New York City garbage barges; and even disguised vessels in order to avoid port inspections (Bloomfield, 1966, pp. 148 & 152). After the stock market crash of 1929, many luxury yachts were sold for a fraction of their value and their beautiful interiors were ruined when they were filled with the cases of alcoholic beverages by bootleggers (Behr, 1996, p. 132). When the rumrunners encountered one of the rehabil-itated World War I Navy destroyers, some of them tried to attract these vessels into running aground in shallow waters. If the lighter rumrunning boats succeeded in this maneuver, they could make their way over the shallow bottom and escape with their contraband cargoes (Gurney, 1973, pp. 85 & 90).

Weather conditions also served as a factor for the rumrunners as well as a lack of vigilance by the authorities. In mid-December of 1922, Jacob Shaw, a construction company watchman at Cold Spring Inlet, near Cape May, New Jersey, noted that a storm off the Jersey Coast had apparently given an opportunity for a large bootlegging schooner to slip into shore and to land its cargo. He saw the vessel docked at the local fishing wharf and cases being removed. They were loaded onto two large trucks, which had neither lights nor license plates. Bootlegging in this manner was facilitated along the coast because of the existence of a number of roads that lead directly to the beach. Moreover, since these points along the coast were no longer patrolled, they made ideal landing places. ("Orders All to Jail in Volstead Cases," *NYT*, December 16, 1922, p. 25).

Of course, the use of bribes was another popular method of delivering rum cargoes. One of the notorius rumrunners in New York City was William Vincent Dwyer. He was known as "Big Bill" Dwyer, not because of his physical appearance, but because of the breath and scope of his illegal operations. At various times, he held interests in oceangoing vessels, nightclubs, hotels, gambling casinos, racetracks, breweries, and professional ice hockey and football teams. His offices were located in well-known office buildings on Broadway and he had an estate in Belle Harbor, Long Island. Dwyer grew up on lower Tenth Avenue and got his start in rum-running through an older neighborhood friend, George Shevlin. Shevlin owned numerous saloons and with the advent of prohibition he needed help in obtaining liquor supplies. Dwyer proved adept in all aspects of smuggling. In garages, he built underground areas for concealing heavy trucks that used special elevators. In order to bring liquor to the shore, he used a fleet of eighteen speedboats equipped with surplus airplane engines. With such engines his fleet of "rumrunners" could outrace most other boats. He formed successful alliances with underworld gang leaders and was responsible for corrupting numerous police and Coast Guard personnel (Kobler, 1973, pp. 260-262).

During the mid-1920s, Dwyer and his associates were able to control the crews of four Coast Guard vessels. Dwyer enlisted the services of one coastguardsman to entrap others. Vulnerable crewmen would then be wined and dined. This pattern of seduction began when "Dwyer provided a sumptuous dinner, theater tickets, a girl and a hotel suite. The tender of a bribe on that following day usually met no resistance, "neither the pay nor the working conditions in the Coast Guard then being very attractive" (Kobler, 1973, p. 265). In this way, Dwyer was able to recruit dozens of coastguardsmen. In at least one well-known case, members of the Coast Guard were actually paid to off-load a shipment of 700 cases of scotch and champagne. This took place on the afternoon of December 27, 1924. On other occasions, the corrupted crews would only intercept those small-scale rumrunners who had refused to pay Dwyer a protection fee of two dollars per case (Kobler, 1973, p. 265). "At other times Coast Guard ships simply looked the other way as 'black ships' steamed straight into New York, unloading" their cargoes of liquor onto carts waiting on local docks (Behr, 1996, p. 144).

In another serious incident involving coastguardsmen and graft, the entire crew of CG-219, based in Monroe, Michigan, were charged with illegally disposing of previously confiscated beer, wine, and whiskey. In this case, the cutter had stopped one rumrunner and seized its cargo and then in plain sight of the crew of this vessel, the coastguardsmen unloaded the liquor onto the boat of another crew of smugglers. The coastguardsmen were brought to justice when the original rumrunners filed a complaint with prohibition officials (Engelmann, 1979, p. 118). In essence, the coastguardsmen had acted like pirates. They had robbed one rumrunner and sold to another, thereby violating the tenets of the "honest" rumrunner's code. According to the research performed by Engelmann (1979), the rules for honest bootlegging and rum-running included:

> Thou shalt not use denatured or wood alcohol in 'cutting' or diluting good liquor;
> thou shalt mind thine own business;
> thou shalt not cooperate with police authorities;
> thou shalt not cooperate with newspaper reporters;...
> thou shalt not steal from other rumrunners;
> thou shalt not default on debts because of capture by police;
> thou shalt not use counterfeit money to pay for liquor;
> thou shalt not undercut another's market. (p. 94)

Clearly, the forces aligned to take advantage of the Prohibition laws were formidable and the enforcement of Prohibition presented the Coast Guard with a serious challenge. Indeed, Rear Admiral Frederick C. Billard, the Commandant of the Coast Guard, declared that "the fight against liquor smuggling is one of the most complex naval operations ever executed; thousands of miles of coast have to be patrolled" (Allen, 1979, p. 47). Throughout the Prohibition period, the two most common tactics carried out by the Coast Guard to interdict liquor trafficking were trailing and picketing. The latter tactic involved the establishment of a blockade of the rum boats through constant sea patrols. Trailing involved following or shadowing suspected rumrunners, whether they be the smaller speedboats or the mother ships waiting on rum row. In this way, they sought to make it more difficult for the offshore craft to transfer their cargoes to the smaller boats (Allen, 1979, p. 47). Of course, once a transfer had been completed, it was a matter of intercepting the smaller boats within territorial waters. In addition, on some occasions Coast Guardsmen in civilian clothes manned a captured rum launch, went out to Rum Row and purchased liquor, thus establishing proof of the offshore vessel's intent to land its cargo illegally in the United States (Allen, 1979, p. 47).

On one hot Sunday afternoon in July 1924, a Coast Guard vessel sighted two swift rumrunners in the vicinity of the Coney Island beach. The cutter pursued the two speedboats in full view of a hundred thousand bathers in the water and lolling on the sand. The three boats raced at full speed, with the smugglers firing pistols and submachine guns and the cutter trying to hit the rumrunners with three-inch shells, none of which fell within a hundred yards of the targets (Asbury, 1969, p. 245). Meanwhile, two policemen, who were obviously caught up in the excitement, ran to the end of the famous Steeplechase Pier and began firing their revolvers into the air until they ran out of ammunition (Asbury, 1969, p. 245). About 23 years earlier, at the same Steeplechase Park where this incident had unfolded, Carry Nation had addressed an enthusiastic audience about the dangers of drinking alcohol. The location was filled with beer gardens, sideshows, and amusement park rides, when she told the audience: "Coney Island would not be what it is were it not for the government of New York.... What can you expect of a government run by a lot of beer-smeared, nicotine-faced, beak-nosed devils?" (Madison, 1977, p.127).

Certainly one of the most daring and embarrassing incidents involving the Coast Guard took place on December 21, 1925. It involved patrol boat, CG-2325. The vessel was docked at Pier 18 in Staten Island and had just had its engines repaired. There was no watch on board when bootleggers came on board and proceeded to make three 28 mile round trips to rum row. In this manner, they picked-up and unloaded 1,500 cases of liquor (Allen, 1979, p. 126).

In 1925, the main federal agencies concerned with enforcing the Eighteenth Amendment were the Customs Service, the Coast Guard, the Border Patrol of the Immigration Service, and the Prohibition Unit. The newest of these agencies was the Bureau of Immigration's Border Patrol. It was formed in 1925. During the twenties, while seeking to enforce the Eighteenth Amendment, the Customs Service and the Coast Guard acknowledged the slaying of 36 individuals. The Prohibition Bureau stated that its agents had taken 137 lives. In the same effort, during the twenties, fifty-five prohibition agents lost their lives, five Coastguardsmen, as well as fifteen Customs and Immigration officers (Kobler, 1973, pp. 290-291). It is important to note that none of these totals include the number of local and state police officers slain in neither the line of duty nor the number of individuals who were killed by such police agents.

Throughout the prohibition era various attempts were made to strengthen enforcement efforts by internal reorganization within the Department of the Treasury. For example, prior to April 1, 1925, Customs, Prohibition and the Coast Guard had been placed under the direction of the Assistant Secretary of the Treasury in charge of the Collection of the Revenues; after that date, they were placed under the direction of the Assistant Secretary of the Treasury in charge of Customs, Coast Guard, and Prohibition. The remaining responsibilities of the Bureau were delegated to an Assistant Secretary in charge of Internal Revenue and Miscellaneous. Significantly, the effect of this change was to divide-up control of the Bureau of Internal Revenue in such a way that one Assistant Secretary had clear responsibility for enforcing prohibition laws and another dealt with other matters of concern to the Bureau of Internal Revenue. Moreover, this division of authority in actuality (although not officially), positioned the Commissioner of Prohibition and his immediate superior, the Commissioner of Internal Revenue into subordinate roles! This happened because the administrative power in all matters of organization, general policy, and the drafting of regulations was assigned to the new Assistant Secretary in charge of Customs, Coast Guard, and Prohibition (Schmeckebier, 1929, pp. 11-12).

However, perhaps the most important of the reorganizational changes of 1925 and especially with regard to its impact on the Coast Guard, was the announcement by the Secretary of the Treasury that henceforth the federal government would concentrate on eliminating the sources of the supply, distribution, and sale of large quantities of liquor. The Treasury Secretary noted that it would be inappropriate for his department to organize the very large contingents of officers that are needed for the purposes of engaging in local prohibition law enforcement. He urged local governments (i.e., state, county and municipal) to assume their lawful responsibilities for self-government by undertaking the prompt enforcement of the prohibition law (Schmeckebier, 1929, p. 12). Two years later, a separate Bureau of Prohibition in the Treasury Department was established by Congress. The details of that law were addressed in the previous chapter.

On the West Coast, all national prohibition enforcement efforts were coordinated by a special agent of the San Francisco Division of the Special Intelligence Unit of the Prohibition Unit (Schmeckebier, 1929, pp. 17-18). Illegal liquor trafficking was mainly controlled by Canadian interests. These interests formed the Pacific Forwarding Company of British Columbia to take advantage of America's thirst. In an ingenious scheme to avoid the payment of any import taxes, Canadian liquor was legally shipped from Vancouver to Tahiti and then diverted (by having the Tahitian customs bond canceled) to the rum rows off of Long Beach, California and the coast of Washington. The Canadians had a well-organized system and they were literally able to guarantee delivery through sales agents assigned to San Francisco, Los Angeles and Seattle. According to Whitehead (1963), "no one knows how many hundreds of millions of dollars in profit was realized by the Canadian conspiracy" (p. 83). Only after Prohibition's repeal were federal law enforcement officials able to bring a case against some of these interests. The U.S. government agreed to accept a fine of three million dollars in a plea bargain to end the case (Whitehead, 1963, p. 84).

Extraordinary efforts were undertaken by the Congress, the President, the Treasury Secretary and the Coast Guard to control smuggling and especially, to undermine the "rum row" on the East Coast. The annual budget for the Coast Guard was more than doubled in order to pay for anti-smuggling activities. Treaties were entered into with several European countries so that Coast Guard crewmen could make inspections of foreign vessels outside of the three-mile limit. Between 1924 and 1928, such agreements were made with England, France, Germany, Spain, Italy, Belgium, Norway, Denmark, Sweden, and the Netherlands. Agreements were also entered into with Canada, Panama, Cuba and Mexico. The agreement with Mexico only lasted for a year. These agreements provided that vessels could be seized if there existed a reasonable belief that an offense was being or was about to be committed on the high seas. Vessels could be boarded so long as they were not at a greater distance from the shore than one hour's travel time (the origin of the 12 mile territorial limit) (Schmeckebier, 1929, pp. 14-15).

The specific obligations and responsibilities of the Coast Guard and especially its Intelligence Office were clarified in a memo issued on May 18, 1927 by the Assistant Secretary of the Treasury. The memo not only focused on the duties of the Coast Guard with respect to the prevention of unlawful attempts to import liquor, but also on the interdiction of narcotics. The memo indicated that the Commandant of the Coast Guard now had 11,000 officers and men, many radio stations, and 277 life-saving stations under his control as well as the hundreds of vessels noted above to prevent smuggling. The Coast Guard's Office of Intelligence was responsible for collecting and classifying the latest information concerning the movements of all ships and personnel engaging in smuggling activities. In addition, the Intelligence Office was charged with keeping other enforcement services and military branches informed about captures and other relevant matters. Notice of important seizures had to be immediately reported to Washington and the evidence turned over to the jurisdiction's collector of customs. Additional clerical support for the preparation of these sensitive reports was to be provided by personnel reassigned from the Prohibition Bureau (Schmeckebier, 1929, pp. 27-28; 34).

A tragic incident involving the Coast Guard and smugglers during Prohibition occurred on August 7, 1927, less than 20 miles from the island of

Bimini. Patrol boat CG-249 under the command of Boatswain Sidney C. Sanderlain with a crew of six was under orders to travel from its base in Ft. Lauderdale to Bimini in the British Bahamas. They had a special passenger, Secret Service Special Agent Robert K. Webster. He was planning to link-up with his British counterparts in order to investigate a group of counterfeiters who were operating in the region. Counterfeit U.S. currency was being used to purchase imported liquor. On the high seas, the cutter encountered a suspicious speedboat with two men aboard. One of the men was Horace Alderman, a convicted liquor smuggler. At the time of the encounter, he was out on bail for the charge of alien smuggling. The crew treated the encounter in a routine fashion and Alderman pulled a weapon. Alderman first killed Boatswain Sanderlain and wounded other crewmembers after Agent Webster failed in an attempt to overpower him. In his attempt, Webster was shot and killed. Four days later, Motor Machinist Mate First Class Victor A. Lamby died from his wounds. The remaining crewmembers managed to subdue the two men. Alderman's partner, Robert Weech became a witness for the prosecution. Two years later, Alderman was hung for his crimes in a hanger at the Coast Guard base in Ft. Lauderdale (Schreiner, Jr., 1990, pp. 36-50).

By November of 1928, the Commissioner of Prohibition reported that numerous rum rows had been successfully smashed (Schmeckebier, 1929, p. 69). The build-up of the Coast Guard fleet had helped the service capture "three hundred thirty booze boats in 1926, almost as many in 1927, and one hundred ten in 1928 in a special two-month drive off the coast of Florida" (Asbury, 1969, p. 263). However, this apparent success was greatly undermined in some areas of the country due to extensive participation in collusion by governmental agents and/or their incompetence. For example, in the years 1928 and 1929, federal law enforcement personnel seized a total of 366 vessels in the Detroit River area. Each of these boats were processed under federal forfeiture guidelines and then docked at a government marine storage facility. Some of them had been seized and forfeited more than once. The confiscated boats were left unguarded and over time all but one of these boats were stolen by gangs! Subsequently, some of these stolen boats would be sold back to their original owners (Engelmann, 1979, pp. 113-114).

Furthermore, there was still a large amount of smuggling originating from European ports, from the French islands of St. Pierre and Miquelon off the Canadian coast, and from Central American and Mexican ports (Schmeckebier, 1929, pp. 69-70). Prohibition gave St. Pierre and Miquelon a level of prosperity "that is still remembered with nostalgia. They are the one place in the world where their benefactor, Al Capone, even at this remove intime, remains a hero. Many of the houses still standing there are made out of the wooden cases champagne bottles originally came in" (Behr, 1996, p. 130).

Moreover, it was reported that huge amounts of liquor were still entering over the northern land and water border between the United States and Canada, notwithstanding the constant patrols by the Customs Service and Coast Guard. Although the Prohibition Bureau and the other federal agencies had specifically identified Detroit as a major entry and distribution point, only a small percentage of liquor (less than 5 percent) was being intercepted (Schmeckebier, 1929, pp. 69-70; Asbury, 1969, p. 264). Worst of all, corruption continued to flourish. One of the most extensive scandals involved members of the Customs Service assigned to Detroit.

In 1928 and 1929 a grand jury revealed that bootleggers and smugglers disbursed annually a corruption fund of approximately two million dollars. About one hundred agents were involved...and their individual monthly take was said to average seventeen hundred dollars.... In addition customs men received lump sums for "free nights" on the border, when the smugglers were permitted to run in as much liquor as they could handle. (Asbury, 1969, p. 184)

The background for such wholesale collusion was due, at least in part, to the failure of Congress to recognize the critical role that the city of Detroit played in the evasion of prohibition. In 1928, the *New York Times* reported that Detroit's second biggest industry was commerce in illegal liquor and that the city was the liquor capital of the United States. The *Times* pointed out that nowhere else in the country was there such a narrow and easily navigable water boundary between Canada and the United States. After the War of 1812, the boundary line was drawn right down the middle of the Detroit River with its tiny islands being equally divided between the two nations. These features provided numerous hiding places and points of departure for smuggling operations. Conditions were just about perfect for such transactions. A speedboat from the Canadian side of the Detroit River could reach the American side in about three minutes. Moreover, the force of customs officers in the entire area was only 90 men and the *Times* concluded that patrols were "hopelessly overmatched by the liquor people" (Mowry, 1963, pp. 105-107).

However, the eventual unraveling of prohibition had a lot to due with simple greed and the overwhelming demand for alcoholic beverages. Greed was not solely restricted to rumrunners and assorted bootleggers of one stripe or another. Greed also influenced thousands of druggists and doctors who regularly filled and wrote prescriptions for whiskey. Of course, many of the prescriptions were forged. In addition, the *Volstead Act* had other loopholes. Fruit juices could be made at home and farmers could make cider. Many publications appeared describing how to distill alcohol in teakettles, coffee pots, and washbasins. New stores opened that specialized in the sale of the equipment and supplies used by home brewers. Moreover, at least five hundred commercial breweries had permits to produce near beer. The process for producing the weaker brew first requires producing it at the usual strength. Considerable amounts of real beer were simply shipped with near beer labels. Thus, production was becoming so decentralized that effective enforcement was simply impossible (Severn, 1969, pp. 112-115).

In 1929, James M. Doran, a new Prohibition Commissioner informed Congress that any serious attempt to enforce prohibition would cost at least 300 million dollars. In that year, Congress allocated 12 million dollars to the Prohibition Bureau. Further appropriations were made to the Customs and Coast Guard services as well as to the U.S. Attorneys Office, so that the total allocation exceeded 30 million dollars (Kobler, 1973, p. 338).

One tragic incident involving a rumrunner took place at 2 A.M. on the morning of December 29, 1929. The incident began in the foggy waters of Narragansett Bay, just off of Newport, Rhode Island, when a coast guard vessel's searchlight discovered sacks of liquor on board the deck of the 50 foot speedboat the *Black Duck*. Her fittings indicated that her principal function was rumrunning. She was built well, painted gray and of low visibility. Maxim silencers muffled her two nearly new Detroit Aero Marine 300 horsepower engines. Moreover, the vessel was equipped with a smokescreen device. Although the Coast Guard signaled for her to stop her engines, she kept going and was fired upon by the cutter's machine gun. Three of her four crewmen were killed and the fourth member was wounded. The *Black Duck* was found to have had 383 cases of liquor on board. A Coast Guard investigation hearing was held that lasted six days. The official board of inquiry concluded that the firing of the machine gun (a three second burst of 21 rounds) was necessary in order to stop the speedboat and recommended that no further action should be taken (Allen, 1979, pp. 246-257). Allen (1979) noted several contradictions in the official records of the case and the matter generated significant levels of unfavorable publicity for the federal government and particularly, the United States Coast Guard.

The incident caused Andrew Mellon, the Secretary of the Treasury, to comment that the Coast Guard was acting "entirely within their instructions and observing their duty in what they did" (Allen, 1979, p. 265). However, Congressman Fiorello LaGuardia stated that the case of the *Black Duck* is indicative of how Prohibition has led to many unpleasant consequences including the demoralizing of conditions within the Coast Guard as well as the Customs Service. He said: "The Coast Guard ten years ago was one of the finest branches of the government service. The honesty, the courage, the cleanliness of Coast Guard men was traditional and held up as an example.... As soon as that service came in contact with Prohibition, it became contaminated" (Allen, 1979, p. 272). Within three weeks of the incident, a Rhode Island grand jury decided that no criminal charges were to be brought against any of the coastguardsmen. They heard testimony from 17 witnesses before making their decision. Finally, on March 4, 1930, a federal grand jury sitting in Providence, Rhode Island, voted that no federal criminal charges would brought against Charles Travers, the lone survivor of the *Black Duck*. The grand jurors added that he had "been punished enough by the Coast Guard, which shot off one of his thumbs" (Allen, 1979, pp. 275-276).

By the end of the twenties, frustration with the way prohibition enforcement was proceeding had caused the Treasury Secretary to recommend the idea of involving other military branches. In the Secretary's 1930 annual report, a specific proposal was made for the United States Army to seal off America's Canadian borders except for a few carefully selected checkpoints to be decided on by the President! Furthermore, it was urged that additional Army units should be posted along America's coastlines (Asbury, 1969, p. 264). Near the end of the twentieth century, the Department of Defense (formerly the Department of War) was designated the lead agency in the detection and monitoring of aerial and maritime transit of illegal drugs into the United States, although members of the military were expressly forbidden from making arrests (BJS, 1992, p. 146). However, in the 1920s the military forces of the United States had only a limited role in the interdiction of illegal alcohol, except of course, for the major role played by the U.S. Coast Guard.

Throughout the twenties, the lack of cooperation among the federal agencies and local law enforcement was conspicuous. They simply did not trust one another. Older career employees in both the Customs and Coast Guard had particular disdain for the new Prohibition Unit. But members of these services also complained about one another. According to retired Coast Guard Lieutenant Joseph Slovick: "A lot of the time, when we had seized some liquor we didn't bring it into the Customs house during the daytime because we didn't want any contact with the customs men [because] they would keep it for their own purposes, or to sell" (Behr, 1996, p. 145).

In 1927, A. Bruce Bielaski, a former high ranking Prohibition Bureau supervisor, told the press that he knew that Coast Guard crews: had been paid to look the other way; had assisted in the actual transfer of cargoes; and had protected smugglers by giving false information to other military vessels about their whereabouts (Behr, 1996, p. 143). Although bribery and graft found its way into every federal law enforcement agency concerned with prohibition enforcement, "the Customs Border Patrol was distinguished by the pervasiveness of graft in its ranks" (Engelmann, 1979, p. 115). In Detroit, "Border Patrol inspectors allegedly screened new members for character—or rather, lack of it. Life in the patrol was made unbearable for honest agents. One witness to the Border Patrol graft testified that one inspector, Daniel Shimel, had been offered $50,000 by rumrunners if he would resign from the patrol, 'because he was one of three honest men on the force'"(Engelmann, 1979, p. 115). Customs Inspector Shimel gave up his position after he received death threats from his fellow agents. In Detroit, the revelation of the collusion among bootleggers, rumrunners and customs officials ultimately led to the firing or resignation of almost the entire force (Engelmann, 1979, p. 115).

Little wonder that during prohibition, Coast Guard morale reached the lowest point in its history. Some coastguardsmen were not only being recruited by various bootleggers, but in some cases bootlegging themselves. Their counterparts in the Customs Service and Prohibition Unit were also accepting graft. Furthermore, routine humanitarian missions were being affected. The traditional safety and rescue mission of the Coast Guard was being interfered with as a result of fake "mayday" (distress) signals that were sent by smugglers. Consequently, Coast Guard vessels were being detoured away from the favorite sea lanes of the smugglers; and occasionally, some ships were being drawn into ambushes (Behr, 1996, p. 144).

Clearly, enforcement of the prohibition law was problematic from its outset. A notable early case involved the discovery that a moonshiner's still was in full operation just five miles north of Austin, Texas. The still was located on the farm owned by U.S. Senator Morris Sheppard, a key author of the 18th Amendment (Mowry, 1963, p. 91). Moreover, the land and water borders of the United States provided an 18,700 mile temptation for the bootleggers and smugglers of that era. In theory, the Coast Guard's effort to blockade the rum rows was designed to virtually stop the flow of liquor from abroad. While such efforts succeeded in some areas, it could not totally stem this flow. On the other hand, overall enforcement efforts were being steadily increased. The *Jones Act of 1929* stiffly increased penalties for violating the prohibition law. By the early 1930s, the number of federal convictions more than doubled and the rate of incarceration had quadrupled. Some states adopted "habitual criminal" statutes. In Michigan, a thirty-year old woman with three children automatically received a life sentence because of her fourth prohibition conviction. Such events did not meet with the public's favor. Demands for repeal were raised by new interest groups and through the reincarnation of older groups. After the incident involving the *Black Duck*, irrate citizens protested the deaths of the vessel's crew outside Boston's historic Faneuil Hall and attacked a nearby Coast Guard recruiter (Perret, 1982, pp. 404-406).

Of course, the Coast Guard could do nothing about the clandestine manufacturing of the domestic varieties of liquor, commonly referred to as "bathtub gin." As has already been noted the law itself contained a variety of loopholes including the fact that doctors were free to prescribe alcoholic drinks and druggists were empowered to fill these prescriptions.

Furthermore, millions of gallons of industrial alcohol were being diverted, watered down, flavored, bottled and sold with bogus whiskey labels and stamps. Federal and state enforcement agencies were underfunded, understaffed, and oftentimes unenthusiastic in rendering mutual aid to one another. For example, although the states were eventually encouraged to initiate and lead policing efforts, "by 1927 their financial contribution to the cause was about one-eighth of the sum they spent enforcing their own fish and game laws" (Allen, 1979, p. 189). In courts, certain days were set aside so that guilty pleas could be received for prohibition violations. In many cases, the small fines paid on such days enabled bootleggers to return to their trade without much interruption in business (Severn, 1969, p. 129). Moreover, the prohibition problem soon became a racketeering problem of significant proportions. Finally, the prosperous economic bubble of the twenties itself blew-up and ushered in this nation's worst period of depression. The temper of the age was now expressed by the famous American humorist, Will Rogers: "What does prohibition amount to, if your neighbors' children are not eating? It's food, not drink, that is our problem now. We were so afraid the poor people might drink—now we fixed it so they can't eat" (Severn, 1969, p. 167).

The Anti-Saloon League, which had played a very large role in the enactment of prohibition in 1919, found itself incapable of sustaining the necessary momentum for its continuation. The League had adapted business managerial techniques to accomplish its primary objective, but it was not able to reconcile competing views and to enunciate a clear strategy for a dry America. However, the League is today remembered for its pioneer role in how to go about running an effective single-issue campaign. Moreover, "by the late twentieth century countless observers of American politics were wondering how the nation could survive the single-issue, interest group political structure the league had promoted" (Kerr, 1985, p. 282).

These events and other factors, such as the change in public opinion expressed in the 1932 general elections retired America's "Noble Experiment." After the 21st Amendment had been officially ratified to repeal the 18th Amendment on December 5, 1933, President Franklin Roosevelt expressed the hope that "this return of individual freedom shall not be accompanied by the repugnant conditions that obtained prior to adoption of the 18th Amendment and those that have existed since its adoption" (Allen, 1979, p. 279). It seemed that the only accomplishment for all of this effort was that the word "saloon" had become a taboo. The institution, of course, has flourished ever since, whether it is known as the corner bar and grill, cocktail lounge, tavern, or by the name of the popular TV show, "Cheers."

However, the repeal of Prohibition in 1933 did not terminate the Coast Guards work to deter smugglers. In order to evade taxes, a variety of merchandise was still being bootlegged. Today, the Coast Guard is currently in the forefront of most law enforcement efforts to deter illegal drugs and aliens from entering into the United States. Repeal of the 18th Amendment also did not end the federal government's concerns about other illegal substances, especially narcotics. At the start of the 1930s, prohibition enforcement on the federal level, of the narcotics variety, was in the capable hands of Harry J. Anslinger. Anslinger served as the Treasury Department's Commissioner of Narcotics for 32 years. He advocated harsh laws against the sale, possession and use of all habit-forming drugs. Despite his unflagging campaign against illicit drugs, Anslinger is credited with having insured that an adequate supply of such drugs was available for medical use during and after World War II. With the aid of drug manufacturers, he arranged for the stockpiling of drugs in the gold vaults of the Treasury Department (Krebs, 1975). The following chapter highlights additional events during Anslinger's career and the eventual establishment of the U.S. Drug Enforcement Administration.

ENDNOTE

1. Newton, Joseph Fort. The Message of the Citizenship Conference to the American People in Fred B. Smith, ed. *Law vs. Lawlessness: Addresses Delivered at the Citizenship Conference, Washington, D.C. October 13, 14, 15, 1923.* New York: Fleming H. Revell Co., 1924, p. 185.

Part 3

POST-WORLD WAR II DEVELOPMENTS

Chapter 11

THE ESCALATION OF THE DRUG WAR

"Any officer authorized to execute a search warrant relating to offenses involving controlled substances... may, without notice of his authority and purpose, break open an outer or inner door or window of a building, or any part of a building...." Public Law 91-513 October 27, 1970.[1]

This chapter deals mainly with: (1) the events leading-up to the establishment of the Drug Enforcement Administration (DEA); (2) the DEA's separate relationship with the Federal Bureau of Investigation despite the fact that both agency heads are under the supervision of the Attorney General of the United States and are located within the same federal branch—the Department of Justice; and (3) issues related to the media's coverage of drugs. Some of the recommendations of President Reagan's Commission on Organized Crime are also presented. In addition, several of the ironies associated with the conduct of the nation's drug war are mentioned.

Harry Jacob Anslinger was born on May 20, 1892 in Altoona, Pennsylvania. He attended public school in Altoona and the Pennsylvania State College from 1913 to 1915. He graduated from the George Washington College of Law in Washington, D.C. in 1930 (Krebs, 1975). Anslinger became the acting commissioner of the Federal Bureau of Narcotics (FBN) on July 1, 1930. In 1930, as a result of the *Porter Act*, the FBN was created as a new division of the Treasury Department. In order to strengthen the Bureau's small forces against major narcotic traffickers, Anslinger took the opportunity to join and ultimately lead a seven-year effort for a new prohibition against marijuana. The final congressional debate about this legislation was notable because the event coincided with a glaring misstatement of fact by a future chief justice of the Supreme Court, Fred Vinson. Representative Vinson responded affirmatively to a question about whether the legislation to heavily tax marijuana was endorsed by the American Medical Association. In fact, the AMA's spokesperson, Dr. William C. Woodward had taken the exact opposite position at a previous hearing (Gray, 1998, pp. 79-81). Anslinger was able to maintain his position as the head of the FBN for more than thirty years and with vigor equal to J. Edgar Hoover's, he routinely confounded and outmaneuvered his adversaries throughout numerous presidential administrations (Gray, 1998, p. 73). The *Porter Act* gave the FBN commissioner the power to approve the manufacture of narcotic pharmaceuticals. Only a relatively small segment of the pharmaceutical industry obtained approval to market these drugs. Industry spokesmen readily supported Anslinger's efforts on behalf of the FBN and their respective companies ultimately enjoyed huge financial success (Gray, 1998, pp. 74-75).

In 1942, Anslinger reported that there was proof that Japan had violated its international commitments for years in its promotion of the opium trade. He stated: "Wherever the Japanese army goes, the drug traffic follows. In every territory conquered by the Japanese a large part of the people become enslaved with drugs" (Krebs, 1975, p. 40). During World War II, the FBN and federal investigatory units from the Coast Guard, Bureau of Customs and the Internal Revenue Service as well as all the branches of the armed forces were involved in the suppression of drug trafficking. The heroin shortage in the United States led to an increased number of thefts from pharmacies, hospitals, and other sources of drugs. Consequently, the use of barbiturates also became an added source of potential substance abuse ("DEA Briefing Book," 1998).

In an effort to assess the actual hazards of marijuana use, Mayor LaGuardia appointed a special committee to study the problem in New York City. The findings of the committee were published in 1944. The committee reached the conclusion that "the publicity concerning the catastrophic effects of marijuana smoking in New York City is unfounded and that marijuana is a minor nuisance rather than a major menace" (Ferguson, 1975, p. 81). However, the American Medical Association urged that public officials should "disregard this unscientific, uncritical study and continue to regard marijuana as a menace" (Ferguson, 1975, p. 81).

The post-war years brought new drug problems to the United States. Cocaine had been virtually nonexistent since 1930, but began showing up at U.S. ports of entry, and was traced to clandestine factories in Peru. Until 1946, each new drug that came along, including synthetic drugs, required separate legislation before it could be controlled. Recognizing the inefficiency of this arrangement, the FBN was given blanket jurisdiction over all drugs ("DEA Briefing Book," 1998).

In the 1950s, Mexican opium made its way to New York, where it was refined into heroin, and then distributed to major cities throughout the country. FBN agents began to see a rise in addiction in major metropolitan areas during this time, as well as a drop in the median age of drug offenders. Both the *Boggs Act of 1951* and the *Narcotics Control Act of 1956* imposed harsher penalties, as well as mandatory prison sentences, for narcotics violations ("DEA Briefing Book", 1998). In part, these tougher controls were instigated by a new campaign conducted by Commissioner Anslinger that erroneously linked international heroin trafficking to Red China. In fact, "Far Eastern heroin was, and continues to be, the business of Chinese Nationalists, Triads, Thais, and Burmese insurgents–not the People's Republic, which routinely executes drug traffickers" (Abadinsky, 1997, p. 60). "Triads," refers to the various ethnic Chinese criminal organizations that have arisen during the twentieth century to engage in international drug trafficking. These criminal enterprises are named for the common symbol associated with such illegal groups, the triad. The triad is "an equilateral triangle representing the three basic Chinese concepts of heaven, earth, and man. In the United States, Triad members have been associated with tongs, benevolent associations that bridge the worlds of legitimate business and crime" (Abadinsky, 1997, pp. 236-237).

For most of Anslinger's career with the FBN, he advocated strict marijuana controls. His crusade regarding this particular substance began in the mid-1930s when he associated the drug with "an epidemic of crimes committed by young people" (Krebs, 1975, p. 40). According to Himmelstein (1983), it was Anslinger's goal that by dramatizing the potential dangers of marijuana abuse that local and state police agencies would be motivated to become the primary enforcers of the new marijuana prohibition laws. Instead, the economic climate of the 1930s prevented most states from undertaking this role. Consequently, the FBN became a victim of its own advocacy and had to add marijuana enforcement to its agenda. However, the use of marijuana did not become widespread until the 1960s when a generation of Americans belonging to the middle and upper classes began to experiment with hithertofore "forbidden fruits." For example, such celebrity children as Robert Kennedy, Jr. and R. Sargent Shriver, III, were arrested for possession of marijuana (Abadinsky, 1997).

Perceptions about America's social upheaval and experimentation with drugs in the early 1960s led to a new and tougher approach to fighting drugs. Accordingly, in 1966 a new federal enforcement unit, the Bureau of Drug Abuse Control (BDAC), directed by John Finlator, was created within the Food and Drug Administration. Its responsibility was to control stimulants such as methamphetamine and various hallucinogens. In 1968, the Johnson Administration consolidated the FBN and BDAC to establish under the Department of Justice, the Bureau of Narcotics and Dangerous Drugs (BNDD). Following this, Richard M. Nixon was elected president, partly on his promise to restore law and order to the nation ("DEA Briefing Book," 1998).

However, not all attempts to contend with the nation's drug problems were entirely criminal in nature. Respectively, in 1961 and 1966, California and New York developed civil commitment programs for drug addicts. Confinement for treatment was to be followed by a period of parole or after-care. New York's program (commonly known as "NACC" for the Narcotic Addiction Control Commission) was scuttled in the 1970s as a very costly failure. At the same time, the federal government increased its contributions to various treatment programs tenfold. Significantly, the 1960s and 1970s also spawned the development of the "therapeutic-community." In these programs, former addicts were recruited as counselors to help other addicts recover. The best known examples of these approaches to the drug problem are Synanon and Daytop Village (Abadinsky, 1997, p. 62).

Nelson A. Rockefeller served nearly four terms as governor of New York, although his political goal was to become the president of the United States. He created NACC during the midst of a come from behind gubernatorial race that cost $5.2 million, nearly ten times the amount spent by his campaign opponent Frank O'Connor. O'Connor was a well-known district attorney from Queens County, but he ultimately proved no match when faced with the aggressive Rockefeller style and fortune. As part of Rockefeller's campaign tactics, his personal wealth enabled him to monopolize television viewers with adds: "showing a syringe entering the main line, or hoodlums walking menacingly on dark, rain-slicked streets. The voice-over was that of Nelson, and it rasped: 'Want to keep the crime rate high? Vote for O'Connor'" (Collier & Horowitz, 1976, p. 354). By 1972, NACC had spent nearly three-fourths of its funding for the construction of new residential treatment facilities and despite huge payrolls, had little to show for the effort. "Of 5,172 individuals treated and released under the NACC's compulsory treatment program, only 141 managed to stay drug-free at the end of a year and a half, which meant each cure had cost New Yorkers about $1.6 million" (Collier & Horowitz, 1976, p. 473). In 1973, after acknowledging the failure of NACC, Rockefeller announced and had enacted a new program that featured mandatory life sentences for persons involved in drug trafficking. He also created 100 new judges to deal with the higher caseloads that would inevitably ensue as a result of the stricter laws. A cynic might speculate that the promise of these new judgeships helped to entice some of the members of the state legislature who were lawyers to adopt these new laws (Collier & Horowitz, 1976).

On October 27, 1970, Congress passed the comprehensive *Drug Abuse Prevention and Control Act*, which replaced more than 50 pieces of drug legislation created since 1914. Title II of the Act, known as the *Controlled Substances Act*, gave Congress the authority to regulate interstate commerce for drugs. It also established five schedules that classify controlled substances according to their potential for abuse. Drugs were placed into categories according to how dangerous they were, how great their potential for abuse, and whether they have any legitimate medical value. During this period, BNDD's budget more than quadrupled. Its agent force grew to 1,361 by February 1972, and its foreign and domestic arrest totals doubled. In addition, BNDD had regulatory control over more than 500,000 registrants licensed to distribute legal drugs. Furthermore, it had established six of the most up-to-date forensic laboratories in the world ("DEA Briefing Book." 1998).

Finally, the Drug Enforcement Administration (DEA) was formally created on July 1, 1973 within the Department of Justice. Its establishment was spurred by the growth of cocaine processing in South America and heroin refining in Southeast Asia. The activities of the BNDD, the Office of the Drug Abuse Law Enforcement, and the Office of National Narcotics Intelligence were absorbed under the newly created DEA. Nixon had created the latter two offices for assistance in fighting the drug war. Thus, in 1973, just a year prior to his sensational resignation from office, Nixon merged the BNDD with his two new special offices in order to form the Drug Enforcement Administration (DEA). The intended purpose for these changes was to unify drug investigations, to create a single federal drug intelligence data base, and to establish clear liaison between federal drug agents and their state and local, as well as foreign, counterparts. However, while all these plans were initiated, the work of the U.S. Customs Service, FBI and Coast Guard remained separate ("DEA Briefing Book," 1998). The official genealogy of the DEA is depicted in *Table 11.1* and its table of organization is presented in *Table 11.2*. A summary of the current role of eleven different federal agencies concerned with narcotics control in the United States, including the DEA, is found in Appendix B.

In 1982, the FBI was specifically granted concurrent jurisdiction with the DEA in the field of drug enforcement. Moreover, the DEA director was obligated to report to the FBI director. According to Buck Revell, the former associate director of the FBI in charge of investigations and a 30-year veteran of that agency, President Reagan had actually proposed the merger of the DEA and the FBI in the early part of 1982. The intent to consolidate the two agencies was officially announced by Attorney General William French Smith and his Associate Attorney General, Rudy Giuliani. In fact, although at that time two high ranking FBI agents were assigned to the posts of acting DEA administrator (Bud Mullen) and deputy administrator (Jack Lawn), the merger was never completed because of resistance by DEA officials and for other bureaucratic reasons. The process was further complicated by the difficulties Bud Mullen had in obtaining Senate confirmation as the DEA's permanent director and his decision to give up his position after only one year as Administrator (Revell & Williams, 1998).

Table 11.1
DEA GENEALOGY

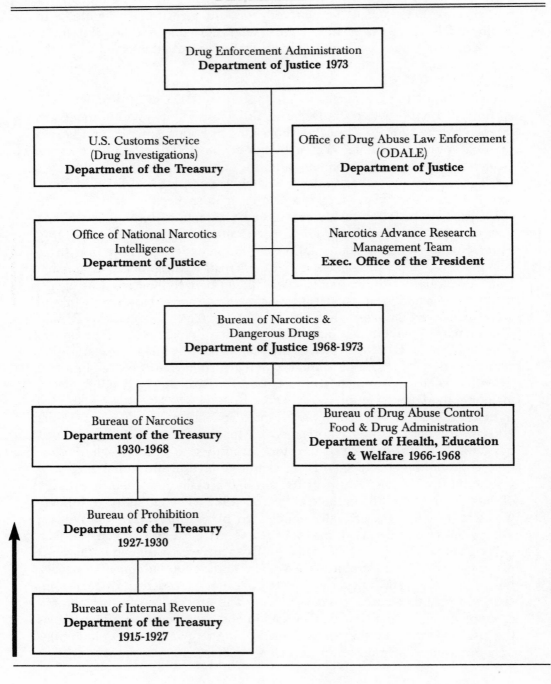

Drug Enforcement Administration
Department of Justice 1973

U.S. Customs Service
(Drug Investigations)
Department of the Treasury

Office of Drug Abuse Law Enforcement
(ODALE)
Department of Justice

Office of National Narcotics
Intelligence
Department of Justice

Narcotics Advance Research
Management Team
Exec. Office of the President

Bureau of Narcotics &
Dangerous Drugs
Department of Justice 1968-1973

Bureau of Narcotics
**Department of the Treasury
1930-1968**

Bureau of Drug Abuse Control
Food & Drug Administration
**Department of Health, Education
& Welfare 1966-1968**

Bureau of Prohibition
**Department of the Treasury
1927-1930**

Bureau of Internal Revenue
**Department of the Treasury
1915-1927**

Table 11.2
DEA ORGANIZATIONAL CHART

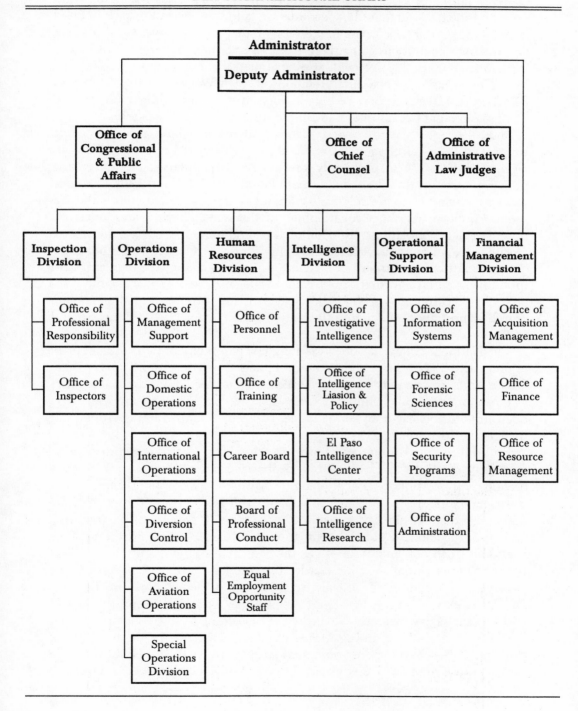

In 1988, after six years of effort, Ed Meese, Reagan's new Attorney General announced that the plan to merge the two agencies was being withdrawn. Revell stated that the consolidation failed because of a "lack of good faith on the part of Jack Lawn, inattention on the part of Webster and Mullen, and my own inability to bring them together and make it happen" (Revell & Williams, 1998, p. 224). Revell also attributed this outcome to the fact that Meese may have had a strained relationship with Webster. During that era, FBI Director Webster had received much greater favorable publicity and Congressional approval than had Meese (Revell & Williams, 1998, p. 224).

Since 1971, the armed services of the United States have provided some support to the federal agencies responsible for drug interdiction. *The Posse Comitatus Act of 1876* specifically prohibited the military from exercising police powers on the U.S. civilian population. In 1982, the *Posse Comitatus Act* was amended to permit state and local law enforcement officials to request military assistance for training, intelligence gathering, and investigation of drug law violations. In addition, the amendment provided for the use of military equipment to enforce drug laws. In 1989, Congress enacted a law designating the Department of Defense as the lead agency for detecting and monitoring aerial and maritime transit of illegal drugs. However, the military is still prohibited from making arrests and from conducting civilian searches throughout the nation (Bureau of Justice Statistics, 1992, pp. 86 and 143).

The National Guard has been assisting law enforcement in its drug control efforts since 1977. Since state governors usually have authority over State Guard units, restrictions on its use at the state and local level are not as strict as those for the regular military branches. However, their assistance has also been limited to providing surveillance, equipment, and training (Bureau of Justice Statistics, 1992, p. 143).

Both Presidents Reagan and Bush provided increased funding for supply-side control efforts. Such measures emphasized law enforcement and interdiction over prevention, education, and treatment. The latter measures comprise the demand-side of drug use reduction efforts. During this period, the demand reduction efforts received no more than 30 percent of the total federal antidrug budget. At the time of the Reagan administration, Vice President Bush personally served as the chairman of the South Florida Task Force of the National Narcotic Border Interdiction System. This Task Force consisted of hundreds of officials from the Coast Guard, Customs Service, and DEA as well as representatives from other divisions within the Justice and Treasury Departments. Nevertheless, according to studies conducted by the U.S. General Accounting Office (GAO) during the 1980s, the flow of drugs into the United States remained steady. In 1991, the GAO reported that no more than one percent of the total of illegal drug imports had been interdicted (Falco, 1992, pp. 3-5). Currently, the U.S. Customs Service has estimated that the flow of drugs has been halted by 10 to 20 percent, but privately, "some border agents put the figure as low as 2 or 3 percent" (Johnson, 1998, p. 3).

By the mid-1980s the political rhetoric regarding substance abuse had clearly reached a new high. Congressman Henry Hyde called for the firing squad in those cases where narcotics agents were implicated in drug trafficking. Future presidential candidate, Patrick Buchanan, the well-known co-host of the CNN talkshow "Crossfire," stated that he favored the execution by hanging of those drug traffickers who sold illegal drugs to children (Trebach, 1987, pp. 131-132). Several months after his CNN comments, Buchanan became the director of communications for President Reagan. In 1999, Congressman Hyde was head of the powerful House Judiciary Committee and the leader of the prosecution team that tried President Clinton in the Senate after his impeachment by the House. In 1986, President Reagan and other leading White House officials volunteered to take urine tests to set an example for the nation. Various candidates for local and national office quickly adopted the idea. The media's attention to the drug problem also reached zenith levels. During the summer of 1986, news reports indicated that at least four children had reported their parents to the police for using drugs (Trebach, 1987, p. 135).

Today, the DEA is in the forefront of America's longest war thanks in large part to the Reagan and Bush years. In 1995, its special enforcement agents were in fifty different countries seeking to arrest narcotic traffickers and producers (Booth, 1996, pp. 206-207). In that same year, the DEA's asset forfeiture program was responsible for the seizure of property worth more than $645 million. In order to qualify for seizure, an asset must be determined to be a tool for, or the proceeds of, illegal activities such as drug trafficking, organized crime, and money laundering ("DEA Briefing Book," 1998). Interdiction spending has more than doubled since 1979, but for all this effort the street price of a gram of cocaine has decreased eightfold over the same period. Furthermore, more than 60 percent of the estimated 300 tons of cocaine that enter the United States each year are believed to pass through the US-Mexican border. Moreover, it was reported that the interdiction missions of the DEA, FBI, Immigration and Naturalization Service, U.S. Customs, and others were being hampered by poor communication and interagency turf wars (Johnson, 1998, p. 3).

Before considering a selected group of America's current initiatives in prohibition enforcement (to be discussed in the remaining chapters), it is, perhaps, useful to pause in order to consider a few other historical ironies and oddities that occurred in the years just prior to the creation of the DEA.

For example, in the mid-1950s, Robert F. Kennedy used to visit the FBN at its New York City headquarters located at 90 Church Street in lower

Manhattan. According to statements made by attorney Howard J. Diller to author David Heymann: "In the Federal Bureau of Narcotics, Bobby discovered a kind of fantasy existence that enabled him to escape the vagaries of his humdrum workaday life.... He'd enjoy the company of agents. They were tough, they drank, they played around—he thought he was like that, too" (Heymann, 1998, pp. 98 & 100). Diller was an agent in the FBN for five years (Margolick, 1989). Kennedy was the chief counsel of the Senate's Subcommittee for Investigations during the 1950s, also known as the McLellan Committee. He later became the Attorney General of the United States when his brother, John F. Kennedy was elected president. In 1968, five years after John F. Kennedy's assassination, Robert Kennedy was assassinated when he was a U.S. Senator from New York State and a promising presidential candidate.

In 1963, the same year that John F. Kennedy was slain in Dallas, Mabel Walker Willebrandt died at the age of 73 from cancer. Willebrandt was known as the "Prohibition Portia," because of her staunch efforts on behalf of the 18th Amendment. She served as Assistant Attorney General for eight years beginning in 1921 when she was placed in charge of all cases involving federal tax law violations as well as the enforcement of the 18th Amendment. Her duties also included the supervision of the Bureau of Federal Prisons. She was the first woman to hold a permanent appointment as an Assistant Attorney General of the United States. Willebrandt and former Labor Secretary Frances Perkins were the first two women to attain cabinet or sub-cabinet rank in the federal government. In order to gain legal experience prior to her federal appointment, Willebrandt worked as a public defender without receiving any salary in more than 2,000 cases. It was New York's Governor Alfred E. Smith who first referred to her as "that Prohibition Portia" during his 1928 presidential campaign. She was so eloquent in her speeches on behalf of the election of President Herbert Hoover that Smith singled her out for special attention ("Mabel Walker Willibrandt Dies," *New York Times*, April 9, 1963, p. 31).

In June 1971, President Nixon announced a new war on drugs in a televised speech. The BNDD and U.S. Customs received substantial budgetary increases. Many famous celebrities including Elvis Presley enlisted in the campaign. Currently, the National Archives maintains a website that features numerous photos of Presley meeting Nixon in the oval office of the White House (Illustrations 11.1 and 11.2). Later, Presley, ended a highly successful performing career as a result of a drug overdose. The DEA was only in its first season when Gerald Ford became president of the United States on August 9, 1974. One month after taking office, Ford granted Nixon a "full, free and absolute pardon" for all crimes he had committed against the United States during his term in office (Blum, 1991, p. 474).

Illustration 11-1. Elvis Presley met President Nixon in the Oval Office of the White House on December 21, 1970. In this photo, the famous rock singer is holding law enforcement badges awarded to him, and photographs of his wife and child. Photo courtesy of the National Archives and Records Administration.

Illustration 11-2. President Nixon and Presley pose for historic photograph in front of the military service flags in the Oval Office. Photo courtesy of the National Archives and Records Administration.

Perhaps, the greatest irony regarding the period relates to the legacy of the punitive Rockefeller drug laws of 1973. During the past ten years, the costs of imprisonment in New York have doubled and there is little relief in sight. In 1997, 47 percent of the inmates entering New York's prisons were there for drug crimes, whereas in 1980, the figure was only 11 percent. Moreover, 90 percent of these new inmates are either black or Hispanic. In response to the position that these laws helped to lower crime rates in recent years, John Klofas, chairman of the Criminal Justice Department at Rochester Institute of Technology, has pointed out that crime rates have varied erratically during the past 25 years. For example, they greatly increased during the crack epidemic of the 1980s. New York's Chief Judge, Judith Kaye has called for the laws to be revamped because they "have proven less than effective" (Craig, 1998, p. E5). In 1998, an editorial in the *Times Union* (Albany, NY) after weighing aspects of the legacy of the Rockefeller era, called upon state legislators to draw a sharper distinction between prison terms for pushers and addicts ("Punishment and Treatment," March 25, 1998, p. A8). It is also useful to point out that President Ronald Reagan's own Commission on Organized Crime, after a three-year study, indicated that reducing demand for drugs was an essential priority of government and that it could best be accomplished through the establishment of a rational system of sentencing for drug offenses. Among the many recommendations made by the Commission was that "such a system should provide a sentence of probation and a fine for a first offense involving mere possession of drugs. The terms of probation should include a requirement to remain drug-free, to be verified, if necessary through periodic drug testing" (President's Commission on Organized Crime, hereinafter cited as PCOC, 1986, p. 485).

The President's Commission on Organized Crime

The Commission on Organized Crime was established by Executive Order 12435 on July 28, 1983. The Commission was headed by Federal Court Judge Irving R. Kaufman and charged with making a full and complete national and regional analysis of organized crime together with recommendations which could be undertaken to improve law enforcement efforts directed against organized crime. The Commission was authorized to issue appropriate subpoenas for the testimony of witnesses and to obtain and disclose electronic surveillance data that had been previously gathered by law enforcement agencies. It's most important finding was that "drug trafficking and abuse together constitute the single most serious organized crime issue confronting this Nation" (PCOC, 1986, p. 3).

In view of this major finding, the Commission urged state governments to adopt various laws modeled after the following federal statutes, if they had not already done so:

1. *The Bail Reform Act of 1984;*
2. *The Racketeer Influenced and Corrupt Organizations Act;*
3. *The Continuing Criminal Enterprise Law;*
4. *Title III of the Omnibus Crime Control and Safe Streets Act of 1968;* and
5. *The Currency and Foreign Transactions Act.*

In addition, the Commission recommended that, where appropriate, states consider "statutory use and derivative use immunity" for witnesses as well as the adoption of statewide grand juries (PCOC, 1986, pp. 411-412). In particular, the Commission urged state and local law enforcement agencies to vigorously enforce the laws prohibiting possession of drugs. It noted that states could fund this effort by implementing effective asset forfeiture programs (PCOC, 1986, p. 485). The Commission struck a realistic chord when it pointed out that "although the drug problem is a national one, its immediate effects are felt most at State and local levels. To respond effectively to the drug problem, State and local jurisdictions will have to increase expenditures for such critical resources as prison facilities, increased manpower, and sophisticated equipment" (PCOC, 1986, p. 479).

The involvement of the U.S. Coast Guard was cited in three specific recommendations. These included: (1) evaluating the expanded use of Coast Guard aviation capabilities in drug interdiction; (2) the establishment of user fees as a means to supplement the Coast Guard's budget; and (3) the expansion of Navy assistance to Coast Guard interdiction efforts, whenever and wherever possible (PCOC, 1986, p. 467).

Media Hype, Censorship and Mistakes

The public's knowledge about drugs is very much influenced by what it hears and sees. In August 1989, President George Bush devoted his very first national televised address to one single issue. He used the phrase "war on drugs" and for the next several months the media featured many reports and editorials that included this imagery. Of course, previous leaders had also used similar rhetoric to declare wars on poverty and illiteracy. Moreover, almost every aspect of prohibition enforcement during the 1920s and the earlier temperance drives in various states had its declarations of war. As a rhetorical device, the theme of war may present a powerful message that can serve to promote social cohesion by binding together the masses against a common enemy. However, according to Dwight Heath, a Brown University professor of anthropology, Bush purposefully used this bellicose language in order to "recast himself as a 'tough guy' who identified a major threat, announced a firm stand, and promised to take forceful action" (Heath, 1992, p. 269). One direct consequence of such an approach is that it tends to add support for drug control policies that involve more show than substance. Thus, it is more exciting to hear about foreign and domestic interdictions (arrests and seizures), than news about the need for treatment and more drug abuse education programs. Similarly, the speechmaker who uses such phrases as "zero tolerance" and "a drug free society" is bound to earn a round of applause, since such terminology sounds a lot more forceful than calling for a "needle exchange."

Throughout the last decade of the twentieth century various surveys showed how for many years the use of drugs (legal and illegal) had been glamorized in movies, recordings, television, and ads. By the end of the century, the only advertisements that seemed to be appearing with any regularity in the media had to do with benefits and side effects of over-the-counter and prescription medicines. Other types of commercials had been banned, either through the settlement of lawsuits or by the introduction of new rules. In addition, the television and movie industries had undertaken self-censorship to reduce the visual portrayal of drug use in their productions.

Even documentary style programs were caught-up in this exercise in "political correctness." For example, in 1998, Anheuser-Busch had sponsored the production of a 30-minute show entitled "An American History of Beer." The program was scheduled to be shown for two consecutive days in mid-July of 1998 on The Learning Channel. Instead, the head of Discovery Networks decided that it should not run, thereby overruling The Learning Channel's vice president in charge of programming. The only direct hint at advertising that would have appeared in the production was an opening message from the chairman and CEO of Anheuser-Busch and the Budweiser logo. The logo shows a black-and-white photo of men posing next to barrels of beer.

About a year earlier, the well-known and acclaimed CBS program "60 Minutes" featured a special documentary film entitled "The Connection." The program was broadcast over satellite television channels throughout the world. The film had dramatic footage of a drug "mule" said to be carrying millions of dollars worth of heroin to London for Columbia's Cali drug cartel. The special documentary won eight journalism awards, including three from the United States. In December of 1998, a panel of media experts concluded that the film was a fake. In particular, it was pointed out that actors had been paid to portray drug dealers and the producer's hotel room had been decorated to look like a drug kingpin's jungle hideout. The production company that made the film, Carlton Communications, said it would return the awards and refund the fees it received from the networks that bought the program (Reid, 1998). In 1981, Janet Cooke, a *Washington Post* reporter, won a Pulitzer Prize for her story entitled an "8-Year-Old Heroin Addict Lives for a Fix." It was later learned that she had written an entirely fictional story and that the prestigious award would be returned (Szasz, 1987).

As earlier chapters have attempted to indicate, the use of censorship as well as the publication and widespread dissemination of false or misleading stories related to the drug problem did not begin in the twentieth century. On the contrary, they have roots in the propaganda campaigns of the prohibitionists of many different eras. For example, in the nineteenth century the famous painting of George Washington, glass in hand, celebrating the founding of the United States was altered. The glass was removed and the decanter on the table was placed under a hat! (Sournia, 1990, p. 121). In the future, it can be expected that media mistakes, whether they are intentional or accidental, will likely occur due to an overzealous regard for keeping pace with the intensification of governmental enforcement initiatives.

The following chapter deals with the here and now of prohibition enforcement. It emphasizes the current policies and practices that are being used to control drug abuse.

ENDNOTE

1. Excerpted from *Title II, sec. 509, of the Comprehensive Drug Abuse Prevention and Control Act of 1970.*

Chapter 12

CURRENT ENFORCEMENT STRATEGIES

"The easiest thing to do is make an arrest. The hardest
thing is to stop it. Enforcement will never stop it."[1]

CHIEF JOHN HILL, NEW YORK CITY POLICE
NARCOTICS DIVISION

This chapter highlights some of the approaches currently being used to address the nation's drug problem, some of which have been characterized by both media and police as involving "zero tolerance" attributes. Special emphasis is provided to several of the initiatives featured in the *1998 National Drug Control Strategy*. In addition, the Drug Enforcement Administrations (DEA) response to the recent upsurge of methamphetamine trafficking and abuse is addressed.

Chapter 13 entitled "The Enforcement Debate" highlights various aspects of drug enforcement policy and the final chapter presents recommendations for a united approach to prohibition enforcement.

The Community Prosecution Program (CPP)

On June 3, 1996, the U.S. Attorney for the District Columbia, Eric Holder Jr. inaugurated a Community Prosecution Section within his office. In 1998, Holder became a U. S. Deputy Attorney General. The project targeted the District of Columbia's (D.C.) Metropolitan Police Department's Fifth District in the northeast corner of the city, an area known for its high levels of violence and drug trafficking. Seventeen assistant U.S. attorneys were specifically assigned to handling the arrests of persons within the Fifth Police District, while two additional assistant U.S. attorneys were posted to work within the Fifth District's police station. These two federal prosecutors began their duties by joining in routine police patrols and making inquiries about how they could be of assistance. In addition, they regularly attended community meetings as did the leaders and other members of the new Community Prosecution Section (Swope, 1998).

The federal prosecutors learned firsthand about the fears of community residents and most particularly, their concern for quality of life issues. The prosecutors discovered that members of the community viewed marijuana possession and sale as serious problems and they personally received hundreds of complaints concerning other types of drug dealing. In response, the members of the Community Prosecution Section began working with patrol officers and investigators as well as initiating roll call training which focused on arrest, search and seizure procedures. The roll call sessions were held around the clock (e.g., at 6 A.M., 2 P.M. and 10 P.M.). In addition, police officers have been afforded an opportunity to meet in the station with prosecutors to review arrest and search warrant applications, rather than having to travel downtown. Closer relationships between the prosecutorial staff and the police have resulted and new ideas have been generated. For example, prosecutors now request that suspects released to the community after arraignment be directed to stay out of the patrol beat where they were arrested. This procedure makes it harder for drug dealers to return to the same neighborhoods where they feel most comfortable and if they live in such a neighborhood a curfew is recommended as a condition of release. Furthermore, an effort is being made to have residents in drug-infested areas provide either oral or written victim-impact statements during the sentencing process. Thus, the sentencing judge will have a more precise view of an offender's behavior in the community (Swope, 1998).

In May of 1998, there were plans to expand the program to all seven of the District of Columbia's police districts. Metro Police Captain Ross Swope considers the Community Prosecution Section project to have engendered a level of commitment and cooperation among the police, prosecutors and the community that previously had not existed. He also feels that the two recent initiatives by the community prosecutors dealing with conditions of release and victim-impact statements "have tremendous potential" (Swope, 1998, p. 14).

In Boston, a similar community prosecution project has been initiated and incorporated into a wider program generally known as the "Comprehensive Communities Program". The federal government through its Bureau of Justice Assistance within the Office of Justice Programs of the U.S. Department of Justice, was responsible for initiating the CPP concept. The idea involves integrating law enforcement, social programs, other agencies and individuals in order to control crime and improve the quality of neighborhood life. A major stimulus for its development was the crack epidemic and deteriorating urban conditions taking place in the early 1990s. Its two basic principles are:

1. Communities must take a leadership role in developing partnerships to combat crime and violence; and

2. State and local jurisdictions must establish truly coordinated and multidisciplinary approaches to address the problems related to crime and violence and the conditions that foster them (Kelling, et. al., 1998, p. 1).

Boston's CPP involves intensive efforts to decentralize neighborhood planning in order to bring about community policing and community mobilization. In addition to these specific efforts as well as its community prosecution program, a drug court and two service provider networks were created to change the way services were delivered to youth and offenders in certain areas of Boston. The provider networks involve alternatives to incarceration for juvenile and young adult offenders and the creation of a partnership between the Boston Police Department and the local Boys and Girls Clubs. The latter network is responsible for placing club social workers in a police station in order to help identify and refer troubled youths to the Boys and Girls Clubs or other appropriate agencies (Kelling, et. al., 1998, p. 6).

In all, the federal government has sponsored CPP initiatives in 16 different cities. Intensive evaluations of six of these sites have already been completed. These sites include: Baltimore; Boston; Fort Worth; Salt Lake City; Seattle; and Columbia, South Carolina. The assessment concluded that in each of these target sites, partnerships have been formed and are broader than one would have expected. In particular, the evaluators found that in Baltimore, trash has been removed, crack houses have been shut, and properties have been put into receivership to be managed on behalf of neighborhoods. Associations are being formed to help renters buy homes in Baltimore neighborhoods that were formally abandoned. In Columbia, police can now park their patrol cars in public housing developments without fear of vandalism and in Salt Lake City and Forth Worth, residents are asking for a say in local government and an opportunity to voice their opinions about local problems.

However, while most sites simply channeled CPP funding to their preexisting drug courts or to ones that were already in the planning stages, Baltimore was able to create new support services (e.g., supervision of community work) for its drug court clients (Kelling, et. al., 1998, p. 9).

The main feature of Salt Lake City's CPP was the creation of Community Action Teams (CATS). Each CAT is a neighborhood-based, problem-solving team comprising a community-oriented police officer, a probation officer, a city prosecutor, a community mobilization specialist, and a community relations coordinator. Community representatives were invited to participate in the CAT on an as-needed basis to help with specific problems. Its CPP was administered out of the mayor's office and a new Pre-Probation Program in the Juvenile Court was developed (Kelling, et. al., 1998, p. 6).

Other federally sponsored anticrime programs that included elements of comprehensiveness and community involvement in the 1990s were:

"Operation Weed and Seed"; "Pulling America's Communities Together" (PACT); and "Safe Futures." The overall strategy of each of these initiatives is that public-private partnerships are preferable to "big government" solutions because they leverage resources and encourage tailoring programs to local conditions. Their underlying assumptions are that: people in trouble tend to have multiple problems; fragmented services waste resources; prevention may be a cost-effective alternative to punishment; and that large building projects (e.g., new prisons) are insufficient to solve social problems (Kelling, et. al., 1998, p. 1).

Drug Courts

Across the nation, drug courts have been established to offer drug addicts a chance to receive help and turn their lives around. In the past, surveys have indicated that defendants who have been convicted of drug possession typically commit a similar offense within 2 to 3 years. However, recidivism among all drug court participants has ranged between 5 and 28 percent and less than 4 percent for persons who have successfully completed a rehabilitation program. Savings have been achieved when participants who came into the program unemployed and on public assistance obtained employment during the course of their treatment. Rockland County, New York instituted a drug court system in 1998 after a two-year planning period. If a person is arrested for possession of drugs, the drug court judge has the ability to refer the drug abuser to a 12-step rehabilitation program instead of a jail sentence. Abusers can obtain free counseling and treatment that they could not otherwise afford. Moreover, participants who complete court-mandated treatment may have their charges dismissed. On the other hand, participants who fail to follow program guidelines can have their cases transferred to the regular criminal courts for prosecution. The average cost for treatment ranges between $1,200 and $3,000, depending upon the types of services provided. It is expected that the program will result in the following savings: reduced police overtime; reduced witness costs; less jury expenses; reduced caseloads for criminal court judges; and less medical expenses for the care of drug addicted infants (Keeperman, 1998).

One of the nation's first drug courts opened in Miami in 1989.[2] Subsequently, in addition to Rockland County, New York, such courts have opened in such major metropolitan areas as Denver and the District of Columbia. In 1997, approximately twenty thousand defendants appeared before the nation's 215 drug courts and many more such courts were in the planning stages. Moreover, in the summer of 1998, federal funds amounting to $27 million were slated to go to more than 150 jurisdictions in order to create drug courts. Separate drug courts have been designed for juveniles, women and drunk drivers. However, the fundamental characteristics of such courts are that they serve nonviolent drug-law offenders and direct them into tough, court-supervised treatment programs instead of prisons or jails. On average, over 70 percent of drug-court participants stay in treatment. In 1997, the National Drug Court Institute was established in order to provide training for judges and support staff ("The National Drug Control Strategy, 1998," p. 37).

In 1994, the Bureau of Justice Assistance within the U.S. Department of Justice published an overview of the use of drug night courts in Cook County, Illinois. The drug night court program was begun as an emergency measure to cope with rapidly expanding caseloads. By the end of 1990, the Cook County Circuit Court had established eight trial parts which operated in the evening to process narcotics cases. The study concluded that the use of special night courts could dramatically cut processing time for drug cases. In 1990, the night courts disposed of almost double the number of cases than had been originally anticipated. On the other hand, more lenient sentencing, more pleas, and a decrease in the use of private attorneys accompanied such economies. The private attorneys appeared in fewer night cases because many of them were also working in the day courts. In their place, public defenders were used. Randolph Stone, a University of Chicago law professor who was the Public Defender for Cook County when the drug night courts began, has opposed the concept of drug night courts for the following reasons:

> First, it is another Band Aid or quick-fix approach to a fundamental problem in the criminal justice system, namely the absence of adequate and balanced funding. Second, drug night courts enhance the sense of "apartheid" in our legal system. Third, the segregation of drug cases encourages judges, prosecutors, and defenders to dehumanize the accused citizen in their efforts to dispose of cases. (*Drug Night Courts*, 1994, pp. 3-4)

These are stinging criticisms. The fact that they were contained in a government report is, however, heartening. It indicates that an effort is being made to learn the truth about new programs. When a court system becomes so overworked that it merely resembles a production line and follow-up services are not provided for probationers, it can hardly be considered a model for other jurisdictions to follow.

Juvenile drug courts have also been established. In a typical juvenile drug court program, youth who meet certain eligibility requirements are offered the option of participating in the program instead of traditional case processing. Such requirements usually include indications that the juvenile has a substance abuse problem and has not engaged in violent behavior. The judge maintains close oversight of each juvenile by scheduling progress meetings with the juvenile and other family members. Both the young person and family members are required to participate in an intensive treatment program. The heart of the juvenile drug court is a drug court team, which works together to foster successful treatment. Team members include: the judge, prosecutor, public defender, treatment provider, probation officer and other agency personnel who may be needed depending upon the nature of the particular case (Kimbrough, 1998, pp. 11-12).

In most cases, the inclusion of a citizen's role in the work of these types of courts has been omitted. Chapter 14 revisits the potential of drug courts and suggests a way to undo this oversight.

Anti-Tobacco Strategies

At the end of the twentieth century, local jurisdictions and the federal government were concerned not only about the traditional hazards involving drug abuse, but also about teen drinkers and smokers. Teen smoking was high on President Clinton's agenda and the U.S. Surgeon General had pointed out that cocaine use was thirty times more likely to occur among smokers than nonsmokers. In 1998, Utah's Third Judicial District developed a Tobacco Court through the pioneering efforts of Juvenile Court Judge Joseph Anderson. The Tobacco Court, the first of its kind in the nation, works out of the Small Claims Court with volunteer judges. They have the authority to levy fines as much as $250, require community service, and send youthful smokers to a special education program. The educational program is called "Stop Teen Smoking" and is one of the few substance abuse programs that concentrate exclusively on smoking. The program reinforces healthy choices through activities and is heavily reliant on parental participation. If teens resist the efforts of the court, they can have their driving privileges suspended (Biele, 1998). Several federal agencies are also involved in increasing awareness among youth of the dangers of tobacco use. In particular, the Food and Drug Administration (FDA) has oversight responsibilities for enforcing regulations that reduce youth access to cigarettes and smokeless tobacco products and the Centers for Disease Control and Prevention carries out the "Research to Classrooms" project to identify and expand school-based tobacco-prevention efforts ("The National Drug Control Strategy, 1998," p. 34).

Underage Drinking Enforcement

Prohibition enforcement efforts directed at underage drinking has taken on new significance due to the fact that more teens die in alcohol-related motor vehicle accidents than from any other cause. Alcohol abuse is also implicated in other types of teenage fatalities including drownings and suicides. In addition to conducting drunk driving patrols and sobriety check-points, the most common strategies used by local police to control teenage drinking include: undercover stings, "Cops 'N Shops," party patrols, and walk-throughs (Little & Bishop, 1998).

An undercover sting typically involves the use of a paid or volunteer minor who attempts to buy alcohol from retail stores and other businesses where alcoholic beverages are sold. Authorities in Alabama have success-fully used sting operations to limit sales to underage consumers. The Cops 'N Shops program involves officers posing as employees or customers in and around shops in order to arrest any underage buyers or persons who may make purchases on behalf of minors. The program also includes the use of signs in shops announcing the existence of the program. Party patrols involve officers attending parties where alcohol is likely to be given to minors or merely patrolling nearby. Walk-throughs are similar to party patrols in that officers may either covertly or overtly visit establishments where alcohol may be sold to minors. Police need to consider the applica-ble administrative and constitutional criminal procedural rules when they conduct either party patrols or walk-throughs without a previously obtained search warrant (Little & Bishop, 1998).

The Office of Juvenile Justice and Delinquency Prevention (OJJDP), a division of the U.S. Department of Justice, has produced a guide to assist states in dealing with underage drinking. The guide contains materials on promising approaches, descriptions of current initiatives, lists of relevant agencies, and an annotated bibliography. The document is entitled *Combating Underage Drinking: A Compendium of Resources* and is available through OJJDP's Web sit at www.ncjrs.org/ojjdp/underage/. Over the years, OJJDP has awarded millions of dollars to jurisdictions and agencies that have demonstrated innovative ideas for addressing underage drinking.

Community Policing

The concept of community policing owes its modern usage to the work of Herman Goldstein (1990) who developed "a problem-oriented" approach to law enforcement. The basic tenets of problem or community-oriented polic-ing involves the identification of specific neighborhood problems, the devel-opment of a plan to address said problems as well as the implementation of the plan. Feedback is collected to fine-tune operations and above all, each phase of the process involves appropriate community representatives. The effectiveness of the police role in the process is measured in terms of the degree to which public cooperation and satisfaction with the resolution of their problems and concerns have been achieved. Since so much of the strat-egy involves communication with the public, this approach has come to be known simply as "community policing." Some police scholars have referred "to community policing as the philosophy and problem-oriented policing as an analytical tool to deal with the causes of crime" (Thibault, et. al., 1998, p. 211). In 1998, the executive office of the President of the United States specifically defined community policing as "an operational philosophy for neighborhood problem-solving in which officers interact with residents on an ongoing basis regarding matters of public concern" ("The National Drug Control Strategy, 1998," p. 35). Since its inception, police officials and policy analysts have varied in their views about whether community policing must involve all members of an agency or merely a part of an agency.

During the 1990s, many innovations in police work have been made under the banner of community policing. For example, during the 1990s neighborhood service teams were established in Garland, Texas. The team consisted of personnel from the police and fire departments, the planning department, housing and neighborhood services. Citizens were asked to identify problems. The residents of an apartment complex near an elementary school were concerned about drug activity. A 25 percent reduction in serious crime was achieved when the Garland Police Department and other team participants: adopted a zero-tolerance enforcement approach, enforced criminal trespass, evicted drug offenders, and code enforcement officials were recruited to assist in making certain that housing improvements were made (Thibault, et. al., 1998, p. 207).

Sherman (1989) has developed the term "hot spots" to refer to locations that make heavy demands on police due to repetitious calls for service. In Jersey City, New Jersey it was discovered that drug hot spots accounted for just 4.4 percent of the points on the city's map, but that 86 percent of the city's drug arrests involving sales were taking place at these locations. Conditions improved at some of these locations after police met with area residents and instituted close surveillance, foot patrols, and other forms of police presence. When targeting such hot spots, it is best to concentrate attention on a few locations in order to conserve police resources (Thibault, et. al., 1998, pp. 209-210).

Perhaps, the most well-known illustration of the community policing initiative for reducing drug-related crime has involved the fulfillment of a campaign pledge made by President Clinton. Under his administration, the U.S. Department of Justice has created the Community Oriented Policing Services Program (COPS). Its dramatic goal was to add a hundred thousand new police officers onto the streets in the towns and cities of America for the express purpose of reinforcing efforts to reduce drug-related crime and violence. In President Clinton's message that accompanied the submission of the *1998 National Drug Control Strategy to Congress,* he made reference to the COPS program and indicated that such efforts were "making a difference:

violent crime in America has dropped dramatically for 5 years in a row" (p. 3).

In 1995, Boston began to implement "Operation Ceasefire." The operation was designed to deter and control gang-related violence. The Boston Gun Project Working Group in accordance with the principles of problem-solving policing developed the plan. In 1997, "Operation Ceasefire," was an Innovations Government program award winner. The John F. Kennedy School of Government runs the awards program at Harvard University. Similar operations have been used in Lowell, Massachusetts and Minneapolis, Minnesota. Chapter 14 presents further details about this creative government initiative that helped to reduce the city's youth homicide problem.

In 1998, Mastrofski and his associates issued an interim report on community policing. They concluded that cooperation between the police and citizens created a feeling of security among neighborhood residents. It also showed that the police supervisor's role had changed from controlling officers to supporting them.

Drug Testing

Another strategy for dealing with drug enforcement concentrates on the police themselves. By the mid-1980s, the practice of testing police personnel for suspected use of illegal substances became commonplace. Although the practice is often considered an unwelcome invasion of personal privacy by police and their unions, the United States Supreme Court has upheld it. Drug testing for railroad workers after accidents and safety violations as well as for U.S. Customs officers assigned to law enforcement duties were upheld respectively in *Skinner v. Railway Labor Executives Association,* 109 S. Ct. 1402 (1989) and *National Treasury Employees Union v. VonRaab,* 109 S. Ct. 1384 (1989). In each case, the Court considered the deterrence value of drug testing and indicated that the employees had fair warning that the screening for drugs would be carried out. In a related case, the New York State Court of Appeals in 1988 upheld random, periodic drug screening for the members of the New York City Police Department's Organized Crime Control Bureau. Departmental policies vary regarding the consequences for testing positive. During the last two decades of the twentieth century, police departments throughout the country have developed the following types of drug screening programs:

1. Random testing for all personnel on a routine basis.
2. Mandatory testing for all preemployment applicants.
3. Testing for pre-service and in-service officers based on reasonable suspicion of illegal drug use or alcohol abuse.
4. Testing of officers seeking or undertaking sensitive assignments (e.g., nar-

cotics enforcement, organized crime, etc.).

5. Elective testing to prove abstinence. (Thibault, et. al., 1998, p. 299).

In 1986, in the case of *Caruso v. Ward*, the random testing of police officers in New York was barred. In 1985, drug testing based on reasonable suspicion that drug abuse had been or was occurring was upheld by the District of Columbia Court of Appeals in the case of *Turner v. Fraternal Order of Police*. The latest trend in drug-testing is to extend it to welfare recipients.

In 1997, the New York State Legislature authorized a substance abuse screening program for persons receiving financial assistance from the state. During the summer of 1998, procedures were developed to test all adult welfare recipients for possible drug and alcohol addiction. According to Jack Madden, a state official assigned to speak with the press about the program, the ultimate goal of the screening process is self-sufficiency for the welfare client. The plan calls for an initial statewide screening through a questionnaire and if that raises questions, welfare recipients will be required to attend an in-person substance abuse assessment to be conducted by certified counselors. The counselors will be empowered to order drug tests, if necessary. A rehabilitation program will be required for persons who are not able to meet their mandated work assignments because of their substance abuse problems. Significantly, welfare benefits will be terminated for persons who refuse to participate in the screening process and benefit levels reduced for their children who live at home (Stashenko, "Welfare Screening Program," *The Daily Gazette*, July 1998). One editorial described the new rules as reasonable and not Draconian, since it will give those who fail at treatment several chances before benefits are lost permanently. In particular, "it will also help to protect children and other household members by providing vouchers for such things as utilities and auto repairs—rather than cash for such things as whiskey and cocaine" ("OK to Screen for Addiction," *The Daily Gazette*, July 1998).

In addition, new federal laws have attempted to establish drug-free workplaces and schools. The *Federal Drug Free Workplace Act* requires all employers with federal contracts above $25,000 to certify that they will provide a drug-free workplace by undertaking the following steps:

1. providing publications and education about drug awareness;
2. requiring notification to the employer by the employee if he or she is arrested for violations occurring in the workplace;
3. requiring convicted employees to participate in a drug-abuse assistance or rehabilitation program; and
4. notifying employees of possible sanctions that might be taken against them by the company.

The *Drug Free Schools Act* states that financial aid provided by the federal government can be withheld from students convicted of drug violations.

FBI and DEA Initiatives

The two most well-known federal agencies involved in fighting drug abuse are the Federal Bureau of Investigation (FBI) and the Drug Enforcement Administration (DEA). Throughout most of its history, the FBI did not work drug cases because of J. Edgar Hoover's fear that exposure to illegal drugs might corrupt his agents (Kessler, 1993, p. 117). According to Buck Revell, formerly the FBI's special agent in charge of the Dallas office and the Bureau's associate deputy director of investigations, the DEA mainly goes after transactions, "whereas we go after an organization" and "we attempt to take out the hierarchy and obtain forfeitures of all their assets" (Kessler, 1993. p. 95). At the time of Revell's statement, the DEA had 3,500 agents working drug cases compared to 1,200 in the FBI. In addition to its participation in a variety of drug trafficking investigations, the FBI has also recognized the need to engage the community. For example, in 1988 it created the Drug Demand Reduction Program whereby agents talk about the dangers of drugs to community groups. Moreover, under a program called "Operations Safe Streets," minority agents and support staff from the District of Columbia office act as role models by tutoring elementary school students and taking them on field trips. In a Junior G-Man Program, weekly meetings are held in which law enforcement topics are discussed as well as the importance of taking responsibility for one's own actions (Kessler, 1993, pp. 119 & 353).

Under the leadership of former FBI Director Judge William Webster, the FBI began working drug cases in 1982 and narcotics enforcement became one of the FBI's priority programs in 1987. Since it made little sense to have two major federal law enforcement agencies leading the drug war, it was originally planned that the DEA would be merged into the FBI. However, all kinds of reasons have been offered to delay the plan over the ensuing years and the overlapping jurisdictions of the two agencies are still in existence (Kessler, 1993, pp. 117-118). Floyd I. Clarke, a former deputy director of the FBI, has expressed criticism over the amounts of time wasted on interagency conflicts (Kessler, 1993, p. 119).

During the 1990s considerable efforts were made to reduce jurisdictional conflicts and new DEA agents are currently trained at the FBI Academy in Quantico, Virginia. All DEA agents must submit to a urinalysis test designed to detect the presence of controlled substances (Schmalleger, 1997, p. 40). Louis Freeh, a former FBI special agent, federal prosecutor and judge was appointed to head the FBI in 1993. At the time of his appointment, President Clinton referred to him as a legend in law enforcement. As director he demonstrated an ability to embrace new technology, diversify his staff and undertook the difficult task of diffusing sister agency feuding by insisting upon cooperation and the sharing of resources. However, in recent years

Freeh and the FBI have been criticized for various types of mismanagement including the erroneous arrest of Richard Jewel for the Atlanta Olympic bombing incident and the slow reaction to correct FBI crime lab conditions after FBI chemist Frederic Whitehurst's revelations (Gibbs, 1997).

At the FBI Academy, the DEA operates a clandestine methamphetamine lab school commonly referred to as the "DEA Clan Lab School." Its purpose is to certify DEA special agents and other police investigators in how to safely gather evidence at such sites. Some of the hazards faced by police and other persons who enter into or near a clan lab are:

1. confrontations with violent meth cooks, under the influence of their product;
2. fire and explosion from flammable solvents and other chemicals;
3. inhalation of toxic vapors;
4. skin contact with chemicals; and
5. exposure to reactive chemicals.

With funding from the Office of National Drug Control Policy, the DEA has begun to provide clan lab certification training schools to state and local police officers. According to DEA Special Agent Michael Cashman, the investigation of clandestine methamphetamine labs "is one of the few instances where the evidence and the crime scene can hurt or even kill the investigator" (Cashman, 1998, p. 42).

Methamphetamine is inexpensive and relatively easy to manufacture. In many communities, its use has taken the place of crack cocaine. On the street, it is known as speed, crystal, crank or dope (Cashman, 1998). In 1998, the National Institute of Justice released a report on adult and juvenile arrests. It found that nearly 40 percent of adults arrested in San Diego during 1997 were using methamphetamines at the time of their arrests. Overall the study (based on more than 30,000 urine tests and interviews in 23 metropolitan areas) found that between 50 and 75 percent of arrested persons tested positive for drugs. The study indicated that methamphetamine use is spreading to rural communities (Chen, 1998).

The discovery and seizure of meth labs and related investigations have become a major activity of the DEA in recent years. For example, between January 1, 1994 and September 30, 1997, the DEA was involved in the detection and seizure of over 2,400 of these labs throughout the United States. State and local law-enforcement agencies, especially in California and Texas, were involved in thousands of additional lab seizures. Significantly, 98 percent of the seizures are methamphetamine labs. Clan labs contain highly toxic and flammable materials and chemicals. Police officers may encounter a lab unexpectedly during routine domestic violence calls or traffic stops, since they can be set-up in nearly any location; for example in private homes, apartments, motel rooms, storage lockers and even in recreational vehicles (Cashman, 1998). In one case, a woman in California was found guilty of second-degree murder "when her three children burned to death after her methamphetamine cooking process turned her mobile home into a toxic inferno" (Doane, 1998, p. 40). In Arizona in 1997, a four-year-old died in an apartment where his parents were preparing methamphetamines. One of the reasons for the resurgence in the production of this chemical may have to do with the Internet. "Now all a methamphetamine manufacturer has to do is turn on the computer, point and click to find a recipe, and point and click to find the chemicals. If the meth cook has any questions during the manufacturing process he can simply visit one of the...chat pages" (Cashman, 1998, p. 44).

In addition to the increasing amount of lab seizures by the DEA agents, arrests involving methamphetamine rose from 2,824 in 1995 to 4,341 in 1997. DEA has established special enforcement operations to target high-level meth traffickers as well as the rogue chemical companies that produce ephedrine, one of the chemicals needed to manufacture methamphetamine. On October 3, 1996, President Clinton signed into law the *Comprehensive Methamphetamine Control Act of 1996.* The law expands general controls over certain chemicals used to produce methamphetamine and establishes higher maximum penalties for the manufacture, import, export, possession or distribution of chemicals or equipment used in methamphetamine production. The law also permits courts to order those convicted under its provisions to pay the cost of cleanup of the illegal lab site (Doane, 1998).

The National Drug Control Strategy

In 1988, Congress passed the *Anti-Drug Abuse Act.* Its long-term purpose was the creation of a drug-free America. A key provision of the law was the establishment of the Office of National Drug Control Policy (ONDCP). The ONDCP was to set policies and oversee their implementation in the field of drug abuse prevention. Its directors were quickly labeled "Drug Czars" by the media and the very first person to hold this office was William Bennett. In 1989, Bennett described a belief that still serves as the basis for current thinking. He said "no single tactic—pursued alone... can work to contain or reduce use" and no "silver bullet" is available to solve the nation's drug-abuse problem. Throughout the 1990s annual reports were issued and each shared the commitment to maintain and enforce drug control laws ("The National Drug Control Strategy," 1998, pp. 2-3; hereinafter referred to as "The 1998 Strategy").

In the mid-1990s, executive orders assigned ONDCP responsibility within the executive branch for leading drug-control policy and established the ONDCP director as the President's chief spokesman for drug-control. The introduction to the federal government's *1998 National Drug Control Strategy* that was submitted to Congress and the people of the United States by President Clinton contained the following comment: "Drug abuse spawns global criminal syndicates and bankrolls those who sell drugs to young people. Illegal drugs indiscriminately destroy old and young, men and women from all racial and ethnic groups and every walk of life. No person or group is immune" ("The 1998 Strategy," p. 1). The document provided a ten-year plan to reduce drug use and its consequences. It claimed to be democratic, outcome-oriented, comprehensive, long-term, wide-ranging, realistic and based on scientific facts. It set forth five broad goals and thirty-two supporting objectives. These goals and objectives were originally set-forth in the *1996 Strategy* and concerned the following concepts: (1) the need for prevention and education to protect children from the dangers of drugs, alcohol and tobacco; (2) the provision of treatment to assist the chemically-dependent; (3) strengthening law enforcement to bring traffickers to justice as well as shielding America's frontiers from drugs; (4) undertaking international cooperation to confront drug cultivation, production, trafficking and use; and (5) the development of scientific research to reduce the supply of illegal drugs. In particular, it noted that the common phrase "war on drugs" was misleading. It stated that "cancer" was a more appropriate metaphor, since like drug abuse cancer is a long-term proposition. Moreover, drug control efforts require continuous energy and resolve whereas wars are expected to end as quickly as possible ("The 1998 Strategy," pp. 2-3).

An important objective of this strategy was improving the ability of High Intensity Drug Trafficking Areas (HIDTA) to counter drug trafficking. HIDTAs consist of regions with critical drug-trafficking problems that are detrimental to other areas of the United States. The ONDCP director in consultation with the Attorney General, heads of drug-control agencies, and state governors designates them. In 1998, there were seventeen such regions and their executive committees were composed of primarily local, state, and federal law enforcement officials. Some of the regions included: Los Angeles; San Francisco; Southeastern Michigan; Miami; Puerto Rico-U.S. Virgin Islands; and Washington-Baltimore. Their purposes were to assess regional drug threats, design strategies to address the threats, and develop integrated initiatives. Since their inception, they have helped to facilitate intelligence sharing and joint operations against trafficking organizations as well as to coordinate prevention and treatment initiatives in support of enforcement operations ("The 1998 Strategy," p. 35).

Another example of an effort to encourage a coordinated effort among law enforcement agencies cited in the *1998 Strategy* are the Organized Crime Drug Enforcement Task Forces (OCDETF) that were first initiated in 1982. These task forces target foreign and domestic trafficking organizations, money-laundering activities, gangs, and public corruption. A typical task force consists of special agents, attorneys, and support personnel from eleven federal agencies and participating state and local departments. In addition, the FBI has established 157 Safe Street Task Forces to address violent crime, most of which is drug-related. Furthermore, the Bureau of Alcohol, Tobacco, and Firearms (ATF) has targeted armed groups of traffickers through its Achilles Program which oversees twenty-one task forces in areas where drug-related violence is severe ("The 1998 Strategy," p. 36).

The federal government through its Department of Education also sponsors the Safe and Drug-Free Schools and Communities Program (SDFS). This initiative helps local school districts to provide various drug and violence-prevention programs. School-based prevention programs that are in widespread use include: the Hilton Foundation's Project Alert; Drug Abuse Resistance Education (D.A.R.E.); the University of California's Self-Management and Resistance Training (SMART); and LifeSkills. In addition, the National Guard has conducted prevention programs like Adopt-A-School and the ATF conducts Gang Resistance Education and Training (GREAT) in schools. Drug-prevention programs have also been sponsored by: the National Institute on Drug Abuse; the Substance Abuse and Mental Health Services Administration; the Center for Substance Abuse Prevention; the National Highway Traffic Safety Administration; the Centers for Disease Control and Prevention; the National Institute on Alcohol Abuse and Alcoholism; and the Office of the Justice Programs of the Department of Justice. Moreover, many civic groups (e.g., Mothers Against Drunk Driving and Students Against Destructive Decisions) and religious organizations have inaugurated programs dealing with substance abuse prevention and treatment ("The 1998 Strategy," pp. 32-34 & 36).

In 1998, the centerpiece of President Clinton's initiative to reduce youth drug use by 50 percent over a ten year period was the "National Youth Anti-Drug Media Campaign." In 1997, the Congress appropriated $195 million for the campaign. The entire campaign is budgeted at $2 billion to be spread over a five-year period. The program is to be funded equally by the federal government and by donations consisting of airtime and advertising space from media outlets throughout the country. Former House Speaker Newt Gingrich joined President Clinton in the announcement of the campaign and said that the rest of the federal funding would be made available. The objectives of this strategy are to discourage drug use by youth aged nine to seventeen through the creation of primarily television, radio and print media ads. While public health advocates suggested the campaign's funds could be better invested, some congressional Republicans said the money should be spent on more aggressive interdiction of drugs. The ads were designed to accurately depict drug use and its consequences and to encourage parents to communicate with their children about the hazards of drug use. For example, one television ad shows a female teenager wielding a frying pan and wildly smashing it into nearby objects. This is followed by the explanation that this is what drugs do to your brain. Another depicts a younger child recounting her mother's warnings not to play with matches. However, when she's asked whether her mother has warned her about drugs, she remains silent ("The 1998 Strategy," p. 31; Shogren, 1998).

The National Institute of Justice's study released in 1998 entitled "Report on Adult and Juvenile Arrests,î revealed both regional and generational differences in drug use. For example, cocaine use nationally was two to ten times more likely among males 36 or older than males between ages 15 and 20. Marijuana use was concentrated among youths. In addition, the use of methamphetamine surpassed cocaine and marijuana use among persons arrested in San Diego, a city that borders the nation of Mexico. Thus, drug enforcement is a complicated problem. According to Jeremy Travis, director of the National Institute of Justice, the research arm of the U.S. Department of Justice: "There is no single national drug problem. We have lots of different local drug problems" (Chen, 1998).

Drug enforcement is also an expensive phenomenon. The approximate federal budget for the *1998 National Drug Control Strategy* was $16 billion. The recommended approximate funding for 1999 is $17.1 billion, an increase of 6.8 percent or $1.1 billion over the level adopted in 1998. A summary of the drug control spending from 1996 and projected through the year 2003 is presented in Table 12.1. More precise amounts are presented in Table 12.2 beginning with the year 1998 and the amounts are displayed by federal department. Specific highlights of the increased budget requests for 1999 include: $50 million by the Department of Education to fund about 1,300 professional drug-prevention coordinators for America's 6,500 middle schools; $146 million by the Department of Heath and Human Services (HHS) for an anti-tobacco initiative that will target cigarette smoking for underage youth; $49.4 million to provide 200 new special agents for the DEA as well as 78 new support workers in order to control methamphetamine and heroin trafficking; 1,000 new Border Patrol agents and related equipment at a cost $163.2 million; $66.4 million for various high-tech non-intrusive inspection devices; and 32.8 million for additional U.S. Coast Guard patrol craft and equipment.

Current Role of U.S. Coast Guard

The U.S Coast Guard (USCG) is currently a division of the Department of Transportation. The Department of Transportation also includes among its organizations the National Highway Traffic Safety Administration and the

Prohibition Enforcement

Table 12.1
SUMMARY OF THE NATIONAL DRUG CONTROL BUDGET
FY 1996 – FY 2003

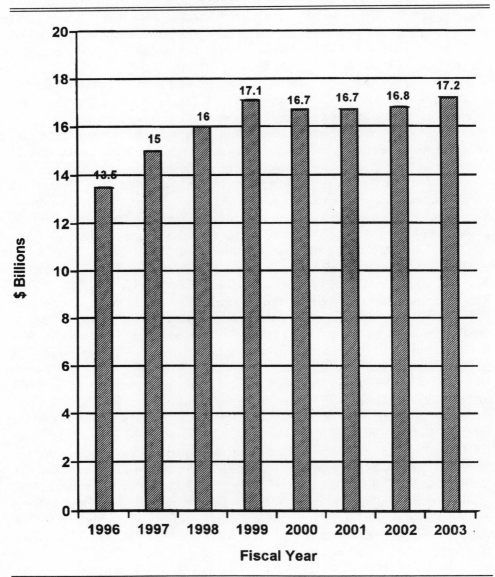

Source: The National Drug Control Strategy, 1998, p.55.

Table 12.2
PROPOSED DRUG SPENDING BY DEPARTMENT ($ MILLIONS)

DEPARTMENT	FY 98 EN-ACTED	FY 99 RE-QUEST	PLANNING LEVEL				% Change 98-03
			FY 00	FY01	FY02	FY03	
Defense	$ 847.7	$ 882.8	$ 870.0	$ 886.1	$896.2	$ 911.8	+8%
Education	685.3	739.7	741.7	743.9	746.1	748.5	+9%
HHS	2,522.5	2,812.9	2,812.9	2,812.9	2,812.9	2,812.9	+12%
Justice	7,260.5	7,670.0	7,317.3	7,234.8	7,242.5	7,443.5	+3%
ONDCP	428.2	449.4	449.4	449.4	449.4	449.4	+5%
State	211.5	256.5	263.5	270.5	278.5	286.5	+35%
Transportation	455.0	515.2	528.9	514.9	514.9	514.9	+13%
Treasury	1,327.9	1,388.1	1,317.0	1,322.9	1,337.2	1,359.2	+2%
Veterans Affairs	1,097.2	1,139.1	1,183.1	1,226.9	1,275.3	1,375.7	+25%
All Other	1,141.6	1,215.9	1,217.0	1,236.4	1,258.2	1,280.7	+12%
TOTAL	**15,977.4**	**17,069.8**	**16,700.9**	**16,698.8**	**16,811.3**	**17,183.2**	**+8%**

Source: The National Drug Control Strategy, 1998

Federal Aviation Administration (FAA). Besides engaging in various humanitarian efforts, the Coast Guard enforces federal laws on the high seas and waters subject to U.S. jurisdiction. The Coast Guard shares responsibility with the U.S. Customs Service for interdicting smuggling in coastal waters and for interdicting air smuggling. As we have already seen, it has been involved with the interdiction of contraband smuggled over water for over 200 years. In recent years, the USCG has contributed enforcement assistance (e.g., training, equipment, and operational and technical support) as part of America's overall international drug control strategy, which is designed to reduce production and destabilize trafficking. In order to identify airborne drug smugglers—radar, aircraft lookouts, and other tracking tools are used to detect the movements of suspect aircraft. Information is shared with a variety of other federal agencies that cooperate in drug enforcement including: the DEA; Immigration and Naturalization Service (INS) Border Patrol; FBI; U.S. Marshals Service; Customs Service; FAA; IRS; Bureau of Alcohol, Tobacco and Firearms (BATF); Secret Service; and the Department of State Diplomatic Service (Bureau of Justice Statistics, 1992, pp. 143–44).

The Coast Guard regularly patrols the sea-lanes between the Bahamas and south Florida. In 1990, the USCG seized large amounts of marijuana and cocaine in the district that covers the southeastern part of the United States and the Caribbean. In that year, 17,567 pounds of marijuana and 67,906 pounds of cocaine were seized. The mid-Atlantic districts seized 12,700 pounds of hashish (Bureau of Justice Statistics, 1992, p. 147).

In 1992, the U.S. Coast Guard had more than 135 seagoing vessels and 180 aircraft for patrolling the oceans. These efforts were supplemented by Navy surveillance patrol activities. Sometimes a Coast Guard team may be assigned to Navy ships patrolling in waters where smuggling is suspected and board if necessary. In order to reduce the ability of smugglers to use foreign territorial seas as safe havens, the Coast Guard has instituted a procedure whereby foreign law enforcement personnel accompany USCG vessels. The foreign law enforcement officers can authorize the Coast Guard to continue pursuit of smugglers in foreign waters (Bureau of Justice Statistics, 1992, p. 147).

Occasionally, good will trips may indirectly support the overall international drug control strategy. The Coast Guard Cutter *Resolute*, based in St. Petersburg, Florida, visited the small Nicaraguan community of Puerto Cabezas in 1997. It was the first such U.S. ship to visit the country since 1979. According to Mark Machowiak, USCG Petty Officer 3rd Class, "Nicaragua's poor economy, lack of law enforcement and isolated geography makes it a haven for drug smugglers" (Machowiak, 1998, p. 17). The vessel and its crew delivered medical supplies and other goods to the village of 1,500 people, where 90 percent are unemployed. Crewmembers also helped to restore a large school building. Machowiak (1998), also reported that the visit helped to bring together U.S. State Department, Coast Guard and Nicaraguan officials to discuss possible solutions involving drug trafficking.

In general, the post-Cold War era has permitted various military units to become more active in domestic concerns. The various branches of the National Guard are now free to focus on counterterrorism and counterdrug operations. For example, Stratton Air National Guard Base is located in upstate New York, near the cities of Albany and Schenectady. In recent years, a special unit consisting of 140 soldiers with a budget of $6 million is assigned to counterdrug efforts. The unit uses UH-60 Blackhawk helicopters and fixed-wing aircraft equipped with night-vision and thermal-imaging equipment to find marijuana fields. The unit also lends its high-tech help to local police agencies to detect the locations of people in buildings during drug raids (Gardinier, 1998). Additional millions are being spent by local and state governments for their own enforcement initiatives.

Summary of the Current Role of Police in Drug Abuse

Police currently use a variety of both informal and formal procedures to contend with the problem of drug abuse. Informal means include: warnings; escorting the inebriated home; arranging for a cab or relative to deliver an inebriate home; and in some cases providing a place for such persons to rest and recover until they could arrive home safely. Moreover, police also tend to refer nondisorderly inebriates to civil detoxification and mental health centers. These centers are common divisions of most community hospitals and county public health systems. Their patients include persons who abuse a wide array of drugs and other dangerous substances. A large percentage of substance abusers arrive at these and other treatment centers on a voluntary basis.

The formal involvement of police is more widely known due to the keeping of arrest records and the involvement of other official agencies of social control. Generally, the police have traditionally tried to eliminate the supply of drugs to the user and to arrest those individuals found to be in possession of drugs. The use of multijurisdictional task forces, consent searches, buy and bust operations, the destruction of crops, the pursuit of drug money, asset seizures, and various types of stings are probably the most common types of formal police involvement in the pursuit of drug traffickers.

At the local level, police efforts include several well-known educational and nontraditional approaches including: classes taught by police officers in local classrooms; obtaining municipal help to improve physical street conditions (e.g., cleaning up vacant lots and demolishing abandoned buildings); a liberal use of no trespass signs; and the distribution of police beeper numbers in order to encourage citizens to report drug dealing.

Today, the availability of new technologies has dramatically changed traditional enforcement strategies in the battle against narcotics. Some of these innovations involve greater levels of governmental intrusion than others. For example, new infrared technology can now detect the number of people and their locations in buildings and ion scanning equipment can detect cocaine residue on money. Today, the U.S. Customs Service is prepared to use x ray and/or magnetic imaging machines as alternatives to strip searches. In such cities as New York, Baltimore and Los Angeles, the use of computers to analyze crime statistics has increased police performance (De La Cruz, 1998). In addition, police now have available computer technology for conducting drug market analysis (DMA). DMA provides location-specific information about where drugs are sold and enables police personnel to access the information quickly. The technology permits maps to be generated that can be used in preparing probable cause affidavits for obtaining search warrants (Hebert, 1993).

The concept of "zero tolerance" has fostered the use of "checkpoints" for the control of drunken drivers, drug users and illegal gun owners. While some of these developments are more intrusive than others, a lot depends upon the discretion, skill and knowledge of the agents of enforcement. The drug traffickers who frequent America's interstate highways are constantly challenging police skills in the field of drug interdiction. In 1919, a young

Army officer named Dwight D. Eisenhower first began to envision such roads throughout the United States for faster travel and military deployment. Today, the DEA's Operation Pipeline has been designed to help with the interdiction problem on our nation's highways.

Operation Pipeline is active in every state. Its headquarters is the El Paso Intelligence Center (EPIC). It's personnel track smugglers, scan criminal databases to link cases, and provide necessary information to officers in the field 24 hours a day. EPIC has access to the appropriate databases of the DEA, FBI, and U.S. Customs and keeps track of all the police calls regarding highway stops made to the center. The center receives about 30,000 calls each year. The program got its start when state troopers in New Mexico and New Jersey noticed a trend during the course of making routine traffic stops. They found that by carefully studying the vehicles and drivers stopped that they could detect smugglers and make drug seizures. According to Lt. Col. Ronnie Jones, deputy superintendent of operations for the Louisiana State Police, the key to successful highway interdictions is to stop as many vehicles as possible. Since 1990, 1.5 million pounds of marijuana and more than 207,000 pounds of cocaine have been seized from highway travelers (Huppke, 1999, p. F1).

Clearly, the law enforcement apparatus marshaled against drug users and traffickers is unparalleled. Nevertheless, there exists a continuing problem of what to do about drug abuse, especially in view of the fact that an estimated nine out of 10 drug shipments on the interstate highways manage to get through without detection (Huppke, 1999, p. F1). The following chapter considers the conflicting points of view regarding prohibition enforcement as well as the social hypocrisy engendered by some of the current enforcement strategies.

ENDNOTES

1. Quoted from pp. 141-42, Skolnick (1992).
2. The drug court initiative did not arise overnight. At least since the early 1970s, individual jurists have experimented with carefully tailored sentencing alternatives in order to address the needs of drug-addicted defendants. For example, in the early 1970s, New York State Supreme Court Justice Abraham I. Kalina consistently offered suspended sentences and a term of probation for nonviolent defendants who plead guilty in cases involving the sale of small amounts of heroin to undercover police officers so long as it was shown that such sales were conducted to support their heroin addiction and that the defendant had gained admittance into a recognized residential treatment program. In 1971, the author served as an aide to Justice Abraham Kalina in the Special Narcotics Trial Part in Brooklyn Supreme Court.

Chapter 13

THE ENFORCEMENT DEBATE

"A law should be enforced whether it be a good law or a bad law. If it be a bad law it should be enforced in order that the people may see that it is a bad law and repeal or modify it. If it be a good law it should be enforced in order that the people may have the protection of it."[1]

FLORENCE E. ALLEN
JUSTICE OF THE SUPREME COURT OF OHIO (1923)

Traditionally, in the area of vice control, police administrators have insisted that "the police do not make the law; they just enforce it." If the laws pertaining to certain prohibited sexual activity between spouses were actually enforced, the majority "of all married couples in this country would have been, at one time or another, technically guilty of a felony" (Lentini, 1977, p. 3). Similar contradictions arise whenever police are directed to enforce criminal statutes concerned with the protection of public morality.

More than 700 years ago, St. Thomas Aquinas wrote: "Private sin is different from public crime, and only the latter lies in the province of man-made law." Nevertheless, in most American communities, the sale and use of certain substances, gambling, prostitution, public drunkenness, and other categories of self-abuse are outlawed. As we have already seen, the enforcement of many of these laws presents a profound dilemma for police and the public. At the time of this book's preparation the entire criminal justice system seemed to be focused on just one of these categories of crime—drug enforcement. Moreover, an overwhelming amount of both local and national media coverage appeared devoted to establishing the fact that drugs were the number one cause of adult and juvenile crime. Yet, research findings are still inconclusive about the precise causes of crime. At best, we can conclude that crime is a complex social phenomenon that has causes deeply rooted in a variety of social ills. Significantly, drug addiction is more likely to be one symptom of these ills, rather than their predominant source. In addition, it now appears that alcohol and not heroin, cocaine or crack, is the drug most closely associated with violent crimes. In 1998, the National Center on

Addiction and Substance Abuse (NCASA) at Columbia University reported that 21 percent of state prison inmates doing time for violent crimes were under the influence of alcohol and not any other substance at the time they committed their crimes. By contrast, only 3 percent were under the influence of cocaine or crack alone and 1 percent were under the influence of heroin alone. Similar figures were obtained for jail inmates (NCASA, 1998).

Previous chapters have closely examined the numerous enforcement issues associated with alcohol enforcement. In this chapter, the overall problem of substance abuse will be treated as one aspect of the problem of victimless crime enforcement. The issue of drug law reform is so charged in American culture at the present time that its placement within this general category may, perhaps, encourage a more objective examination of the issue and possibly lead to a new mission or agenda for the nation with respect to the drug problem. It represents a distinct challenge for the new millennium.

Police have exhibited inconsistent activity in the area commonly labeled "crimes without victims" or "victimless crimes," and the public has openly defied many victimless crime laws. Many researchers have described the increasing social service nature of modern police work, as well as the role conflicts inherent in the enforcement of these laws. A clarification of the police role in victimless crime appears to be long overdue.

A "victimless crime" is any illegal act in which the parties to the offense do not consider themselves to have been injured or victimized by the behavior. The participants believe that their behavior is a private exchange over which the law should have no control. Consequently, they seldom report their conduct to the police. Schur (1965) has defined victimless crime as "the willing exchange, among adults, of strongly demanded but legally proscribed goods or services" (p. 169). Other criminologists have emphasized the low visibility, indifferent public response, and inconsistent law enforcement regarding victimless crimes.

Victimless crimes include: the sale of illegal services and products or substances; the receipt and use of such services or goods; and such self-abusive acts as vagrancy or the juvenile offense of being a "runaway." Estimates of the percent of all victimless crime arrests range from 40 percent to over 50 percent of the total annual arrests in the United States. Nationwide, there appears to be a distinct trend to repeal vagrancy and public intoxication penal laws. In their place have been substituted mental health or social service regulations that seek to divert these cases to community-based treatment facilities and programs. Moreover, some state courts have ruled that the older types of penal laws regarding vagrancy and public intoxication are unconstitutional.

The enforcement of victimless crime laws seem to rely on the assumption that society is harmed by private immorality and that the police, as society's most numerous and visible moral defenders, must enforce the laws and thereby preserve the common morality. Generally, the police must act as the complainant in all court proceedings against victimless crime defendants. Of course, as we have already seen, the premise for the establishment of laws prohibiting drug sales and their possession as well as for the establishment of a wide array of drug courts, is that drug cases are not victimless crimes but instead that the community as a whole is the victim of drug dealers and their networks.

The current police role in the field of victimless crime can be summarized under five major functions. Police are enforcement agents of victimless crime statutes when engaged in proactive police work (e.g., when police seek out such crime on their own initiative); crime preventers when engaged in reactive patrol activities (e.g., by responding to citizen complaints); peace-keepers when exercising discretion in the handling of victimless offenders (e.g., symbolically upholding the moral standards imposed by society by responding to the scene, but not making an arrest); service agents when victimless offenders become harmed (e.g., administering first aid to those persons who have been overdosed or assaulted); and protectors of the rights of victimless offenders during field contacts with them.

After the Twenty-first Amendment had been officially ratified to repeal the Eighteenth Amendment on December 5, 1933, President Franklin Roosevelt expressed the hope that "this return of individual freedom shall not be accompanied by the repugnant conditions that obtained prior to adoption of the 18th Amendment and those that have existed since its adoption" (Allen, 1979, p. 279). However, present day prohibition enforcement involving other substances still requires the cultivation of informants or tipsters, without which the only possible witnesses would be those police who must hide their identity in order to enforce the law. Today, police of every rank may be encouraged to participate in vice control work. In some jurisdictions, vice enforcement is rigidly practiced through the maintenance of arrest quotas and individual officers are encouraged by threats and rewards to assure adequate production.

The opportunity for police to become corrupted as a result of their involvement with victimless crimes is almost unavoidable, given the tremendous sums of money involved. Moreover, the enormous latitude enjoyed by vice officers in conducting undercover investigations contributes additional opportunities for scandal. Numerous police agencies have been the subject of journalistic disclosures about the offer and receipt of payoffs and bribes to officers working in vice control, although less publicized is the fact that no amount of vice enforcement will ever eliminate the behavior in question. Moreover, both FBI and DEA agents have been caught participating in drug trafficking (Monk, 1998, p. 340). For most of the duration of Hoover's control over the FBI, he kept his agents away from undercover drug investigations because he feared that such work might lead to controversy that could embarrass the bureau (Kessler, 1993, p. 2). Skolnick (1992) concludes that although "the possibilities of corruption exist in any form of enforcement against criminal activity, it is particularly in drug enforcement that agents and officers encounter large sums of cash and drugs with great market value" (p. 148).

Moreover, the enforcement of modern day prohibitions involving controlled substances has an insidious side well-known to defendants, prosecutors, and judges. Unless police are using undercover "buy and bust" tactics, they must rely on surveillance methods to actually see narcotic transfers in order to be able to obtain sufficient probable cause for making arrests. This need has been known to cause police to perjure themselves. Judges consistently suppress evidence of drugs and other types of contraband when they are convinced that police officers have fabricated information related to their search and seizure procedures. In addition, it is not uncommon to hear about complaints from neighborhood residents that police have planted drugs in their homes or in their clothing. "Some cops resort to this when they know someone's selling but they can't catch the dealer in the act. Others don't report all the drugs and money they confiscate when they do catch someone" (Davis, et. al., 1998, p. 113).

The major effect of vice control seems to be in the areas of supply and demand. For example, police authorities consistently concentrate on street prostitutes, but seldom arrest the higher-priced call or party girl. Similarly, police usually concentrate on the most visible or public forms of gambling. The country club set is relatively immune from a vice raid. Furthermore, successful drug enforcement causes drug prices to rise due to limited supply and a constant demand. These practices lead to discrimination. Significantly, while members of the middle and upper classes can readily afford to conceal their vices, lower-class members cannot. As lower class members seek to fulfill their wants in visible and vulnerable places, the police may easily apprehend them. If jailed, their exposure to other offenders and loss of employment may lead to further criminality.

Moreover, as police expand their interdiction efforts and seize ever-increasing amounts of illicit drugs, a phenomenon known as "the Darwinian Trafficker Dilemma" arises. According to Skolnick (1992), this occurs when law enforcement efforts successfully undermine the operations of marginally efficient suppliers, but permit more sophisticated traffickers (i.e., the fittest) to survive. They are "the best organized, the most corrupting of authorities, the most ruthless and efficient" (Skolnick, 1992, p. 143). In addition, if diminished supplies of one type of drug happen or its cost rises, drug abusers are likely to substitute another drug. For example, by the early 1990s, crack cocaine emerged to replace marijuana in California (Skolnick, 1992, p. 146).

The social hypocrisy engendered by the present police role contributes little to a community's welfare. It appears to be a chief source for the weakening and even corrupting of the institutions of the law. It is known that dedicated police have become overwhelmed by the mental stress arising out of their responsibilities to police the morals of the community and by the temptations of vice itself.

A suggested future role of police in the realm of victimless crime enforcement is urged that would substitute the concept of "referral" for that of "arrest." Such a projected role adopts the view that at least some police should be relieved of their present law enforcement functions with respect to victimless crime statutes. It assumes that the nonvictim offender is involved in a medical and personal moral difficulty and can best be aided by agencies outside the criminal justice system. Such a new approach would enable more police energies to be spent on the detection, identification, and arrest of violent offenders, terrorists, and white-collar criminals, rather than in the protection of the private virtues of Americans. Moreover, it would provide greater resources for the important goals of prevention and treatment.

The establishment of a supportive role, in contrast to a punitive one, in the field of crimes without victims will require:

- Decriminalization of prostitution and the charge of public intoxication.
- Legalization of almost all forms of gambling.
- Repeal of Sunday closing laws.
- Repeal of all laws concerning sex acts between competent consenting adults in private.
- Diversion of all nondangerous addict offenders from the criminal justice system.
- Creation of new community treatment programs for drug addicts, gamblers, runaways, and prostitutes.
- Special training for police regarding referral/release to families and social agencies.
- Adoption of clear policies and procedures for the exercise of police discretion involving referral.

The distinction between legalization and decriminalization is important. Legalization permits the act while retaining some form of social control; decriminalization repeals all laws on the subject and leaves control entirely to one's private conscience. Any discussion about which acts society ought to criminalize should weigh the benefits and harms that could result. In addition, it should be kept in mind that, whereas official controls and sanctions emphasize that a law has been broken, the supportive role turns attention to the causes in the hope that appropriate treatment strategies will be found.[2]

Additional Arguments in Support of Eliminating Victimless Crime Enforcement

Various advantages for the adoption of a nonpunitive position in the field of crimes without victims have already been presented. Others include:

- Protecting the domain of individual privacy.
- Freeing of police resources for deployment against nonconsensual crime.
- Freeing court and jail resources for the trial and detention of more serious cases.
- Eliminating the need for selective enforcement of victimless crime laws and the possible disregard for due process rights.[3]
- Eliminating certain secondary crime often associated with victimless crime (e.g., blackmail, bystander assaults, mistakes in warrant enforcement, etc.).
- Eliminating prohibitions which may have actually encouraged the practice of "forbidden pleasures" (e.g., youth gangs may honor members who regularly defy the law).
- Furthering respect for law and generating millions in tax revenue.

Moreover, it is important to recognize that heroin and other addictive drugs do not cause crime, rather it is the poor users need to pay for these drugs at extortion-level prices that may contribute to the commission of property crimes. Furthermore, while drug use itself may not be the reason for the launching of a criminal career, it "tends to intensify and perpetuate criminal behavior" (Inciardi, 1996, p. 268). In addition, although drugs are commonly abused, the majority of the users of all types of legal and illegal drugs are not materially harmed by their drugs. Significantly, drugs only "affect people in the context of how an individual uses them, and once that human element is brought into the equation, all our well-documented foibles come into play" (Trebach, 1996, p. 256). The harmful effects of prisonization will be eliminated and the opportunities for productive living may be restored. William Halstead, one of America's most famous surgeons and a founder of the John Hopkins Medical School, was a regular user of morphine throughout most of his successful career. Most addicts can function normally if adequately supplied with drugs.

Monk (1996) calls attention to the need to take into account the intricate relationship between drugs and race in modern American society. He cites a variety of statistics to indicate that many more blacks than whites are being convicted and incarcerated for the possession of crack cocaine.

The existence of some types of deviance may actually serve useful purposes within society. The selection of persons for the "deviant" or "criminal" label offers a community the opportunity to demonstrate moral outrage, clarify group norms, develop its bonds, and preserve its identity. "Like a war, a flood, or some other emergency, deviance makes people more alert to the interests they share in common and draws attention to those values which constitute the 'collective conscience' of the community. Unless the rhythm of group life is punctuated by occasional moments of deviant behavior, presumably, social organization would be impossible" (Erickson, 1966, p. 4).

Nevertheless, there appears to be sufficient amounts of serious deviancy without having to single out the prostitute, the addict, or illegal public gambler for arrest and prosecution. In fact, such deviancy may act as a needed "safety valve" for society's discontented. For example, since prostitution usually involves little emotional attachment, it may provide a beneficial outlet for some persons without having to weaken family ties. Moreover, the law of supply and demand is applicable. Strict police enforcement may curtail the availability of prostitutes, but the effect would be to raise what customers are charged and the higher profits might encourage additional persons to enter the "oldest profession." Furthermore, when persons who participate in victimless crimes are themselves seriously victimized, but fear to report such wrongs, the opportunity for the community's "collective conscience" to be stirred is decreased. In addition, those victimless crime participants are further removed from their society's social fabric.

Arguments in Support of Preserving Victimless Crime Enforcement

On the other hand, various compelling reasons support the existence of victimless crime statutes and the present police role of enforcement. Police administrators in several big cities have attributed major decreases in violent crime to aggressive law enforcement and prosecution including illegal drug transactions and other types of victimless crime. Police costs are always high. The evils sought to be controlled are real ones. Victimless crime laws seek to protect perpetrators and their families. The tragic suffering of the latter group is sometimes overlooked in briefs for legalization or decriminalization. Alternative treatment programs are needed and their efforts may decrease the addict's need to steal. However, the offending conduct must remain prohibited or more people will be free to experiment and become addicted. Even debates and news coverage about the legalization of dangerous substances can send a wrong message to vulnerable youth. For example, news coverage of individuals smoking marijuana in California's legal cannabis clubs may imply to some youth that using drugs may be "fun" (Sanders & Constantine, 1998, p. 27). According to Inciardi (1996): "there is extensive physiological, neurological and anthropological evidence to suggest that people are of a species that has been honed for pleasure....and the pursuit of drugs is found across time and across cultures. Moreover, history and research has demonstrated that 'availability creates demand'" (p. 269).

Mere drunkenness or addiction is not a crime. It is only when drunken or addicted persons exhibit their condition publicly or disturb or injure others that they become offenders and subject to the criminal sanction.

Vice enforcement assists society in the control of more serious crime. The connection between organized crime and the existence of gambling, narcotics trafficking, and prostitution is well documented. Arrest and criminal convictions are essential in order to destabilize and to take the profits out of organized crime.

The lack of a complainant is not a valid reason for the repeal of a law. Many people do not report offenses, even though they have been harmed. This is more common when the offender and the victim are known to each other. Assaults between family members and friends often go unreported. The reluctance to notify the police of illegal conduct is quite understandable if the reporting party might be subject to arrest as an accessory to the vice act.

Disrespect for laws will not be eliminated through the abolition of victimless crimes. Legalizing prostitution, gambling, and/or drug dealing still requires governmental regulation. Undoubtedly, the new rules will be broken and selectively enforced. Furthermore, merely because some laws are not universally obeyed is no reason to call for their repeal. Society has a legitimate right to outlaw any act it may deem wrong. The criminal law permits a community to actualize its sense of outrage.

In February 1998, *The Police Chief*, an official publication of the International Association of Chiefs of Police (IACP), published a rather unique article entitled "A Police Chief's Guide to the Legalization Issue." The article was co-authored by Darrell Sanders, the IACP president in 1996-97 and Thomas A. Constantine, the administrator of the U.S. Drug Enforcement Administration (DEA). The article provided an overview of the reasons for the successful passage of propositions in California and Arizona in 1996 that legalized certain drugs for medical use. In California, the *Compassionate Use Act of 1996* permits individuals to use and obtain marijuana for various medical conditions. In April 1997, the Arizona proposition was sufficiently amended so that Sanders and Constantine were able to declare that the law no longer presented an immediate problem for law enforcement. However, they stated that since the passage of the California measure (also known as "Proposition 215"), that the state's police agencies had become concerned over their ability to arrest and prosecute marijuana dealers and buyers. In addition, "since the passage of that measure, there has been a growing number of the so-called 'Cannabis Buyers Clubs' opening...under the pretext of providing marijuana to seriously ill people" (Sanders & Constantine, 1998, p. 25). In particular, the article noted that the California measure contained confusing and misleading wording so that voters believed that they were approving compassionate pain relief, rather than endorsing an initiative that essentially made marijuana legal for all residents of the state.

Portions of the remainder of the article featured a summary of four major arguments for opposing drug legalization and a list of 20 ways for police chiefs to educate themselves and others about the dangers of drug abuse. The predominant theme of the lattermost list was that police chiefs should enlist the support of as many groups and organizations as possible to curtail the legalization movement. Moreover, one of the items on this list directly encouraged law enforcement officials to "organize a grass-roots political drive" (p. 29) so that legislators could learn law enforcement's views against drug legalization. The final page of the article included a list of resources that could be referred to for the purpose of responding "from a law enforcement perspective to many of the false claims and myths created by those who would legalize drugs" (Sanders & Constantine, 1998, p. 30).

While the adoption of such state propositions has no direct legal bearing on existing federal drug laws and their enforcement, Sanders and Constantine are obviously worried. Moreover, their advice further erodes the old adage that "the police do not make the law; they just enforce it." After their publication and remembering the other efforts made by key law enforcement officials (e.g., Harry Anslinger, etc.), an updated adage is necessary; perhaps, indicating that "the police not only enforce the law, but help to shape it."

The federal law enforcement stakes are high in the field of narcotics enforcement. According to Gray (1998), the current annual federal law enforcement bill is $16 billion. Gray (1998) believes that the continuance of marijuana as a prohibited substance with no exception for medical usage is necessary to maintain this level of funding. Basing his estimates on figures published by the U.S. Department of Health and Human Services in August 1996, Gray notes that the elimination of marijuana from the enforcement sphere would mean that "the number of illegal drug users instantly drops from thirteen million to three million, and the drug war shrinks from a national crusade to a sideshow" (Gray, 1998, p. 174).

Reconciliation of the Opposing Viewpoints

Suggestions for eliminating victimless crime enforcement or for maintaining the status quo oversimplify a very complex issue, especially with respect to drug abuse. Elliott Curie (1994) has argued that that the only hope to reduce drug use and drug-related crime in America is to do battle with its deepest social roots: poverty, family disintegration, and racial discrimination. He carefully examined the application of the traditional strategies involving law enforcement, treatment, and legalization and concluded that new approaches are needed. In many ways, his insights offer a useful compromise regarding the police role in victimless crime enforcement. His four major recommendations involve:

1. Adopting more reasonable sentences.
2. Focusing on drug traffickers, not users.
3. Providing serious help for abusers within the justice system.
4. Shifting law enforcement priorities toward longer-term community security (e.g., community-oriented policing).

In 1764, Cesare Beccaria wrote that the seriousness of crime should coincide with the certainty of appropriate punishment. He contended that a well-conceived criminal code would greatly help to deter crime by its appeal to humanity's ability to weigh the consequences. Later, the influences of psychology and psychiatry contributed to the development of a rehabilitation model for sentenced offenders. Until very recently, much of the thinking in the field of victimless crime has been leaning in the direction of Beccaria's deterrence model because correctional programs have been deemed largely unsuccessful. It is now becoming rather self-evident that attempting to deter personal abuses and excesses only through conviction and the threat and use of imprisonment are highly inappropriate for many victimless offenders. It is becoming increasingly understood that

> the law is obviously not the minimum standard for millions of individuals. Tough law and order stands by local and national leaders are contradictory and often self-serving. To suggest that penalties should be raised instead of lowered goes against the great tide of evidence built up in other countries.... No amount of deterrence will control a socially desired activity, the Prohibition Acts being the most obvious example. (Kiester, 1972, pp. 74-77)

Today, restitution as a type of punishment has become a popular recourse for less serious offenses. It involves some payment or services by a wrongdoer to the victim for the damage done. Often, the granting of probation is made contingent upon a promise to recompense the victim. Restitution permits the offender to do something constructive and does not alienate him from society. It considers not only the theoretical harm to society that must be repaid, but also the actual harm to the victim that should be repaid. However, many lower class drug addicts, prostitutes, and gamblers are ordinarily not in a position to participate in such equitable systems of justice. It is a callous act to require police enforcement of these offenses when one of society's more promising methods for establishing justice, cutting crime and aiding victims is of so little value. Fortunately, the public is generally supportive of other types of rehabilitation programs. Recent research findings indicate that policymakers have consistently overestimated public attitude regarding punitiveness and underestimated public support for rehabilitation (Applegate et al., 1997).

The San Francisco District Attorney's Office presently offers first-time prostitutes and customers an alternative to the endless cycle of arrest, jail, release, and rearrest. In collaboration with law enforcement and public health as well as a variety of private social service agencies, the office provides counseling and other assistance to the women offenders. Their male customers are provided the opportunity to pay a fine and attend an educational program in lieu of more serious penalties and prosecution. Since the program began in 1995, 1,350 women and girls have received services that have helped them leave prostitution, and only 4 of the 1,300 customers who have completed the program have been rearrested. Moreover, of the 165 women who have enrolled in substance abuse programs, 68 successfully completed the program and found legal employment ("First Offender Prostitution Program," 1998, p. 32).

The massive deployment of our nation's police forces against victimless crime appears to be based primarily on the intuition of our lawmakers. Although many persons feel that morality is a proper subject for governmental control, its regulation should not automatically be considered a police function. Research efforts may reveal more appropriate methods for coping with victimless crime. There is a lack of quantitative and verified information that defines the nature and extent of victimless crime. Studies concerning the effectiveness of the current application of criminal justice resources are needed.

James Inciardi, one of the staunchest advocates against drug legalization, has concluded that the focus on the war on drugs should be shifted. He believes "that we do indeed need drug enforcement, but it is stressed far too much in current policy. Cut it in half, and shift funds to criminal justice based treatment programs" (Inciardi, 1996, p. 269).

Underlying a nonpunitive police role in the area of victimless crime is the assumption that controlling crime and safeguarding morals are separate and distinct entities. Such a role supports the view that laws should only be enacted after problems of enforcement have been carefully considered. It needs to be appreciated that the first line for social control is seldom the police and in many cases should never be a police matter. The protection of society's virtue is a matter for the family, the church, the community, peer groups, and public opinion. Energies and resources devoted to the strengthening of these institutions are more appropriate than police interventions that may lead only to criminal sanctions. However, it is usually essential to provide special legal protection for the immature and disabled. In their article, Sanders and Constantine (1998) noted that the California proposition authorizing marijuana for medicinal purposes specified no age limit. "If the first priority of a free society is to safeguard the individual's rights, security, and property, Americans must decide whether the police are to go on frittering away their energies in fruitless attempts to enforce morality, or to use their time and resources to keep our streets and homes safe. We cannot have it both ways" (Kiester, 1972, p. 73).

It is for all of these reasons that a reduced enforcement role for the police is advocated in the field of victimless crime. Neither drug legalization nor decriminalization may be appropriate or necessary, rather police and prosecutors should work with concerned members of the community regarding enforcement needs. The problems associated with substance abuse and other categories of victimless crime represent the millennium challenge. Will new prevention programs and referral programs become available? Will the present punitive system of drug enforcement be exercised with greater caution and discretion? The concluding chapter discusses a variety of approaches for harnessing the resources of the community and thereby directly addresses the millennium challenge. Currie (1994) has stated "We will never...punish our way out of the drug crisis. We can, however, use the criminal-justice system, in small but significant ways. The real job is to define what we want the police and the courts to accomplish" (p. 148).

Success in the reform of vice control may ultimately be a question of money and education. Police are unable to refer people to agencies they do not know exist, they are not encouraged to use, or that are simply not available due to lack of funding. Apparently, many people only want "vice" out of view and are willing to rely on the existing methods, personnel, and agencies of control. As long as such complacency exists, the police role in victimless crime will continue to be defensive (at times), ambiguous (too aggressive or lax), and very expensive.

ENDNOTES

1. Allen, Florence E., The Courts and Law Enforcement in Fred B. Smith, ed. *Law vs. Lawlessness: Addresses Delivered at the Citizenship Conference, Washington, D.C. October 13, 14, 15, 1923.* New York: Fleming H. Revell Co., 1924, p. 55.

2. Although drug-prohibition policies have many problems, overall they have managed to send a message to the majority of American society that at least hard drugs are dangerous and should be avoided. Moreover, it is now well recognized that alcohol and nicotine, the two most widely used and legal drugs are responsible for untold amounts of suffering in this country. For these and many other reasons, the author believes that mere decriminalization is not the answer to the nation's drug crisis. Controls are necessary, but the present system of draconian controls creates more harm than good. J. Inciardi and D. McBride have com-

prehensively addressed the pros and cons of the legalization/decriminalization debate in *Handbook of Drug Control in the United States* (Westport, CT: Greenwood Press, 1990). In addition, for an insightful overview of the many contradictions in America's criminal justice system see D. Forbes, *False Fixes: The Cultural Politics of Drugs* (Albany, NY: State University of New York Press, 1995).

3. On the federal level not all laws are equally enforced. In particular, Immigration and Naturalization Service (INS) officials and federal prosecutors are reluctant to arrest economic migrants (undocumented alien workers) and the U.S. employers who rely on migrant labor. According to former U.S. attorney Alan Bersin, as a matter of policy, the U.S. attorney's office does not prosecute economic migrants, rather they are returned to their county of origin. (See Michael Huspek, "Desperation and Death Along Border," *The Sunday Gazette*, 7/12/98, p. F4.)

Chapter 14

THE UNITED APPROACH

"Uncle Sam can, and will, shoulder the importing end
and the sources of internal supplies, but prohibition will
never be satisfactorily enforced until you see that there
is a rebirth of responsibility in your local communities."[1]

MABLE WALKER WILLEBRANDT
ASSISTANT ATTORNEY GENERAL OF THE
UNITED STATES (1923)

This chapter recommends a united approach to coping with the nation's drug problem. It involves at least a five-prong effort. Firstly, there needs to be sufficient drug rehabilitation facilities so that all drug abusers and persons at risk of drug abuse have available "treatment on demand." Secondly, the energy of carefully trained and screened police volunteers is needed for undertaking a wide range of tasks regarding substance abuse prevention. Thirdly, the federal government should make available existing resources for the advance training of police volunteers and offer incentives to local communities to recruit retired military personnel to assist in training and supervising police volunteers. Fourthly, the new front-line police occupational position of "Drug Control Police Specialist" needs to be created. This position is recommended in order to replace the current informal, often happenstance, and primarily reactive response of the nation's police with respect to intoxicated and addicted persons. The primary role of drug control police specialists would be to seek out drug addicts in the community and refer them to the most appropriate treatment agencies and facilities. In carrying out their responsibilities, these specialists would be expected to work in a systematic (formal), proactive and creative manner. Finally, the manner in which most local police are trained and qualified for service needs to be altered in order to create a more professional police occupation. The foregoing recommendations are addressed in this chapter in separate sections and through a consideration of the following related topics: demand-side strategy; harm reduction; community mobilization; street drug enforcement programs; problem-oriented policing; citizen-oriented policing; and the realities of the police subculture.

236

Presently, the war against illicit drugs is being fought primarily within and without the land borders of the United States in order to focus on both the demand and supply sides of the problem. This is the same policy that was practiced during the period from 1920 to 1933 with respect to alcohol prohibition. More importantly, then as well as now, the laws regarding prohibition were selectively enforced. In the early 1920s, the federal government permitted liquor sales on commercial steamships that catered to the upper classes, but not in the saloons of lower class neighborhoods. In addition, raids on upper-class nightclubs that sold liquor were unusual. Today, it is becoming increasingly understood that drug purchase and consumption patterns differ substantially depending on the drug involved. For example, crack users are more likely to know numerous dealers, live on the street or in a shelter, and purchase the drug in their own neighborhood (Riley, 1997). Yet, throughout the 1980s and 1990s, the federal government has punished crack cocaine users far more harshly than powder cocaine users. The cost of a vial of crack is much less than powder cocaine. "In some cities, a vial of crack now costs less than a single admission to the movies, well within the reach of most teenagers" (Falco, 1992, p. 6). The net result has been the incarceration of a highly disproportionate number of minority group members as compared to white Americans.

The addition of funding for reducing the demand side of drug abuse was highlighted by two key events during 1988: the passage of the *Anti-Drug Abuse Act of 1988* and a candid statement by the U.S. Navy's highest ranking officer, Admiral Carlisle A. H. Trost, the former chief of naval operations. The federal law adopted in 1988 established the Office of National Drug Control Policy and the Admiral's statement was to the effect that America's combined armed forces and law enforcement establishment could not stop the smuggling of illicit drugs into the United States even if they did nothing else. Admiral Trost declared that they could not halt smuggling because "the economic incentives are so potent and the network of communications from farm to market via thousands of boats and small planes is so extensive" (Halloran, 1988, p. 10). Furthermore, large container ships present an even greater avenue for the arrival of illicit drugs. On a daily basis, a dozen or more of these vessels may arrive at each of the major port cities of America. The U.S. Customs chief inspector for the port of Los Angeles, Wayne Kornmann, has stated that less than two percent of these containers are examined (Gary, 1998, p. 151).

The recent demand reduction strategies also derived from the approach and philosophy known as "harm reduction" or "harm minimization." Such an approach begins with the acknowledgement that some drug users may be so hardcore that their substance abuse may require extensive treatment, rather than arrest and incarceration. This strategy was developed in the

Netherlands and the United Kingdom during the 1970s and early 1980s in response to the need to stem the spread of the HIV virus among drug abusers. In brief, advocates on behalf of harm reduction favor various treatment programs (e.g., methadone maintenance) and needle exchanges. They also are concerned about the human rights of drug users and the need to better integrate them into society, "rather than isolating them in separate clinics, programs, markets, and neighborhoods" (Nadelmann, 1992, p. 88).

At the same time, a variety of new enforcement strategies have been introduced to strengthen local enforcement efforts. Chapter 12 presented a selected overview of these developments (e.g., drug courts, etc.). Significantly, many of these approaches have been consistent with Jane Jacobs' classic statement that "the public peace—the sidewalk and street peace—of cities is not kept primarily by the police, necessary as police are. It is kept primarily by an intricate, almost unconscious, network of voluntary controls and standards among the people themselves, and enforced by the people themselves" (Jacobs, 1961, pp. 31-32).

Some of the most promising new strategies involving law enforcement may be categorized as follows: (1) Street Drug Enforcement Programs; (2) Problem-Oriented Policing; (3) Citizen-Oriented Policing. These types of strategies are especially useful for contending with drug abusers found in economically depressed communities. In such areas, the residents are unlikely to have the benefit of the necessary social and financial supports for receiving the treatment that is essential for overcoming their addictions. Significantly, in such neighborhoods and public housing projects, residents may be highly accustomed to seeing drugs being illicitly used and sold. "Treatment is often unavailable as there are no Betty Ford clinics for the desperately poor" (Skolnick, 1992, pp. 155-156). It is in such disadvantaged settings, that each of these community-policing strategies may prove to have their greatest potential. These alternative approaches are addressed below.

The three aforementioned strategies will be placed into a special context involving recommendations for direct citizen participation in the field of drug abatement. This is important because except for being constantly advised to address the hazards of drug issues with their children and being urged to serve as perfect role models, the general public has been typically left out of America's longest war. However, it is essential that communities engage in a united approach when dealing with social problems. Such a model consists of combining community mobilization, suppression (police interventions), and social service interventions (Howell, 1998, p. 14). The recommendations in this chapter seek to do this in a manner that complements regular police efforts and initiatives, so that traditional police hostility to community involvement may be reduced.

Community Mobilization

A successful method for fostering community participation involves a widespread, but rather little known police resource—volunteer police officers. They represent an untapped reservoir of help for substance abuse abatement.

Auxiliary police are typically unpaid dedicated volunteers. They are recruited, selected, trained, supervised, regulated (usually by the same or similar rules which apply to regular police), equipped (arms optional), and assigned by regular police departments. Although there may be a rank structure within the auxiliary police unit and members may possess all the powers of peace officers, any member must immediately comply with the lawful orders of any regular police officer. In most departments, they are considered to be unsalaried volunteer members of the agency.

Auxiliary Police History

How best to protect the health, safety and welfare of the public is a complex problem involving a myriad of private and public interests and initiatives. In the United States, as we near the end of the twentieth century, over 17,000 local, state and federal law enforcement agencies have been established for these purposes. However, such responsibilities have not always been in the exclusive hands of government.

In England, at least since the reign of Edward I (1272-1307), large towns were officially policed by a constable and a security force consisting of unpaid citizens. Since the late 1600s, the local citizens who perform in this capacity have been designated as "special constables." Today, about 15,000 special constables perform routine patrol duties alongside regular constables.

In the United States, the terms "reserves" or "auxiliary" refer to citizen volunteer police officers. They were first organized into significant units at the time of World War I, although unpaid "posse" members had been recruited in frontier towns during the nineteenth century. Currently, there are over 4,000 auxiliary police officers in New York City and at least 100,000 more nationwide. Ohio has the most volunteer officers in the United States and California ranks second. They have, respectively, 18,000 and 13,000 volunteer police officers. Reserve deputies in Georgia attached to the Fulton County Sheriff's Department made a vital contribution to the security of the 1996 Summer Olympics held in Atlanta. Eight state police/highway patrol agencies use reserve troopers. Appendix C describes various aspects of the New York City Auxiliary Police Program.

Coast Guard Auxiliaries, Park Hosts and SAMs

The following information about the U.S. Coast Guard Auxiliary, volunteer campsite park hosts, and downtown safety and maintenance officers or SAMs is presented in order to carefully distinguish these groups from municipal, county and state auxiliary police units. However, they can also serve as an important community resource for drug abatement activities. The National Park Service as well as many state, county and local parks and forests rely on volunteer hosts to help keep campgrounds open. The Coast Guard Auxiliary has no law enforcement authority, but provides several important functions related to marine safety. Furthermore, SAMs are typically hired by downtown private business districts in urban areas as a type of hospitality corps. The contributions of these innovative services are worthy of note.

The Coast Guard Auxiliary was formed through an act of Congress in 1939 in response to the increasing number of recreational boats then in use. Auxiliary members receive the same basic training as Coast Guard members and they are qualified to stand watch aboard a Coast Guard vessel or at a Coast Guard station. Members deploy their own vessels on a regular basis in order to patrol for the safety of other boaters. When any of these are so used, they are considered to be government property. The U.S. Coast Guard Auxiliary has three primary functions: public education, the provision of courtesy marine examinations, and on-water operations (Kastberg, 1998).

Public education addresses boating skills and seamanship classes for adults as well as coastal navigation courses for basic and advanced boaters. Courses on water safety are provided for young adults and school-age children. The courtesy marine examinations consist of free safety inspections for required safety equipment and adherence to federal safety regulations. Since the Coast Guard Auxiliary has no law enforcement authority, the inspections offer boaters an opportunity to have any questions answered without fear of receiving any fines. On-water operations involve activities such as search and rescue, safety regatta patrol, marine parades and checking aids for navigation (Kastberg, 1998).

Campground hosts are recruited for unpaid volunteer positions throughout the national parks and other park systems. At Virginia's Shenandoah National Park, host duties include registering campers, checking site availability and answering questions. In general, they become extra eyes and ears for the park rangers. If there is a problem requiring emergency assistance (e.g., medical, animal, or persistent rule breaker), they can contact park rangers by radio. They work at least four hours a day, five days a week. Sometimes they must intervene when campers make too much noise, park on the grass or destroy plants. However, such matters can usually be handled with an appropriate mix of firmness and diplomacy. They use their own recreational vehicles or trailers, but receive free sites and hookups for water and electricity. Many veteran hosts develop expertise regarding wildlife and they are greatly appreciated by regular park employees and visitors (Baker, 1998).

The Downtown Business Improvement District in Washington, D.C. employs a hospitality corps, known as SAMs, to patrol a 110-block zone from the White House to the MCI Arena. They wear cherry red coats and captain's hats and carry walkie-talkies to call for police or paramedics. They are unarmed, but may carry a broom to sweep the public sidewalks around downtown businesses. The SAMs have no official connection to the District of Columbia government, since they are paid for by the Business Improvement District. Their most common task is to provide directions to downtown visitors and workers. However, their presence obviously helps to deter crime. Similar organizations have been established in New York City, Dallas, Philadelphia, Phoenix and in other large cities (Johnson, 1998).

In many respects, the activities of these and similar kinds of paid and unpaid workers appear to be far removed from the world of the drug lords. However, tourists, boaters and campers have clearly benefited from their services.

Street Drug Enforcement Programs

These programs basically involve increasing police personnel hours and interagency cooperation for the purpose of narcotics control. Emphasis is placed on the identification of sellers, users and crack houses, as well as the development of tactical plans and operations in order to make arrests or obtain court orders for property seizures. Special tactics include saturation patrols, "Trojan Horse" runs (undercover buys by means of a van or similar conveyance) and "reverse sting" operations in which undercover officers pose as drug dealers. Law enforcement agencies may pool their resources and create joint narcotics task forces in order to generate the necessary intelligence to locate and identify the purchasers and sellers of illegal drugs. These types of programs have been carried out in both urban and suburban areas. For example, the cities of Lynn, Massachusetts (population 80,000), and New York (population over 7 million) have instituted specific street drug enforcement programs that have resulted in substantial increases in narcotics arrests (Hayeslip, 1989).

While this strategy may at first sound punitive in scope and therefore inconsistent with the path laid out in the previous chapter, its focus is aimed at providing "the breathing room that might enable a stricken community to regain enough sense of security to begin to work effectively on its larger problems" (Currie, 1993, p. 204). Significantly, Currie (1993) advocated that "what drug ridden communities most need is help in protecting their residents from victimization by highly visible and volatile drug dealing and by the crime and violence that pervades street drug culture. Making the reduction of violence and open drug dealing our first priority could both save lives and reduce the fear that now paralyzes many poor neighborhoods" (p. 204).

Auxiliary police personnel recruited from the same communities experiencing extensive amounts of drug abuse could effectively assist police departments engaged in street and crack enforcement strategies by:

1. providing detailed information about the location of street sales and the identification of drug sellers;
2. staffing drug hotlines to obtain additional information about drug sales and providing treatment information to drug users;
3. augmenting the resources needed to carry out the civil procedures necessary for the proper implementation of asset seizures (e.g., crack houses);
4. where laws so provide, conducting field investigations for applicants seeking public housing;
5. assisting in the enforcement of building and fire codes; and
6. maintaining crime prevention building patrols within every housing project (public or private) concerned about drug-related crime.

Problem-Oriented Policing

Since staging police sweeps and other types of street drug enforcement efforts may be short-lived or otherwise come to lose their crime deterrent effect over time, such initiatives need to be coupled with longer-term strategies. Both "problem-oriented" and "citizen-oriented" policing may fulfill these longer-term community security needs. Under the former approach, police identify problem areas and collect and analyze relevant data as the first step in developing prevention or enforcement strategies. Fundamental to this effort is the compilation of local and regional crime statistics and trends. In addition, periodic surveys are conducted of community residents in order to learn about community problems and the effectiveness of policing strategies. It is not uncommon for such studies to determine that a community is in need of improved educational, medical, daycare, housing, and/or recreational facilities.

In Houston, Mayor Lee P. Brown broadened this concept when he was Houston's police chief. He referred to it as "neighborhood-oriented policing." The basis for his approach was that the war against drugs could be successful only through the involvement of the community. He listed four distinctive steps for the fulfillment of this strategy: (1) the development of a partnership between the people of each neighborhood and the police; (2) the identification of local problems; (3) the formation of joint solutions; and (4) the joint carrying-out of the activities necessary to resolve the problems (Brown, 1988).

One of the most well-known examples of problem-oriented policing emerged from the Boston Gun Project's planning phase. Key members of the planning team were selected from: the Boston Police Department's Gang Unit, the departments of probation and parole, the U.S. Attorney's and county prosecutor's offices, the Office of the State Attorney General, school police, youth corrections, and social services. They created "Operation Ceasefire" and it involves two types of enforcement strategies: direct assaults upon illicit firearms markets and "pulling every lever" when violence erupts. A central goal of the project was to deter chronic offenders from committing further acts of violence. The "pulling levers" strategy is designed to send a direct message to gang members that crime is costly. Team members first meet with gangs around the city, visit detention facilities, and speak to school assemblies. The groups are informed that the city is not going to put up with violence any longer and if the warning isn't heeded an overwhelming crackdown is delivered on the gang's activities. These consequences (the levers) might include strict enforcement of trespassing and public drinking statutes, serving outstanding warrants, cultivating confidential informants, delivering strict probation and parole supervision, seizing drug proceeds and other assets, seeking higher bail, focusing prosecutorial attention on all gang-related crimes, and even the possibility of additional sanctions from federal enforcement agencies (e.g., ATF, DEA, INS, etc.) The program was successful because the gang members discovered that the team was credible. It was actually able to deliver the promised responses. In addition, communication was maintained with the targeted gang as the strategy unfolded and the members of the project regularly met to assess progress and select appropriate responses. "Operation Ceasefire" could be implemented with respect to other crime problems, such as street drug markets (Kennedy, 1998).

Auxiliary police personnel could be used not only to carry out appropriate surveys and other forms of data collection, but also to staff local task forces whose object is to obtain any needed resources for the community. Moreover, members of the auxiliary could serve as the primary liaison between police and neighborhood residents, especially during the critical partnership development phase of planning. In a program like "Operation Ceasefire" auxiliaries could also protect and assist those gang members who seek to become reintegrated into community life.

The prevention of children and adolescents from joining gangs is probably the most cost-effective strategy for drug abatement available. In the United States, the number of cities with youth gang problems has increased from an estimated 286 cities with more than 2,000 gangs and nearly 100,000 gang members in 1980 to about 4,800 cities with more than 31,000 gangs and approximately 846,000 members in 1996 (Howell, 1998, p. 1). The Bureau of Alcohol, Tobacco and Firearms (ATF) has implemented a school-based gang prevention curriculum, know as "Gang Resistance Education and Training" (GREAT). Initial evaluation has shown positive results. For example, students who completed the program reported lower levels of gang affiliation and delinquency, including drug use, minor offending, property crimes, and crimes against persons (Esbensen & Osgood, 1997).

While auxiliaries could be used to expand the delivery of GREAT and related curriculums offered to youth, it must be emphasized that the evaluations of strictly educational programs often turn-out to be less than desirable. In 1994, a review of eight previous studies involving DARE (the well-known Drug Abuse Resistance Education program) concluded that DARE was not as effective as had been previously believed. Moreover, it questioned the use of law enforcement personnel as teachers of the program, noting that there had been no studies on whether this is an effective use of police personnel (Abadinsky, 1997, p. 213). In 1999, in a related example, researchers at the Johns Hopkins School of Public Health reported that driver education classes do not appear to be producing safer drivers. After a careful examination of several previous studies, they could find no evidence that teenagers who enrolled in the classes had fewer accidents or committed fewer traffic infractions than those who did not attend such classes. Moreover, they indicated that these types of classes might actually be contributing to the nation's accident problem by putting more young drivers on the road ("Classes Don't Make Drivers Safe: Study," 1999, p. A6).

Citizen-Oriented Policing

This approach directly seeks to harness the talents and experiences of local residents in order to decrease crime. The support of community groups is sought for tougher laws, clean-up projects and more jails. In Seattle, for example, citizens were encouraged to set up their own drug hotline (Hayeslip, 1989).

One of the most popular strategies involving citizen-oriented policing has been the establishment of "Neighborhood Watch" programs. One of the earliest of these was the citywide "Home-Alert" organization in Oakland, California. The objective of the program was protection through participation and cooperation, with each member of the group agreeing to observe and report any suspicious behavior occurring in the neighborhood. Information about the Home Alert Program was spread through mass mailings, newspaper articles, television broadcasts and the publication of a monthly newsletter to keep members informed of crime conditions and prevention activities. Within six months, more than 1,000 groups were active in Oakland (Whisenand, 1977).

Unfortunately, the success of many efforts to harness the latent energies of community members has been short-lived. In some instances, block meetings have been held and special street signs erected proclaiming the existence of a "Neighborhood Watch," but in reality the group merely existed in name, rather than in fact. In Minneapolis, the police department tried to maintain interest in a watch program by having police go door to door in order to chat with community residents about local crime conditions, but only a few officers actively participated (Sherman, n.d).

Some hotline programs have been unsuccessful due to the fear people have about the adverse consequences if they report a crime to the police. They fear that they may be arrested (especially if they are undocumented aliens) or victimized through retaliation if they should be identified. Nevertheless, most police agencies heavily rely on the tips provided by informants in order to control all forms of vice.

Throughout the 1990s, the Office of Juvenile Justice and Delinquency Prevention (OJJDP), within the U.S. Department of Justice, has developed and funded a variety of programs ranging from working with high-risk youth in public housing projects to helping communities fight the growing violence of youth gangs. Many of these programs involve training for law enforcement agents and others concerned with the coordination and daily operation of the various segments of the juvenile justice system. Many of these programs feature elements consistent with the attributes of citizen-oriented policing (Munson, 1988).

The use of auxiliary police personnel would appear to be a natural type of citizen-oriented strategy for reducing crime associated with drug abuse. Conceivably, having auxiliaries serve as their bridge to community groups might alleviate many of the frustrations which police have encountered with regard to community organization. Yet, this strategy is rarely included in community drug enforcement initiatives. Moreover, there is not a single reference to auxiliary police in the 1998 policy guide and ten-year strategy produced by the Office of National Drug Control Policy. Nevertheless, units of auxiliary police could be assigned to:

1. provide presentations to children and their parents about the nature of drugs;
2. reassure potential informants and other tipsters about the confidentiality of their communications to police hotlines;
3. serve as role models for youth at risk;
4. play an active role in crisis intervention and recreational programs that seek to divert youth from drug use and sales;
5. sponsor community forums in order to give diverse sections of the com-

munity the opportunity to share concerns about local drug problems;
6. energize participants in neighborhood watch groups by planning and implementing programs to maintain community interest;
7. establish and operate boys' and girls' clubs in selected housing projects and other neighborhoods;
8. take an active role in programs that promote user accountability (e.g., by helping to monitor methadone maintenance programs) and assist the new drug control police specialists;
9. work closely with alternative school programs by supervising clubs and other after-school activities;
10. staff storefront police stations for the purposes of building community solidarity;
11. instruct and organize "citizen police academies";
12. serve as departmental liaisons to civilian anticrime patrols and contract security guard employees and agencies;
13. help to educate shop owners and tavern employees about the nature and misuse of false identity cards;
14. provide a better alternative to the "designated driver" campaign; and
15. serve as aides to court probation officers to assist in the work of night drug courts.

Most of the foregoing are self-explanatory. However, additional comment is needed regarding: the use of citizen police academies; the provision of storefront stations; "designated driver" program; and the creation of auxiliary police units to assist in the work of drug night courts.

Citizen police academies (CPAs) offer abbreviated versions of some of the curriculum actually presented to new police recruits. Generally, classes are held at least one evening a week for about a ten-week period. Different topics are presented during each class. In 1993, two sessions of the New York City CPA was devoted to the following issues: police secrecy and cynicism as well as quality-of-life issues (e.g., graffiti, open-air drug dealing, panhandlers, etc.) (Clark, 1993). Storefront (mini) police stations can actually reduce open-air drug dealing and strengthen ties between residents and the police by providing a highly visible, accessible and permanent police presence in drug-infested neighborhoods.

The U.S. Department of Transportation currently uses a public affairs commercial with the theme that "friends do not let intoxicated friends drive." It urges that one person in every group of drinkers should remain sober and serve as the group's "designated driver." The program was used in Scandinavian nations in the mid-1980s and was introduced to the American public by the Alcohol Project at Harvard University's School of Public Medicine. The head of the project was able to convince Hollywood writers to include the concept in their television scripts. However, critics of this approach have pointed out that, in reality, the "designated driver" is most likely to become the person who has had the least number of drinks and that the stories and ads infer that "it's okay to get plastered as long as someone else is driving" (Harris, 1994, pp. 165-166). Younger drinkers may think that they can drink without regard to possible health consequences. Auxiliary police officers could help point out these problems at appropriate public meetings and could be on-call to serve as drivers upon request.

In the previous chapter, the option of drug night courts was addressed. In 1994, the U.S. Department of Justice issued a favorable report about the success of the system used in Cook County, Illinois. However, it also disclosed a variety of serious flaws including production line tactics. In addition, the system can lead directly to prison for many low-level minority addict dealers when they are given probation but not treatment for their serious drug problems. According to public defender Tim Lohaff, probation gives "them just enough rope to hang themselves (Gray, 1998, p. 27). The night courts were established to deal with the huge number of cases generated by "zero tolerance" police work. Volunteer police officers could be used to deal with inquiries from family and friends about these cases and they could play a key role in helping to insure that probationers receive necessary treatment. The deployment of police drug control specialists could help to reduce the caseloads of these courts by reaching drug users before they are initially arrested or later returned to court because of probation violations.

The enumerated functions for the police auxiliaries are directly and specifically geared to help communities achieve sufficient cohesiveness in order that citizens will be: better protected in their environments; less likely to become a crime statistic; and empowered to resist drug dealing. Moreover, unlike many regular police who do not live in the areas they police, the auxiliaries typically do. Their leadership and potential contributions should not be overlooked.

The types of community policing strategies that have been presented are labor intensive. Carefully selected and trained auxiliaries are an obvious solution and they can be recruited without making cutbacks in other critical governmental services. In 1991, after high level government officials proposed the use of an auxiliary police force in Sydney, Australia, hundreds of citizens immediately expressed interest. At that time, the president of the Retired Police Association of New South Wales, said he believed that former police officers were ideally suited to become auxiliary police and to be involved in their training (Quinn, 1991, p. 7).

The Realities of the Police Subculture

All of the foregoing recommendations for the expansion of a citizen's role in drug prohibition enforcement have been carefully selected so as to avoid infringing upon the time-honored duties of regular police. Few, if any, of these proposals call upon citizen auxiliaries to engage in any type of traditional "crimefighting." The reasons for this are plain. Police union leaders are unlikely to support any type of drug enforcement strategy that empowers citizens to act in their place. According to Champion and Rush (1997), even "the practice of using retired cops as volunteers may be viewed by the police union as 'scab labor': uncompensated labor that would otherwise be performed by regular hires" (pp. 363-364).

In the past, the strategies which police have adopted to reach out to the community were primarily designed to strengthen a limited number of local crime prevention goals. These included: improved street lighting, property identification, home and business security surveys, and special crime or neighborhood watch programs that may or may not have had a citizen patrol component. When the idea of calling upon the community for assistance has been seriously urged, it has often been as a last resort. Furthermore, at such times, the call has typically consisted of only asking citizens to respond to a toll free hotline or e-mail address. Not surprisingly, the police often receive numerous calls that have little validity or value.

Although reserves and auxiliary units have been recruited by many police agencies, they are sometimes viewed as competitors because patrol officers feel that the unpaid volunteers threaten their jobs. Perhaps, the biggest threat posed by the use of auxiliary police may relate to what has been called the "prime directive of patrolling." According to Bayley (1994), the concept refers to the need of police agencies to have officers available for any emergency. It is based on an unspoken fear that there may come a time during the course of a given shift that a big incident may develop that might cause the police to lose control due to the lack of human resources. In order to avoid this possibility, departments seek to maintain a reserve capacity. This is typically accomplished by seeking to have the maximum number of patrol units in the field. It seems logical that if properly qualified and trained auxiliaries were available this issue would be more or less resolved since they could be summoned to handle routine assignments while the regular police are reassigned to the big incident. On the other hand, the presence of such a reserve of auxiliary personnel might be interpreted to mean that there would be less need to have extra regular patrol units always available and ready for service. Indeed, this issue is also an unspoken, but very real fear of the regular police. In addition, it might also mean that regular officers would then be free to spend more time on their calls and thus, perhaps, render greater service by performing more concentrated work. Significantly, most unions (of any type) tend to routinely resist the notion of more work. Moreover, part-time volunteers, no matter how qualified and trustworthy, are still outsiders and their deployment can upset a very delicate and sensitive arrangement. "The phrase 'out of service' is revealing. The primary purpose of patrolling is not to handle requests from the public adequately, it is to be available.... Not being able to regain control is the worst nightmare of a police commander" (Bayley, 1994, p. 45).

Despite such considerable drawbacks, the united approach requires police officers, supervisors, and their respective unions to directly address their secret concerns about both the fear of losing control and the use of volunteers. If they choose to do so, it may be possible to utilize auxiliary police or volunteer reserves for the purposes of drug abuse prevention and drug abatement. The federal government could provide a big boost in this direction by recognizing the potential contributions of volunteer police. This could be done through the establishment of an auxiliary training division at one or more of their national or regional law enforcement training centers. The centers could teach leadership development, appropriate reporting techniques, handling drug offenders, crime prevention and surveillance skills. The course of study could also be made available to the volunteer members of the National Park Service, Civil Air Patrol, U.S. Coast Guard Auxiliary, and other groups with more limited policing responsibilities. Thus, volunteers could be sent for extra training in much the same way as the National FBI Academy provides extra training for local police.

The federal government could also provide financial support for the supervision and inservice training of local auxiliary police units. A program could be established through congressional action modeled on the Defense Department's original "Troops to Teachers Program." Thus far, this program has helped to place 3,000 veterans from all branches of the armed forces into positions within local school districts. Significantly, for each veteran who qualified by October 1, 1995, school districts received an incentive grant of up to $50,000 to help pay their salaries during a five-year period. Over 31,000 persons retire each year from the military, many of them relatively young (Hewitt & Siew, 1998). Just as some of them have become schoolteachers, others could draw upon their military training and help to train and supervise new volunteer police personnel.

The regular use of auxiliary police personnel would appear to be a natural type of community policing anti-drug strategy. If governments were to recognize their potential, the forces marshaled against substance abuse could be doubled or even tripled in a short amount of time. In the United Kingdom, a major study involving special constables (volunteer police) found that nearly 80 percent of the regular police agreed that they were a useful supplement to the regular force (Leon, 1991, p. 668). Synergism occurs when people and governmental organizations channel their energies toward a common purpose and accomplish what they could not accomplish alone. Citizens who are auxiliary police or who have been trained by them (e.g., through CPAs) may serve as a tremendous reservoir in the prevention of drug abuse. Hundreds of thousands of potential volunteers are waiting for the call.

The Role of Drug Control Police Specialists

Of course, the use of trained volunteers cannot be the sole basis for a revised strategic plan regarding substance abuse and control. Additional professional human resources are also needed. One of the first statements made by Barry McCaffrey, when he was the incoming director of the White House Office of National Drug Control Policy, was that "we must focus as a priority on reducing consumption among the three million hard core users who consume 75% of the total tonnage of illegal drugs" (McCaffrey, 1996, p. 326). He further pointed out that by encouraging the use of treatment programs among such hard core addicts that reductions in: drug trafficking; associated violence; costly emergency room visits (over 500,000 in 1995); and related property crimes would take place (McCaffrey, 1996).

Such priorities cannot be obtained with the use of existing resources. Sufficient treatment facilities must be available to meet the demand and an entirely new corps of police professionals is needed. They would be attached to local police departments and serve as "drug control specialists." Every local law enforcement agency should consider their immediate employment. According to David C. Lewis, Professor of Medicine and Community Health at Brown University: "Part of the problem with the war on drugs is the punitive social atmosphere created by the law enforcement process that has criminalized drug use—with an increasingly harsh, get-tough policy but with little actual success" (Lewis, 1992, p. 165).

The recruitment of drug control police specialists could serve to help communities achieve the following goals: (1) the reduction of harm; (2) the furtherance of safety; (3) the provision of care for those who need it; (4) the diversion of cases out of the criminal justice system through effective problem solving; and (5) the enhancement and promotion of interventions involving informal mechanisms of social control.

These new specialists would possess all of the powers of regular police officers and receive all of the appropriate training. This is essential not only because of the violence associated with drug trafficking, but because 60% of the people who use heroin and cocaine are already involved in the criminal justice system (Clinton, 1996). One of the reasons for the lack of success of New York's mandatory drug treatment program in the 1970s was the fact that narcotic parole officers were unarmed and did not have peace officer status. Many of the paroled addicts failed to report and the "officers" found it very difficult to apprehend them (Abadinsky, 1997). However, such specialists should have regular law enforcement authority and training, not strictly for the purpose of arresting parole and probation violators, but rather so that they could be considered equal partners with the police and have access to police information and other resources in order to better accomplish their special purpose.

The establishment of these positions would greatly help to elevate police work to that of a profession. The employment of drug control police officer specialists is in keeping with the philosophy of Chief August Vollmer, perhaps, the nation's leading police reformer. When he was the police chief of Berkeley, California, during the first quarter of the twentieth century, he believed that "the policeman who knew the people on his beat was in an excellent position to identify problems and refer them to other community professionals for treatment" (Carte & Carte, 1975, p. 34). In 1921, Vollmer was reported to have remarked to his new officers: "you can prevent people from doing wrong; that's the mission of a policeman.... I'll admire you more if in the first year you don't make a single arrest. I'm not judging you on arrests. I'm judging you on how many people you keep from doing something wrong. Remember... you're to listen to people, you're to advise them...." (Carte & Carte, 1975, p. 45).

Fred Kohler, who served as Cleveland's police chief from 1903 to 1913, might if he were alive today, also have given his support to this concept. In December 1907, Kohler had adopted a policy that he referred to as the "Golden Rule." In that year, it became the police department's official policy that all minor offenders (e.g., intoxicated persons) would be either escorted home or warned, rather than arrested (Richardson, 1974, p. 79).

Individuals recruited for these positions would need to possess solid educational backgrounds and skills in at least four fields: substance abuse education; family counseling; crisis intervention; and investigation techniques. Their primary task would be to seek out drug addicts in the community and refer them to the most appropriate treatment agencies and facilities. A poll of police chiefs and county sheriffs across the nation found that 42 percent were in favor of more drug and alcohol prevention programs (Brown, 1995).

The role of the drug control police specialist needs to be carefully distinguished from that of community service officers (CSOs) and the interesting proposal made by David Bayley, an internationally recognized authority on criminal justice and policing, calling for the creation of neighborhood police officers (NPOs). In Santa Ana, California, CSOs have been used to handle calls for service that do not involve police emergencies, but may only involve referring and advising. They are uniformed, but do not carry weapons. According to Bayley (1994), effective crime prevention requires a wide range of skills that the average police officer is unlikely to possess. These include: the ability to assess and diagnose social problems and coordinate "among private police, citizens, volunteers, commercial interests, welfare agencies, architects and builders, politicians and legislatures, and a host of other government departments" (Bayley, 1994, p. 129). Bayley (1994) asserts that "crime prevention will not take place if it is tacked onto the existing duties of patrol officers and detectives" (p. 146). Therefore, he calls for the establishment of a vast new frontline uniformed specialization within policing to be known as the Neighborhood Police Officer (NPO) who would not be responsible for handling emergency calls nor would they be available on a 24-hour a day basis. They would have sergeant rank and maintain hours based on their own schedules (Bayley, 1994, pp. 147-151). "The primary function of NPOs would be the diagnosis of security needs and the formulation of plans to meet recurring needs before they become law-enforcement emergencies.... NPOs would concentrate on consultations with people who have incipient problems and the after-care of crime victims" (Bayley, 1994, p. 147).

In some respects the new drug control police officer specialists might resemble the proposed NPOs. NPOs and drug control specialists would certainly share many of the same goals and need to be well educated in order to perform their assignments. However, drug control specialists would be unlike NPOs because of at least three reasons: (1) the need for unique counseling skills; (2) the need to focus on one particular purpose (substance abuse); and (3) the need for plainclothes attire. Moreover, since NPOs would be engaged in all manner of problem solving, they might have to utilize various law enforcement approaches on a more frequent basis than the police drug control specialists. On the other hand, both positions would look upon any enforcement method (be it criminal or civil), as more of a means than an end in itself. Bayley (1994) notes that within a problem-solving framework, enforcement is best "used instrumentally to achieve change in a particular situation" (p. 114).

Drug control police specialists are needed because the number of people who need drug treatment is estimated to be 3 or 4 times the number of people receiving treatment. Moreover, drug treatment has positive effects on drug users. Significantly, since most people who enter drug treatment do so reluctantly and the criminal justice system has been shown to effectively influence individuals with drug problems to seek treatment, the services of these specialists should prove helpful (BJS, 1992, pp. 109 & 111). It is important to consider that the goals of treatment are not confined to reducing the drug consumption of individuals in treatment but are much broader. These goals include:

1. reducing the demand for illegal drugs;
2. reducing street crime;
3. changing users' personal values;

4. developing education and vocational capabilities;

5. improving the user's overall health; and

6. reducing fetal exposure to drugs (BJS, 1992, p. 111).

At many local community colleges in the United States, courses in substance abuse and family counseling, human services (or social work) and criminal justice are available. The establishment of this new entry-level specialist position should quickly cause such colleges to draw upon their curriculums in order to create the most appropriate and desirable sequence of courses for this new type of position.

If it is true that "drug related street violence is more connected to drug criminalization than to the pharmacological effects of the drugs themselves" (Lewis, 1992, p. 166), than the use of police drug control specialists in non-punitive roles would seem to be a highly appropriate initiative for the sake of safer communities. Lewis has cited a variety of studies that directly contradict the common perception that drugs "cause" violent crime. For example, a study of adolescents in Miami found that about 60 percent of the violence was related to the commission of crimes carried out in pursuit of money to buy drugs. Moreover, a study of cocaine-related murders in New York City found that most of these cases involved territorial disputes among drug dealers. Ironically, an important exception to this pattern was the finding that alcohol intoxication directly influences violent behavior (Lewis, 1992, p. 178). Simply stated, the police can best hope to reduce demand for drugs by helping addicts obtain the necessary drug treatment.

Police Professionalism

In 1929, Police Commissioner Grover Whalen stated that there were 32,000 speakeasies in New York City (Cashman, 1981, p. 43). The operators and owners of these speakeasies were "dependent on corrupt policemen and agents who drank too much of their liquor and extorted too much of their profit" (Cashman, 1981, p. 44). In the same year, Whalen also recognized that the complexities of social life demanded a new approach to police training. He knew his force lacked a well-organized program for the education and the training of its members. Thus, was born the College of the Police Department of the City of New York. Faculty members from the College of the City of New York (CCNY), New York University and Columbia University collaborated in its establishment (Whalen, 1929). While the school never awarded college degrees, it did contribute to increasing the effectiveness of the police and standardizing police methods. Today, graduates of its successor institution, the New York City Police Academy, may receive 30 college credits when enrolling in a traditional college. Nevertheless, only a handful of big city departments, such as New York City

Table 14.1
SCHEMATIC OUTLINE OF THE ORGANIZATION OF THE COLLEGE (1931)

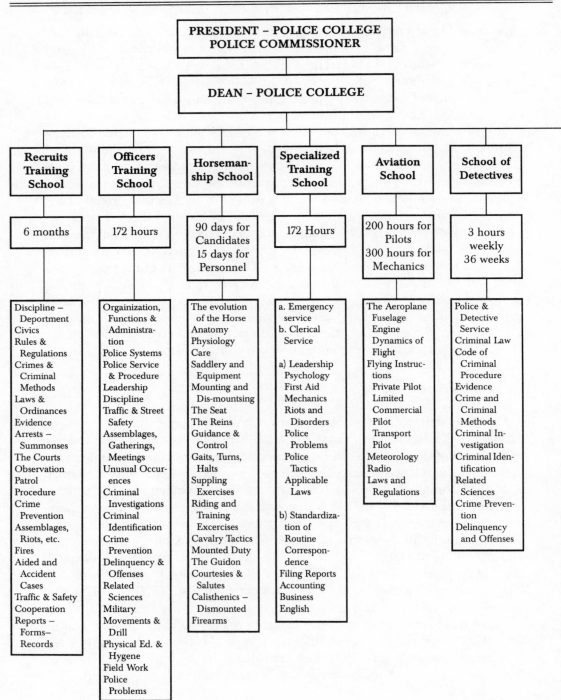

PRESIDENT – POLICE COLLEGE POLICE COMMISSIONER		
DEAN – POLICE COLLEGE		

Recruits Training School	Officers Training School	Horseman-ship School	Specialized Training School	Aviation School	School of Detectives
6 months	172 hours	90 days for Candidates 15 days for Personnel	172 Hours	200 hours for Pilots 300 hours for Mechanics	3 hours weekly 36 weeks
Discipline – Deportment Civics Rules & Regulations Crimes & Criminal Methods Laws & Ordinances Evidence Arrests – Summonses The Courts Observation Patrol Procedure Crime Prevention Assemblages, Riots, etc. Fires Aided and Accident Cases Traffic & Safety Cooperation Reports – Forms– Records	Orgainization, Functions & Administra-tion Police Systems Police Service & Procedure Leadership Discipline Traffic & Street Safety Assemblages, Gatherings, Meetings Unusual Occur-ences Criminal Investigations Criminal Identification Crime Prevention Delinquency & Offenses Related Sciences Military Movements & Drill Physical Ed. & Hygene Field Work Police Problems	The evolution of the Horse Anatomy Physiology Care Saddlery and Equipment Mounting and Dis-mountsing The Seat The Reins Guidance & Control Gaits, Turns, Halts Suppling Exercises Riding and Training Excercises Cavalry Tactics Mounted Duty The Guidon Courtesies & Salutes Calisthenics – Dismounted Firearms	a. Emergency service b. Clerical Service a) Leadership Psychology First Aid Mechanics Riots and Disorders Police Problems Police Tactics Applicable Laws b) Standardiza-tion of Routine Correspon-dence Filing Reports Accounting Business English	The Aeroplane Fuselage Engine Dynamics of Flight Flying Instruc-tions Private Pilot Limited Commercial Pilot Transport Pilot Meteorology Radio Laws and Regulations	Police & Detective Service Criminal Law Code of Criminal Procedure Evidence Crime and Criminal Methods Criminal In-vestigation Criminal Iden-tification Related Sciences Crime Preven-tion Delinquency and Offenses

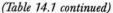

(Table 14.1 continued)

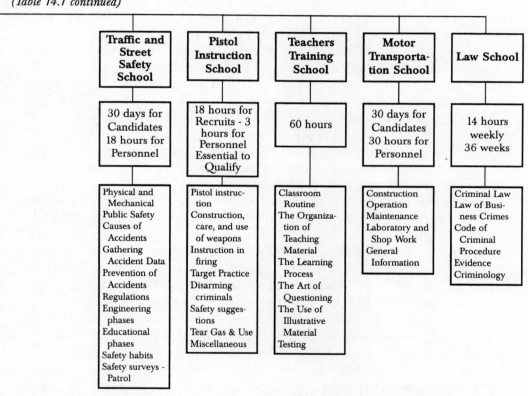

Traffic and Street Safety School	Pistol Instruction School	Teachers Training School	Motor Transportation School	Law School
30 days for Candidates 18 hours for Personnel	18 hours for Recruits - 3 hours for Personnel Essential to Qualify	60 hours	30 days for Candidates 30 hours for Personnel	14 hours weekly 36 weeks
Physical and Mechanical Public Safety Causes of Accidents Gathering Accident Data Prevention of Accidents Regulations Engineering phases Educational phases Safety habits Safety surveys - Patrol	Pistol instruction Construction, care, and use of weapons Instruction in firing Target Practice Disarming criminals Safety suggestions Tear Gas & Use Miscellaneous	Classroom Routine The Organization of Teaching Material The Learning Process The Art of Questioning The Use of Illustrative Material Testing	Construction Operation Maintenance Laboratory and Shop Work General Information	Criminal Law Law of Business Crimes Code of Criminal Procedure Evidence Criminology

and Chicago, now require the possession of a two-year college degree or its equivalent in order to compete for police officer positions. An outline of the 1929 organization of the "College" is presented in Table 14.1.

Responsible police officials should carefully examine the police-training model in the United Kingdom if they are truly serious about adopting community-policing techniques. In the United Kingdom, police training involves a two-year developmental process. During this training, the police are regularly sent into communities for firsthand experience and then adequate time is made available for debriefing about their experiences. Such sessions are considered crucial for the recruit's understanding and development as a professional police officer. In addition, field training involves a criminal justice system's perspective. Early in their training, recruits are assigned to meet with representatives from probation, parole and social service agencies. At the end of two years and only after the successful completion of all of the various stages or modules of training are recruits deemed eligible for regular assignment. Permanent status is only awarded after an additional year of satisfactory performance (Champion & Rush, 1997, pp. 81-82). A similar approach to training could be established throughout the United States under local sponsorship and control by using the programs and facilities of community colleges and related institutions.

While some important steps related to police professionalization were made during the last few decades of the twentieth century, much remains to be done. For example, there is currently no national police officer certification exam, nor is there a national police college. There are, however, four national military colleges. Moreover, not a single state currently sponsors a specific police college. However, many fine criminal justice college programs do exist. For example, John Jay College of Criminal Justice in New York City and the College of Criminal Justice at Northeastern University in Boston are internationally respected. Moreover, throughout the State of California there exist many well-known schools and programs in the field. Nevertheless, there are still very few higher educational institutions in the United States that are specifically accredited by state agencies to provide police training certifications for preservice students.[2] Thus, unlike the legal and medical professions, police currently lack national testing as well as a wide variety of preservice schools to select from. Significantly, the disparate and sporadic nature of police higher education may account for the maintenance of the traditional criminal approach to handling drug cases.

New Mission

The start of a new millennium should offer new hope for old problems. Perhaps, officials entrusted with coping with America's drug problems may be willing to develop a new mission with respect to prohibition enforcement after the year 2000. Such a mission should expand the role of citizen volunteers at all stages of the law enforcement process. In addition, the envisioned new mission would include the selection of full-time salaried drug control police specialists and new auxiliary police training coordinators (perhaps, recruited from the ranks of retired military personnel). The combination and addition of these types of personnel could foster the birth of vitally needed programs, make better use of existing ones, and help to restore confidence among police and community groups.

The new mission may help to bring an end to the seemingly hopeless year-in, year-out-criminal approach that has dominated this field for more than eighty years. While the ideas presented may require the elimination of some of the more draconian aspects of current prohibition enforcement, the overall strategy is concerned with obtaining a realistic accommodation that steers clear of the legalization versus decriminalization debate. The focus is on harm reduction and the use of penal sanctions primarily for violent predators and the true "drug lords." However, these improvements cannot be made unless the current workers in the system are also convinced about the merits of the new mission.

From its beginning, this book has attempted to place prohibition enforcement into its appropriate historical, legal and political contexts. Much of the materials have focused on the so-called professionalization of criminal justice, especially starting in the 1920s. Criminal justice officials have the responsibility to carve out not only a new mission for civilians in the fight against drugs, but to iron-out new roles for themselves. Each of the major institutional players—police, prosecutors, courts, and corrections need to examine their current strategies.

At the beginning of the twentieth century, Pound urged the need to have the office of prosecutor removed from politics. He called for the reform of the criminal courts, separating the bench from politics, and improved methods of bench and bar discipline (Pound, 1930). In France and Italy, judges are civil servants who have successfully passed a competitive examination. Most remain in their judicial posts for the remainder of their professional careers, rising to higher courts based entirely on their merit (Friedman, 1998, pp. 82-83). Pound concluded that the system of probation, despite its insufficient resources was "one of the outstanding good features of our criminal justice" (Pound, 1930, p. 197). Overall, he was especially concerned about the lack of cooperation in the administration of justice. Pound's insights are still valid and need to be thoughtfully studied and reconsidered.

Moreover, the work of Rufus King's joint AMA-ABA research committee on narcotics drugs begun in the 1950s should be revisited in order to carefully review the nature of the national drug program. He was especially concerned over the fact that enforcement of narcotics prohibition was mainly targeting small-time dealers and users, rather than major traffickers (Gary, 1998, p. 86).[3] In addition, the report of the Shafer Commission should be carefully reviewed and updated. In 1972, the Commission's report concluded that personal use of marijuana should no longer be a crime. President Nixon had expected the opposite conclusion, especially since he had appointed a former Republican governor, Ray Shafer, to head the commission (Gray, 1998, p. 97). Certainly, the recently approved initiatives in some states involving the medical use of marijuana should be closely monitored.

Sadly, America's experimentation with various types of drug prohibitions and the need for a vast enforcement apparatus seem likely to continue well into the next millennium, not only because of political considerations, but also because of a seemingly endless fixation with the need to maintain classes of "forbidden fruit." Unfortunately, the heavy hand of prohibition enforcement has even erased a drug users' one last chance to exercise self-control. Although America is a vastly different country than it was in 1900 and its addict population no longer basically consists of middle-aged southern white women hooked on a mix of alcohol and opium known as laudanum, a lesson from that era is instructive. In that year addiction peaked and was followed by a steady drop. The passage of the *Pure Food and Drug Act of 1906* required manufacturers to list ingredients on the label. Significantly, "when people began to realize their favorite nostrums were laced with addictive drugs, they stopped using them" (Gray, 1998, p. 44). Today, the illicit nature of drug sales doesn't lend itself to appropriate labeling, thus all users or potential users are denied one last opportunity to exercise common sense. Nevertheless, a two billion-dollar national media advertising campaign has been planned and initiated in the hope of accomplishing a similar purpose. The problem is that such important messages may just blend in with all the other types of hype that appears in the media! One minute or less commercials cannot substitute for the need for many more specialists and aides in the field of substance abuse and control.[4]

CONCLUSION

Throughout history various attempts have been made to restrict or to permanently outlaw various pleasure-giving substances. In the fifth century BC, Plato expressed his personal vision of the ideal state and listed what he considered to be the most appropriate use of alcohol. Plato recommended: (1) that no one under 18 be permitted to drink wine; (2) that persons under 30 might use wine but only in moderation: and (3) he placed no limits for persons who had reached age 40. Over fifteen hundred years ago, a Chinese emperor decreed that drinkers should lose their heads. One thousand years ago, the Egyptian ruler, Caliph Hakim ordered that all vineyards be destroyed and wine imports forbidden (Sournia, 1990, pp. 6 & 119). In the seventeenth century, merely visiting a coffeehouse in what are now Egypt, Saudi Arabia, and Turkey was a capital offense (Heath, 1992, p. 275). However, none of these historic events or policies achieved any degree of permanence. America's Constitutional ban on alcoholic drinks lasted a little more than thirteen years and similar controls on alcohol in Canada, Finland, Iceland, India, and Russia have each met a similar fate (Heath, 1992, p. 281).

Nevertheless, America's twentieth century prohibitions on other substances are being enforced with considerable tenacity. For example, in 1981, the U.S. Supreme Court upheld the constitutionality of a 40-year prison sentence imposed on a Virginia man for possession and distribution of marijuana worth about $200. The Court's decision reversed rulings by two lower federal courts that had declared that the sentence violated the Eighth Amendment's provision against the imposition of cruel and unusual punishment. The lower federal courts were of the opinion that the sentence was too harsh in proportion to the crime (Szasz, 1987, pp. 334-335).

In a discussion that centered upon racial matters, America's favorite talk show host, Oprah Winfrey, indicated that America was at a serious crossroad when she said: "I understand a lot of what that conflict is about. It's about people truly not understanding one another" (Lynch, 1998, p. 5). She believes that solving problems requires coming to really know people and having knowledge of "each other's hearts" (Lynch, 1998, p. 5). Now more than ever before, national leadership is needed to provide this type of perspective for dealing with many of its most persistent problems including substance abuse.

Currently, substance abuse may be the most costly of all criminal activity. If the social costs of lost job productivity, property losses, and medical treatment are added to the sums needed for policing, the total has been estimated at nearly $60 billion per year (Schmalleger, 1997, p. 60). It is now time to seriously consider moving away from a criminal-police-military approach. The stakes are not only high for members of this generation, but for its future members as well. As we have seen, it is one thing to pass a law and quite another to enforce it. The time has come to appreciate that merely enacting laws will not automatically strengthen family values and personal morality. "The legal system plays a part, to be sure, in the moral constitution of society, but it is a secondary, symbolic, and derivative role" (Friedman, 1998, p. 189).

The events involving national prohibition demonstrated how a national voluntary movement that was initially aimed at elevating morality and contributing to the general welfare might cause more harm than good for the average citizen. The attempt to control the drinking habits of Americans was considered a "noble experiment." Enforcement efforts were very weak at the state and local levels of government. Municipal police forces primarily engaged in serious efforts to regulate the sale and distribution of alcoholic beverages only after being prodded by the criticisms of organized groups. On the federal level, sufficient resources for policing prohibition were never provided and often never requested. Moreover, various attempts to target major violators (e.g., organized liquor traffickers) also failed due to "the performance of men in public office, by lack of funds and by opposition to the law" (Merz, 1931, p. 250). In order to overcome public resistance to the law, Presidents Harding, Coolidge and Hoover made numerous appeals to the general public regarding the need to abide by the law of the land. In one of his last speeches, Harding declared that respect for the law must be shared by the influential citizen and "the humbler citizen, else the temple will collapse" (Merz, 1931, p. 245). Coolidge reiterated this sentiment when he stated: "The complementary duty to enforcement of the law is obedience to the law" (Merz, 1931, p. 246). Finally, Hoover proclaimed: "that the problem of law enforcement is not alone a function or business of government. Every citizen has a personal duty in it" (Merz, 1931, p. 244).

Over 80 years later and on the eve of the new millennium, leaders and citizens are confronted anew by the inherent difficulties regarding prohibition laws and their enforcement. The key leaders are now different as are most of the citizens, but some key issues remain the same. For example, in the 1920s, there were many illicit stills and distilleries; today, there are many clandestine drug labs producing methamphetamines and crack cocaine. Padlock injunctions were use in the twenties and they are in vogue today. Then and now, the courts have been overwhelmed by drug cases and the prisons were filled to more than their capacities. In the 1920s, radio signals, automobiles and high-speed motorboats helped move illicit alcohol to the marketplace and across borders; drug traffickers still use these tools as well as private and commercial aircraft, personal cell phones and pages. Furthermore, undercover police work was commonplace then and is standard practice today. Tainted alcohol was sold and consumed and tainted drugs are now being used. Over 100 years ago mandatory temperance instruction was included in public school curriculums; today instruction concerns a wider range of abused drugs. In the early 1900s, it was advocated that police should play a more positive role in society and maintain a social-work orientation (Walker, 1977, p.79). This need existed then, and still exists today. On the other hand, while in the 1920s, there was widespread disrespect for the liquor law, today there is widespread support for most laws regarding controlled substances. If public officials can successfully harness this support, a breakthrough will be achieved in the field of drug enforcement. This chapter has set forth guidelines for how public support can be used.

The occurrence of deviancy by others, such as at the time of Charles Tighe's violent conduct on the streets of Manhattan in 1921, caused others to become involved in a variety of different ways. Some were simply bystanders who stayed for "the show," while others tried to assist their neighbors. Some victims had the courage to report the brutality that they had experienced. Substance abuse is now so common in some areas that it borders on not even being considered especially deviant. Nevertheless, it is a social problem of immense proportions and like the people in the Tighe case, we must do something.

Jerome H. Skolnick, the Claire Clements Dean's Professor of Law, within the Jurisprudence and Social Policy Program at the University of California, Berkeley, has written: "Neither moral exhortation nor an unprecedented expansion of law enforcement, or military intervention can or should be used to address what is essentially a health and social problem" (1992, p.156).

ENDNOTES

1. Willebrandt, Mabel Walker. The Department of Justice and Some Problems of Enforcement in Fred B. Smith, ed. *Law vs. Lawlessness: Addresses Delivered at the Citizenship Conference, Washington, D.C. October 13, 14, 15, 1923.* New York: Fleming H. Revell Co., 1924, p. 92.

2. Perhaps, a slight trend may be underway to change this. In New York State, both Jamestown Community College and the State University of New York at Canton do provide some limited training for well-qualified preservice students. Similar programs also exist in California, Florida, Texas, Michigan, Minnesota, New Mexico and Vermont. In addition, the U.S. Dept. of Interior has certified about 25 colleges to offer seasonal park ranger training.

3. Rufus King may have played an interesting role in Anslinger's eventual retirement. In 1961, King provided an NBC radio audio tape of a debate he had had with Anslinger in July of 1959 to a White House official, Dr. Peter Bing. In a May 4, 1996 interview with author Mike Gray, King related that Bing, who was the assistant White House Science Advisor at that time, told him that President Kennedy "listened to that tape and he heard Anslinger ranting and raving, and he and Bobby made up their minds he had to go" (Gray, 1998, pp. 90-91).

4. The Substance Abuse and Mental Health Services Administration has published *The National Directory of Drug Abuse and Alcoholism Treatment and Prevention Programs.* The directory includes information about substance abuse treatment and prevention programs at the local, regional, and national levels. It includes the types and levels of care available as well as the range of services offered at each facility. This guide could assist Drug Control Police Specialists to locate appropriate treatment and prevention programs in many different geographical areas. Moreover, the directory may be obtained without charge from the National Clearinghouse for Alcohol and Drug Information, P.O. Box 2345, Rockville, MD 20847, or by calling 800-729-6686.

Appendix A

NEW YORK TIMES ARTICLE ON SENTENCING OF TIGHE*

TWO TO FOUR YEARS FOR TIGHE, CLUBBER

Judge Crain Says Sentence of Detective Sergeant Should Be a Warning to the Force

NO PITY FROM HIS VICTIM

Woman "Sorry for Him in a Way, But, He Treated Me Awfully And Said Awful Things."

Detective Sergeant Charles Tighe was sentenced yesterday by Judge Crain in General Sessions to not less than two years and not more than four years at hard labor in State prison for abusing and beating Mrs. Emma Lennon of 561 West Fiftieth Street on the night of July 28, when Tighe "ran amuck," in the Court's language, at Coen's saloon, 600 Ninth Avenue, and beat a number of men, women and children. The maximum penalty under the law was five years.

Judge Crain said that he wished the sentence to be taken as a warning that similar punishment would be meted out to similar offenders. Before passing sentence he listened to a plea in behalf of Tighe by his lawyer, Samuel Furstenberg, and to several character witnesses. Judge Crain then called on Mrs. Lennon, who was in court, to tell how she felt toward the defendant.

"I am sorry for him in a way," she said, "on account of his family, but he treated me awfully and said some awful things to me."

Judge Crain turned to Tighe, who had been free on bail of $2,000 and who seemed to be confident of a light sentence.

"The complaining witnesses, a reputable married woman, was returning from the bank," said the Judge. "She had a right to be where she was. You took hold of her, as you had no right to do. You spoke to her as you had no right to do, and you forced her into a room, as you had no right to do. Your conduct was ungentlemanly, unbecoming a police officer and contrary to the law."

"You ill-treated several other persons, at least one other of them being a woman. In all likelihood you were under the influence of liquor. That is the most charitable interpretation of your conduct. You were mentally unbalanced from drink, and to use a colloquial expression, 'ran amuck.'"

"Your record on the police force is a bad one, and it is rather surprising to me

* New York Times, October 15, 1921 p. 3

262

that you have remained on the force. I realize that you automatically lose your position on the police force. I also recognize the regrettable circumstance that policemen are sometimes accused of brutality and lawlessness calculated to bring the police force into disrepute. The majority of the members of the force are faithful and brave, and our citizens justly rely on them for protection. There was apparently no malice in your assault upon Mrs. Lennon, because you had never seen her before, so that your conduct is attributable to your being mentally unbalanced through drink, and a desire to show your authority."

"Your punishment is in part a warning to members of the Police Department that if they overstep the law and act brutally toward citizens they will be punished in a manner that is commensurate with the gravity of the offense."

Tighe, who is 32 years old, had been in the Police Department between nine and ten years. He is married and has one child. At the time of the beating and blackjacking in front of Coen's saloon, when Mrs. Lennon was beaten, he was a member of the staff of Chief Inspector William J. Lahey. Tighe had been repeatedly on trial on charges of brutality at Police Headquarters.

Appendix B

NARCOTICS CONTROL

The Role of United States Agencies

A comprehensive drug control and anticrime strategy can be carried out only if U.S. agencies have clearly defined domestic/international roles and cooperate closely in all elements of the strategy. The agencies listed below have been given the following international responsibilities for drug control or anticrime by statute and, in some cases, by the authority vested in the Director of the Office of National Drug Control Policy.

1. The Director of the Office of National Drug Control Policy is charged with the responsibility for formulating and coordinating national drug control policy. The Office is responsible for establishing and promulgating objectives/policies, the National Drug Control Strategy, coordinating the implementation of policies, and overseeing the fulfillment of the assigned drug control program responsibilities.

The Director recommends to the President changes regarding organizations, management, budgets, and allocations of personnel in federal departments and agencies. The Director also reviews agency budgets prior to their submission to OMB.

2. The Department of State is the lead agency for international narcotics control and anticrime policy formulation and implementation. It is responsible for coordinating the international narcotics control and anticrime assistance activities of all U.S. Government agencies operating overseas.

The Secretary of State has designated the Assistant Secretary for the Bureau for Narcotics and Law Enforcement Affairs (INL) as State's primary focal point for all international narcotics and international criminal matters. The State Department's role, carried out by INL, is both diplomatic and programmatic.

The Bureau of International Organizations works with INL in coordinating the involvement with the agencies of the UN system on drug control or anticrime issues.

Regional bureaus, such as the Bureau of Inter-American Affairs, the Bureau of South Asian Affairs, and the Bureau of European Affairs, are responsible for guiding the operation of the U.S. diplomatic establishments of their areas.

3. The Department of Justice has the lead role in enforcing U.S. laws in the public interest and in narcotics cases, developing prosecutions against traffickers. Justice, and together with the State, (Office of the Legal Adviser), is also responsible for the negotiation and implementation of extradition treaties and Mutual Legal Assistance Treaties (MLATs). Justice, through the Office of Professional

264

Development and Training (OPDAT) and International Criminal Investigation Training Assistance Program, (ICITAP), provides assistance with the Administration of Justice Programs.

The U.S. Drug Enforcement Administration (DEA) is the primary federal drug enforcement agency for counternarcotics. Its main responsibility is to enforce the Controlled Substances Law and regulations of the U.S. and bring organizations or individuals violating these laws to justice. DEA is also engaged in recommending and supporting enforcement programs aimed at reducing the availability of illicit controlled substances and precursor chemicals in the domestic and international markets.

Overseas, in addition to their investigative work with foreign enforcement organizations, the DEA provides technical support to these organizations to reduce narcotics manufacturing/trafficking through training and the sharing of law enforcement techniques. DEA also collects and analyzes drug-related intelligence, coordinates drug-related intelligence sharing with foreign enforcement agencies, and works with governments to seize drug-related assets.

The Federal Bureau of Investigation (FBI) collects, analyzes and disseminates domestic law enforcement related intelligence on criminal organizations. The FBI conducts long-term domestic investigations aimed at dismantling criminal organizations and their support mechanisms, such as money laundering, public corruption, organized crime, etc.

The Immigration and Naturalization Service is responsible for facilitating the entry of persons legally admissible as visitors or as immigrants to the United States; granting benefits under the Immigration and Nationality Act, as amended, including providing assistance to those seeking permanent resident status or naturalization; preventing unlawful entry, employment, or receipt of benefits by those who are not entitled to them; and apprehending or removing those aliens who enter or remain illegally in the United States and/or whose stay is not in the public interest.

The ICITAP is responsible for law enforcement training of foreign police. It is an arm of DOJ, but has no program funding of its own. INL provides funding for any law enforcement training in both narcotics and crime programs.

The OPDAT is responsible for criminal justice training programs for public prosecutors and for providing commentary on draft legislation requested by foreign governments.

The U.S. Marshals Service, in drug-related matters, is responsible for apprehending most federal fugitives, operating the Federal Witness Security Program for endangered governmental witnesses, and seizing, managing and selling property forfeited to the Government by drug traffickers and other criminals.

4. The Department of the Treasury is the lead U.S. Government agency for financial crimes enforcement, and is responsible for administering and enforcing the Bank Secrecy Act. Treasury has been designated by Congress as the lead agency for negotiating international agreements on money-laundering cooperation (Kerry Amendment) and has chaired the U.S. delegation to the Financial Action Task Force created by the 1989 Economic Summit. Treasury receives and analyzes more than 7 million financial transaction reports annually, and provides information to a number of enforcement agencies within Treasury, Justice and other federal departments.

The U.S. Customs Service has the authority for investigating a wide variety of international criminal activities, including smuggling of contraband, violations of intellectual property rights, drug trafficking, and money-laundering violations. Customs' efforts include programs designed to combat illegal transportation of contraband through the ports of entry of the United States concealed in commercial cargo, in international containers, in passenger baggage and by individual couriers. The Customs Service also employs a sophisticated electronic interception and apprehension of aircraft and personnel.

Customs provides training and technical assistance to foreign governments and participates in joint enforcement operations with source, transit, and bank haven countries.

The U.S. Secret Service has the authority for investigating a wide variety of international financial crimes, including credit card fraud, counterfeiting of U.S. currency and financial instruments. Secret Service efforts include programs to help foreign governments to detect counterfeit U.S. currency in foreign banks.

The Bureau of Alcohol, Tobacco and Firearms (BATF) has the authority to investigate the illegal flow of firearms from the United States. The use of firearms is inherent in international criminal activities. BATF is committed to identifying the source of firearms and stemming the availability of these illegally obtained firearms from the United States. BATF's efforts include programs designed to prosecute unlawful sources of firearms through the use of the Federal firearms laws, and to locate sources through the use of traces of firearms seized during domestic and foreign law enforcement efforts.

The Internal Revenue Service (IRS) directs its investigation of crimes toward major money laundering organizations. In addition to its investigation of tax-related violations and its assistance in multiagency asset seizure and forfeiture actions, the IRS has statutory authority to investigate nearly all violations of the Bank Secrecy Act, as well as transactional money laundering violations under the provisions of Title 18 of the United States Code. Additionally, the IRS's Detroit Computing Center processes nearly 7 million financial transaction documents, such as the Currency Transaction Reports (CTRs), each year and maintains these reports in a financial database for subsequent retrieval and analysis.

The Federal Law Enforcement Training Center (FLETC) is a domestic training center for Treasury and Justice agencies. FLETC also provides training for foreign officials on international money laundering and financial fraud.

5. The U.S. Coast Guard (USCG), as principal maritime enforcement agency for the United States, contributes to the counternarcotics strategy in several key ways. First, it employs aircraft and cutters in a broad array of interdiction strategies against marine and air smugglers, and participates in a variety of joint-agency and joint-nation operations. Second, it plays an integral role in the intelligence process, collecting and analyzing raw data from both open and sensitive sources, and through the exchange of information with cooperating agencies and nations. Third, Coast Guard shares its maritime expertise with countries affected by criminal organizations through an extensive program of classroom and on-site training. Finally, frequent assistance is given to countries that lack extensive roadways and aircraft resources by providing Coast Guard aircraft logistic support.

6. The Department of Defense (DOD) has been designated as the lead agency for detection and monitoring of aerial and maritime transit of illegal drugs into the United States. Selected U.S. Commands have been directed to execute these responsibilities and three Joint Task Forces have been created to assist in the coordination of DOD resources in support of interdiction agencies. DOD provides training and technical assistance to foreign governments in conjunction with the Department of State. DOD is also responsible for integrating various federal assets into an effective communications network.

7. The Agency for International Development (AID) is responsible for the design and implementation of development assistance programs worldwide. AID assists the coca/cocaine producing countries to diversify their economies away from coca dependency and towards open, outward market economies.

In the short term, it is AID's responsibility to alleviate the negative economic and social dislocation which will result from successful drug control programs. In the longer run, AID's mandate includes ameliorating severe poverty, achieving lasting growth, sharing the benefits of growth more broadly, and strengthening democratic institutions and respect for human rights. AID also sponsors antidrug education programs which are designed to build institutions overseas to address the growing problem of drug abuse. AID also is responsible for funding Administration of Justice programs to strengthen host nation capability to prosecute criminal cases in court and to develop and implement laws to deter criminal elements.

8. The Intelligence Community's role is to collect and produce counternarcotics and anticrime strategic intelligence in support of all appropriate federal agencies. The community also supports the requirements of law enforcement and interdiction agencies for timely, actionable tactical intelligence.

To support the President's counternarcotics efforts further, the Director of the Central Intelligence Agency (CIA) established the Counternarcotics Center (CNC) in April 1989. (In 1994, the CNC's mandate broadened to include all international crime issues. The name of the center was changed to the Counternarcotics and Crime Center to reflect its expanded mission). The center brings together the analytic, collection, and technical elements of the CIA to afford more focus to its agency-wide efforts regarding the international crime, including narcotics trafficking. It also functions as a community center by bringing representatives from the law enforcement and national security agencies together to address intelligence problems of common concern.

Finally, the Center is creating ways to provide more information of direct use to law enforcement agencies, while, at the same time, providing improved and more timely strategic assessments to policymakers. In support of the President's national drug control policies, the Center has drafted a classified counternarcotics strategy (and is working on an international crime strategy) for the intelligence community.

The U.S. Information Agency (USIA) is the lead agency for anti-narcotics and crime international information initiatives. Through its offices overseas, USIA seeks to build international support for enhanced government/private sector actions against crime and the drug trade by disseminating information on the global nature and consequences of crime. USIA also provides information about U.S. efforts to address our narcotics and crime problems to international audiences.

10. The National Institute on Drug Abuse (NIDA), an Institute of the Public Health Service of the Department of Health and Human Services, has the lead responsibility in the U.S. Government for drug abuse research. It is an important source of expertise in demand reduction for the international narcotics program and provides various technical services funded by INL, e.g., epidemiology studies, clearing house publications, household surveys, community correspondents group proceedings, etc.

11. The Department of Agriculture (USDA), Agricultural Research Service, assists in the development of crop substitution programs and in environmental studies on the impact of the use of herbicides upon illicit narcotics crops.

Appendix C

A NEW YORK CITY AUXILIARY POLICE WEBSITE

Values:
In partnership with the community and the New York Police Department we pledge to:

- Maintain a high standard of integrity and competence and render our services in a professional and courteous manner.
- Assist in crime prevention by our uniform presence which also creates a sense of safety to citizens of our community.
- Assist in improving police community relations by participating in police service to the community.
- Maintain our skills and be prepared to act as an effective adjunct to the Police Department in the event of civil defense emergency or natural disaster.

NYC Auxiliary Police Officers are:

Unpaid volunteers men/women of this city, who are registered with New York State as part-time peace officers. They are employees/members of this department when signed in on the roll call sheet. They go on patrol in uniform to help make the streets safer for the citizens of New York City. We are unpaid professionals who serve our community.

As NYC Auxiliary Police Officers we perform such duties as:

- Uniform patrol with a partner in residential and commercial areas
- Special event details (parades, marathons, block parties, street fairs, etc)
- Patrol perimeter of mall and shopping centers
- Subway platform and stairwell
- House of worship patrol
- Senior Citizens escorts
- School and church crossings
- Assist in traffic and crowd control
- Observing and reporting dangerous street conditions
- Assisting Vice (liquor and cigarette sales to underage youths program)
- Assisting the NYPD in any way possible.

Training:

NYC Auxiliary Police Officers receive 16 weeks of training. (1) one or (2) two days a week, and undergo a background investigation. The training course includes:

- Patrol functions
- Types and techniques of patrol (automobile, foot)
- Traffic control
- Crowd control
- Social Science
- Victimology
- Citizen contacts
- Criminal Law
- Penal Law
- Criminal Procedure Law
- Laws of arrest
- Use of physical and deadly physical force
- Self Defense Training
- First Aid Training
- NYC Transit System Training
- Portable Radio Communications Training
- Field Training

New York City has 3,600 Auxiliary Police Officers today, and the numbers are still growing larger. As Auxiliary Police Officers we can make that difference. Auxiliary Police Officers are a special breed, because it takes a special person to become an Auxiliary Police Officer. We are unpaid professionals who go out there with pride, commitment and respect. Be safe and god bless.

Telephone Numbers: Auxiliary Police Headquarters, Queens 212-AUX-1000, 718-520-9243
63rd Precinct Auxiliary Police 718-258-4453

WORKS CITED

Trial Transcripts

New York City Court of Special Sessions, Charles Tighe (Defendant), October 8, 1921, Roll 366, John Jay College of Criminal Justice Library.

Newspapers Cited

The Christian Science Monitor
The Daily Gazette (Schenectady, NY)
The New York Times
Times Herald Record (Middletown, NY)
Times Union (Albany, NY)
Rockland Review (Rockland County, NY)
Sunday Telegraph (Sydney, Australia)

Books Cited

Abadinsky, Howard. *Drug Abuse: An Introduction.* Chicago: Nelson-Hall, 1997.

Allen, Everett S. *The Black Ships: Rumrunners of Prohibition.* Boston: Little, Brown, 1979.

Anderson, Jervis. *This Was Harlem: A Cultural Portrait, 1900-1950.* New York: Farrar, Straus, Giroux, 1982.

Asbury, Herbert. *The Great Illusion: An Informal History of Prohibition.* Westport, CT: Greenwood Press, 1968.

Bayley, David H. *Police for the Future.* New York: Oxford University Press, 1994.

Becker, Howard S. *Outsiders: Studies in the Sociology of Deviance.* New York: Free Press, 1963.

Behr, Edward. *Prohibition: Thirteen Years that Changed America.* New York: Arcade Publishers, 1996.

Benjamin, Daniel K. & Miller, Roger Leroy. *Undoing Drugs: Beyond Legalization.* New York: Basic Books, 1991.

Blocker Jr., Jack S. *Retreat from Reform: The Prohibition Movement in the United States 1890-1913.* Westport, CT: Greenwood Press, 1976.

Blocker Jr., Jack S. *American Temperance Movements: Cycles of Reform.* Boston: Twayne Publishers, 1989.

Bloomfield, Howard V. L. *The Compact History of the U.S. Coast Guard.* New York: Hawthorn Books, Inc., 1966.

Blum, John M. *Years of Discord: American Politics and Society, 1961-1974.* New York: W.W. Norton & Co., 1991.

Bodenhamer, David J. *Fair Trial: Rights of the Accused in American History.* New York: Oxford University Press, 1992.

Booth, Martin. *Opium: A History.* New York: St. Martin's Press, 1998.

Bopp, William J. & Schultz, Donald O. *A Short History of American Law Enforcement.* Springfield, IL: Charles C Thomas, 1972.

Bowen, Catherine Drinker. *Miracle at Philadelphia: The Story of the Constitutional Convention May to September 1787.* Boston: Little, Brown & Co., 1966, Republished 1986.

Boyer, Paul. *Urban Masses and Moral Order in America, 1820-1920.* Cambridge, MA: Harvard University Press, 1978.

Carte, Gene E. & Carte, Elaine H. *Police Reform in the United States: The Era of August Vollmer, 1905-1932.* Berkeley, CA: University of California Press, 1975.

Cashman, Sean D. *Prohibition: The Lie of the Land.* New York: Free Press, 1981.

Champion, Dean J. & Rush, George E. *Policing in the Community.* Upper Saddle River: NJ: Prentice Hall, 1997.

Chapin, Bradley. *Criminal Justice in Colonial America, 1606-1660.* Athens, GA: The University of Georgia Press, 1983.

Cherrington, Ernest H. *The Evolution of Prohibition in the United States of America.* Montclair, NJ: Patterson Smith, 1920, 1969.

Clark, Norman H. *The Dry Years: Prohibition and Social Change in Washington.* Seattle: The University of Washington Press, 1965.

Coffey, Thomas M. *The Long Thirst: Prohibition in America 1920-1933.* New York: W.W. Norton & Co., 1975.

Collier, Peter & Horowitz, David. *The Rockefellers: An American Dynasty.* New York, NY: Signet, The New American Library, Inc., 1976.

Corradini, Robert E. *Saloon Survey of New York City: Prohibition and Saloons and Liquor Stores.* Westerville, OH: The World League Against Alcoholism, (1925).

Crump, Irving. *The Boys' Book of Policemen.* New York: Dodd, Mead & Co., 1917.

Currie, Elliott. *Reckoning: Drugs, The Cities, and the American Future.* New York: Hill and Wang, Paperback Edition, 1994.

Davis, Eric; Martin, James; Holcomb, Randy; & Fisher, Luchina. *The Slick Boys: A Ten-Point Plan to Rescue Your Community by Three Chicago Cops Who Are Making It Happen.* New York: Simon & Schuster, 1998.

Deakin, Thomas J. *Police Professionalism: The Renaissance of American Law Enforcement.* Springfield, IL: Charles C Thomas, 1988.

Duis, Perry H. *The Saloon: Public Drinking in Chicago and Boston 1880-1920.* Urbana, IL: University of Illinois Press, 1983.

Einstein, Izzy. *Prohibition Agent No. 1.* New York: Frederick A. Stokes Co., 1932.

Engelmann, Larry. *Intemperance: The Lost War Against Liquor.* New York Free Press, 1979.

Erikson, Kai T. *Wayward Puritans: A Study in the Sociology of Deviance.* New York: John Wiley and Sons, 1966.

Everest, Allan S. *Rum Across the Border: The Prohibition Era in Northern New York.* Syracuse, New York: Syracuse University Press, 1978.

Faber, Eli & Rowland, Eileen. *Trial Transcripts of the County of New York 1883-1927.* New York: The John Jay Press, n.d. (Pamphlet)

Ferguson, Robert W. *Drug Abuse Control.* Boston: Holbrook Press, 1975.

Fogelson, Robert M. *Big-City Police.* Cambridge, MA: Harvard University Press, 1977.

Friedman, Lawrence M. *Crime and Punishment in American History.* New York: Basic Books, Harper Collins Publishers, 1993.

Friedman, Lawrence M. *American Law: An Introduction,* Second Edition. New York: W.W. Norton Garner, & Co., 1998.

Gerald W. *The Police Role in Alcohol-Related Crises.* Springfield, IL: Charles C Thomas, 1979.

Gervais, C.H. *The Rumrunners: A Prohibition Scrapbook.* Thornhill, Ontario: Firefly Books Ltd., 1980.

Goldstein, Herman. *Problem-Oriented Policing.* New York: McGraw-Hill, 1990.

Gray, Mike. *Drug Crazy: How We Got Into this Mess and How We Can Get Out.* New York: Random House, 1998.

Greenberg, Douglas. *Crime and Law Enforcement in the Colony of New York 1691-1776.* Ithaca, NY: Cornell University Press, 1976.

Gurney, Gene. *The United States Coast Guard: A Pictorial History.* New York: Crown Publishers, Inc., 1973.

Haller, Mark H. *Eugenics: Hereditarian Attitudes in American Thought.* New Jersey: Rutgers University Press, 1963.

Hamowy, Ronald. *Dealing with Drugs: Consequences of Government Control.* Lexington. MA: Lexington Books, D.C. Heath & Co., 1987.

Harris, Jonathan. *This Drinking Nation.* New York: Four Winds Press, Macmillan, 1994.

Hickey, Thomas J. *Criminal Procedure.* Boston: McGraw-Hill, 1998.

Himmelstein, Jerome L. *The Strange Career of Marijuana: Politics and Ideology of Drug Control in America.* Westport, CT: Greenwood Press, 1983.

Hofstadter, Richard. *The Age of Reform: From Bryan to F.D.R.* New York: Vintage Books, 1955.

Holli, Melvin G. *Urban Reform in the Progressive Era.* In Lewis L. Gould (Ed.), *The Progressive Era* (pp. 133-151). Syracuse, NY: Syracuse University Press, 1974.

Inciardi, James A. Should Drugs be Legalized? in Richard C. Monk *Taking Sides: Clashing Views on Controversial Issues in Crime and Criminology,* 4th Ed., Guilford, CT: Dushkin Publishers Croup/Brown & Benchmark Publishers, 1996.

Inciardi, James A. *Handbook of Drug Control in the United States.* Westport, CT: Greenwood Press, 1990.

Jacobs, Jane. *The Death and Life of Great American Cities.* New York: Vintage Books, 1961.

Kerr, K. Austin. *Organized for Prohibition: A New History of the Anti-Saloon League.* New Haven, CT: Yale University Press, 1985.

Kessler, Ronald. *The FBI.* New York: Pocket Books, 1993.

Kiester, Edwin Jr. *Crimes with No Victims.* New York: Alliance for a Safer New York, 1972.

Kobler, John. Ardent Spirits: *The Rise and Fall of Prohibition.* New York: G.P. Putnam's Sons, 1973.

Kyvig, David E. *Repealing National Prohibition.* Chicago: The University of Chicago Press, 1979.

Lentini, Joseph R. *Vice and Narcotics Control.* Beverly Hills, CA: Glencoe Press, 1977.

Leon, Clare Katherine. *Special Constables: An Historical and Contemporary Survey.* Unpublished Ph.D. Dissertation, Bath University, 1991.

Lichtenstein, Perry M. & Small, Saul M. *A Handbook of Psychiatry.* New York: W.W. Norton & Co., 1943.

Lubove, Roy. *The Progressives and the Slums: Tenement House Reform in New York City 1890-1917.* Pittsburgh, PA: University of Pittsburgh Press, 1962.

Lyman, Susan E. *The Story of New York: An Informal History of the City from the First Settlement to the Present Day, Revised Edition.* New York: Crown Publishers, 1975.

Macht, Norman L. *Baseball Legends: Babe Ruth.* New York: Chelsea House Publishers, 1991.

Madison, Arnold. *Carry Nation.* Nashville, TN: Thomas Nelson Inc., 1977.

McBain, Howard L. *Prohibition: Legal and Illegal.* New York: The Macmillan Co., 1928.

McWilliams. John C. The History of Drug Control Policies in the United States in James A. Inciardi, *Handbook of Drug Control in the United States.* Westport, CT: 1990.

Merz, Charles. *The Dry Decade.* Seattle: The University of Washington Press, 1931, 1970).

Monk, Richard C. *Taking Sides: Clashing Views on Controversial Issues in Crime and Criminology, 4th Ed.,* Guilford, CT: Dushkin Publ. Group/Brown & Benchmark Publishers, 1996.

Monk, Richard C. *Taking Sides: Clashing Views on Controversial Issues in Crime and Criminology, 5th Ed.,* Guilford, CT: Dushkin Publ. Group/Brown & Benchmark Publishers, 1998.

Morgan, Edmund S. *The Puritan Family: Religion and Domestic Relations in Seventeenth-Century New England. New Edition, Revised and Enlarged.* New York: Harper & Row, 1944, 1966).

Morgan, H. Wayne. *Drugs in America: A Social History, 1800-1980.* Syracuse, NY: Syracuse University Press, 1981.

Mowry, George E. *The Twenties: Fords, Flappers and Fanatics.* Englewood Cliffs, NJ: Prentice-Hall, 1963.

Murray, Robert K. *The Harding Era.* Minneapolis: University of Minnesota Press, 1969.

National Center on Addiction and Substance Abuse (NCASA). *Behind Bars: Substance Abuse and America's Prison Population.* New York: NCASA at Columbia University, 1998.

Nelli, Humbert. *The Business of Crime.* New York: Oxford University Press, 1976.

New York State Police. *The New York State Police: The First Fifty Years 1917-1967.* Albany, NY: New York State Police, 1967. (Pamphlet)

Oliver, Willard M. *Community-Oriented Policing: A Systemic Approach to Policing.* Upper Saddle River, NJ: Prentice Hall, 1998.

Parrish, Michael E. *Anxious Decades: America in Prosperity and Depression 1920-1941.* New York: W.W. Norton & Co., 1992.

Perrett, Geoffrey. *America in the Twenties: A History.* New York: Simon and Schuster,1982.

Pound, Roscoe. *Criminal Justice in America.* New York: H. Holt, 1930.

Powers, Richard Gid. *Secrecy and Power: The Life of J. Edgar Hoover.* New York: The Free Press, 1987.

Ratcliffe, S.K. (1926, June). Crisis of Prohibition. *Contemporary Review,* 129, 712-721.

Revell, Oliver & Williams, Dwight. *A G-Man's Journal: A Lengendary Career Inside the FBI—From the Kennedy Assassination to the Oklahoma City Bombing.* New York: NY: Pocket Books, 1998.

Richardson, James F. *Urban Police in the United States.* Port Washington, NY: Kennikat Press, 1974.

Rosen, Ruth. *The Lost Sisterhood: Prostitution in America, 1900-1918.* Baltimore: The Johns Hopkins University Press, 1982.

Rothman, David J. *The Discovery of the Asylum: Social Order and Disorder in the New Republic.* Boston: Little, Brown & Co., 1971.

Rothman, David J. *Conscience and Convenience: The Asylum and Its Alternatives in Progressive America.* New York: Little, Brown & Co., 1980.

Sann, Paul. *The Lawless Decade: A Pictorial History of a Great American Transition: From the World War I Armistice and Prohibition to Repeal and the New Deal.* New York: Bonanza Books, 1957.

Schmalleger, Frank. *Criminal Justice: A Brief Introduction, 2nd Ed.* Upper Saddle River, NJ: Prentice Hall, 1997.

Schmeckebier, Laurence F. *The Bureau of Prohibition: Its History, Activities and Organization.* Washington, D.C.: The Brookings Institution, 1929.

Schreiner, Samuel A., Jr. *Mayday! Mayday!.* New York: Donald I. Fine, Inc., 1990.

Schulz, Dorothy Moses. *From Social Worker to Crimefighter: Women in United States Municipal Policing.* Wesport, CT: Praeger, 1995.

Semmes, Raphael. *Crime and Punishment in Early Maryland.* Montclair, NJ: Patterson Smith, 1938, 1966.

Senna, Joseph J. & Siegel, Larry J. *Essentials of Criminal Justice, Second Edition.* Belmont, CA: West/Wadsworth Publ. Co., 1998.

Severn, Bill. *The End of the Roaring Twenties: Prohibition and Repeal.* New York: Julian Messner, 1969.

Sherman, Lawrence, "Repeat Calls for Service: Policing Hot Spots," in Dennis Jay Kenney, ed., *Police and Policing.* New York: Praeger,1989.

Sinclair, Andrew. *Era of Excess: A Social History of the Prohibition Movement.* New York: Harper Colophon Books, 1964.

Slosson, Preston W. *The Great Crusade and After 1914-1928.* Chicago: Quadrangle Paperbacks, 1930, 1971.

Smith, Fred L., Ed. *Law vs. Lawlessness.* New York: Fleming H. Revell Co., 1924.

Sournia, Jean-Charles. *A History of Alcoholism.* Cambridge, MA: Basil Blackwell, 1990.

Stefoff, Rebecca. *The U.S. Coast Guard.* New York: Chelsea House Publishers, 1989.

Stone, Lawrence. *Family, Sex and Marriage in England 1500-1800.* New York, 1977.

Sullivan, Mark. *Our Times 1900-1925.* New York: Charles Scribner's Sons, 1939.

Szasz, Thomas. "The Morality of Drug Controls," pp. 327-351 in Ronald Hamowy *Dealing with Drugs: Consequences of Government Control.* Lexington, MA: D.C. Heath & Co., 1987.

Theoharis, Athan G. & Cox, John Stuart. *The Boss: J. Edgar Hoover and the Great American Inquisition.* Philadelphia: Temple University Press, 1988.

Thibault, Edward A., Lynch, Lawrence M. & McBride, R. Bruce. *Proactive Police Management, Fourth Edition.* Upper Saddle River, NJ: Prentice Hall, 1998.

Thompson, Roger. *Sex in Middlesex: Popular Mores in a Massachusetts County,* 1649-1699. Amherst, MA: The University of Massachusetts Press, 1986.

Timberlake, James H. *Prohibition and the Progressive Movement 1900-1920.* Cambridge, MA: Harvard University Press, 1963.

Trebach, Arnold S. Should Drugs be Legalized? in Richard C. Monk *Taking Sides: Clashing Views on Controversial Issues in Crime and Criminology, 4th Ed.,* Guilford, CT: Dushkin Publ. Group/Brown & Benchmark Publishers, 1996.

Trebach, Arnold S. "The Need for Reform of International Narcotics Laws." pp. 103-136 in Ronald Hamowy *Dealing with Drugs: Consequences of Government Control.* Lexington, MA: D.C. Heath & Co., 1987.

Walker, Samuel. *A Critical History of Police Reform: The Emergence of Professionalism.* Lexington, MA: Lexington Books, D.C. Heath & Co., 1977.

Walker, Stanley. *The Night Club Era.* New York: Blue Ribbon Books, Inc., 1933.

Whitehead, Don. *Border Guard: The Story of the United States Customs Service.* New York: McGraw-Hill, 1963.

Willebrandt, Mable Walker. The Department of Justice and Some Problems in Enforcement in Fred B. Smith, Ed. *Law vs. Lawlessness,* New York: Fleming H. Revell Co., 1924.

Wrobleski, Henry M. & Hess, Karen M. *Introduction to Law Enforcement and Criminal Justice, 5th Ed.,* St. Paul, MN: West Publ. Co., 1997.

Government Documents

Bureau of Justice Statistics (December 1992) *Drugs, Crime, and the Justice System: A National Report.* Washington, D.C.: U.S. Dept. of Justice, Office of Justice Programs.

Drug Night Courts: The Cook County Experience. Washington, D.C.: Bureau of Justice Assistance, U. S. Department of Justice, August, 1994.

Esbensen, F. & Osgood, D.W. (1997) *National Evaluation of G.R.E.A.T.* Research in Brief. Washington, D.C.: U.S. Dept. of Justice, National Institute of Justice.

Howell, James C. (August 1998) *Youth Gangs: An Overview.* Juvenile Justice Bulletin. Washington, D.C.: U.S. Dept. of Justice, Office of Juvenile Justice and Delinquency Prevention.

Mastrofski, Stephen, Parks, Roger B., & Worden, Robert E. (1998) *Community Policing in Action: Lessons From an Observational Study.* Research in Brief. Washington, D.C.: U.S. Dept. of Justice, National Institute of Justice.

National Drug Control Strategy, 1998. Washington, DC: Office of National Drug Control Policy, 1998.

National Household Survey on Drug Abuse: Main Findings 1994. Washington, D.C.: U.S. Dept. of Health and Human Services, Substance Abuse and Mental Health Services Administration, September 1996.

President's Commission on Organized Crime. *America's Habit: Drug Abuse, Drug Trafficking, and Organized Crime.* Washington, D.C.: U.S. Government Printing Office, 1986).

Kelling, George L.; Hochberg, Mona R.; Kaminska, Sandra Lee; et. al. (June 1998). *The Bureau of Justice Assistance Comprehensive Communities Program: A Preliminary Report.* Washington, D.C.: National Institute of Justice, U.S. Dept. of Justice, 11 pp.

Riley, K. Jack. (December 1997). *Crack, Powder Cocaine, and Heroin: Drug Purchase and Use Patterns in Six U.S. Cities.* Washington, D.C.: U. S. Department of Justice, National Institute of Justice, 46 pp.

Sherman, Lawrence (n.d.) *Neighborhood Safety.* Washington, D.C.: National Institute of Justice: Crime File Study Guide, 4 pp.

Whalen, Grover A. (1930). *The New York Police College.* New York: New York City Police Department.

Journal Articles

Applegate, B.K., Cullen, F.T. & Fisher, B.S. (1997, September). Public Support for Correctional Treatment: The Continuing Appeal of the Rehabilitative Ideal. *Prison Journal, 77* (3), 237-258.

Baker, Beth (1998, September). Home Away from Home: Volunteers Welcome Campers to Nation's Parks. *NRTA Bulletin, 39* (8), 12-14.

Bilchik, Shay. (1998, December). From the Administrator. Juvenile Justice: *Journal of the Office of Juvenile Justice and Delinquency Prevention, 5* (2), 1.

Bohm, R. (1986). Crime, Criminal and Crime Control Policy Myths. *Justice Quarterly, 3* (2), 193-214.

Brown, Lee P. (1995, August 1). Why the United States Will Never Legalize Drugs. *Vital Speeches of the Day, 61* (20), 628-629.

Carter, Robert L. (1996, March 1). The Criminal Justice System is Infected with Racism. *Vital Speeches of the Day, 62* (10), 290-293.

Cashman, Michael. (1998, February). Meth Labs: Toxic Timebombs. *The Police Chief, 65* (2), 42-47.

Clark, Jacob R. (1993, October 31). Pulling Back the Blue Curtain. *Law Enforcement News, 19* (388), 1 & 6.

Clinton, Bill. (1996, October 15). The War Against Crime: Improve the Opportunity for Community Based Strategies. *Vital Speeches of the Day, 63* (1), 1-5.

Colvin, Mark. (1982, June). The 1980 New Mexico Prison Riot. *Social Problems, 29* (5), 449-463.

Doane, George. (1998, February). Responding to the Methamphetamine Problem. *The Police Chief, 65* (2), 36-40.

Driscoll, Charles B. (1925, December). *McNaught's Magazine.* Vol. 4, p. 170.

Falco, Mathea (1992, Summer). Foreign Drugs, Foreign Wars. *Daedalus: Journal of the American Academy of Arts and Sciences, 121* (3), 1-14.

First Offender Prostitution Program–Diverting Offenders from Repeat Involvement. (1998, July). *National Institute of Justice Journal,* (236), 32.

Gibbs, Nancy. (1997, April 28). Special report: The FBI. *Time. 149* (17), 28-35.

Greenberg, Martin A. (1982, May). The Police Role in Victimless Crime. *USA Today,* 31-33.

Greenberg, Martin A. (1989, October). Auxiliary Police and Drug Abuse Prevention. *The Police Chief, 56* (10), 117-118.

Greenberg, Martin A. & Cooper, Ken. (1996, November 15). Unused Secret Weapon Against Terrorism. *Law Enforcement News, 22* (455), 12 & 15.

Hayeslip, D. Jr. (1989, March/April). Local Level Drug Health, Enforcement: New Strategies. *NIJ Reports,* (213), 2-7.

Heath, Dwight B. (1992, Summer). U.S. Drug Control Policy: A Cultural Perspective. *Daedalus: The Journal of the Academy of Arts and Sciences, 121* (3), 165-194.

Hebert, Eugene E. (1993, April). NIJ's Drug Market Analysis Program. *National Institute of Justice Journal,* (226), 2-7.

Hewitt, Bill & Siew, Walden. (1998, November 23). In the Trenches. *People Weekly, 50* (19), 143-144.

Kimbrough, Robin J. (1998, December). Treating Juvenile Substance Abuse: The Promise of Juvenile Drug Courts. Juvenile Justice: *Journal of the Office of Juvenile Justice and Delinquency Prevention, 5* (2), 11-19.

Lewis, David C. (1992, Summer). Medical and Health Perspectives on a Failing US Drug Policy. *Daedalus: The Journal of the Academy of Arts and Sciences, 121* (3), 165-194.

Little, Bobby & Bishop, Mike (1998, June). Minor Drinkers/Major Consequences: Enforcement Strategies for Underage Alcoholic Beverage Law Violators. *FBI Law Enforcement Bulletin, 67* (6), 1-4.

Lynch, Lorrie. (1998, Oct. 9-11). Oprah's New Mission. *USA Weekend,* 4-6.

Mackowiak, Mark. (1998, April). Operation Handclasp. *Profile, 41* (6), 16-17.

McNamara, Joseph. (1997, June 15). The Drug War. *Vital Speeches of the Day. 63* (17), 537-538.

McCaffrey, Barry R. (1996, March 15). The So Called War on Drugs: What We Must Do. *Vital Speeches of the Day, 62* (11), 325-326.

Munson, D. (1989, March/April). OJJDP Funds 21 New Projects During Fiscal Year 1988. *NIJ Reports,* (213), 8-12.

Nadelmann, Ethan A. (1992, Summer). Thinking Seriously About Alternatives to Drug Prohibition. *Daedalus: The Journal of the Academy of Arts and Sciences, 121* (3), 85-132.

Ratcliffe, S.K. (1926, June). Crisis of Prohibition. *Contemporary Review, 129,* 712-721.

Sanders, Darrell & Constantine, Thomas A. (1998, February). A Police Chief's Guide to the Legalization Issue. *The Police Chief, 65* (2), 23-30.

Sechrest, Dale K. & Burns, Pamela. (1992, September). Police Corruption: The Miami Case. *Criminal Justice and Behavior, 19*(3), 294-313.

Skolnick, Jerome. (1992, Summer). Rethinking the Drug Problem. *Daedalus: Journal of the American Academy of Arts and Sciences, 121* (3), 133-159.

Stone, Robert. (1990, July). Fighting the Wrong War: How the President's War on Drugs Repeats the Mistakes of Vietnam. *Playboy, 37* (7), 68-70, 167.

Swope, Ross E. (1998, April 30). Community Prosecution: A Missing Link. *Law Enforcement News. 24* (488), 14.

"The Letter of the Law: For Delaware Sex Offenders, It's 'Y'." (1998, April 30). *Law Enforcement News, 24* (488), 16.

Newspaper Articles

(Only signed and more recent articles are listed here. Earlier cites have been integrated into the body of various chapters, especially in Part 2.)

Biele, Katherine. (1998, July 13). Utah Starts Tobacco Court in Bid to Curb Teen Smoking. *The Daily Gazette*, p. A7.

Chen, Edwin. (1998, July 12). President Targets Drug Users. *The Daily Gazette*, pp. A1 & A11.

Classes Don't Make Drivers Safer: Study. (1999, January 6). *The Daily Gazette,* p. A6.

Craig, Gary. (1998, June 21). Drug Laws' Legacy at Core of Debate. *Times Union,* p. E5.

De La Cruz, Donna. (1999, January 2). Residents, Officials Applaud NYC's Plummeting Crime Rate. *The Daily Gazette,* p. B6.

Green, Alice P. (1998, September 27). New York's Drug-Sentencing Policies Too Severe. Letter. *The Sunday Gazette,* p. F2.

Greimel, Hans. (1998, December 4). Oregon Lights Up with Marijuana Law. *The Daily Gazette,* p. A6.

Halloran, R. (1988, July 23). Navy's Top Officer Says Military Cannot Halt Influx of Latin Drugs. *The New York Times,* p.10.

Hughes, Gary. (1999, February 21). Take Dead Aim. *The Sunday Gazette,* p.F1.

Huppke, Rex W. (1999, January 17). Drug Smuggling on Interstates a Challenge for Cops. *Sunday Times Union,* p. F1.

Jackson, Derrick Z. (1997, November 11). Outrage for Woodward, Silence for Blacks. *Times Herald Record,* p. 57.

Johnson, Kyle. (1998, August 27). `Drug Czar's' Plan to Shoe Up Leaky Border Meets With Skepticism. *The Christian Science Monitor,* p. 3.

Johnson, Mark. (1998, December 13). Courtesy Patrols Burnish Cities' Images. *Times Union,* p. F1.

Kastberg, Sabrina. (1998, August 2). Watching the Waters. *The Times Union: A Special Promotional Supplement,* p. 8.

Keeperman. Ben. (1998, July 29). New Rockland Court Officers Hope for Addicts. *Rockland Review,* pp. 1-2.

Krebs, Albin. (1975, November 18). Harry J. Anslinger Dies at 83; Hard-Hitting Foe of Narcotics. *The New York Times,* p. 40.

Levinson, Arlene. (1998, December 29). AP Poll: Clinton Scandal Ranks as Top Story of '98. *The Daily Gazette,* p. D4.

Mable Walker Willebrandt Dies; Lawyer for U.S. in Prohibition. (1963, April 9). *The New York Times,* p. 31.

McCaffrey, Shannon. (1998a, December 25). Holiday Clemency Refused by Pataki. *The Daily Gazette*, p. B4.

McCaffrey, Shannon. (1998b, December 27). Alliance Seeks to Ease State's Drug Penalties. *Times Union*, p. D7.

Punishment and Treatment. (1998, March 25). Editorial. *The Times Union* (Albany, NY), p. A8.

Queary, Paul. (1998, October 23). Marijuana Measures Aim at Compassion of Voters. *The Daily Gazette*, p. A8.

Quinn, Sue. (1991, August 25). Hands Up! Who Wants to Volunteer? *Sunday Telegraph* (Sydney, Australia), p. 7.

Reid, T.R. (1998, December 6). Panel Concludes Prize-Winning Drug Film was a Fake. *The Sunday Gazette*, p. A9.

Researchers in Spain Serve Bronze Age Beer. (1998, November 28). *The Daily Gazette*, p. D1.

Rohde, David. (1998, October 9). Calling System Like 'Torture,' Grand Jurors Urge Changes. *The New York Times*, p. B5.

Tripp Seeks Donations for 'Growing' Legal Fees. (1999, January 9). *The Daily Gazette*, p. D14.

Williams, Timothy, (1999, February 21). NYC Seizure of Cars Driven in DWI Cases Starts Monday. *The Sunday Gazette*, p.137.

Websites

Drug Enforcement Administration, Briefing Book. *DEA History*. September 29, 1998; at www.usdoj.gov/dea/pubs/briefing/1_2.htm

Federal Bureau of Investigation, Office of Public and Congressional Affairs. *A Short History of the Federal Bureau of Investigation*. June 10, 1998; at www.fbi.gov/history/hist.htm

The Office of National Drug Control Policy at http://www.whitehousedrugpolicy .gov (This site has the full text of many of the office's policy initiaves and programs and links to related sites.)

U.S. State Department. *Narcotics Control: The Role of United States Agencies*. September 29, 1998; at HYPERLINK http://www.state.gov/w...otics_law/control.html www.state.gov/w...otics_law/control.html

NAME INDEX

SUBJECT INDEX